National Theatre Connections
2025

National Theatre Connections 2025

TEN PLAYS FOR YOUNG PERFORMERS

YOU 2.0
Normalised
Brain Play
Saba's Swim
No Regrets
The Company of Trees
Their Name Is Joy
Ravers
Mia and the Fish
Fresh Air

Edited by
NATIONAL THEATRE

methuen | drama
LONDON · NEW YORK · OXFORD · NEW DELHI · SYDNEY

METHUEN DRAMA
Bloomsbury Publishing Plc
50 Bedford Square, London, WC1B 3DP, UK
1385 Broadway, New York, NY 10018, USA
29 Earlsfort Terrace, Dublin 2, Ireland

BLOOMSBURY, METHUEN DRAMA and the Methuen Drama logo are trademarks of
Bloomsbury Publishing Plc

First published in Great Britain 2025

Introduction copyright © National Theatre 2025
Resource material copyright © National Theatre, 2025

YOU 2.0 © Alys Metcalf, 2025
Normalised © Amanda Verlaque, 2025
Brain Play © Chloë Lawrence-Taylor and Paul Sirett, 2025
Saba's Swim © Danusia Samal, 2025
No Regrets © Gary McNair, 2025
The Company of Trees © Jane Bodie, 2025
Their Name Is Joy © May Sumbwanyambe, 2025
Ravers © Rikki Beadle-Blair, 2025
Mia and the Fish © Satinder Chohan, 2025
Fresh Air © Vickie Donoghue, 2025

NATIONAL THEATRE and CONNECTIONS typographical font style are used with the
permission of the Royal National Theatre.

The authors asserted their right under the Copyright, Designs and Patents Act, 1988,
to be identified as authors of this work.

Cover artwork: Photography by Tami Aftab.
Art direction and design by the National Theatre Graphic Design Studio.

All rights reserved. No part of this publication may be: i) reproduced or transmitted in any form, electronic or mechanical, including photocopying, recording or by means of any information storage or retrieval system without prior permission in writing from the publishers; or ii) used or reproduced in any way for the training, development or operation of artificial intelligence (AI) technologies, including generative AI technologies. The rights holders expressly reserve this publication from the text and data mining exception as per Article 4(3) of the Digital Single Market Directive (EU) 2019/790.

Bloomsbury Publishing Plc does not have any control over, or responsibility for, any third-party websites referred to or in this book. All internet addresses given in this book were correct at the time of going to press. The author and publisher regret any inconvenience caused if addresses have changed or sites have ceased to exist, but can accept no responsibility for any such changes.

No rights in incidental music or songs contained in the work are hereby granted and performance rights for any performance/presentation whatsoever must be obtained from the respective copyright owners.

All rights whatsoever in this play are strictly reserved. Application for performance, etc. should be made before rehearsals begin to the respective playwrights' representatives listed on page 595. No performance may be given unless a licence has been obtained

A catalogue record for this book is available from the British Library.

A catalog record for this book is available from the Library of Congress

ISBN: PB: 978-1-3505-4206-8
ePDF: 978-1-3505-4214-3
eBook: 978-1-3505-4207-5

Series: Plays for Young People

Typeset by RefineCatch Limited, Bungay, Suffolk
Printed and bound in Great Britain

For product safety related questions contact productsafety@bloomsbury.com.

To find out more about our authors and books visit www.bloomsbury.com
and sign up for our newsletters.

Contents

Head of Young People's Programmes Introduction vii
Connections Dramaturg Introduction viii
Connections 2025 Synopses x

YOU 2.0 by Alys Metcalf 1
Character Plot 46
Main Narrative Beats 48
Workshop Notes 50

Normalised by Amanda Verlaque 65
Character Plot 100
Main Narrative Beats 101
Workshop Notes 102

Brain Play by Chloë Lawrence-Taylor and Paul Sirett 113
Character Plot 156
Main Narrative Beats 157
Workshop Notes 158

Saba's Swim by Danusia Samal 171
Character Plot 205
Main Narrative Beats 206
Workshop Notes 208

No Regrets by Gary McNair 221
Character Plot 258
Main Narrative Beats 265
Workshop Notes 267

The Company of Trees by Jane Bodie 281
Character Plot 321
Main Narrative Beats 322
Workshop Notes 324

Their Name Is Joy by May Sumbwanyambe 337
Character Plot 388
Main Narrative Beats 389
Workshop Notes 391

Ravers by Rikki Beadle-Blair 403
Character Plot 442
Main Narrative Beats 444
Workshop Notes 445

Mia and the Fish by Satinder Chohan 459
Character Plot 506
Main Narrative Beats 507
Workshop Notes 509

Fresh Air by Vickie Donoghue 521
Character Plot 569
Main Narrative Beats 570
Workshop Notes 572

Participating Companies 587
Partner Theatres 591
National Theatre Connections Team 593
Performing Rights 595

Head of Young People's Programmes Introduction

National Theatre Connections

We are delighted to welcome you to the Connections 2025 anthology – marking the 30th year of this remarkable nationwide youth theatre festival.

Every year, Connections gives youth theatres and school groups the unique opportunity to stage new plays, which have been written specifically for young people, and to perform them at leading theatres across the UK. Over the last thirty years, we have worked with some of the UK's most exciting contemporary playwrights, and are so pleased to be able to continue this in 2025, with ten brilliant new plays. Over the last three decades, Connections plays have chronicled the changing landscape for young people, creating a canon of work, permanently available to schools, colleges and youth theatres.

At the beginning of their rehearsal process, companies take part in the Connections Directors' Weekend – an opportunity for the directors to work with the playwright of their chosen play and a leading theatre director. Notes from these workshops accompany the plays in this anthology, giving an insight into the playwrights' intentions, creative inspiration and tangible techniques and exercises for exploring the text.

Connections is not just the National Theatre's programme: it is run in collaboration with fantastic Partner Theatres across the UK, who work with every company to develop and transfer their production. Their festivals celebrate the brilliant work that has been created and amplify the voices of young people. This year, over 250 companies from across the country are taking part in Connections, with over 5,000 young people involved in every aspect of theatre making.

Over the last thirty years we have been lucky enough to work with a huge range of schools, youth theatres and venues across the UK who have supported and shaped the programme. On the value of Connections, last year our friends at Sherman Theatre said: 'Young people's creativity is truly celebrated, positive cultural experiences are fostered and the whole theatre ecology, locally and nationally, is nourished by this partnership, which is the first step on a creative path for so many young people.'

We hope you enjoy this year's plays, as Connections continues to be a celebration of the power of young people and of theatre.

Kirsten Adam
Head of Young People's Programmes
November 2024

Connections Dramaturg Introduction

Thirty years ago, Connections was born, and like all first-time parents our chests filled with pride, as we beamed, marvelled and bristled with anticipation at the wonder and potential of our creation. Further still, just like novice parents, none of us thought to project so far into the future as to imagine that one day we'd be responsible for creating something that would go on to circumnavigate the sun thirty times and counting. Fully grown and playing its part in the world. However, here we are: Connections has endured and it is having an impact.

Acknowledging landmark milestones is essential as they provide the opportunity to do many important and necessary things that help maintain a healthy sensibility, including the chance to reflect, re-evaluate, reset, celebrate and mark the many achievements and the even greater number of lessons along the way. Don't worry, I'm not going to use the remainder of this introduction to document all thirty years' worth of recollections. However, I would like to spend a moment to think about teenagers and what that holds for us now compared with 1995.

Recent (as in the last ten to fifteen years) findings in neuroscience have been transformative in giving us an understanding and a language for taking on board the notion of the 'teenage brain'. I don't have empirical evidence, but I would assert that attitudes and perceptions of teenagers have changed for the better over the last thirty years. Of course, context is crucial, and everything is relative – but on the whole, understanding is deeper and attitudes more sophisticated when engaging with teens. Where once there was a propensity to herd everyone between thirteen and nineteen together, behind the one all-encompassing shield – marked approach with caution, but only if absolutely necessary, and better if you can wait until they've got over it – now there's a greater inclination to take the time to try and see the person, the one unique and miraculous individual that is still growing, still learning and still with so much potential, that can only be fulfilled over time and with great care. When you encounter a teen, you're encountering someone at a crucial stage of development in their lives, where positive interaction can stimulate fruitful outcomes, powerful and important enough to last a lifetime, for both parties. In short, through greater understanding there has been a shift in mindset which in turn has led to a shift in attitudes and behaviours, and this is vital.

In 1995, you could look up and a new century was in sight – the future was bright, the adults were sorting the world out. Fast forward three decades, 2030 is in sight and the stakes are high, the future is by no means guaranteed, for which the adults are largely responsible – the sorting out has become falling out on a global scale. It is clear that if the future is to be secured, it will undoubtedly be because of the collective efforts of the next generation, the teenagers of today. We are in their hands.

So, nurturing is crucial, and it is apparent that Connections provides an ideal vehicle for daily fostering and facilitating of positive interactions for thousands of teenagers, directors, teachers, parents and carers across the whole of the UK.

The plays in this collection set out to see, listen and actively engage with teenagers and the amazing brains they possess – in a mutually respectful, provocative and fundamentally creative way. Presenting worlds where nothing of any value can ever and must never be taken for granted but must be fought for and actively maintained through vigilance and care. The worlds in these plays are challenging, populated by homophobes, insensitive rampant capitalists, grieving gamers, lost people, lost souls, the hyper-anxious, reticent, quiet and over-controlling, the violently angry and aggrieved – lonely, regretful and criminal, committing crimes against humanity and against the planet. They are also simultaneously astonishingly empathetic, vibrant, upbeat, inventive, funny, defiant, joyful and hopeful. They make fun, create drama, go deep and rise high above the clouds to new heights – providing new horizons, fresh insight and re-energised faith.

What teenagers have is passion, energy and desire. What you have when you are thirty, is experience, knowledge and agency. Combine all of this and it's a potent mix. Connections is that cocktail, and every performance is a bubble of possibility exploding within and beyond borders – set to make a positive impact, powerful enough to last a lifetime and illuminate the future.

So here's to being thirty, to being a teenager and to our playwrights, who together create thousands of stories and millions of reasons for us to be cheerful and not fearful about the future.

Ola Animashawun
Connections Dramaturg
November 2024

Connections 2025 Synopses

A note on casting

At National Theatre Connections we think long and hard about every play that we add to the selection. The writers whose plays make up our portfolios offer their plays as stories about humanity. We want the plays to be for everyone, and to tell stories about a wide range of experiences from around the world.

We are proud to continue to offer plays that challenge young people to experience life in someone else's shoes, and transport them to different times, places and emotional landscapes. We encourage our playwrights to keep the casting options for their plays as open as possible. For all plays in the portfolio, all parts can be played by D/deaf and disabled performers and, apart from where the playwright states otherwise, by actors of any gender or ethnicity. If your group doesn't exactly match the apparent casting requirements of a play in terms of race, ethnicity or gender, and you would like to produce it, we would still encourage you to do so. Any queries or changes regarding casting should be checked with the Connections team and we will advise accordingly.

Where locations are specified, rather than being preoccupied with accents, we recommend focusing your energies on finding the emotional truth of these settings.

Character Plots and Main Narrative Beats – Making Plays More Accessible

To make each play easier to navigate, we have created **Character Plot** and **Main Narrative Beats** documents. They provide a clear, simplified overview of the play, which may be especially useful for:

- Quickly understanding the play's structure before reading it in full
- Identifying which play best suits your group of young people
- Supporting casting decisions by showing how characters appear throughout the play
- Helping young people engage with the story in a clear, accessible way.

Thank you to our Connections 2025 Associate Director, Freyja Winterson for creating these documents. Special thanks to the team at Hackney Shed, for inspiring and informing this work.

Character Plots

Each Character Plot lays out:

- **Scenes** (listed along the top axis)
- **Characters** (listed on the left-hand side)
- A **tick mark** for each scene a character appears in

We hope that this makes it easier to cast your production to suit your group's needs, and may help towards your rehearsal planning and preparation.

For No Regrets by Gary McNair, the character plot is formatted differently, as it does not have named characters. Instead, it offers scene breakdowns for three different company sizes – explained in detail on p258.

Main Narrative Beats

The Main Narrative Beats document provides a simple breakdown of key plot points, and we hope that this offers an accessible entry point into each play. This helps:

- Quickly assess if a play is right for your group
- Introduce the story to your company in a clear, digestible way.

These resources are designed to remove barriers to engaging with the plays, and we hope that it makes your process and the experience for your participants more inclusive.

Synopses

YOU 2.0 by Alys Metcalf

Cast size: minimum of eight, no upper limit and potential for ensemble
Suggested age suitability: 13+

Strangers Martha and Isaac find themselves forced into playing YOU 2.0, a new therapy video game designed to help players access their better selves. As they tackle the levels in two-player mode, the pair form an unlikely friendship behind the anonymity of their gaming avatars, but their impact on each other's lives goes much deeper than the game.

Content guidance:

- Discussion of mental health
- Allusion to self-harm
- Mild language
- Discussion of bereavement
- References to chronic illness.

Normalised by Amanda Verlaque

How do you protect a memory against a homophobic bully, when the bully is your own brother?

Cast size: minimum of twelve, potential for additional ensemble roles
Suggested age suitability: 14+

When an environmental campaign is the catalyst for protecting an LGBTQIA+ shrine, a group of friends must confront what comes first – friends or family. As the stakes rise, the battle lines are drawn between being loyal and being an ally – and what does 'normal' really mean anyway?

Content guidance:

- Strong language (you are welcome to remove any swear words if preferred)
- References to the death of a character (unseen, prior to the play starting) in a car accident, and themes of grief
- References to and depictions of homophobia
- Depictions of bullying
- One character gets beaten up (offstage, unseen) and returns bruised.

Brain Play by Chloë Lawrence-Taylor and Paul Sirett

Cast size: ten named speaking characters (five of which are voiced puppets), plus an ensemble
Suggested age suitability: 13+

When Mia's dad suffers a traumatic brain injury and struggles to leave the house, she makes it her mission to find the cure for his symptoms. Delving deeper and deeper into the world of neuroscience, Mia is desperate to make him better, but first she must contend with her own brain.

Content guidance:

- Strong language (you are welcome to remove any swear words if preferred)
- Discussion of brain injury and the associate affects
- Discussion of anxiety, PTSD, obsessive compulsive disorder and mental health
- References to blood
- Discussion of hearing loss
- References to agoraphobia
- At one point a character says 'take him out and shoot him', in jest.

Saba's Swim by Danusia Samal

Cast size: eight named speaking characters
Suggested age suitability: 15+

Seven months ago, Saba walked out of her GCSE mocks and didn't come back. Her friends don't understand why. Now, on prom night, Saba's finally made contact, challenging her friends to track her down via a series of cryptic clues. But when the friends are finally reunited, Saba is different. The way she sees the world has changed. And what she's asking of her friends . . . is it more than they can give?

Content guidance:

- Frequent descriptions of war, bombing and death, including the death of infants
- Descriptions of drowning
- Mild language
- Mention of depression
- Depiction of arson
- Discussion of prison and criminality
- One character smokes on stage.

No Regrets by Gary McNair

Cast size: fully flexible, can be performed by a cast of three to 100 with lots of opportunities to play multiple and varying roles.
Suggested age suitability: 14+

Over the course of five years, playwright Gary McNair spoke to people at all stages and in all walks of life on the subject of regret. This play marks the results of those conversations. A collection of scenes from the silly to the profound, which charts our relationship with the things we should have done but didn't and the things we shouldn't have done but did.

Content guidance:

- Strong language
- Description of violence
- Mention of alcohol and addiction
- One scene of a mugging and stabbing
- References to death.

The Company of Trees by Jane Bodie

Cast size: ten named speaking roles
Suggested age suitability: 14+

When new girl Willow moves into town, the popular gang at school don't welcome her. But when gang leader Taylor has a spectacular gymnastic accident, leaving her bed-bound, her once loyal gang begin to drop away.
    Enter Willow, to share Taylor's solitude, teach her about trees and poems that don't rhyme, and Taylor begins to heal. A play about bullying, bravery, the power of nature, finding friendship, loneliness and Hanoi the giant tortoise.

Content guidance:

- Strong language (you are welcome to remove any swear words if preferred)
- Themes of bullying
- References to physical injury
- References to the loss of a parent.

Their Name Is Joy by May Sumbwanyambe

Cast size: ten named speaking roles
Suggested age suitability: 16+

Set in the summer of 2019, on a spring onion farm in Lincolnshire, *Their Name Is Joy* is a bittersweet coming-of-age drama that explores a terrifying loss of childhood innocence, as experienced by a group of young British casual labourers when they come face to face with the reality of modern-day slavery.

Content guidance:

- Instances of xenophobia and far-right views
- References to starvation
- Discussion of trafficking and modern slavery.

Ravers by Rikki Beadle-Blair

Cast size: 21 named speaking roles, option to combine characters if you need to
Suggested age suitability: 14+

A rag-tag group of self-described 'neeks' (nerds and geeks) gather at midnight in a local park to hold a 'dry rave' (no intoxicants). Will they succeed in redefining 'cool'? Or will the powers that be succeed in shutting down the neek revolution?

Content guidance:

- Depiction of underage drinking
- Moderate language (you are welcome to remove any swear words if preferred)
- Themes of anxiety.

Mia and the Fish by Satinder Chohan

Cast size: 11 named speaking roles, potential for other non-speaking roles
Suggested age suitability: 13+

A modern retelling of the ancient Indian myth Manu and the fish. Mia is a young refugee girl who along with her sister is washed up onto the shores of the UK. Against the backdrop of a freak winter heatwave, as the climate emergency becomes critical, one day Mia happens upon and nurtures a talking fish that she names Samaki. As well as becoming Mia's friend and confidante, Samaki quickly grows and becomes a giant fish, larger than any marine animal the world has ever known and the key to her and her friends' survival in the face of the imminent extinction of humanity.

Content guidance:

- Discussion of the climate emergency
- References to displacement and the refugee crisis
- Mild language.

Fresh Air by Vickie Donoghue

Cast size: 12 named speaking roles
Suggested age suitability: 14+

Students from a pupil referral group are made to go orienteering in what they discover is England's most haunted woods. Stalked by eerie ghost children determined to keep them there for ever, they must learn to confront the here and now to unlock the key to their futures.

Content guidance:

- Moderate language (you are welcome to remove any swear words if preferred)
- Mild gore
- Mild dread throughout
- Ghosts and supernatural elements throughout
- References to mental health
- One instance of a character being choked – in a supernatural context, with no physical contact required.

YOU 2.0

by Alys Metcalf

Alys Metcalf is a Welsh writer with strong links to the Isles of Scilly. She works across TV, theatre and film. She is an alumnus of BBC Cornish Voices and BBC Comedy Room, and trained under the Royal Court Young Writers and Criterion New Writers programmes. Her play *Leopards* opened the new artistic director's season at Rose Theatre and was co-produced by Francesca Moody Productions, Rose Theatre and Kater Gordon. Other plays include *Your Only Live Forever* at Soho Theatre; *Reel Life* at Ustinov Studio, Theatre Royal Bath; and *Unearthed* on a UK tour. Alys Metcalf is currently under script commission with the BBC for a new TV drama and is developing her debut feature film *Little Rock* with Ffilm Cymru and Blue Horizon Productions. She has written several online beginner's guides for popular TV shows, including *Peaky Blinders*, as well as interactive AI story *The Act* for the BBC.

Characters

Martha	*16*
Isaac	*16*
Headmaster	*60s*
Ivy	*12, Martha's sister*
Mrs Edwards	*30s/40s, a geography teacher*
Danny	*16, Isaac's mate*
Lucas	*16, Isaac's mate*
Ruth	*40s, Martha's mum*
Rude Customer	*An entitled customer*

Characters within the video game:

Screw This	*Martha's gaming avatar*
Dead Inside	*Isaac's gaming avatar*
The Game	*An ensemble representing the voice and actions of the game*
Avatar (1–4)	*Warm, energised, patronising, central guides of the video game (This role can be played by one to four actors, depending on cast size, at the director's discretion)*
Disclaimer	*The serious, fast-delivered game disclaimer*
Dancing Deana	*A dance fitness avatar*
Mindless Monster	*A volatile monster*
Little Timmy	*A scared little boy*
Ball of Stress	*A taunting ball of stress*
Mobile Phone	*A taunting mobile phone*
Freud	*Sigmund Freud*
Bingo Caller	*A bingo caller*

With the exception of characters Martha, Isaac, Screw This and Dead Inside, the cast can play multiple roles. Everything pertaining to the video game should be achieved by the ensemble, as physically and creatively as they wish. No screens/projections should be used throughout the play.

(–)	*Denotes an interruption.*
Beat.	*A pause wherein the unspoken causes an emotional shift in character.*

Scene One

A dark stage. A whooshing sound. A 'loading' icon swirls on screen.

The Game   LOADING. LOADING. LOADING.

Cheery-looking **Avatar** *appears, beaming. The 'loading' icon disappears.*

Avatar   Well, hello! And welcome to YOU 2.0, the game-based emotional learning experience, empowering a happier, more balanced, *better* you!

Now, are you ready to level up your life?! Press X if so!

Beat.

Beginning is the hardest thing. But once you get started you won't regret it! So, shall we get going?!

Beat.

A brand new YOU is waiting to meet you!

Beat.

So, what do you think, are you ready to press X?

Beat.

Emotional understanding is just a click away!

Beat.

Come on, press X, you know you're worth it!

Finally, a 'X' sound pings.

The Game   YEYYYY!

Avatar   Congratulations! You've just made the first positive step in taking control of your life!

We now see **Martha** *(sixteen) in her bedroom. She's sitting on her bed in her pyjamas, game controller in hand, looking unimpressed. (The video gaming screen in front of her is in the direction of the audience.) She's wearing a rainbow-coloured woolly hat.*

Martha   What the hell, I didn't press anything?!

Avatar   As you play YOU 2.0, you'll learn key lessons about yourself whilst completing enlightening tasks and expanding your mental and emotional understanding. Your objective is to reach the final level, where you'll be awarded the prize of your best self, YOU 2.0.

Martha   Whoopee.

Avatar   Just before we begin, here's a quick reminder of our player policy!

Disclaimer (*spoken quickly*)   For privacy, protection and GDPR purposes, YOU 2.0, a Do Better Games Ltd creation, does not accept any responsibility for real-life consequences of player decisions. Personal improvement is contingent on the participant's investment in the game, but results are subject to individuals and not guaranteed. YOU 2.0 is not a substitute for seeking professional help.

Martha Alright, chill out.

Avatar Before we get started, you need to choose a player name. For privacy reasons, please choose a pseudonym. And be as playful as you like!

The Game TYPE IN THE BOX BELOW!

Martha *types.*

Avatar If you're happy with the name you've chosen then press X!

Martha *presses X.*

Great to meet you, Screw This! It's time to personalise your avatar!

How we outwardly present ourselves can be a reflection of self-identity. Scroll through the options and select the item that resonates with you most!

Martha Okay, what we got here?

A carousel of colourful accessories appears: a variety of hats, a colourful shield, giant glasses, a cape . . . **Martha** *scrolls through them.*

(*Scrolling through.*) No . . . no . . . no . . . no . . . ah, whatever! This one.

She selects the shield.

Avatar Interesting! Shields are associated with self-protection, used to conceal and defend oneself. What do you think this choice says about you?

Martha Jeez, it really wasn't that deep.

Avatar If you're happy with your choice press X.

Martha Hang on a second!

She scrolls to a hat with a giant bone on top of it.

. . . There we go.

Avatar Boneheads are associated with stubbornness, foolishness and stupidity, what do you think –

Martha Don't care!

The 'X' sound pings.

Avatar Great choice, Screw This, your avatar is ready!

Martha's *cheerful-faced avatar,* **Screw This**, *appears, wearing the bone hat.*

Avatar And now with *that* out the way . . . let's play!

The screen goes dark, except for the swirling 'loading' icon.

The Game LOADING. LOADING. LOADING.

Scene Two

Headmaster's *office, secondary school.* **Headmaster** *and* **Martha** *sit opposite each other.*

Headmaster I'd like to stop meeting like this.

Martha As would I, Headmaster. Truly.

Headmaster Your behaviour would suggest otherwise.

Martha I really think that's a matter of perspective, sir.

Headmaster From Mrs Edwards' perspective you humiliated her in front of the class.

Martha She always assumes we don't know stuff.

Headmaster She's a teacher, that's the basis of her job.

Martha Well, I find it very condescending, sir. Especially being put down a set. I'm acing my grades, I'm miles ahead of the others, it doesn't make sense?

Headmaster Classroom insubordination, bolshy, dismissive behaviour with fellow students, a general refusal to comply with the rules –

Martha So I'm a nonconformist –

Headmaster You're your own worst enemy.

Martha I dunno, sir, some of the girls in my class *really* hate me.

Headmaster (*sternly*) This isn't a joke, Martha. Someone's locker was raided last week, their valuables taken.

Martha Are you accusing me of *stealing*, sir?

Headmaster According to the janitor you were sighted around that area at the time.

Martha Probably getting something out of my own locker? When did this happen exactly?

Headmaster You tell me.

Martha I've no idea.

Headmaster I'm sure you appreciate the serious implications if it's found to be true.

Martha Of course, but I didn't do it.

Headmaster Be that as it may, given your recent poor conduct and while we're looking into the theft allegation, we've made the unfortunate decision to place you on temporary suspension for a week.

Martha (*panicked*) What?! That's not fair! I can't – my mum can't – I mean, that really won't work, sir.

Headmaster You'll spend the week addressing the root of your unruly behaviour and learning how to interact appropriately.

Martha And how do you propose I do that, cooped up at home all day?

Headmaster Ordinarily, we'd engage you in the school counselling service, but since falling victim to recent funding cuts we no longer have one. However, we do have access to a new game-based wellbeing platform.

Martha A what now?

Headmaster We'll supply the gaming equipment. You'll log in once a day at the same time and make sure you complete it.

Martha And what if I don't want to do it?

Headmaster You're smart, Martha. I'm sure you know the answer.
It really would be a shame to lose you.

The school bell rings. **Martha** *looks concerned.*

Scene Three

The next morning. **Martha***'s house. Kitchen.*

Ivy *is dressed in school uniform, shoving schoolbooks into her rucksack.* **Martha***'s wearing her pyjamas and dressing gown, holding a lunchbox.*

Ivy You seen my maths book? Can't find it anywhere.

Martha No, but you're gonna be late.

Ivy *now notices what* **Martha***'s wearing.*

Ivy Why aren't you dressed? You're not ill.

Martha If anyone asks then I am, okay?

Ivy That's weird. What are you up to? Does Mum know?

Martha Listen, you know those jeans I've got?

Ivy The ones you never let me borrow?

Martha They're vintage.

Ivy You got them from a charity shop.

Martha Whatever. If you keep it a secret that I'm home this week then you can wear them.

Ivy You mean a secret from Mum?

Beat.

Martha Alright, then you can have them.

Ivy Deal. I'm gonna wear them on my birthday.

Martha Yeah, about that. Maybe don't hassle Mum about the whole roller skates thing.

Ivy (*annoyed*)   I haven't even mentioned it!

Martha   Alright, good. Now run or you'll miss the bus!

Ivy   So bossy! (*Referring to* **Martha**'s *rainbow woolly hat.*) Where'd you get that hat?

Martha   Nowhere, now go!

She realises she's holding **Ivy**'s *lunch box.*

Martha   Ivy!

She passes it over.

Ivy   It's not last night's pasta, is it?

Martha   You want to waste it?

Ivy (*rolls her eyes*)   Obviously not.

She goes to leave, then –

Hey, where you bunking off to?

Martha   Nowhere. I'll just be in my room.

Ivy   Doing what?

Martha   Playing a video game.

Ivy   Wow. That's *really* sad.

She leaves.

Scene Four

Continued from Scene One. **Martha**'s *bedroom.*

The Game   LOADING. LOADING. LOADING.

Martha   Come on, let's get this out the way.

The Game   NEW PLAYER!

Martha   What?!

Avatar   A new player has joined the game. You have the option of continuing solo, or joining forces to play YOU 2.0 as a two-player game.

Martha   Yeah, no thanks.

Avatar   Aside from mastering the art of teamwork, your differing skill sets and life experiences may help guide you through the levels with greater ease, understanding and, of course, speed.

Martha   Speed? Well, why didn't you say?!

She presses X.

The Game CONNECTING YOU WITH DEAD INSIDE!

Martha I'm sorry, *who*?

Suddenly, avatars **Screw This** *and* **Dead Inside** *(wearing a hooded cape) appear on screen next to each other.*

Avatar Screw This meet Dead Inside, your gaming companion! You must now work as a team until the end of the game, completing each level.

You can only succeed together!

Martha Could've mentioned that *before* I got stuck with the Grim Reaper.

Avatar Please put on the wrist and ankle bands provided in your gaming pack.

Then press X when you're ready!

Martha *shoves on the wrist and ankle bands, then presses X.*

The Game LEVEL ONE . . . THE DOPAMINE DANCE!

Game character **Dancing Deana** *spins onto the screen. Her enthusiasm borders on cringeworthy.*

Dancing Deana Yo yo yo! I'm Dancing Deana! Follow my lead and let's bust out some moves, getting us *into* our *bodies* and *outta* our *minds*!

Dancing Deana *does a freestyle move, then freezes.*

Avatar Dancing is a great way to boost your physical and mental wellbeing, lowering cortisol and raising happy hormones like serotonin and dopamine. Simply follow the arrows on screen to dance like Deana!

Screw This, you're up first!

A pop song strikes up. **Dancing Deana** *starts bopping on the spot, centre stage. Players* **Screw This** *and* **Dead Inside** *appear either side of her.*

Dancing Deana Screw This! Are we ready?! Five, six, seven, eight –

Dancing Deana *does a series of simple moves to the music, dancing on spot. As she moves her arms and legs,* **The Game** *shows instruction arrows, indicating < left > right ∧ up and ∨ down, for the player to follow.*

Martha *starts doing some of the moves, mimicked by* **Screw This**, *who is synchronised with her. She accidentally misses out some of the moves.* **Dead Inside** *stays still.*

Dancing Deana Not bad! Good attempt!

Martha Oi, don't patronise me!

Suddenly **Martha** *concentrates and* **Screw This** *starts doing well.*

Dancing Deana Hey, great progress! You look awesome!

Martha Obviously. This is easy!

Dancing Deana   Your serotonin is surging, your dopamine is looking dope!

Screw This *is now smashing the moves –* **Martha***'s momentarily invested.*

Dancing Deana *pauses.*

Dancing Deana   Wow, Screw This, you deserve a quick break! It's over to you, Dead Inside. In five, six, seven, eight –

Martha *stops, out of breath.* **Screw This** *stands in neutral as* **Dead Inside** *begins to dance.*

They struggle with the moves, skipping loads out – including all the moves using the left arm.

Dancing Deana   Keep going, Dead Inside, practice makes perfect!

That's better. Don't give up!

Dead Inside *gets slightly better but is still missing all the moves on the left arm.*

Dancing Deana   It's the trying that counts. Great effort!

Martha   He's not moving his left arm!

Dancing Deana   Choreography isn't for everyone. But don't worry, now's your chance to break form and show your creativity!

The Game   FREESTYLE TIME!

Martha   Oh God, no.

Dancing Deana   Now let yourself go and feel the flow! Are we ready? Everybody!

In five, six, seven, eight –

Dancing Deana *freestyles on the spot.*

Don't self-censor! Dance like no one's watching! Throw yourself in and feel the flow!

Screw This *and* **Dead Inside** *stand still.* **Martha** *looks flummoxed.*

Dancing Deana   Feel the endorphins!

Martha   Feel like a dickhead!

Dancing Deana   Don't let insecurity and pride stand in your way!

Martha   Who you calling insecure?!

Dancing Deana   Uh oh, if you don't get moving you won't complete the level!

Martha   Arrrggh, fine then!

Martha/Screw This *suddenly start freestyling self-consciously.*

Dancing Deana   Woah, look at you, Screw This! That's it, unleash yourself!

Dead Inside, I need more from you! Remember you're working as a team!

Martha   Yeah come on!

Dead Inside *barely moves, except for stomping their feet and moving their right arm up and down.*

Dancing Deana   Uh oh, looks like your collective happy hormones are dropping!

Martha   Have you only got the one move?! What's wrong with you?!

A surge down sound.

The Game   HORMONE LEVELS CRITICALLY LOW!

Martha   For God's sake!

She suddenly unleashes herself – into fast, energised, manic dancing.

Slowly, a surging up sound. It climbs and climbs as **Martha** *exerts herself.*

The Game   HORMONE LEVELS RISING!

Dancing Deana   Wow! Keep it up!

Finally, a ding-ding noise of success!

Way to go! Dopamine target reached!

Martha *collapses in a heap, sick from exertion.*

The Game   YEYY! YOU DID IT!

The music stops. **Dancing Deana** *disappears.*

Avatar   Congratulations, you've completed the first level! And didn't you look groovy? Remember, no one wants to stagnate in life. Moving your body figuratively and literally helps you move forward!

Martha *rips off the bands, throws them across the room. Flops on her bed, exhausted.*

The Game   REFLECTION SECTION!

Avatar   Take a moment to reflect on how moving your body made you think and feel. You can share your thoughts with your fellow player by typing in the text box below.

Martha (*annoyed*)   I do have a few *thoughts* actually.

Disclaimer   A reminder that we advise caution in sharing any real names or personal information which can be used to identify you or your location.

The Game   TYPE YOUR MESSAGE BELOW!

Screw This *and* **Dead Inside** *face each other. (When they speak their voices are upbeat and free of sarcasm.)*

Martha (*types/speaks her message*)   Hi, Dead Inside. What the . . .

Screw This   Hi, Dead Inside! What the heck is your problem?!

A brief pause.

Dead Inside   . . . Someone's got a temper!

Martha (*typing*)   Yeah 'cause you –

Screw This   Yeah 'cause you sabotaged the game!

Dead Inside   . . . I didn't! Not on purpose, anyway!

Martha (*typing*)   You weren't even . . .

Screw This   . . . You weren't even trying! You barely put your dead heart into it!

Dead Inside   . . . I was!

Martha (*typing*)   Hello?! You . . .

Screw This   Hello! You only moved the one arm!

Dead Inside   . . . Yes, because the other one is injured!

We now see **Isaac** *in his bedroom – his left arm is bandaged. He's wearing pyjamas, holding the game controller. In the following section,* **Martha** *and* **Isaac** *continue to type before their respective avatars speak (though there doesn't need to be big pauses between their typing and the avatars talking).*

Isaac   That's thrown them.

Martha   Good excuse.

Screw This   What's wrong with it?!

Isaac   Um. . . .

Dead Inside   Fell off my bike, cut it open!

Martha   Damn it, why did I choose two-player!

Dead Inside   But I'll try my best!

Screw This   I really need this game to be over!

Dead Inside   Just stop playing then?!

Screw This   I can't, it's compussery!

Isaac   What?

Martha (*realising the typo*)   Agh!

Screw This   Compusslarary!

Martha   No, agh!

Dead Inside   Compulsory?

Martha   Yeah.

Screw This   Yes!

Dead Inside   . . . Why?!

Martha   An excellent question.

Screw This   My school's making me! I'm suspended!

Dead Inside   What did you do?!

Screw This   Nothing! Appaz I have a bad attitude!

Dead Inside   Which school?!

Martha   Alright, creep.

Isaac   Wonder if that's creepy?

Screw This   FYI not meant to share personal info!

Isaac   Fair enough.

Screw This   Why are you playing?!

Isaac   Where to begin?

Dead Inside   . . . For fun!

Martha (*scoffs*)   Fun?! Whatever, Dead Inside. That's the biggest load of –

Screw This   That's the biggest load of doodoo I've ever heard!

Isaac   Doodoo? Are we five?

Martha   Doodoo? No, I meant load of . . .

Screw This   Load of doodoo!

Martha   So it's censored out profanities. Alright, *game*, then how about . . .

Screw This   Flip off!

Isaac   Excuse me?

Screw This   Flipping female canine!
Faeces of a bull!
Faeces for brains!
Twit face!

Isaac   I'm sorry?

Screw This   Cockerel slurper!

Martha   That's original.

Isaac   What's happening?

Screw This   Bollards!
Stupid prick!

Martha (*thrilled*)   Aha!

Isaac *looks offended.*

Martha (*smugly*)   Forgot to censor *that* one didn't they?!

Isaac (*deflated*)   I really don't need this.

Dead Inside   Okay, enjoy the game!

Isaac *puts down the controller, stands to leave his bedroom.*

Martha   What?! Wait, no, no, no, don't go! I wasn't . . .

Screw This   I wasn't talking to you!

Isaac *pauses.*

Martha   Crap, are they still there? I can't finish this without them!

Avatar   If you've finished sharing your reflections then click X to load the next learning!

Martha *clicks. Her* **Avatar** *faces out, in a ready stance.*

The Game   Screw This, READY!

Isaac *stands, unsure.* **Martha** *looks anxious.*

Martha   Come on, please.

Avatar   Over to you, Dead Inside. Press X to continue your journey together. A happier you is just around the corner!

Isaac *hesitates.*

Scene Five

A week before. School classroom. **Mrs Edwards** *stands before her students.*

Mrs Edwards   As a matter of fact, the *smaller* the earthquake, the more *frequently* they occur. And of course, the name of the instrument used to measure their seismic waves is. . .?

A stumped room.

Clue's in the word *seismic*? Anyone? We did cover this.

The bell rings. The classroom starts to empty.

It's a seismograph. Alright off you go, if you haven't already. Oh, actually, Isaac, can you stay behind a moment please?

Isaac *looks surprised.*

Isaac   Yes, miss.

Miss Edwards *busies herself while the class clears.* **Danny** *and* **Lucas** *playfully jostle* **Isaac**.

Danny   Ooh, he's in trouble!

Lucas   Has the angel-boy finally lost his halo?

Isaac (*laughs*) Hardly an angel.

Lucas Whatever, you're so squeaky-clean I can see my reflection.

Danny Hey, you coming to Jordan's later?

Lucas Gonna watch that shark film.

Isaac *Jaws*?

Lucas No the other one. The big one.

Danny The megalodon one. Meant to be shit. But good shit.

Mrs Edwards (*from across the room*) No swearing!

Danny Sorry, miss.

Isaac (*quietly*) If I make it out alive then, yeah, I'll be there.

Lucas (*to* **Danny**) He's gonna flake again.

Danny Don't flake this time. Serious. (*Points to* **Isaac***'s bandaged arm.*) And don't use that thing as an excuse either. You don't need an arm to watch a film.

Isaac Alright, alright, I'll be there.

Lucas You better.

Danny Lucas needs you to comfort him. He's a right wuss with horror films.

Lucas I'm not!

Danny Whatever. (*To* **Isaac**.) Later, man!

Danny *leaves, trailed by* **Lucas**.

Lucas (*to* **Danny**) Hey, I'm not a wuss.

Isaac*'s now alone with* **Mrs Edwards**. *An awkward moment. Then* **Mrs Edwards** *softens.*

Her manner is kind, concerned.

Mrs Edwards I'm sorry. I always hate the ambiguity of asking a student to stay behind.

Isaac That's alright. Have I done something, miss?

Mrs Edwards No, or rather . . . maybe that's the issue, the *not* doing. I hear you've cancelled all your extra-curricular activities?

Isaac Because of my arm, miss. I fell off my bike –

Mrs Edwards Yes, I understand. But that happened last week and this has been going on for a while.

Isaac Has it?

Mrs Edwards I've noticed you generally seem less involved . . . enthused, than you used to be.

Isaac Sorry, miss . . . if I've not . . . I guess I've just been busy.

Mrs Edwards (*not unkindly*) Oh, I see. With what? Perhaps. . .with your thoughts?

Isaac *struggles to answer.*

Isaac I'll be okay, miss.

Mrs Edwards Well, in case you ever decide you're not feeling okay, I have a proposal. A bit of a fun one. Something a little different. A little, how should I put this? Out of the box.

Scene Six

The game, continued. **Martha** *and* **Isaac** *are in their rooms. He hesitates, controller in hand, then presses X.*

Avatar What do you say, Dead Inside, are you in?!

Isaac (*sighs*) . . . I've gotta try something.

He presses X. **Dead Inside** *poses in a ready stance.*

The Game DEAD INSIDE READY!

Martha Great! They're still here.

Avatar Before we move onto the next game, let's take a quick moment to talk about –

The Game DIFFICULT EMOTIONS!

The Game *can visually and creatively accompany the following speech to make it more dynamic. This could take the form of animated graphics in a self-help video.*

Avatar Life can be unpredictable. Sometimes it's going well . . . and sometimes it knocks us sideways. Either way, uncomfortable emotions, such as worry, fear, anger and sadness, can make it harder to cope.

Under enough emotional pressure, it's possible for the brain's *fight or flight* response to become overly sensitive, causing us to react with heightened anxiety, stress and even aggression when faced with everyday challenges.

But we're not powerless. Through mindfulness and self-awareness, we can rewire our brains and embrace a more balanced approach to life.

The first step is to acknowledge these feelings, rather than bury them.

Martha I acknowledge that I feel bored.

Avatar Over time, this will help you learn what your triggers are.

Isaac I know what mine is.

Avatar One useful technique to help deal with emotional pressure is box breathing. Before we begin the next game, take a moment to breathe in for four seconds, then hold your breath for four seconds, breathe out for four seconds, then hold again for four seconds.

Let's try it now!

Isaac *does the following,* **Martha** *doesn't.*

The Game   *IN*, TWO, THREE, FOUR, *HOLD*, TWO, THREE, FOUR, **OUT**, TWO, THREE, FOUR, *HOLD*, TWO, THREE, FOUR!

Avatar   Do you feel calmer?!

Martha/Isaac   No/Kind of.

Avatar   Excellent! Now on with the game!

The Game   LEVEL TWO! THE MINDLESS MONSTER!

Avatar   We can't always control what thoughts pop into our heads. But we can try to reframe the unhelpful ones!

In this game, select the right strategies to battle the Mindless Monster's dark thoughts, taking him from mindless to mindful!

The Game   LET'S PLAY!

Screw This *and* **Dead Inside** *avatars face the* **Mindless Monster** *in poised stances, as if ready to fight. The set-up looks a bit like the 2D video game* Street Fighter.

The Game   ROUND ONE!

Lively music starts up. **Mindless Monster** *lets out a frustrated whine.*

Mindless Monster   Ugh! I hate the way I look today! I'm such a monster!

Isaac   Sounds like self-doubt.

Martha   Okay, *select a strategy.*

Isaac   Okay, what have we got?

Martha (*scrolling through options*)   *Retail therapy*, no . . . *Take a risk*, no.

Isaac (*scrolling through options*)   *Change appearance*, no . . . *Practise positive self-talk?*

Dead Inside *lunges towards* **Mindless Monster**, *sending them the command.*

Dead Inside   PRACTISE POSITIVE SELF-TALK!

The command hits **Mindless Monster**, *transforming him to a slightly happier state.*

Mindless Monster   At least with my nice strong teeth and sharp claws I can kill and eat whatever I want!

Martha   Nice one, Dead Inside. I'll go . . . *show self-compassion.*

Screw This *lunges forward, sending self-compassion.*

Screw This   SHOW SELF-COMPASSION!

Mindless Monster (*happier still*) It's been a long day, no wonder I feel beastly! Maybe I need a rest!

A ding-ding-ding noise.

The Game ROUND TWO!

Mindless Monster *huffs.*

Mindless Monster Why don't I live in a big cave like the other monsters?! My cave sucks!

Isaac *Take a bath*, no . . . *Create a to-do list* . . .

Martha Okay, how about . . .

Screw This (*lunging forward*) CHALLENGE THE THOUGHT!

Mindless Monster (*upbeat*) I guess having a bigger cave wouldn't make me a better monster. And mine's a pretty decent size already!

Dead Inside (*lunging forward*) PRACTISE GRATITUDE!

Mindless Monster At the end of the day, I'm lucky to even *have* a cave to live in!

A ding-ding-ding noise.

The Game ROUND THREE!

Mindless Monster *stomps his feet and roars.*

Mindless Monster GRRR! Someone just ordered me about! They think I'm beneath them!
I'm so mad!

Martha Of course you are!

Isaac But what's the context?

Martha (*scrolling*) *Take a time out* . . . *Examine own insecurities* . . . screw off!

Isaac Maybe they weren't *ordering*. It's all about interpretation.

Screw This (*lunging*) ASSERT DOMINANCE!

Isaac Assert dominance?!

Martha Yeah, you show 'em!

Isaac Screw This, what are you doing?!

Mindless Monster *grows tall and growls.*

Mindless Monster GRRRR! ORDER ME AGAIN, I DARE YOU!

The Game UH OH, ANGER INCREASING!

Martha (*confused*) But you've got to stand up for yourself!

Isaac Quick, gotta calm him down!

Dead Inside (*lunging*)   BREATHE!

Mindless Monster *takes a deep breath.*

Mindless Monster   That slowed down my fight or flight response. But I'm still annoyed!

Isaac   What else then?! . . . Aha!

Dead Inside (*lunging*)   CONSIDER OTHER PERSPECTIVES!

Mindless Monster   Perhaps they weren't undermining me. Perhaps my sense of status and self-worth felt threatened due to underlying insecurities.

An end of game noise.

The Game   YEYYYYY!

Avatar   Congratulations, you made the Mindless Monster mindful!

The next time you find an unhelpful thought popping into your head, try remembering the three Cs. Catch it, check it, change it!

The Game   REFLECTION SECTION!

Avatar   It's time to reflect on the ways you might challenge your unhelpful thoughts. Now both players know each other a little better, you have the option of enabling speak mode! Press X to continue.

Isaac   Guess two-player is less lonely. Okay.

He presses X.

The Game   ENABLING SPEAK MODE!

Martha   No, I don't want to speak!

Avatar   Another friendly reminder to exercise caution and discretion around sharing personal information.

Martha   Wait, where's opt-out? Why is there no opt-out?!

The Game   PLAYERS CONNECTED!

Martha *and* **Isaac** *can now hear each other. Throughout their conversation,* **Screw This** *and* **Dead Inside** *stay facing each other, in a static holding state, occasionally adjusting to a new position.*

Beat.

Isaac   Hello?

Um. Hello?

Beat.

Guess it's not working?

Martha   Actually it is.

Isaac Oh ... Sorry.

We don't have to talk, if you don't want to.

Martha Do you want to talk?

Isaac I dunno. Might help?

Martha To discuss game tactics?

Isaac Uh ... sure, that too, I guess. Interesting choice by the way ... *Assert dominance*.

Martha You taking the piss?

Isaac Just wondering why you chose it. Like, what's your thinking behind that?

Martha No offence but can we skip the whole *reflection* thing? I've just gotta finish this game and get back to school before my mum finds out I'm suspended.

Isaac Okay ... if you want.

Martha I know there's a place for all this introspective, self-discovery stuff, but I've got enough on my plate and I won't be patronised by a rudimentary, impersonal, rolled-out for dummies video game.

Isaac You missed out thematically confused and with terrible graphics.

Martha Right? It's super-outdated.

Isaac I know, like, what is this? *2012*?

Beat.

Even if it's stupid I'll take a distraction right now. My school thinks I'm off sick this week having minor surgery on my arm. I forged this whole letter from my dad.

Martha You're bunking off?

Isaac I guess I just wanted a break from people?

Martha To play a crappy video game?

Isaac It's gotten a bit weird at home on my own, like, I think I actually need distractions. I remembered the game. My teacher suggested it to me the other day –

Martha Your teacher hates you –

Isaac And I thought, what the hell. Got nothing to lose.

Martha Because you're *dead inside*?

Isaac That's just a joke. Couldn't think of a username.

Martha Behind every joke there's some truth.

Isaac I thought you didn't want to get reflective?

Martha Touché.

Avatar If you've finished sharing your reflections then click X to load the next game!

Martha Come on, then, let's blitz this.

Isaac I chose two-player for the company, not to be bossed about to a finish line.

He presses X.

The Game DEAD INSIDE, READY!

Martha Alright. Keep your cape on.

She presses X.

The Game SCREW THIS, READY!

Scene Seven

The Game LEVEL THREE – THE NIGHT WATCHERS!

Avatar One way to maintain a healthy body and mind, increase memory, emotional wellbeing and resilience is by practising good sleep hygiene. Using your anti-nap zapper, help Little Timmy get a good night's rest by fending off the incoming threats to his sleep!

Little Timmy, *a young boy in bed, yawns.*

Little Timmy I'm so, so sleepy!

He closes his eyes to sleep. **Screw This** *and* **Dead Inside** *guard his bedroom. A lullaby plays.*

Suddenly, **Ball of Stress** *enters the room, heading towards* **Little Timmy**, *who wakes up.*

The Game LOOK OUT! BALL OF STRESS!

Ball of Stress Stress stress stress stress stress!

Little Timmy Aggghh!

Martha Quick, shoot it!

Dead Inside *and* **Screw This** *fire their anti-nap zappers at* **Ball of Stress**. *Eventually it dies and fades away.*

Little Timmy Phew, goodnight!

Little Timmy *goes back to sleep.*

Next, a giant **Mobile Phone** *enters.*

The Game LOOK OUT! BLUE LIGHT!

Mobile Phone Scroll me, scroll me, scroll me!

Little Timmy *wakes, reaches for the phone.*

Little Timmy . . . Ooh, cat videos!

Dead Inside *and* **Screw This** *zap* **Mobile Phone**.

Isaac   Take that!

Eventually it dies.

Mobile Phone   Battery low! Noooo!

Little Timmy   My phone's died!

He goes back to sleep.

Oh well! Night night!

Next **Cup of Coffee** *enters the room.*

The Game   LOOK OUT! CAFFEINATED DRINK!

They zap at it.

Suddenly, the voice of **Martha**'s *mum,* **Ruth**, *outside her room.*

Ruth (*offstage*)   Martha?!

Startled, **Martha** *stops playing the game.* **Screw This** *stops shooting, freezing on the spot.*

Martha   Crap!

Isaac   What?

Martha (*to self*)   How do I pause this?! Aghh! Why won't it pause?!

Isaac   What you doing?

Martha   Muting you.

Isaac   Why what's happening?

Martha (*pressing mute*)   Mute.

Isaac (*silently*)   Hang on . . . Hello? Hello?!

He is now on mute and we can only see, not hear, him playing the game. The game temporarily disappears from stage.

Ruth *appears in* **Martha**'s *bedroom.*

Ruth   Thought I heard you –?

Martha   Mum, how come you're home?

Ruth   Forgot my glasses, I'm on a break. Same question to you?

Martha   It's . . . I'm sick.

Ruth   Really? What's wrong?

Martha   Sore throat. Aches.

Meanwhile, **Isaac** *is manically tapping the controller buttons, looking stressed.*

Ruth   Oh. I'm sorry love. I could've, well, I might've been able to take the day off –

Martha   No, it's fine, honestly. I just need sleep.

Ruth   I'll be home as soon as I can. We're a bit busy.

Martha   Take your time, I've got homework anyway.

Ruth   Okay, love.

Noticing the rainbow-coloured hat **Martha***'s wearing.*

Ruth   That's a nice hat.

Martha   A friend gave it to me.

Ruth   That's sweet. Are you cold? I'll put the heating on.

Martha   I'll do it. You better get back.

Isaac *stands up with his controller, concentrating on the screen, hammering the buttons, stressed.*

Isaac (*silently*)   Come on come on come on!

Ruth   Alright, well, see you later, love.

Martha   See you later, Mum.

Ruth *leaves.* **Martha** *breathes a sigh of relief. She shivers, wraps herself in her blanket.*

She picks up the controller.

Where were we?

She unmutes the game. It reappears. **Little Timmy** *is jumping up and down on the bed.*

Little Timmy   Wooopeeee!

Isaac (*exasperated*)   Aghhh!

The Game   GAME OVER!

Martha   What!

Isaac   Where've you been?

Avatar   Uh oh! Looks like Little Timmy will be up all night! To progress to the next level you'll need to restart and complete this game. But don't worry, failure makes us stronger! Take a quick moment to reflect on what you'll improve and do differently before the level restarts.

Martha   What happened?!

Isaac   You left halfway through, that's what happened.

Martha   Something came up, I thought you could handle it.

Isaac   No need to be rude, this isn't compulsory for me.

Martha Meaning?

Isaac Meaning I don't have to play it.

Martha Then go if you like! I don't care.

Isaac Really? 'Cause you can't finish without me.

Martha I think I said I don't care?

Isaac Sounds a lot like self-sabotage.

Martha Don't therapise me!

Isaac If you *have* to play this then you might as well get something out of it. Or it's even *more* of a punishment.

Martha I don't need anything out of it.

Isaac That sounds pretty defensive.

Martha Says the guy pretending he's playing for fun. What are you hiding?

Isaac Nothing.

Martha Are you an incel or something? What the hell's your problem?!

Isaac If you must know my mum died.

Martha *is taken aback.* **Isaac** *squirms.*

An uncomfortable beat.

Isaac Sorry.

Martha Why are you sorry?

Isaac For making it awkward.

Martha It was already awkward.

Beat.

So, are you sad then?

Isaac Well, obviously.

Martha No I mean, are you playing this game because you're sad? Because you know a grief counsellor would be better.

Isaac I had one for the first few months. Then life carried on, my friends forgot, or, I don't know. It's been a year and a half and everyone's stopped talking about it. It's easier to just pretend everything's normal.

Martha Sounds like hard work to me. Enough to drive you crazy.

It's an honest moment, in which they both slightly soften.

Avatar It's time to repeat the level. Press X when you're ready!

They hesitate.

Martha Maybe I was a bit defensive. If you want to go, I respect that.

Isaac Don't be nice to me because my mum died.

Martha I'm not, I'm just saying.

But if you play on, I promise to be less of a dick.

Beat.

Isaac *presses X.* **Dead Inside** *poses in a 'ready' stance.*

The Game DEAD INSIDE READY!

Martha *sighs with relief.* **Screw This** *poses in a 'ready' stance.*

The Game SCREW THIS READY!

Scene Eight

School yard. **Danny** *stares into a phone, recording a video.* **Lucas** *sulks behind him.*

Danny Isaac, tried you like three times, man. Why you not picking up?

Lucas Maybe his arm fell off in surgery?

Danny Ignore Lucas, he's just salty 'cause Abigail turned him down.

Lucas She didn't? I didn't even ask her.

Danny You're coming to the party this weekend, yeah? Kyra thinks you're coming, which means Brianna's coming, which means I'm counting on you.

Lucas He'll bail. That's what he does now.

Danny Anyway, hope the arm's good. Figure you'll be ok by the weekend, right? Strong guy like you.

The school bell rings.

Ah, prison calls. Gotta go!

(*Points camera at* **Lucas**.) Say bye, Lucas.

Lucas Bye, bailer.

Danny Love ya, man.

He finishes the video.

(*Tuts at* **Lucas**.) Salty, man, you're so salty.

Scene Nine

The game, continued. This scene runs like a montage in which we see fast-paced snapshots of various games and conversations as time passes and **Martha** *and* **Isaac** *move through the levels, getting increasingly into the game.*

The Game   LEVEL SEVEN – THE VAULT OF VULNERABILITY!

Avatar   Showing vulnerability is a sign of strength, not weakness. It can help break down barriers, build bridges and connect us with one another.

In this game, scale the Mountain of Troubles and collect enough courage coins to unlock the vault of vulnerability.

Dead Inside *runs on the spot (in profile, as if in 2D, like Super Mario) ahead of* **Screw This**.

Martha   Coin above your head, jump!

Dead Inside *jumps.*

Isaac   Damn, missed it!

Martha   I've got it.

Screw This *jumps. A ding sound, as they collect a coin.*

Isaac   Watch out, emotional curveball! Duck!

Screw This *and* **Dead Inside** *squat down as an emotional curveball rumbles overhead.*

The Game   REFLECTION SECTION!

Isaac   Those curveballs were crazy!

Martha   I know, they came out of nowhere!

Isaac   So, I'm guessing there's nothing you want to share? You know, be *vulnerable* about?

Martha   Ummm . . . nothing really springs to mind?

Isaac   Yeah . . . (*Lying.*) Me neither.

Martha   Great! Let's play!

The Game   LEVEL EIGHT – ANXIETY BINGO!

Bingo Caller   Being eaten alive!

Martha/Isaac   Eighty-five!

Bingo Caller   Fear of bees!

Isaac   Fifty-three!

Bingo Caller   Becoming poor!

Martha   Got it! Number four! BINGO!

The Game   REFLECTION SECTION!

Isaac   . . . Losing friends, chronic illnesses like my mum's. Oh, and the dark.

Martha   I hate the dark.

Isaac   Really? What else makes you anxious?

Martha   I dunno . . . nothing else really.

Isaac   Come on, I feel like I've told you loads!

Martha   I'm thinking.

Isaac   There must be something that keeps you up at night?

Martha   Spiders, I guess?

The Game   LEVEL NINE – FREUD OR FRAUD!

Freud *stands, wearing glasses.*

Avatar   Identify which quote is renowned psychoanalyst Freud and which is fraud!

Freud   *Time spent with cats is never wasted.*

Avatar   Or quote B:

Freud   *No one is so brave that he is not disturbed by something unexpected.*

Martha   That one, that one's Freud!

Isaac   Agreed.

The Game   INCORRECT!

Freud   Commiserations! Those were in fact the words of the renowned ruthless Roman general Julius Caesar. Now let's explore why your unconscious mind might have chosen this answer.

The Game   REFLECTION SECTION!

Isaac   We're clearly psychopaths.

Martha   Or evil tyrants with mummy issues.

Isaac   What's your mummy issue?

Martha   I was joking.

Isaac   Come on, everyone has parent issues. What about your dad?

Martha   If you must know, he lives in Florida with his new wife. But I'm okay with it. We get on better without him.

Isaac   Okay.

Martha (*sarcastic*)   No, you're right, I need *serious* therapy.

Isaac   There's nothing wrong with that.

Martha   Then why don't you get some?

Isaac   I don't think Dad could handle it. He's been a mess. He's only just picked himself back up again.

Martha But you're his son, surely he'd support you?

Isaac Of course he would. He'd go out of his way to get me help and then secretly tear himself apart that I'm not coping. He cares so much about being a good dad. Too much. He worries that he's letting Mum down.

I didn't even tell him when I hurt my arm. I just bandaged it myself.

Martha Really? I'd be throwing up everywhere. I hate blood.

Isaac Is that an anxiety of yours? It can't just be spiders.

Martha Hey, stop trying to catch me out!

The Game LEVEL TEN – SNAKES AND SOCIAL LADDERS!

Dead Inside *and* **Screw This** *are halfway through the game.*

The Game YOU ROLLED TWO! MOVE TWO PLACES!

Dead Inside *moves forward two places.*

The Game YEY! YOU'VE BOUGHT A HOUSE! CLIMB THE PROPERTY LADDER!

Dead Inside *climbs the ladder.*

The Game SCREW THIS, TIME TO ROLL!

YOU ROLLED FOUR! MOVE FOUR PLACES!

Screw This *moves forward four places.*

The Game UH OH! SOCIAL SHAME SNAKE!

SLIDE DOWN TEN PLACES!

REFLECTION SECTION!

Martha Seriously, you should meet the people at my school. Talk about social ladders, they're so stuck up.

Isaac Like how?

Martha Just trust me, everyone's super-privileged and spoilt. They all look down their noses. Even the teachers have it in for me.

Isaac Is that why you're suspended?

Martha Um . . . I guess so, yeah?

The Game LEVEL ELEVEN – MINDCRAFT!

Avatar Using the building blocks, craft a dream environment in which to thrive and survive!

The blocks assemble into the shape of a house.

The Game   REFLECTION SECTION!

Isaac/Martha   Toilet!

They both run off.

Then run back in.

The Game   LEVEL TWELVE – IMPOSTER PALACE!

Avatar   There's an imposter syndrome hiding somewhere within the palace. Work as a team to flush it out!

The Game   LEVEL FOURTEEN! LEVEL SEVENTEEN! LEVEL TWENTY-ONE!

Avatar   When spiralling in panic, use the five, four, three, two, one technique to focus the mind. Simply list five things you can see, four things you can touch, three things you can hear, two you can smell and one you can taste! Try it now!

They're looking around their rooms, listing things.

Isaac   An orange rug –

Martha   A laundry basket –

Isaac   A glow in the dark star on the ceiling I've never taken down –

Martha   A poster of a whale that's faded in the sun –

Isaac   Womble the bear –

Martha   A teddy bear?

Isaac   My seventh birthday present. Mum made him a waistcoat.

Martha   That's sweet.

Isaac   Knitting was kind of her thing. Gloves, scarves, hats –

Martha   She sounds wholesome. What was she like?

The Game   LEVEL TWENTY-THREE! RESILIENCE RACEWAY!

Screw This *and* **Dead Inside** *are side by side in racing cars.* **Martha** *and* **Isaac** *now seem genuinely invested in the game.*

Martha   Big corner!

Screw This *and* **Dead Inside** *turn the corner.* **Screw This** *skids.*

Isaac   I'm losing control!

Martha   Hold down R1, stops it skidding!

They turn another corner. **Screw This** *no longer slides.*

Isaac   Nice!

A row of item boxes with question marks on them briefly appear – then disappear as **Screw This** *and* **Dead Inside** *drive through them, causing jingly sound effects.*

Martha Yes! Got a power boost!

Isaac Save it till we need it!

The Game WATCH OUT!

A siren sounds. Suddenly the **Fun Police** *drive up behind them.*

The Game UH OH! THE FUN POLICE!

Martha Might have to use that power boost sooner than we thought. You ready?

Isaac/Martha Three, two, one!

A surging sound, as **Screw This** *and* **Dead Inside** *lean back in their cars, ready to power boost.*

Then, a loud, power-boosting whoosh.

Blackout.

Scene Ten

Later that week. **Martha***'s house. Kitchen.* **Ivy** *holds a pair of roller skates; she's wearing* **Martha***'s jeans.*

Ivy Oh my God, I love them, I love them, I love them!

Martha The roller skates or my jeans?!

Ivy Both! (*Examining the roller skates.*) They're proper good ones. How'd you afford them?

Martha I won a poetry competition at school.

Ivy Genius.

Martha The thing is, Mum doesn't know I bought you them. And I don't want her to feel bad.

Ivy I'll only wear them when she's out.

Martha Promise?

Ivy Promise! Gonna try them in the park. You coming or still hiding in your room?

Martha Got a few levels left, then I'm done.

Ivy Aren't you bored?! It's been like a week.

Martha You know, it's actually been alright.

Ivy Can you at least change your pyjamas? No offence but you stink.

Martha Alright. I'll catch you up.

Ivy Okay, weirdo, gotta roll!

She runs off with the roller skates. **Martha** *smiles after her.*

Scene Eleven

Days later. **Isaac** *and* **Martha***'s respective bedrooms. They're friendly, jovial.* **Martha***'s huddled under her duvet.* **Dead Inside** *and* **Screw This** *are facing each other in the reflection section state.*

The Game REFLECTION SECTION!

Isaac Pretty sure I've broken my R1?

Martha Collateral damage. That's what happens when you totally smash it!

Isaac We have kind of smashed it. You know there's only two levels left?

Martha Wow. (*Secretly disappointed.*) Thank God for that.

Isaac Soon we'll be (*mimicking game*) 'awarded the prize of out best selves'! Whatever that means.

Martha It means I'll no longer be angry and you'll no longer be sad. Just like that. Magic.

Isaac You're still an enigma to me.

Martha Not this again. I've told you loads!

Isaac That you have a sister, that your dad lives abroad, that you're suspended, though I'm not *entirely* sure why.

Martha Yeah, see, loads.

Isaac But I don't really *know* you, know you.

Martha We're not allowed to share personal info.

Isaac Why do you think you're angry? You can be honest with me.

Beat.

Martha *looks like she's about to confide.*

Isaac Okay, while you think I'm gonna find some painkillers. Arm's throbbing like mad. Back in a bit.

Isaac *runs off.* **Martha** *lies back on her bed. After a moment, her phone rings.*

Across stage, we see **Ruth** *on her mobile, wearing a waitress apron. We hear the noise of a busy restaurant in the background.*

Ruth (*worried*)   Martha, are you at home?

Martha   I, umm –

Ruth   I've just had a call from your headteacher checking in on you. Why didn't you tell me you're suspended?!

Martha   I . . . I'm sorry.

Ruth   I'm working a double shift, I can't come back right now. But I hope it's not true, Martha, what they said.

Martha   No, Mum, it's not.

Ruth (*sadly*)   I must've dropped the ball. It's my fault, stretching myself too thin. I haven't been paying enough attention.

Martha   Please, Mum, it's not your fault –

Rude Customer *approaches* **Ruth**.

Rude Customer   Excuse me, I'm waiting here! The name's Peterson.

Ruth   Of course, Mr Peterson, my apologies. Your table's just over by the window. (*To* **Martha**.) Martha, I've got to go.

She hangs up the phone. **Martha** *looks horrified.*

Isaac *comes back into the room.*

Martha   You stupid idiot, Martha! You stupid, stupid idiot! You can't do anything right, you pathetic loser!

She buries her head in her hands. It looks like she's about to cry.

Isaac   Martha?

Martha   How do you know my name?

Isaac   You just said it. Are you okay?

Martha   I'm fine! Just give me a second.

Beat. **Isaac** *waits while* **Martha** *struggles to calm down.*

Isaac   Maybe . . . maybe you could try the listing technique, you know five things you can see –

Martha   I'm not doing that!

Isaac   Then what about breathing?

Martha   I am breathing!

Isaac   The box breathing, you know, in for four, hold for – ?

Martha   You're making it worse! Ah, I'm such an idiot!

Isaac What happened, Martha?

Martha Stop using my name, we don't even know each other!

She picks up her controller.

The Game SPEAK MODE DISABLED.

Martha *flops onto her bed, burying her face.*

Isaac *hesitates. Then types.* **Dead Inside** *talks to* **Screw This** *on screen.*

Dead Inside My name's Isaac! I'm sixteen and I'm an idiot too!

Martha *looks at the screen, picks up her controller. The stage goes dark on the pair as we focus solely on* **Screw This** *and* **Dead Inside**. *Through their next section of dialogue they periodically change stances/positions. Their voices remain unfalteringly upbeat.*

Dead Inside You wanna tell me what's going on?! You can talk to me!

Screw This I'm a screw-up, that's what!

Dead Inside I'm sure that's not true!

Screw This Yes, it is! You don't know me! Even when I'm trying my best I ruin everything!

Dead Inside Don't be hard on yourself!

Screw This Why not! I'm a stupid female canine! Ahhh!

Dead Inside Ha ha ha!

Screw This You know what I mean! I'm horrible!

Dead Inside Horrible to yourself!

Screw This Because I deserve it! I'm selfish and impatient and rude!

Dead Inside Come on!

Screw This I really hate myself sometimes!

Dead Inside Why don't you try that thing about the unhelpful thoughts?!

Screw This Oh my God stop!

Dead Inside I know it's cringe! Just humour me! What was it, again?!

Screw This The three Cs?!

Dead Inside Yeah that's it! Catch it, check it, change it!

Screw This Don't want to!

Dead Inside You're your own worst enemy!

Screw This I've heard that before!

Dead Inside Okay, then I'll do it for you!

You say you're selfish, but you bought your sister an amazing gift, which was probably really expensive!

Screw This   I shouldn't have done that!

Dead Inside   It was super-nice! And you say you're impatient, but you let me talk about my mum loads! You ask loads of questions! TBH I've told you things I've never told my friends!

Screw This   It's easier with strangers, especially ones you can't see!

Dead Inside   And you say you're rude! Okay, well, maybe sometimes you are! But I think it's just defensiveness! You think the worst of yourself, so you assume everyone does too!

But what do I know!? I'm not Freud!

Screw This   No, you're not!

I appreciate it though!

Dead Inside   Any time!

Beat.

Screw This   Hey, I was thinking! I know we're not meant to . . .!

Dead Inside   Meant to what?!

Screw This   Like, the game says not to . . .!

Dead Inside   Not to what?!

Screw This   But I was just wondering. . .!

Screw This/Dead Inside   Do you wanna meet up?!

Scene Twelve

A cold day in the park. **Martha** *loiters, wearing a winter coat and the rainbow-coloured knitted hat.* **Isaac** *appears. He looks shocked to see* **Martha**.

Martha (*warm but nervous*)   Isaac? Hi!

Isaac (*awkwardly*)   Hi.

Martha (*babbling*)   I'm so relieved you're not a creepy old dude! I mean, talk about stranger danger, it's pretty stupid to meet IRL. I told my sister my location and everything but still. I was suddenly having doubts, like, what if this is all some elaborate catfishing?! Were you worried too? You told your dad, right?

Isaac *nods gravely.*

Martha   Well . . . I guess we've been lucky.

A stiff beat. **Martha** *tries to ease the tension.*

Anyway . . . You look different without your goth cape. I was going to wear the giant bone, but it's kinda cold –

Isaac (*abruptly*) Where'd you get that hat?

Martha . . . My hat?

Isaac That knitted hat. Where did you get it?

Martha I don't know, a charity shop? It's freezing isn't it?

Isaac You go to Ridgewood Academy, don't you?

Martha (*disappointed*) Oh. Yeah, I do.

Isaac Yeah. Me too.

A loaded beat.

Martha (*self-consciously*) I suppose that makes sense . . . same big school, same video game.

Don't think I recognise you? I'm guessing you're in top set for everything?

Isaac I only know you go there because I recognise that hat.

Martha What?

Isaac You stole my bag!

Martha I think you've confused me with someone else?

Isaac You stole it from my locker! Is that why you're suspended?

Martha No, I already told you why!

Isaac That hat was in my bag, just admit that you took it!

Martha So what if I did?!

Isaac What do you mean *so what*?!

Martha I mean, if you don't want your stuff stolen then maybe close your locker.

Isaac So it's *my* fault?!

Martha Maybe stop treating your possessions so carelessly and they won't go missing.

Isaac Don't turn it around on me, it's theft! What is your problem?!

Martha What's *yours*? Are you enjoying this? This *righteous* little power trip?!

Isaac God, you're so defensive!

Martha No, I'm not!

Isaac Why did you steal it?! Answer me!

Martha None of your business!

Isaac It's exactly my business! Tell me why you took it!

Martha I don't know!

Isaac You just do it for the thrill? Is that it?

Martha Yeah, that's it!

Isaac Then no wonder you're so ashamed of yourself. No wonder you don't have any friends.

Martha What?

Isaac You heard.

Martha *looks upset, but replaces it with anger.*

Martha Well, don't worry, you can ignore me now too! Just like everyone else!

Isaac Maybe there's a reason for that, maybe you are a screw-up after all!

Martha You don't even know me!

Isaac You're right, I don't. And I don't want to either.

Martha *looks stung.*

Isaac I don't care about the money. Just give me the hat.

Martha *throws it at* **Isaac**'s *feet.*

He picks it up.

Isaac (*sadly*) My mum made it for me. It took her ages. And I was always too embarrassed to wear it.

Some days I feel crazy, wondering if she was even real. Wondering how everyone can act so normal when the world has totally changed.

So I keep it in my bag to look at it, whenever I feel like I'm going mad.

It reminds me how much she cared.

Martha Isaac . . . I didn't know that.

Isaac Last week I felt so alone. And then you took it.

Martha I'm . . . I'm sorry –

Isaac Save it. You're the reason my arm's like this.

Martha . . . What? What are you talking about? You fell off your bike.

A haunting realisation for **Martha**.

(*Horrified.*) Isaac. What did you do?

Isaac *hangs his head, barely meeting her eye.*

Isaac Good luck with the game.

He leaves. **Martha** *stands alone, shrunken in shame.*

Scene Thirteen

Martha's *house. The living room.* **Martha** *is slumped in front of the TV, listless.* **Ivy** *comes in.*

Ivy You can't mope around forever. Your energy is really exhausting.

Martha *ignores her.*

Ivy So you got suspended, it's not the end of the world! And Mum believes you, she knows you wouldn't steal. We're not that desperate.

Come get some fresh air? I'll show you the spin I can do on my skates!

Well, *almost* do.

She turns off the TV.

Martha?! You better snap out of this, or people at school are gonna think you're actually guilty.

Martha It doesn't matter. I won't be going there any more.

Ivy Why? You didn't do it and they don't have any evidence?! That's like a *wrongful conviction*. It happened to this murderer on the podcast I'm listening to, except he wasn't *actually* a murderer.

Martha It's too late.

Ivy No it's not, fight your corner! It's a *miscarriage of justice*!

Martha I never finished the video game.

Ivy Your video game?! What's that got to do with anything?

Martha It's two-player. I can't do it alone.

Ivy Are you asking me to play with you?

Martha (*regretful*) I need to take the roller skates back.

Ivy My roller skates?

Beat.

Martha (*remorseful*) I didn't win a poetry competition. And now I need that money back.

I'm sorry, Ivy. I'm really sorry.

I just wanted you to have a good birthday.

Ivy (*realising*) Oh.

Beat.

It's really stupid, what you've done.

Martha (*sadly*) I know.

Ivy   Like *really* stupid.

Martha   I know.

Ivy   But it's kinda thoughtful too. In a weird way, like it came from a good place. So tell them the truth. The school. Maybe they'll forgive you.

Martha   I can't.

Ivy   Don't be proud, Martha. It's just how it is. Tell them the truth and they'll understand.

And maybe tell Mum too. I hate keeping secrets from her.

Martha   She'll feel terrible.

Ivy   I know, but at least she'll understand.

You know it's ok to show a bit of vulnerability from time to time.

Martha (*remembering*)   Level Seven.

Ivy   What?

Martha   *The Vault of Vulnerability*.

Ivy   Yeah, I don't know what that means.

Martha   You need courage coins to unlock it.

Ivy   That bloody game again.

Martha   I just feel so ashamed.

Ivy   Well, you shouldn't. I don't. Shame takes up *way* too much energy.

Just be honest, Martha.

And maybe take a shower?

Scene Fourteen

Screw This *and* **Dead Inside** *stand side by side, in the last positions they were in.*

Avatar   If you've finished reflecting, press X to begin the next level!

Beat.

If you've finished reflecting, press X to begin the next level!

Screw This *talks to* **Dead Inside** *on screen (still in an upbeat voice).*

Screw This   Isaac? I don't know if you're there and I understand if you never want to talk to me again! But I'm so sorry about the hat! When I grabbed the bag, I thought maybe a wallet would be in there, if I was lucky! Nothing sentimental!

I know that's still wrong! I just mean . . . I hate that I caused you to . . . that I made you feel like that! It's awful!

The truth is, things have been really difficult lately! Remember Anxiety Bingo on Level Fifteen?! Well, what makes me anxious is number four! *Becoming poor*!

In fact, we already are! Mum works crazy hours and we still can't afford our bills! My sister goes to the breakfast club at school but I'm too embarrassed to go! I already feel like people judge me and they don't understand what it's like! Like the pressure and the shame and stuff! It makes me angry and I can't always control it!

I wanted money for my sister's birthday present! She never complains but I know she misses out! But don't worry, I'm getting the money back and first thing on Monday I'll bring the bag to the headmaster's office and tell him what I've done!

I'm so sorry, Isaac, about everything! Please don't hurt yourself again!

I know you feel desperate and alone, but I promise it's not the answer!

You need to talk to your dad! I bet he'll be relieved you can be honest with him! He can get you proper help! I'm going to tell my mum the truth too!

And confide in your friends! You shouldn't have to pretend around good friends! I wish I'd confided more in you!

Anyway, thanks for playing the game with me! Especially after I called you a *stupid prick*!

I'll miss having someone to talk to!

Take care of yourself!

Bye!

Scene Fifteen

A house party. **Teenagers** *mill about talking, dancing. Music plays.* **Isaac** *arrives, looking awkward.* **Danny** *bounds over, trailed by* **Lucas**. **Danny** *hugs* **Isaac**.

Danny   Isaac!

Lucas   Well, look who's back from the dead! Thought you'd finally grace us with your presence.

Isaac   Thought I'd see what all the fuss was about!

Lucas   Nice week off?

Danny   He had surgery, mate.

Lucas   Oh yeah. Did it hurt? Did they give you morphine?

Isaac   I'm on the mend.

Danny   Good to hear it! You're a hero.

Lucas   I'd have surgery if it got me a week off school.

Danny   Lucas, wanna get our boy a drink?

Lucas Why can't you do it?

Danny Abigail's in the kitchen.

Lucas's *face lights up.*

Lucas Back in a bit.

He darts off.

Danny (*bright again*) It's good to see you!

Isaac Same, mate, same.

Danny Lucas is paranoid you're phasing us out.

Isaac Why would I do that?

Danny Exactly. I mean, I was worried for a minute, to be fair. You went all weird and quiet. Like a zombie robot.

Isaac Sorry about that. It's all good now anyway. I'm back.

Danny Yeah?

Isaac Yeah, I just.

He gathers the courage.

To be honest, I've been really struggling since Mum died. Like some days I just feel really overwhelmed. Like it's impossible to do regular things and sometimes I –

Danny Mate –

Isaac What?

Danny No offence but is this really the place? We're at a party.

Isaac Oh.

Danny Sorry, I mean, *obviously* you can talk to me about it, obviously. Any time. But . . . bit heavy for right *now*, isn't it?

Isaac Of course. Sorry.

Danny I've got your back, man. Hey, we're doing a beer pong tournament, you wanna team up?

Isaac Sure.

Danny Legend. I'll let the guys know.

He wanders off. After a moment, **Isaac** *takes out his phone and makes a call.*

Isaac Hi, Dad. . .any chance you can pick me up?

Yeah, but it kind of sucks. Plus, I don't have any friends here.

Great. Let's go somewhere for food. Somewhere we can talk.

Yeah, there's just some things I need to say.

Scene Sixteen

Headmaster *and* **Martha** *sit opposite each other. She's holding* **Isaac**'s *bag, looking sullen.*

Headmaster That's the bag?

Martha

Headmaster Well. I'm sure you have an excellent explanation as to why it's in your possession?

Martha Sort of, headmaster. It's complicated.

Headmaster I suppose you never touched that wellbeing game, either?

Martha I almost finished it, sir.

Headmaster Oh. Well, either way this whole debacle leaves me little choice, Martha.

Martha You mean, *expulsion*, sir?

Headmaster Indeed, it's a criminal matter! We'll inform the owner of the bag, then the ball's in his court whether or not to press charges.

Martha It's just . . .

Headmaster Just what?

Martha The thing is . . . (*She sighs, giving up.*) Never mind.

Suddenly, **Isaac** *bursts into the room.*

Isaac Sorry to interrupt!

Headmaster Isaac, what excellent timing! Martha here has just handed in your bag –

Isaac (*seeming happy with relief*) Yes, you found it!

He grabs the bag and looks inside.

You absolute legend, where was it?

Martha (*surprised*) I . . . sorry?

Isaac And everything's still in here! Guess they thought nothing was worth taking!

Martha . . . They?

Isaac The people who stole it. Where did they dump it?

Headmaster (*confused, to* **Martha**) Hang on a minute, you mean it wasn't you?

Martha I . . . uh –

Isaac Of course it wasn't Martha. She's a good friend, she'd never do that!

Martha *smiles, relieved.*

Martha It was on the street, behind some bins.

Isaac Makes sense! There are some crazy opportunists out there!

Martha Yeah . . . some real mindless monsters.

Beat.

Headmaster Well . . . I must say I'm relieved! Expelling a student is a bureaucratic nightmare!

Off you go then.

Martha *and* **Isaac** *go to leave.*

Headmaster Actually . . . as coincidence would have it, you were both guinea pigs for the school's new wellbeing game.

Martha Yes, sir, we played it together.

Headmaster Did you?

Isaac Yes, it gave us the option, sir.

Headmaster How curious.

So go on then, did you learn anything?

Martha   . . . Umm.

Martha *and* **Isaac** *look at each other.*

Isaac We'll need some time for reflection.

Scene Seventeen

School gates. The bell rings. The sound of kids' voices in the courtyard.

Martha You didn't have to do that.

Isaac Turns out Screw This had a pretty good explanation.

Martha You saw it?

He nods.

Isaac, I'm so sorry –

Isaac It doesn't matter, forget about it –

Martha I tried to return the roller skates but Ivy's worn them in too much.

Promise I'll get the money back though, all of it.

Isaac It's only ten quid.

Martha *looks sheepish.* **Isaac** *realises.*

Isaac How much were the roller skates?

Martha . . . Forty-five.

(*Ashamed.*) It wasn't only your locker. Just no one else seemed to notice.

I know, I'm awful.

She shrinks in shame. After a moment, **Isaac** *suddenly moves forwards and hugs her.*

Isaac If they didn't notice then maybe they didn't really need it.

Martha Why are you being so nice to me?

Isaac Because your heart's in the right place. And you give brilliant advice. I talked to my dad. You were right, he can handle it. He didn't fall apart.

He was just *helpful*, actually.

Martha See! That's great. Did you tell him . . . about your arm?

Isaac No, but. That's not going to happen again.

Martha Good. That's really good.

The school bell rings.

Isaac Double maths. You?

Martha Geography. Mrs Edwards. Think I upset her.

Isaac She's pretty cool. Just apologise, she'll forgive you.

Martha I said I'd rather watch glaciers melt than sit through her class.

Isaac . . . Maybe give it some time.

Beat.

You know it's not your fault, the situation you're in?

Martha My attitude is my fault.

Isaac I'm just saying, don't be too hard on yourself. If anyone should feel bad it's the people who make assumptions, instead of seeing that you're struggling. And maybe a video game's good for learning how to deal with your *reactions* to things. But how can you stay *calm* and *resilient* when you have to cope with the same stress every single day? Just seems unrealistic.

Martha I dunno, it's just how it is.

Isaac Well, it shouldn't be. And you shouldn't feel embarrassed.
I was thinking . . . maybe we could go to the breakfast club together?

Martha Don't pity me, I don't want sympathy.

Isaac It's not sympathy, it's support. I'll eat beforehand and we can get to know each other properly, face to face.

Martha . . . Maybe. But not tomorrow. Mum's taken a few mornings off work to be with me. I think it's guilt that she's let us down? Which she hasn't at all, but . . .

It's actually been so nice spending time with her . . . like joking about and . . . even though we're struggling a bit, I just feel really lucky to have a mum like that.

(*Realises.*) I'm sorry, I didn't mean –

Isaac (*kindly*)   No, no, I get it. You are.

Danny and **Lucas** *walk by without stopping. It's a bit awkward, but* **Isaac** *seems unfazed.*

Isaac   Alright?

Danny (*sheepish*)   Yeah, alright.

Lucas (*coughs under his breath*)   Bailer.

Danny (*to* **Lucas**)   Lucas.

Lucas   What? He is!

. . . and they're gone.

Martha   Friends of yours?

Isaac (*shrugs, genuinely unperturbed*)   Not really.

The school bell rings again.

Martha   Can't get in trouble. I'm on thin ice.

Isaac   Alright, better go then.

Beat.

Martha (*smiles*)   You know, maybe not *everyone* at school is stuck-up.

Isaac *smiles. It feels like they both want to say more, but can't. They go to walk off in opposite directions. Then after a moment, they both stop and turn around –*

Isaac   It's just . . . don't you wanna know how it ends?

Martha   . . . You mean, to be *awarded the prize of my best self*?

Isaac   To meet a *better, happier, more balanced YOU 2.0*?

They look at one another, eyes twinkling, an idea forming.

Martha   Now that would be *seriously* pathetic.

They grin widely, with joint understanding, as we hear the sudden noise of the video game 'dinging'. And in the background –

The Game   YEYYYYY!

Blackout.

End.

Character Plot

	1	2	3	4	5	6	7	8	9	10	11	12	13	14	15	16	17
Martha	✓	✓	✓	✓		✓	✓		✓	✓	✓	✓	✓			✓	✓
Isaac				✓	✓	✓	✓		✓		✓	✓			✓	✓	✓
Headmaster		✓														✓	
Ivy			✓							✓			✓				
Mrs Edwards					✓												
Danny					✓		✓								✓		✓
Lucas					✓		✓								✓		✓
Ruth							✓			✓						✓	
Rude Customer											✓						
Screw This	✓			✓		✓	✓		✓		✓			✓			
Dead Inside				✓		✓	✓		✓		✓			✓			
The Game	✓			✓		✓	✓		✓		✓						
Avatar	✓			✓		✓	✓		✓					✓			
Disclaimer	✓																
Dancing Deana				✓													
Mindless Monster						✓											
Little Timmy							✓										
Ball of Stress							✓										
Mobile Phone							✓										
Cup of Coffee							✓										
Freud									✓								
Bingo Caller									✓								

More information about the characters and how much they speak

Martha – Significant dialogue
Isaac – Significant dialogue
Headmaster – Dialogue in two scenes
Ivy – Dialogue in two scenes
Mrs Edwards – Dialogue in one scene
Danny – Dialogue in four scenes
Lucas – Dialogue in four scenes
Ruth – Dialogue in two scenes, could be doubled (play another part)
Rude Customer – A couple of lines, could be doubled
Screw This – Significant dialogue and a long monologue
Dead Inside – Significant dialogue
The Game – Dialogue throughout
Avatar – Could be played by one to four (or more) people, significant amount of text that could be shared
Disclaimer – One line, could be doubled

Dancing Deana – Significant dialogue in one scene, could be doubled
Mindless Monster – Some lines in one scene, could be doubled
Little Timmy – Some lines in one scene, could be doubled
Ball of Stress – One line, could be doubled
Mobile Phone – One line, could be doubled
Cup of Coffee – No lines, could be doubled
Freud – Some lines in one scene, could be doubled
Bingo Caller – Some lines in one scene, could be doubled

Main Narrative Beats

1. The computer game starts, Martha is not impressed, she chooses her player name, 'Screw This'.
2. Martha is in the Headmaster's office, she is in trouble. The Headmaster accuses her of stealing, she is suspended from school and she has to play a wellbeing computer game.
3. At home, Martha and her sister Ivy eat breakfast. Martha bribes Ivy not to tell Mum about being suspended.
4. Martha plays the game. There is a new player called 'Dead Inside', they play together. The first level is fun freestyle dancing, the new player only uses one arm. The new player is Isaac, who chats with Martha via the game. They argue, and then agree to work as a team.
5. At school Isaac is in Geography, Mrs Edwards wants to know why he's stopped going to clubs. Isaac says it's because he hurt his arm falling off his bike. Mrs Edwards suggests he play a new wellbeing game.
6. In their own bedrooms, Martha and Isaac play the game together. It teaches them about difficult emotions. They meet the Mindless Monster. They complete the level and are able to speak directly to each other, they start to become friends.
7. In the game, Martha and Isaac are helping Little Timmy get to sleep. Martha's mum Ruth appears, Martha pretends she's sick. Ruth notices she has a new rainbow hat. When Martha returns to the game. Isaac is cross she suddenly stopped playing. He tells Martha his mum died recently.
8. Isaac's friends Danny and Lucas are trying to call him. Back in the game Isaac and Martha play lots of fun levels, learning about emotions and wellbeing, and sharing their fears.
9. At Martha's house, Martha has bought Ivy a pair of roller skates, they can't tell Mum about them.
10. Back in the game, Martha and Isaac are chatting. Martha's Mum calls, she has found out Martha is suspended. Martha is upset, Isaac tries to cheer her up using techniques from the game. Martha and Isaac decide to meet up in real life.
11. In the park, Martha and Isaac meet up. Isaac asks about the rainbow hat, Martha is wearing. He says it's his hat, his mum made it for him. Martha must have stolen his bag from his locker. Isaac says Martha is the reason his arm is injured, Martha realises he has hurt himself on purpose.
12. At Martha's house, Ivy tries to cheer her up. Martha needs the roller skates back so she can get the money. In the game Martha writes a long apology to Isaac.
13. At a house party, Isaac sees his friends he tries to tell them how he is feeling, they aren't interested. Isaac calls his Dad and asks to talk.

14. In the Headmaster's office, Martha has returned Isaac's bag, she's going to be in trouble. Isaac runs in and lies to protect Martha, they both tell the Headmaster they have played the game together.
15. At the school gates, Martha tells Isaac she stole from other lockers. Isaac forgives her, they decide to carry on playing the game, together.

YOU 2.0

BY ALYS METCALF

Notes on rehearsal and staging drawn from a workshop with the writer led by director Josie Rourke with movement director Jessica Wright, held at the National Theatre, October 2024

How the writer came to write the play

Writer Alys Metcalf knew she wanted to be playful with the format and that she was interested in two strangers connecting first in a faceless form. She knew she wanted to write a play about a young person who grapples with her pride and shame due to coming from an under-privileged background. She wanted to do this in a subtle way and keep the play light and playful. The idea of a video game felt like a brilliant way to explore these themes.

Introductions and aims

Lead director Josie Rourke began by sharing advice which she received from her mentor, Peter Gill: 'The first thing you should do when you are about to direct a play is tackle what you are most scared about, or what you think will take the most amount of time.' E.g: if you are directing *Romeo and Juliet* you've got to start with the fights. She set this out to be the motto for the day, focusing on everything and anything the participants foresaw to be knotty, challenging or time-consuming during their rehearsal process. She invited the group to name what they were worried, scared and felt challenged by within the play.

The two main strands the workshop focused on were about approaching the text and creating a movement language to tackle the world of the video game.

Approaching the play

Rourke suggested that a useful way to approach a text before rehearsals is to identify key story beats (the plot) and the essential traits and the journey the characters go on. *YOU 2.0* has two central characters: Martha and Isaac. Exploring who they are and their previous circumstances to the play can support finding the right young people for the roles and reveal more about the play itself.

Character breakdown and casting

Rourke asked Metcalf some questions in order to find out more about these two central characters.

*Q: **What are the qualities and stories of the two central characters?***
A: The two characters are suffering a similar crisis, but there is a different reaction and emotional response to it. They are both weighed down by shame for different reasons. Martha has a forward energy whereas Isaac has a sense of needing to withhold.

Martha has shields up around her and relies on humour and cynicism, she has hardened edges. Her defences are up so she is ready to defend herself at any moment, even in inappropriate moments. She takes everything very personally, especially when something is a bit challenging. For example, not progressing in a game becomes personal and painful due to the challenges she has faced in life – having to be an anchor at home, needing to be independent and needing to be responsible at all times. She doesn't allow space to be vulnerable. She shuts down arguments. She is incredibly funny and tries to pretend as if everything is rolling off her. She goes on a huge journey which means she ends up opening up to Isaac. She is really worried about her family, and is literally hungry. She needs to be charming, her humour is similar to someone like Paul Merton. Her language is sharp but she is not mean, there is a goofiness to her.

She comes from a single-parent household. Her mum works for a job that she is overqualified for so she is constantly applying for other jobs. Martha's sister is more shielded and gets upset when not receiving gifts because they can't afford it. Martha tries to preserve her sister Ivy's childhood, so she is constantly trying to support her. She is trying to keep everything going and it all starts to come out with missing homework, stealing money from other students and talking back to teachers. She is feeling a huge amount of shame about what she has done, but is desperately hoping she'll get away with it.

Rourke and Metcalf both agreed that Martha is a difficult character to cast – she needs enormous charm as well as sharpness (the danger is that she could easily become too shouty and just play 'angry').

Isaac has always been part of the group, always liked even if not the most popular guy in the group. He is the good guy you go to, he is kind and reliable, gives everyone the benefit of the doubt. He has a good sense of humour too but less sharp than Martha's. He lost his mum and he can't talk about it with his mates. He is struggling and the video game allows him to open up to a stranger; it is easier with Martha than with Isaac's mates who don't have the vocabulary to give him what he needs. Isaac lost his mum a year and a half ago, and he is aware that his dad is really worried about him. His dad isn't coping particularly well with the loss of Isaac's mum either. Isaac doesn't have anyone to talk to since his grief counselling ended and now feels he is expected to be fine. As a result he cuts his arm as an act of self-harm. School doesn't have resources to deal with it, but his teacher notices something is up so she suggests that he could play this game. He isn't suicidal, but he is desperate and isolated. He is also dealing with pride and shame.

*Q: **How is Isaac's withholding different to Martha's?***
A: He holds back, it comes out in silence – he bites his tongue, he doesn't reveal what he is thinking. Martha is more cerebral, whereas Isaac takes what he thinks and isn't necessarily able to share it.

Q: What does the play think about adults?
A: That adults are also vulnerable; they also need help. Life happens at every stage and sometimes adults can't cope either. There is a lot going under the surface, so it's good to consider that when casting Martha's mum.

Q: What about the teachers?
A: Headmaster is definitely more on the comical end to allow lightness to sweep in. He needs an air of authority. He doesn't have a lot of time, maybe he has a golf holiday coming up, he wants the best but he also wants to just get on with it. Maybe he was great, but has been in the system for too long. Mrs Edwards is definitely more layered and intuitive.

Rourke identified the challenge of asking actors to act like they are not coping or playing exhausted. It's important not to let characters become passive, – someone who is not coping will try their hardest to look like they *are* coping.

Q: What do you think about gender-swapping characters?
A: You should work with the cast you've got. It shouldn't be a problem to change the gender of most characters. They are written with specific genders in mind and with certain tropes such as boys being not as good at talking about their feelings, so it's worth bearing those in mind. You could decide whether swapping their genders or asking them to play the other gender might work better for your show.

It feels important that Isaac and Martha are not the same gender.

Rourke advised to keep the characters and their lines truthful to the text. It's probably not helpful to reallocate lines to other characters or create any new characters within the naturalistic scenes. The world of the video game will give your company all the possibilities for ensemble work!

Q: What's your suggestion if your cast is too small or too big?
A: The actors playing Martha, Isaac, Screw This and Dead Inside shouldn't play another part. Multi-roling should work well otherwise if your group is smaller, and could be fun and playful, especially within the game.

If your group is larger than the cast size, then you could use your ensemble to help create the video game. E.g.: they could help with the racing car, with scrolling on the phone. Ensemble can help create/voice the video-game world.

The ensemble could also help keep the stage alive and interesting during set changes.

Q: Do you see Screw This and Dead Inside as specific genders?
A: I'm happy for you to choose how you want to cast it – it's about how Martha and Isaac see themselves.

'Real world'

- Martha (see above)
- Isaac (see above)
- Headmaster (feel free to lean into a bit of a trope; more on this above)
- Ivy (sister, naively oblivious, sassy, surprisingly wise)

- Danny and Lucas (young people who don't have a language to speak about grief, stuck in a pattern of behaviour; shutting conversations down is their way of coping with Isaac's grief)
- Ruth (a woman on the edge, trying to hold it together, trying to be patient and compassionate, working incredibly hard)
- Rude Customer (says it all!)

'Avatar world'

The avatar world characters have their own distinct qualities and actions. Identifying these can support the company to create them physically.

- Voice of the game: You are welcome to explore the accent, but in Metcalf's mind, it's British. You could explore bringing the essence of an American voice but keep it in your cast's accents. Trust your instinct and do whichever feels right for your group.
- Screw This and Dead Inside: (the essential aspect of these two avatars is to find a way to connect them back to Martha and Isaac; for example, they could wear the same coloured clothes as Martha and Isaac)
- Disclaimer (classic disclaimer voice)
- Dancing Deana (fun and playful; below is a useful movement exercise to start exploring their character)
- Mindless Monster: To find what it means to be mindless, you could workshop it with your group e.g. using animal qualities that the young people can borrow to explore the movement of the monster could be useful. Several young people could play the monster!
- Little Timmy (if gender-swapping go with Tilly!)
- Ball of Stress (in Metcalf's mind it's a chaotic line drawing kind of thing)
- Mobile Phone (you can create this in lots of different ways, from costume to just a physicality)
- Sigmund Freud (Freud feels outdated. This is reflecting the game – it's outdated, it's wrong. Martha and Isaac would be just as annoyed by it as your young people performing it might be!)
- Bingo Caller (again, this is not exactly cool with the kids, it's the game trying and failing to connect with teenagers. Anxiety bingo is not so helpful at first glance. It's also very recognisable and playful).

Plot and story beats

Before rehearsals, it could be helpful to identify the story beats and the key emotional events. Rourke suggested that the plot of this play could be summarised as the creation of a friendship that would have never occurred without the events that take place within the play.

Rourke also highlighted what could go wrong when staging *YOU 2.0* – you could do an amazing production of it where no one knows what's actually going on. It's a busy play with many brilliant moments, so finding the story beats is important. What's the key information you need to deliver to take an audience on the journey with you?

The group discussed the events taking place before and during the play. Below are some of their thoughts.

Before the play begins

Before the play begins two young people are in crisis. Martha is in a crisis of wanting to help her family. Driven by poverty, she steals from other students at school. She gets suspended, which she desperately tries to hide from her mum so as not to put pressure on her.

Isaac has lost his mum. There has been a period when his bereavement has been supervised, but this support has gone. It's been decided that everyone, including Isaac, should get on with it. Everyone around him is trying to pretend that everything is ok. E.g.: his friends are not mean, they are just trying to be light and goofy. Before the play begins he has self-harmed and his teacher suspects this, but the school doesn't have the resources to support him, so she offers the game as some help.

The play

The play begins in the video game. We skip the exposition of game being given to Martha and Isaac and instead we meet them straight away. The game is a mechanism to reveal the information about the characters and start their connection.

The big reveals: She stole his bag. She is poor. They know each other. Isaac broke his arm deliberately. At the end, Isaac saves Martha from being expelled.

Emotional beats: Avatar telling the truth to Isaac about Martha's circumstances. Isaac receiving the moment of vulnerability from Martha he's been waiting for, enabling him to understand her more. This happens via the playing of the game and how it feels when they fail or succeed at levels. Each level makes it more emotional and real. Martha goes from needing to finish the game to be allowed to go back to school, to actually enjoying playing with Isaac. Isaac on the other hand plays it voluntarily, to make himself stop thinking.

Challenge: Avatars need to have a shared language with Martha and Isaac that ties them together, whether that's movement, costume or other ways to support clarity for the audience.

Your role is to ensure these emotional beats land so the audience goes on the journey with the characters, allowing the moments of compassion, forgiveness and letting go to truly land. The play ends with two characters who used to block and withhold, starting to share and genuinely connect.

World of the game

The real challenge of this play is the video-game world. Choreographer Jessica Wright worked with participants to explore different ways of approaching the world, giving different tools and movement exercises to start generating movement options.

The **voices of the game** feel important to the dramaturgy and flow of the play. The game has two separate voices: the ones related to actually playing the game and the wellbeing voices that give advice and reflections after each game. Playing with the tone and pace of these different voices is an important differentiation. Alys Metcalf suggested you could think about it like *Blue Peter* meets *Headspace*!

Sometimes the game is wrong. It's wrong on purpose – sometimes the game fails to respond to the specific needs and references of the people playing it.

Movement

Identify before starting with movement:

- Where does the play require choreography?
- Where does it require heightened movement language (how realistic or elevated do you want it to be)?
- Where do you want it to be naturalistic?

Warm-up

Exercise: Moving together as a group

Wright asked the group to start walking around the space. First becoming aware of their bodies – their posture, the neutral pace they fell into. Once everyone settled in she asked the group to pick up the pace and the energy a little bit. She then asked the group to start walking on a grid – no soft curves, just all hard edges, if needed they could stop and wait until they can turn and move again. She encouraged them to keep changing direction.

What do you need to do in your body to pause, to change direction? How do you activate that?

She then asked the group to change their movement every time she clicked. Next, the group started moving in curves, letting go of hard edges and instead moving only in soft curves. The group then moved back into a neutral walk around the space. Wright then asked the group to stop walking and then start walking again at the same time.

What did you notice when trying to stop together?

Wright challenged the group to take more risks, to start stopping at less expected times as a group. She encouraged bravery.

Wright then challenged them to do the same exercise, but walking backwards.

The next level of the exercise was about choosing someone else in the group and keeping them in their peripheral vision.

Wright then asked the group to explore how small they can make the space they are all walking around in. Rules: make the space the group takes up is as small as possible, but without touching one another, keep moving, not getting stuck on the outside. Wright encouraged the group to keep walking and then to do the same exercise of stopping and starting together as a group.

She then asked the group to find more space between themselves and then, as a group, to reach up to the ceiling at the same time and then to go down to touch the ground. Wright then challenged them to keep moving as a group between up and down without a leader, led by them collectively as an ensemble.

Exercise: Getting the body mobile: out of the head and into the body

Wright led a more traditional warm-up sequence which consisted of:

1. Generating heat – rubbing hands together, actively, building the pace more and more. After a few beats stopping, separating the palms and just feeling the energy generated. *Move the palms closer and further away, feeling the energy that moves between the palms. Explore how far it's possible to go and not lose connection between the palms*
2. Start moving palms and hands up and down and around, allowing the body to have a nice stretch – *imagine having a bubble around that you are pushing away*
3. Quick massage of the neck to wake up
4. Brush down the body giving real pressure through the hands – all the way down. *Making contact with your body, waking it up*
5. Ensure feet are in line with the hips. Reach up with your arms towards the ceiling. Throw the arms down. Bend the knees. Slowly bend over, letting your upper body fall to the ground. Slowly move to stretch the legs then back to the ground three times. Slowly start rolling back up and once standing reaching arms to the sky. Repeat a couple of times. Every time go a bit faster, picking up the pace
6. Circle the head in both directions.

Exercise: Opening up the body

(music during warm-up: Dua Lipa and Calvin Harris 'One Kiss')

Start with the right arm, then left, then both at the same time. Each roll repeated a couple of times.

1. Shoulder roll
2. Hand to shoulder roll
3. Full arm roll
4. Reach up and then stretch to the side
5. Reverse order.

Generating material

Exercise: Generating ideas for Dancing Deana

A short warm-up sequence that becomes a movement sequence is a way to start generating ideas and movement as an ensemble. It can use simple instructions that are easy to follow and are fun. The example Wright taught the group was:

1. Four jumping jacks
2. Two grapevines
3. Party jog around the room (any direction)
4. Meet a partner and groove with them. On the eighth beat high five with them.

Wright then asked them to bring the idea of being a fitness instructor to it. Not just completing the moves but also considering how to move and what to communicate with the moves – ENERGY! FUN! KEEP GOING!

Once the moves were set and everyone confident, Wright asked everyone to make their moves more precise, bigger, and bring even more of a fitness energy to it.

Rourke pointed out how a warm-up is a great way to guide people into generating material without noticing. Flowing from warm-up into creating takes the pressure off from the group.

Wright shared the following video with the group as a useful reference for the Dancing Deana: https://www.youtube.com/watch?v=CxgD9P-kMjE

Exercise: Laban

The second exercise was based on a Laban technique. Wright asked everyone to take up enough space to be able to move around.

(Music used during the exercise: *Music for 18 Musicians*: Section VII [Steve Reich] and 'Cirrus' [Bonobo])

1. Imagine you are inside a cube. Mark out the ceiling by reaching to it, then the front wall, side walls, back wall. Wright encouraged the group to make it feel real by continuing to touch the walls, corners and edges of the cube until it was easy to visualise
2. Take a minute to choose five points and locate them in your cube. These points remain fixed. Even if you walk metres away from your fixed points, they will remain there. Make this imagined geography feel very real and the locations specific
3. Move between your fixed points. First move between one to five in order and then start exploring, reaching them out of order. Before you move between fixed points make sure you see them clearly and then move to them
4. Reach number one with the top of your right wrist. Now go through all other points using the top of your right wrist. This can be done with any other parts of your body (back of right heel, inside your arm, shoulder, tip of the nose,

tongue, etc.). This is about now specifying what point of your body you are reaching to these fixed points. Make sure this movement is accurate and clear

5. Explore different ways of using the specific body parts you are reaching with and how you move your whole body with it. It's about solving a problem not about 'doing a move' which leads to unusual and more interesting movements

6. Once you set up a few different body parts to reach the fixed points then start moving between them. For example: one – tip of the nose, two – top of the right wrist, three – left pinky finger, four – inside your arm, five – left ear. Think about whether you are moving directly to it, around it or below it: *what's the direction of it and the intention of it*

7. Next step: Choose body parts individually and create a sequence that's repeatable. Decide on the size of your cube and stick to it. Make your movements within this set size of cube. Aim for clarity and not having transitional movements between points but rather move straight between your fixed points. (Tip: Wright encouraged participants not to set the body parts when they are working as the director, but give the young people the option to find their choices of body parts themselves.)

8. Duration: Think about *what* is moving and *how* it's moving. Add *long* or *short* to what you created. This adds a dynamic to what you have created

9. Sharing: Participants created a big circle and moved from one after the other to share what they created. Wright encouraged them to take up the space and relocate to have enough space to share their movement. Rule: minimum one person or maximum five people can share the space at the same time. Aim is to keep the space charged and energised. No apologising for what you created!

10. Wright asked the group to keep sharing their movement, but now aim to engage with other people in the space. To find their cube, maybe join their cube size, interact and engage as everyone shares their movement in the space. *Keep going and repeating your movement, keeping the space energised, engaging with each other as you are moving through your own sequence.*

Learnings and observations from the group:

- Body parts have natural ways they move. It's great to think about how performative these moves can get. Adding intentions can really help and really set the movements
- Visualising can be really helpful as an approach for young people. Find the way that helps your individual group the best – is it visualising or is it music, what's their way into movement?
- This exercise feels useful for the video-game aspect – it's like hitting a mark, which translates brilliantly for gaming
- Rourke asked Wright about *how to record and retain the sense of movement? How can it be noted and used in staging?* – Wright said she'd record it at the end of a session. She also believes the clearer and more real you visualise the fixed points and the images, the more your body remembers it when you next come back to it.

Exercise: Co-ordination exercise

(Music: 'We Found Love' by Rihanna ft Calvin Harris)

This is a good warm-up to do after a break. Participants got in a circle and repeated the exercise of generating heat between palms, then reaching and stretching to releasing by dropping down, then shaking out of tension.

Wright then asked the participants to stand in lines, with their feet knuckle-distance apart. Arms went forward, up side and down while participants bounced through their knees. Then feet went into turn out, with heels together, and the sequence was repeated. Then the same, but with feet wide apart and facing forwards. Then with feet wide apart and heels turned towards each other. This was repeated a couple of times in line with the beat of the music. It was a joyously chaotic exercise to help wake up the brain post-lunch!

Exercise: Creating groups and shapes

An exercise to help explore ways of bringing video-game characters such as Mindless Monster to life.

Wright asked the ensemble to walk around the space in their neutral state. When she said 'two' they had to create groups of twos in the space without talking. Then in threes, fours, etc. Wright encouraged the group to allow themselves to be able to stay by themselves if they are without a pair rather than rushing around – the aim is to make it feel like the perfect solution is whatever happens in the room instinctively, even if it's not perfect.

Working with partners – needing your partner

In groups of two, the participants were asked to explore different ways of giving their weights to each other: different ways of leaning on or holding each other. It's essential to do this silently, to be intuitive and move without noise and chatter.

Tip from Wright: the more the pairs can connect physically, the more weight they can share with each other, the more stable they will be. Once the group explored this Wright asked them to start moving around the space again. This time when she said 'two' she asked them to meet someone new and silently decide how they will connect and share their weight.

Creating shapes in small groups

(Music during exercise: 'Honeyed Words' by Anna Meredith)

Now in threes, the participants were asked to find a way to create different shapes by finding different points of connection on each other's bodies.

Rules: ensuring that all contact remains respectful and consensual feet always need to be in contact with the ground, hands need to be in contact with the other group members' bodies. Focus is still to play with sharing and transferring weight to each other their weight, putting body weight into the place where you are connected to the other person's body. For example, pushing arms together, holding onto legs, kneeling, sides meeting. Aim is to put your body into physical contact.

Wright then asked the group to start moving around the space again and depending on the number she called out to do the following instructions: two – find a partner and share their weight, three, four and five – in groups of the same number as called, find contact with each other's bodies and create shapes, sharing weight at the contact points? Once the move was completed, everyone started moving around the space again. Repeat and move between numbers. Wright encouraged the participants to take part, but to also find moments to step back and observe.

Additional instruction

Participants continued working with the same principles but this time there were specific instructions: e.g.: three feet, one elbow, two hands, etc. Using these instructions they created a shape and contact within groups.

Exercise: Generate using words

Wright encouraged everyone to think about the language of the game. *How do we show one character with several bodies?*

Ideas from the group:

- Mirroring
- Speaking in unison
- Moving in unison
- Creating formations

Physicalising words:

Wright asked the group to find a new partner and to explore saying and physicalising the following words: *scoop, jab, ring, decay, stroke-punch, fold-draw.*

She asked the pairs to make choices about the following:

- How to say the word? What's the rhythmic intonation?
- What's the movement when saying the word? Which body part is leading? How does the whole body engage?
- How many times does the word and the movement get repeated?
- Does each person in the pair have the same movement? Or could they have the same intonation, but their movement is different?

Addition: Choosing a line from the play and trying to apply the above exercise to it. E.g.: 'Type a line in the box.'

- One person in the pair to physicalise word/sentence, the other one to observe then swap
- Explore word/sentence as a pair.

Tips from Wright:

- When working with movement, she encouraged participants to avoid saying anything but the text.
- She also encouraged movement to be made more abstract, capturing the quality of the word or sentence, without being too literal.
- She suggested that observing each other, both within pairs and other teams, can be a really useful source of inspiration when generating ideas for movement.
- Building up a bank of physical vocabulary and language to draw on with the young companies can help avoid falling back into being too literal.

Exercise: Mirroring in groups of six

The aim of this exercise is to create mirroring that's really precise, to build another tool for the physical vocabulary. It encourages finding a wide-peripheral vision to be able to seamlessly swap between group leaders and mirror, without staring too much at the group leader.

In a group of six, stand so the leader is at the front, one line of three behind them, and a line of two behind them. One person leads and the other five follow. The action to be mirrored can be their morning routine, the action of the word they've been exploring before or freestyling. The aim is to move almost at the same time as the leader. Groups can then try moving through space and changing leaders without speaking.

Exercise: Mirroring and speaking words

Wright then asked participants to merge the mirroring exercise with the exercise they have done before on speaking and physicalising words.

The leader of the group moves, everyone else has to be connected to each other by hands on each other's bodies. Wright then asked the group to travel through the space with the leader using moves and saying the words explored in the previous exercise (scoop, jab, etc.). Other members of the group follow, all connected by hands on shoulder, backs, etc. Leaders can swap out and share the material they made in the previous exercise using words. Tip from Wright: make sure you keep sharing weight as you are connecting to your group leader and each other.

Possible variations:

- Everyone to complete the same movement and word together in unison
- Same movement and words, but movement is in canon
- Group connected by hands and energy leading one way towards one leader – changing leaders after the completion of one word and movement
- Moving one by one completing the same action.

These exercises can be especially useful when bringing characters like Mindless Monster to life in rehearsals. You can build up a bank of materials that can be a useful source throughout the rehearsal process. Wright hoped the group found these exercises a good way in, without the pressure of trying to 'choreograph' anything.

Design, props and scene changes

Rourke asked the group to start thinking about the practical challenges of the play. For example, practically getting a bed on and off stage is a real challenge. Some playwrights think in detail about how it would look on stage, some playwrights offer ideas and leave it to the director to find a staging solution. *YOU 2.0* feels like a play that offers a lot of ideas where finding creative solutions will be useful when staging it!

> **Josie Rourke challenged the group to think about these questions and gave the following advice:**

- What is the minimum requirement for this play? What's the poor theatre version of this play? If you only have five minutes to get in/get out what can you achieve? What do you need?
- She recommended thinking about sound and lighting and what these creative aspects can do to support your production. She pointed out that it's probably a show that needs a lot of sound cues. She asked the participants to consider whether some props could be exchanged for sound effects
- She set the provocation to the group to set themselves a challenge/focus point when directing the play. E.g.: Does it bring the charm of the old video-game world? Having checkpoints can be useful to refer back to throughout the process
- How long should it take to move from scene to scene? Can story be generated/told during scene transitions?
- Identify iconic moments/props/images. What are the things definitely needed to make the show vivid and clear? For example, Isaac's hat is vital and needs to visually pop on stage
- Thinking about specific set pieces: e.g.: bed on stage. Do we need to see a bed to believe it's a bedroom? How else could a production suggest it? Could the location of the bedroom move on stage during the show or should it stay in one area? If the production has a bed on stage, does it need to move? If it does, how can it be moved? Does the bed help comically or scenically?
- It might be worth thinking about the game as a character in itself. It's a real invitation for creativity, but needs clarity and precision. Finding the rules of it and the voices that are part of it is essential. The video-game aspect is also a brilliant way to utilise the whole ensemble.

Question and answer with Alys Metcalf and Josie Rourke

Q: Could the company create the spaces and locations just using their own bodies if we have a large ensemble?
AM: The play has a series of physical demands to suggest the game which is already a challenge. It might be worth thinking about how many languages you want to be using in your show so it doesn't get too confusing.

Q: How far should we go with sound and music?
AM: This feels like a really sound-heavy show, the precision and detail of it is interesting. Thinking about rehearsing with cues can be helpful.

Using a score to support, for example, the montage of playing the game could be brilliant and really help with the pace. Focusing the score on the game rather than naturalistic scenes might be helpful.

Q: How to make the jeans work with two actors who are different sizes?
AM: If jeans don't feel right due to gender or anything else you can change it to a pair of sunglasses.

Q: What do you think about puppets for the game?
AM: You should definitely explore it if that feels fun. If it helps with clarity then go for it!

Q: How do you pronounce the title?
AM: I've been saying You-two-point-O.

Q: When did you (Metcalf) last play a video game?
AM: Probably at Christmas with my nephew, but I subscribe to the older video games, more like Nintendo 64 – a little bit old and a little bit shit. Not the newest version of Xbox, but rather you can see the pixels a little bit, like Mario Kart on N64 or Minecraft. This vibe was the inspiration for the play too, but happy for companies to find their version of it.

Q: Is Martha and Isaac's relationship completely platonic?
AM: I would like it to be. It feels refreshing and less complex, there is so much in the play it probably doesn't need this extra layer. We are seeing a friendship form between Martha and Isaac.

Q: How should we approach young people playing adult characters?
(Can we do it non-naturalistically or should it be naturalistic?)
AM: The world of the video game is already heightened, so it's probably clearer to root the scenes with the adults in reality to help ground the story.

Rourke mentioned as an example a few American sitcoms (*Parks and Recreation, Brooklyn Nine-Nine*, US version of *The Office*) and the ways they are often really observational which could be a useful approach. There is something exciting and charming to see young people playing adults.

Q: Why don't you want projection to be used in the show?
AM: Screens are not the language of this play. By using projection or screens it feels you'd take away from the creating the delight and charm of the play. Screens are all around us which makes it feel essential, but actually this should be a celebration of the young people.

Q: Is this a tech-positive play? Is it a play that criticises it?
AM: I think it's semi-tech positive, but I hope it also highlights that a technological shortcut will never solve the crisis of not having enough mental health professionals. It can be a useful tool but never will be one size fits all and won't replace real human connection.

Q: What do you think about the game overall?
AM: It's kind of rubbish, but it's also really fun. You may learn something, but it may not be what you are expecting to learn. It's also important to not completely disregard the importance of wellbeing and self-help. It's just that this particular game is a bit shabby, not necessarily perfect.

Rourke commented that this thing that's really wonky is still helpful accidentally. It feels like this connects to the idea of the two characters accidentally connecting by playing this not-so-great game within a broken system.

A participant highlighted how the game is imperfect, but it still creates space for friendship. It's like life, it's not perfect and the situation is not great, but you can find the great stuff in it, you can find connection within it.

Q: How to stage the monologue of Screw This?
AM: Allow it to be upbeat and be one tone as if it was read by Siri!

Rourke added that it's a really classy piece of writing so just enjoy it. Trust that the text will do the job and an audience will follow it. Resist the temptation to make it varied, resist the condition to bring the intentions and emotion into what they are saying. Focus on doing one thing and do that brilliantly. It can have musicality in it without bringing the emotional intentions behind it. It sits in a brilliant history of modernist plays – being able to speak in one tone or condition to reveal the writing. This will expose the meaning of the writing. It's an amazing acting and directorial challenge.

From a workshop led by Josie Rourke and Jessica Wright
With notes by Júlia Levai

Normalised

by Amanda Verlaque

Amanda Verlaque is from Northern Ireland and lives between Belfast and Dublin. She worked in TV drama as a script editor, storyliner and producer before starting her writing career, and now writes for stage, screen, audio and VR. Her critically acclaimed play about homophobia, misogyny and coercive control, *This Sh*t Happens All the Time*, was produced by the Lyric and revived by the Grand Opera House. Work in theatre includes *This Sh*t Happens All the Time*, a critically acclaimed play about homophobia, misogyny and coercive control, produced by the Lyric and revived by the Grand Opera House; and *Lolly* an audio play about warring sisters trying to navigate the Covid lockdown, and *Distortion*, a critically acclaimed play about political hypocrisy, homophobia and PR spin, both produced by The MAC. She also adapted and wrote the pilot for *An Irish Country Doctor* based on Patrick Taylor's award-winning novel and she made her directorial debut with *Egg*, her VR short film set during the Second World War. She has been under commission to the Abbey, Ireland's national theatre, and was one of the Irish Theatre Institute's Six in the Attic artists for 2022/23. She is currently part of The Mavens programme at the Mill Theatre, Dublin, and is under commission to Playhouse Derry.

Characters

Approx. 15/16 years old:

Bo – *cis male*

Kieran – *cis male*

Rosa – *cis female*

Reema – *cis female*

Sam – *cis female*

Approx. seventeen/eighteen years old:

Jay – *cis male but could be played by a non-binary or trans male*

Maddie – *cis female*

Clarke – *cis male but could be played by a non-binary or trans male*

Matt – *cis male but could be played by a non-binary or trans male*

Jamesy *(Colm's twin and Bo's older brother)* – *cis male*

Jamesy's gang: age 13 to 16. Numbers to be decided by production team but approx. four. Named members: **Dee** *and* **Mox** – *age 16 and cis male*. Other gang members can be played by any gender.

School kids at the rally and vigil: age range 13 to 18. Numbers to be decided by production team.

Optional considerations

Slur words/banter – can be modified to suit vernacular.

Glossary

Youse = you plural. Peelers = police. Craic = fun/a brilliant time

A note on swearing: Companies are welcome to replace swear words, providing the alternative carries the same meaning and emotional charge.

Scene One: The Meadows Shrine, a Few Days Ago

SFX birdsong. A lush green meadow. Trees and wildflower. SFX a babbling brook. A peaceful place. In among a woodland there's the stump of a felled Rowan tree that's been converted into a shrine, only now it's covered with debris made up of torn photos, a broken lamp jar, cards and flowers. **Jay** *surveys the mess.*

Jay   What is wrong with you people?!

But he is alone and no one hears him. He slowly tidies up, putting the destroyed trinkets, etc. into a bin bag. Once this is done, he takes cards and photos from his bag and arranges them around the stump. He lays fresh flowers. A new lamp jar is produced and he flicks the switch so the little red heart glows inside the glass.

If I've to come here every day I will. Every time it's wrecked I'll fix it. I won't give up.

He sets the lamp jar in among the trinkets and flowers. He takes a moment to survey his work. He blows a kiss, then turns and leaves.

Scene Two: Communal green near a housing estate

SFX of nearby traffic on a busy road. **Bo** *and* **Rosa** *are dribbling a football (the actors are playing with an imaginary ball and will mime their actions) trying to get past each other to where* **Kieran** *stands in goal against a wall. His arms are outstretched even though* **Bo** *and* **Rosa** *are nowhere near him. It's clear that* **Rosa** *is the better footballer. The mood is playful and* **Bo** *and* **Rosa** *exchange light banter throughout.*

Kieran   Bo?

Bo   What, mate?

Kieran   Look at the time.

Bo   What of it?

Kieran   Your Jamesy said you were to meet him.

Bo   Don't be worrying about him. You just watch that goal. (*To* **Rosa**.) So come on, tell me, have I a chance or what?

Rosa   How many times? She's way outta your league, mate.

Bo   Have you asked her?

Rosa   Don't need to. Chrissy Knox isn't interested in you, ya wee runt.

Bo   How do you know? Like, really know.

Rosa   Cos it's me she likes, not you.

Bo   You're a wee liar.

Rosa She's as gay as I am.

Bo You're winding me up.

Rosa So don't believe me. But you're way off the mark, mate.

She tackles the ball from **Bo**.

Bo How am I supposed to get a girl if you keep getting in there before me?

Rosa I can't help it if they prefer me. It's not just footy I'm better at than you.

Rosa *grins at* **Bo** *and pulls a face. He smiles back and kicks the ball directly at her, but she swerves, gains control of the ball and thwacks it past* **Kieran**, *who doesn't move an inch, arms still out wide.* **Rosa** *laughs.* **Bo** *can't help but laugh too.*

Bo Fuck's sake, Kieran!

Rosa Keep up the good work, Kieran.

Kieran I don't think I'm good at this.

Bo What makes you think that?

They laugh and resume dribbling. **Kieran** *remains stock still. He shouts over to* **Bo**.

Kieran You'll have to go soon, Bo. Jamesy's gonna be pissed off.

Bo So what? He's not the boss of me.

Rosa *is impressed.*

Rosa Finally standing up to your big brother, eh?

Bo Always have.

Rosa Whatever. (*Pause.*) Here, I know who *does* fancy you.

Bo Don't say Reema.

Rosa Reema.

Bo Can't go there. Kieran likes her.

Rosa She doesn't feel the same.

Bo Doesn't matter. Wouldn't be right.

Reema *approaches. They greet each other. The footy continues.* **Reema** *watches, bored.*

She snaps some pics. It's obvious it's **Bo** *she's concentrating on.*

Reema You're really good, Bo.

He points at her phone while he attempts to dribble.

Bo I'm shite. Don't be snapping me.

Reema *puts her phone away.*

Reema I didn't know you played.

Rosa He doesn't.

Kieran *comes out of goal.*

Kieran We've just started.

Reema Oh well, practice makes perfect.

Kieran Do you wanna play, Reema?

Reema In these shoes?

Kieran What's wrong with them?

Reema There's nothing wrong with them!

Jay *walks past.* **Bo** *and* **Jay** *glare at each other.*

Rosa/Reema/Kieran Hiya, Jay.

Jay *nods in recognition.* **Bo** *watches him go by.*

Bo He did it again. Eyeballing me. What's his problem?

Rosa Dunno. He's fine with me.

Bo Ever since Colm died.

Reema Maybe Jay doesn't want to be reminded of Colm?

Bo What's that to do with me? I wasn't his twin. Doesn't explain the death stare either.

Reema Here's Jamesy now.

Rosa I better head.

Bo You don't have to worry, Rosa, he won't say anything to you.

Rosa I'm not worried. It's what I might say to him, the homophobic prick.

Bo Sorry, Rosa.

Rosa Not your fault. You coming, Reema?

Jamesy *approaches with his gang in tow (there's approx four gang members at any given time but Jamesy is always with* **Dee**, *his 'right-hand man').*

Rosa *and* **Reema** *pass* **Jamesy** *and his gang.*

Jamesy Alright, Reema, love? Watch yourself there with that one.

Rosa Wise up, bigot.

Jamesy What did you say?

Rosa You heard me. Come on, Reema.

Jamesy's *gang sense trouble.* **Dee** *mimics* **Rosa**.

Dee Come on, Reema.

Jamesy *and his gang laugh.* **Rosa** *tugs* **Reema***'s arm. They head on.* **Jamesy** *turns his attention to* **Bo***.*

Jamesy Where the fuck have you been? Didn't I tell you we've stuff to do?

Bo Sorry, Jamesy.

Jamesy *gets right up into* **Bo***'s face; he enjoys holding court in front of his gang.*

He pokes **Bo** *as he says each word:*

Jamesy Don't. Ignore. Me. Again.

Bo *is scared; he blusters.*

Bo I'm really sorry, bro. The phone must've been on silent. Honest.

Jamesy *takes a moment and seems to accept this. He smiles, wraps his arm around* **Bo** *in a friendly manner.*

Jamesy Too busy chatting up Reema, eh? Eh?

Kieran I like Reema.

Jamesy *guffaws. His gang join in. They circle in on* **Kieran***, who visibly tenses.*

Jamesy Punching well above your weight there. You need to lower your expectations. Find someone on your level. Am I right or am I right, lads?

He and **Dee** *fist pump.* **Kieran** *stares at his feet, doesn't reply.*

Jamesy Lost for words, Kieran?

He taps **Kieran***'s temple as he speaks directly into* **Kieran***'s face.*

Jamesy Lights on but nobody's home? Lift doesn't go all the way to the top?

Dee Good one, Jamesy!

Kieran *remains silent.* **Jamesy** *turns back to* **Bo***.*

Jamesy Don't make me come looking for you again. You hear me?

Bo *nods.*

Jamesy Say, 'I won't, Jamesy. I swear.' Go on, say it.

Bo I won't, Jamesy. I swear.

Jamesy *pushes* **Bo***.*

Jamesy Wee scrote.

He points at **Bo***.*

Jamesy Keep your phone on.

He and his gang exit. **Bo** *and* **Kieran** *watch them go.*

Kieran   Why does he have to be so nasty?

Bo   Takes after Da. Been worse since Colm died.

Kieran   I wish Jamesy was nice like Colm was.

Bo   Me too, mate.

Scene Three: The Meadows Shrine, a Few Days Later

Jay is at the stump. The shrine has been vandalised again and he's seriously pissed off. He aggressively dumps the torn cards, etc. into a bin bag. **Maddie** *arrives, out of breath.*

Jay   What kept you?!

Maddie   What's the emergency?

She puts her hands on her knees and breathes deeply.

Jay   You by the looks of it.

Maddie   I'm here aren't I? What's the rush?

Jay   Look. This mess. Again. What is wrong with that lot?

Maddie   What lot? How many times do I have to say you don't know who did this. It could've been anybody.

Jay   How many times do I have to say it wasn't just anybody. Jamesy is behind this.

Maddie   Makes no sense. Why desecrate the image of your own brother? Especially your identical twin?

Jay   That's probably the reason, knowing the twisted fucker. *That's* the sort of family they are. Remember the funeral? The Da with his crocodile tears who banned me from going? Trust me, Jamesy's behind this. And given the way Bo looks at me I'd say he's up to his neck in it too.

Maddie   You've no proof.

Jay *takes this in.*

Jay   That's why I'm going to catch them in the act. Put a stop to it. Otherwise, I'll be doing this for fucking ever!

Maddie   Leave it, Jay. Jamesy's bad news.

Jay   You think I can't handle myself? I'm not afraid of some coward who vandalises a shrine to his own brother.

Maddie   Please, Jay, that's not what I'm saying. Just don't go looking for trouble.

Matt *and* **Clarke** *arrive and survey the scene.* **Matt** *squeezes* **Jay***'s shoulder, takes the bin bag from him and starts clearing up the mess.*

Matt Aw, mate. This is shit.

Clarke Not for much longer.

Jay Too right. I'm gonna sort this. Jamesy's gonna get what's coming to him.

Matt Don't be picking fights with Jamesy.

Jay If one more person tells me to lay off Jamesy! (*Pause, quieter.*) I'm not standing around watching him take the piss.

Clarke You won't have to. All this is gonna go.

Jay No it's not. It's a shrine, it's not doing anyone any harm.

Matt He means the Meadows, mate. Haven't you heard? It's being redeveloped. New housing.

Maddie Doubt it. The land's protected. It's a green belt.

Clarke It's a money belt.

Jay Not if I've anything to do with it.

Clarke Don't be such a dick, Jay. What are you gonna do? Lie down in front of a bulldozer?

Jay This is me and Colm's place. It's special.

Matt What about building the shrine somewhere else?

Clarke Maybe it's time to move on, Jay.

Maddie Are you being a dick on purpose?

Clarke What? I'm trying to help.

Maddie By being really insensitive?

Clarke It's unhealthy that Jay comes here every day. It's almost a year since Colm died.

Jay Oh is it? I didn't realise that. Thanks for reminding me about my dead boyfriend's anniversary, Clarke.

Clarke I'm just saying.

Jay *dismisses* **Clarke** *with a flick of his hand.*

Jay Whatever. (*Pause.*) If Colm was here, he would definitely do something. Lying in front of a bulldozer isn't such a bad idea, Clarke.

Clarke Wait, what? That's not what I said.

Maddie That's a great idea, Clarke. Colm wouldn't stand for this and he'd get everyone onside too.

Clarke Hang on.

The others ignore **Clarke**, *caught up in the excitement of a plan forming.*

Matt   There'd be protests and campaigns. Like the time he spray painted old Cameron's Merc cos he wouldn't support Pride.

Jay *smiles at the memory.*

Jay   Served the old bigot right. Should've been sacked from teaching centuries ago.

Matt   He nearly had a stroke until he realised it was a skin!

Maddie   Watching him peel it off, the face on him!

They all laugh.

Jay   He knew it was Colm but couldn't prove it.

Maddie, **Jay** *and* **Matt** *mimic Cameron.*

Maddie   I'm getting fingerprint experts down here!

Jay   DNA specialists. You're going to jail!

Matt   You're a disgrace! Should be ashamed of yourself!

They double up in fits of laughter. As the laughter subsides they grow silent. A beat.

Jay   I'm gonna start a campaign, take on the council and the property developers. I'm gonna go large on this, Colm style. Who's with me?

Maddie *and* **Matt** *whoop.* **Clarke** *is subdued but the others don't notice.*

Maddie   We need a plan. Where do we even start?

Jay   I know exactly what to do. It's as if Colm's here right now, guiding me.

Scene Four: School

SFX school noises. **Maddie** *and* **Matt** *stand beside* **Jay** *who's coming to the close of a rousing speech.* **Clarke** *stands back, alone.* **Bo**, **Rosa**, **Reema** *and* **Kieran** *stand to one side, taking it all in.* **Sam**, *the school's radio station reporter, is recording the event.*

Jay   We'll take over the Meadows if we have to. We'll lie in front of the bulldozers if we have to! We're gonna stop another rich developer getting richer at the expense of our hangouts. The Meadows belongs to every single one of us! It's free and it's up to us to keep it that way!

Roar of support.

Jay   Are you with me?

Roar of support.

Jay   The campaign to save the Meadows starts here!

Anon. One Fuck the property developers!

The crowd laughs and cheers.

Jay We'll show the developers *and* the council that they can't mess with us!

Anon. Two Fuck the council!

Roar of approval. SFX bell rings for class. Students start to drift away. **Bo**, **Kieran**, **Rosa** *and* **Reema** *move centre stage.*

Kieran Are they gonna take all the trees away?

Bo Looks like it.

Rosa Not if Jay can help it. That was impressive. Very like your Colm.

Kieran I like the trees and the fields. And the river.

Reema I like decent housing. That's a better cause.

Kieran The trees are lovely.

Reema So's somewhere nice to live. This place is a dump.

Rosa It's not that bad.

Reema Yes it is.

Kieran Colm loved the Meadows.

Rosa That's why Jay's doing this. So we get to keep them.

Reema Oh it's 'we' is it?

Rosa So what if it is? I'm getting involved. What would your Colm do, Bo?

Bo *laughs.*

Bo He'd be a part of it. Probably lead it. Kieran's right, Colm loved the Meadows.

Rosa You gonna take after him then? Join Colm's mates?

Bo Might do.

Kieran Jamesy doesn't like Colm's mates. He'll go nuts if you get involved, Bo.

Bo Right enough.

Rosa Thought you didn't care what Jamesy thinks?

Bo I don't but, like, I'm hardly gonna go out of my way to annoy him, am I?

Rosa *shakes her head, annoyed with* **Bo**.

Rosa Suit yourself, Bo.

SFX class bell rings again. **Bo**, **Rosa**, **Kieran** *and* **Reema** *exit.* **Jay**, **Maddie**, **Clarke** *and* **Matt** *move centre stage. Everyone except* **Clarke** *is upbeat.*

Maddie That was brilliant, Jay, you're a natural!

Matt It feels so good to be doing this!

Jay It does, doesn't it?

Jay *clocks that* **Clarke** *isn't joining in.*

Jay Clarke? You with us?

Clarke I've a class.

Maddie What's up? You're always on for stuff like this.

Clarke There's better stuff to be getting on with.

Maddie Stuff?

He shrugs.

Clarke I dunno. Life?

Matt Don't be a prick, mate.

Clarke I'm not. It's called progress. We can't stop it.

Maddie It wouldn't kill you to show some support.

Clarke Just so Jay can have a shrine? Sorry, mate, count me out.

He exits.

Jay Why's he being such a dick?

Matt I don't know what's up with him.

Maddie Something's not right.

Scene Five: The Meadows Shrine

Cast member takes centre stage with a sign that reads: 'A FEW DAYS LATER'

The campaign is growing in numbers and a crowd is gathering, waiting for **Jay**. **Rosa** *and* **Reema** *are there.* **Sam** *arrives and approaches* **Rosa**. **Sam** *fancies* **Rosa**, *and* **Reema** *watches on, smiling.*

Sam Hi, Rosa.

Rosa Sam.

Sam How's you?

Rosa Good. You?

Sam Yep, good. (*Pause.*) Some turnout, eh?

Rosa Yeah.

Reema *makes a show of waving at* **Sam**.

Reema Hi, Sam!

Sam Yeah, hi, Reema.

Reema I'm good too thanks for asking.

Sam What?

Rosa Wise up, Reema. Ignore her, Sam.

Jay, **Maddie** *and* **Matt** *arrive.*

Sam There's Jay, I better head. See you, Rosa.

She makes her way over to **Jay**.

Reema You're in there, Rosa! Never seen Sam tongue-tied except when she's talking to you.

Rosa You're enjoying this aren't you?

Reema You gonna ask her out?

Rosa Might do.

Reema I think she'd say yes.

Rosa Course she would.

Reema *gives* **Rosa** *a playful dig.*

Reema Mate, the size of your head!

Rosa *returns the playful dig.*

Rosa Shush! Jay's being interviewed.

Maddie *and* **Matt** *stand next to* **Jay** *who's being interviewed by* **Sam**. *Most people have their mobiles on, filming.* **Rosa** *and* **Reema** *watch the interview from the sidelines.* **Bo** *arrives and stands alone, unseen by the others.*

Sam The campaign is really taking off. Are you surprised that so many people care about the environment?

Jay Not really. It's about the future of our green spaces and we know we have to stop ruining them. The Meadows is an ancient, sacred place that's been protected for centuries –

Sam – Until now.

Jay Yeah, until greedy developers got their hands on it. They'll smother it in concrete and glass.

Sam They're not developing all of the Meadows.

Jay So they say. If this is allowed to happen, it'll all go eventually. Where are we supposed to go?

Sam There are plenty of places –

Jay – Where exactly? We're too old for the playpark and too young for the pubs.

Sam You come here a lot don't you?

Jay *nods.*

Sam Every day in fact. Why's that?

Maddie *squeezes* **Jay**'s *arm.* **Jay** *takes a breath.*

Jay I used to hang out with Colm underneath the big Rowan tree.

Sam Who's Colm?

Maddie Are you for real? You know who he is.

Jay He is – was – my boyfriend. When it was destroyed during the big storm all that was left was the stump. It kinda looks like a seat so we called it our special seat, just for us. It's where we grew really close.

Sam And fell in love?

Jay *nods. He gets a bit upset.* **Maddie** *holds onto him, providing support.*

Jay Yes.

Maddie If Colm was here today, he'd be leading this campaign. We're doing this in his memory.

Sam Why isn't he here today?

Jay He died in a car accident. Almost a year ago. You know that, Sam.

Sam *moves her mic to one side.*

Sam I know, but maybe not everyone knows? I'm just helping you get the message across, build support?

She brings the mic up and waits. **Jay** *blows out his cheeks, composes himself.*

Jay Colm loved it here and we loved each other. I turned the stump into a shrine for him, for people to leave flowers and mementoes if they wanted to, so we never forget him. But it's always being vandalised.

Sam Maybe the shrine got damaged by accident?

Jay No, it didn't.

Sam How do you know? Did you see who did it?

Jay *is getting rattled.*

Jay No, but I know who's behind it.

Sam How can you be so sure, if you didn't see who did it? It could still be an accident.

Jay's *had enough of* **Sam**. *He's angry.*

Jay The one thing in the entire place that just happens to be a memorial to a gay guy? It's a hate crime.

Sam Did you report it to the police?

Jay Of course, I did! They've done nothing. Maybe this campaign will stop the developers *and* the homophobes.

Maddie I think you've got enough for your report, Sam.

Sam*'s not finished. She ignores* **Maddie**.

Sam Maybe if you named names the police would have a better chance?

Jay All I'll say is that the bigots were very close to home for Colm.

Bo *exits, unseen.*

Maddie *steps in, takes control.*

Maddie Ok, we're done here. Thanks, Sam.

Sam But I've more questions.

Maddie That's enough for now.

Sam *and* **Maddie** *face each other off for a beat or two. Then* **Sam** *exits.*

Rosa *and* **Reema** *approach* **Jay** *and* **Maddie**.

Rosa Hiyas.

Maddie *and* **Jay** *turn as one.*

Maddie Hiyas.

Rosa I'd like to help.

Jay Close friends only. Sorry.

Reema Wise up, Jay.

Rosa Colm was my friend too, Jay.

Jay I thought Bo was your friend.

Rosa He is.

Jay All he does is shoot daggers at me.

Reema You must've done something to annoy him.

Jay Doubt it. Ask him about the shrine being trashed. Bet he knows all about it.

Maddie Leave it, Jay, will you? Listen, we're glad you're on board. We're planning a huge demo.

Rosa I'm up for that. Count us in.

Reema Us? Sorry but we need housing more than some random field.

Rosa She's just joking, aren't you, Reema?

Reema No, I'm not.

She folds her arms, determined.

Rosa Really?

Reema Yes really.

Rosa *copies* **Reema** *and folds her arms.*

Rosa Bet you'd go if Bo was going.

Reema *shakes her head, mouth open, speechless . . . almost.*

Reema Witch!

She storms off.

Rosa She's just being awkward. That's her way of joking.

Jay She's had a humour bypass.

Rosa She's my mate.

Jay Coulda fooled me.

Rosa She didn't grow up here. She doesn't get how important the Meadows are to us. Plus, her family was housed in the shittiest of shitty estates. Give her a break, she'll come round.

Maddie Fair enough. Jay?

Jay Suppose.

Rosa I'm happy to help out. Gimme a shout?

Maddie *nods and* **Rosa** *heads off.* **Maddie** *and* **Jay** *watch her go.*

Jay What did you have to do that for?

Maddie We need all the help we can get and you need to stop obsessing about Colm's family, cos you've no proof! You've always gotten along with Rosa so stop turning friends into enemies.

Maddie *and* **Jay** *head off.*

Scene Six: Communal Green Near a Housing Estate

Rosa *catches up with* **Reema**. *She tugs* **Reema***'s arm but* **Reema** *shrugs her off.*

Rosa Oh come on, Reema, don't be like this.

Reema What did you have to say that for?

Rosa We'll it's true isn't it? You fancy Bo.

Reema Wise up.

Rosa Lighten up.

Reema Like you, Ms Eco Warrior?

Rosa It's not just that, Reema. You know what's been happening to Colm's shrine. What kind of message does that send?

Reema What's the big deal? It's only some randomers being dicks.

Rosa All it takes is some randomers to get away with it without anyone calling it out for that behaviour to be normalised.

Reema You're not going to give me your 'normalised' speech again?

Rosa Look, I'm sorry what I said about Bo in front of Jay and Maddie.

Reema Showed me up big time.

Rosa I mean it, I'm sorry. But Reema, if I don't stand up for myself we'll be back in the dark ages. Jay's got a point and he has my support.

Reema I thought the campaign was about protecting the Meadows, saving the environment for everyone's benefit?

Rosa It is.

Reema Then what's all this talk about the dark ages and standing up for yourself? It's not meant to be about you, Rosa.

Rosa If it's about an LGBTQ+ shrine being vandalised as well then it is about me.

Reema The shrine.

Rosa Don't mock.

Reema Then don't be such a drama queen about it. 'Dark ages' for fuck's sake. Do I look like I need a history lesson?!

A beat. **Reema** *calms down.*

Reema Look, I'm sorry too.

Rosa Thanks, mate. You'll go to the demo?

Reema Maybe. (*Pause.*) Do you think I'd be in with a chance with Bo?

Rosa I knew it! You could be. Better than pretending to like footie. 'You're really good, Bo; practice makes perfect, Bo.'

Rosa *laughs but* **Reema** *is furious.*

Reema Shut up!

Rosa *stops laughing.*

Rosa Calm down! Can you not take a joke? Fuck's sake, Reema, you're hard work sometimes.

Reema *huffs.*

Reema Go and hug some trees if you want. I want better housing.

She walks off. **Rosa** *shakes her head.* **Sam** *approaches.*

Sam Hi, Rosa, what's up with Reema?

Rosa She's in one of her moods.

Sam She was very smiley last time I saw her.

Rosa Laughing at us, that's why.

Sam Was that cos it was about . . .

Rosa *and* **Sam** *start to flirt.*

Rosa . . . about?

Sam Me . . . fancying you?

Rosa Are you . . . psychic?

Sam *nods.*

Sam I am. I can see us dating.

Rosa Wow. Impressive.

Sam So . . . you wanna do something later?

Rosa Looks like it. Have to say, you're a fast mover.

Sam You're always with Bo or Reema. Didn't want to waste an opportunity to talk to you alone.

Rosa Bold. I like it.

Sam You do?

Rosa I do.

Scene Seven: The Meadows

Matt, **Jay** *and* **Maddie** *arrive at the Meadows to find the fencing has already been erected. Their heads tilt back as they read the sign:*

Matt 'Private property'.

Maddie 'Norton Developments'. That's why Clarke didn't want to get involved.

Jay 'Trespassers will be prosecuted'.

Matt You think it's his dad's company?

Jay This can't be happening.

Maddie How many building contractors called Norton do you know that aren't Clarke's dad?

Jay What are we supposed to do now?!

Jay *sits on the ground, defeated.* **Rosa** *arrives. She sees the sign and the fencing.*

Rosa What the fuck?

Jay We're screwed!

Rosa No we're not.

Jay *points at the sign.*

Jay Do you need glasses?

Rosa Just cos the fence is up doesn't mean we give in. Loads of people are gonna be raging about this so we make the most of it.

Maddie Rosa's right. This could help our campaign.

Matt You can't just give up.

Jay *thinks for a moment then jumps to his feet.*

Jay Get your phones out, I need you to film me.

Maddie *and* **Matt** *get their phones out.*

Jay Ready?

Maddie Yep, go for it.

Maddie *and* **Matt** *start filming, circling* **Jay**. **Jay** *points to the fencing.*

Jay See this? They think they can do what they want. Think this will keep us out? No way. These Meadows have been free for centuries. To the money-grabbing property developers let me say this, you can't fence us in or keep us out for ever. If you agree with us, come join us. It's not too late to stand up for the world we all share.

They stop filming.

Maddie Nice one, Jay.

Jay I have to say, that's made me feel better.

Rosa We need to do more of these, aim for the main news stations. Go large.

Matt Like they'd care what we think. We're hardly their target audience.

Rosa No but they *do* care what our parents think.

Maddie I'll post an Insta with Mum and Dad. Seeing as they started dating here a million years ago!

Matt When dinosaurs ruled the earth!

Jay And no one worried about being gay, trans or whatever cos they were too busy trying to not get eaten alive!

Rosa   The dinosaurs didn't discriminate, everyone tasted delicious!

She checks her phone.

We are getting shed loads of likes.

Matt   If we get older people behind us the developers won't see just a handful of kids making noise.

Jay   Why couldn't Clarke tell us about this? Some mate he is.

Matt   Would you choose your mates over your family?

Maddie   Mates are family too.

Jay   We need a plan B. Once they add that barbed wire we'll be cut to pieces. We can't ask people to climb over it.

Maddie   We can cut it back.

Matt   And get done for destroying their property?

Rosa   They're taking ours. And who says we have to go over it anyway? We just need to know where to go through. You said it, Jay, they can't fence in the entire woodland.

Jay   We can find a way in, set up camp, make them move us by force.

Maddie   We use Insta so everyone can see us 24/7, just in case they play dirty.

Rosa   Stay for as long as we can.

Matt   We need to sort out provisions. We don't know how long this will take.

Jay   You're not gonna starve, Matt.

Matt   Still. Maybe arrange takeaways or something?

Maddie   Have you lost it?

She pretends to be on her phone.

Eh, hello? Yes, is that 'We Deliver Anywhere' pizzas? Could we have a hundred sixteen-inch crazy hot ones to the Meadows please? What's that? Whereabouts in the Meadows? Oh let me think now . . . well if you go past all the big fields until you come to the one with the stump –

Matt *gives* **Maddie** *a playful push.*

Matt   – Haha, very funny. You should be on the stage, Maddie.

Maddie   Don't worry food will be sorted, Matt. What if we decide a set number of days? No one else needs to know that.

Rosa   Just enough to get the message out and pile the pressure on the developers and the council.

Jay   Colm's anniversary is next week, I'd like to do it then if you guys agree.

The others nod.

I've a good feeling about this.

Scene Eight: A Bench Near the River

Jamesy's *on his phone. He's watching* **Jay**'s *interview (we'll find this out in a second).* **Dee** *and* **Mox** *are huddled close to* **Jamesy** *as he watches the video.*

Dee That's not on, Jamesy.

Mox I'd be raging if he said that about my brother.

Jamesy *says nothing, keeps watching.* **Mox** *tried to get closer to* **Jamesy** *but* **Dee** *pushes him out of the way.* **Reema** *passes by.*

Reema Hi, Jamesy.

Jamesy *looks up, sees her, but returns to his phone, ignoring her.* **Reema** *walks on.* **Jamesy** *looks up, has a thought.*

Jamesy Hang on, Reema.

He waves his mobile at her.

C'mere and look at this.

Mox *tries to get back into* **Jamesy**'s *orbit to see the video but* **Dee** *pushes him away again.*

Dee What are you gonna do about it, Jamesy? You can't let that Jay off with this.

Jamesy Shut the fuck up, Dee!

Dee *backs off, afraid.* **Jamesy** *calms down.* **Reema** *sits down beside him and he shows her the interview.*

Reema Yeah everyone's talking about it. They're gonna put houses all over the Meadows. It's causing a big stink, which is a laugh if you knew the dive I live in. But you can't say that to the tree huggers, they'd blame you for killing the planet.

Jamesy Never mind the tree huggers. Why's he saying that about Colm? In front of people?

Reema What about it?

She senses **Jamesy** *is getting irked.*

Jamesy Why is *that queer* making out that Colm was gay?

Reema Cos he was?

Jamesy He wasn't.

Reema It's not really an issue.

Jamesy Yes, it bloody well is!

Reema Okay. Whatever you say. It's just that, well, they seemed to be a couple.

Jamesy *stands up, angry.* **Reema** *is taken aback. She moves away from him while he rants.*

Jamesy That's what he wants people to think. My brother was straight.

If he thinks he can use Colm as a sob story to save some stupid fields? Showing him up, disrespecting the dead? Fuck that. I'm starting my own campaign. I'll do this for Colm.

He spots **Bo** *and* **Kieran** *walking in the distance.*

Jamesy There's my wingman. Oi! Bo!

He waves at **Bo** *and* **Kieran** *to join him.*

Reema You're really gonna start your own campaign?

Jamesy *shrugs. He has no intention of campaigning.*

Jamesy Maybe. (*To* **Bo**.) Have you heard what that Jay's been saying about our Colm? Dragging his name through the mud? I don't want his first anniversary to be ruined.

Bo Don't be causing trouble, Jamesy. He's not doing anyone any harm.

Jamesy Oh, you think so do you? What about the harm done to me? To our family name? I'm glad Colm isn't alive to see this.

Bo You don't mean that!

Jamesy I know the path he takes through the Meadows. I've a wee something planned that'll set the record straight once and for all. You up for that lads?

Dee *and* **Mox** *clap hands, delighted.*

Dee Yeeeeooow!

Kieran What if you get caught?

Jamesy Me? What if *we* get caught. Youse are gonna help me.

Scene Nine: School Common Room, the Next Day

Jay *is nursing a bloodied nose. He has his head back.* **Matt** *is feeding sheets of toilet roll to him as he dabs at his nose.* **Sam** *is there, mic out and at the ready.* **Maddie** *enters, takes in the scene.*

Maddie What happened.

Matt He got jumped by Jamesy and his gang.

Jay And Bo. Told you.

Maddie Mate, I'm so sorry.

She hugs **Jay**.

Sam I need to interview you about this, Jay.

Jay I told you, Sam, no.

Matt From now on anywhere you go, we go too.

Jay Seriously, Matt? I don't want you to be my bodyguard. I can't live like that. (*Pause.*) He was waiting, biding his time! He must've been watching me. For all I know he's been watching me tidy up the shrine then wrecking it all over again when I leave.

Maddie But you're going to report this, right?

Sam If you're going to the peelers then why not give an interview to the school radio? It'll be an exclusive about homophobic hate crime.

Jay It's not the kind of publicity I need right now. Sorry, Sam.

Sam *exits.*

Jay I'm not letting Jamesy get away with this. He was toe to toe with me, Maddie, right in my face. It was like looking at a demonic Colm. Fuckin' surreal.

Maddie What did you say to him?

Jay He said he wanted a word. I said here's two: fuck off.

Maddie *and* **Matt** *laugh in spite of the seriousness of what's happened.* **Jay** *sees the humour in it too and joins in.*

Jay Before I had time to think about what was coming out of my mouth I was asking him why he's obsessed with me, maybe he's queer too. That's when this happened.

He touches his nose and winces.

Matt Fuckin' hell, Jay! Respect!

A beat, then **Jay** *grows serious again.*

Jay I got lucky. He heard cop sirens so he legged it, fuckin' coward. But the look on his face? He really wanted to hurt me.

Scene Nine A: Communal Green Near a Housing Estate, Same Day/Time as Scene Nine

Jamesy *is buzzing. He's entertaining his cronies as he relives what he said and did to* **Jay**.

Even though most of them were there, he still regales them. They crowd around him and he's loving the attention. **Bo** *and* **Kieran** *stand to one side.*

Jamesy Did you see his face? I tell ya, I could smell the fear offa him.

Dee He probably shit a brick!

Mox Shit a whole wheelbarrow full!

Dee He wasn't on his feet for long though was he?

Jamesy *makes a boxing 'one, two' jab, prodding* **Bo** *and some of his mates.*

Jamesy And did you see the dirty looks he was giving you, Bo? Full of hate he was. I hardly had to touch him at all.

He makes the boxing 'one, two' jab again.

One wee tap and he was on the deck. Weak fucker.

He is delighted with himself. His cronies laugh in unison, but not **Bo** *and* **Kieran**.

Jamesy *turns to them.*

Jamesy I saw youse numbnuts shitting yourselves. If you don't step up you'll get a taste of what he got. Just cos the peelers spoiled the fun doesn't mean this is over. I'll see youse at the usual spot later. We're gonna end this shit for good.

He and his gang head off.

Scene Nine B: School Common Room, a Few Minutes After Scene Nine

Jay *is deflated.* **Maddie** *and* **Matt** *tidy away the bloodied toilet roll.*

Jay Some anniversary for Colm this is. Jamesy's ruined it.

Maddie There's only a handful of Jamesys. They can't stop us all.

Jay Ok for you to say. Were you about to be kicked to death?

Maddie Help me out, Matt.

Matt You're leading an amazing campaign, Jay. The developers are all over the news, bad press central.

Maddie Colm's shrine might make it after all.

Jay *brightens at the thought.* **Clarke** *arrives.* **Jay** *darkens again.*

Jay What do you want? Prick.

Maddie I asked him to come.

Clarke Jesus, mate, your face!

Jay What of it?

Clarke Don't be like that.

Jay You here to spy on us?

Clarke Don't, please. I feel like shit.

Matt That's your own fault.

Maddie Hear him out. Tell them, Clarke.

Clarke It's my fault the fencing is up.

Jay All our plans are ruined cos of you!

Clarke I know that. That's why I'm here.

Matt Gonna get your daddy to take the fencing down?

Clarke It's gonna get worse. It won't just be barbed wire keeping you out. I heard my dad on the phone. He's bringing in a security firm. The place will be crawling with them.

Maddie When?

Clarke Tomorrow.

Jay Prick.

Matt Thanks for nothing, mate.

Jay We don't have enough time to get the camp up and running.

Clarke I was thinking, if you plan something quick, it could still count.

Maddie We could get a good-sized crowd gathered for a vigil?

The others like the sound of this.

Clarke Whatever you're gonna do, do it tonight. Cos tomorrow is the beginning of the end for the Meadows.

Scene Ten: Communal Green Near a Housing Estate, Later the Same Day

Bo *sits, head in hands.* **Rosa** *approaches and sits down next to him. The mood is sombre.*

Rosa I heard what happened.

Bo I had nothing to do with it.

Rosa Jay got the living shit kicked out of him!

Bo I swear, I didn't lift a finger.

Rosa Didn't lift a finger to stop Jamesy or help Jay? What would you have done if the peelers hadn't showed up?

Silence. A beat.

Bo   Jay told Jamesy he wasn't afraid of him. Couldn't believe it, no one's ever stood up to him before.

Rosa   You could try it sometime.

Bo   I don't know what to do. I just wish none of this had happened.

Rosa   But it has.

Bo   I want things to be okay between us.

Rosa   That won't happen until this gets sorted.

Bo *nods. A beat.*

Bo   I'm heading back. You coming?

Rosa   Sorry, Bo, I can't be around you just now.

Bo *walks off.* **Rosa** *sits alone.*

Scene Eleven: Street Near the Communal Green

Jamesy *is walking along the street.* **Bo** *approaches him.* **Jamesy** *keeps walking.*

Bo   Did you see my messages?

Jamesy *stops.*

Jamesy   Yeah, I saw them.

There's an awkward silence between them.

Bo   Good, cos I wanted to see you.

Jamesy   I'm all yours.

Bo   Good, cos –

Jamesy *interrupts* **Bo**.

Jamesy   – Spit it out, Bo! I thought it was important, messaging me every five minutes!

Bo   I don't want any more trouble.

Jamesy   What would you know about trouble, you wee sap.

Bo   I want you to leave Jay alone.

Jamesy   Don't be wasting your breath on him.

Bo   He's not doing anyone any harm.

Jamesy   Wrong! He's trying to hijack the memory of our flesh and blood.

Bo   You can't stop people having memories.

Jamesy They're not memories, they're lies! I'm not gonna just sit back and take it, that's why I'm standing up for Colm's reputation. The family name is important.

Bo Then why did you pick on him?

Jamesy What are you on about? I haven't got time for this, Bo.

Bo You did. Da gave him a hard time and you joined in. Afraid Da was gonna do the same to you?

Jamesy Watch your mouth! Colm turned into a wuss. Hanging out with posh gits like Jay, putting ideas into his thick skull.

Bo Da made Colm's life a living hell.

Jamesy We were trying to harden him up. You have to think of Da's reputation.

Bo *scoffs.*

Bo Da's reputation!

Jamesy *pushes* **Bo.**

Jamesy Careful, Bo. You respect Da. Da says respect is the most important thing.

Bo And he's right. But you have to earn respect, by what you do. And I know for sure, you can't punch respect into someone.

Jamesy *closes in on* **Bo***, threateningly. The two brothers stare at each other.*

Jamesy Don't go messing things up for me and Da by doing anything stupid.

Bo I won't, but it's time you stopped acting the hard man for Da.

Jamesy *makes as if he's going to strike* **Bo***.* **Bo** *flinches and* **Jamesy** *bursts out laughing.*

Jamesy Wee scrote. Sometimes I think you're a bigger wuss than our Colm.

He walks off. **Bo** *watches him go.*

Bo Colm wasn't a wuss. Neither am I.

Scene Twelve: Communal Green Near a Housing Estate

Rosa *and* **Sam** *are hanging out at the green. They're flirting with each other.*

Sam I mean it, it's my turn next time. You choose the shittiest films!

Rosa My taste is excellent I'll have you know. And who says there's a next time?

Sam Ha ha. You're hilarious.

Rosa *playfully digs* **Sam***.*

Rosa Hilarious with a side order of taste.

Sam   Get you!

Rosa   Think you already have.

*She and **Sam** lean into each other. **Kieran** walks past with a group of mates. He waves over to **Rosa**.*

Kieran   Rosa!

Rosa *turns her back on **Kieran**.*

Rosa   Ignore him.

Sam   What's going on?

Rosa *doesn't respond.* **Kieran** *breaks from the group and joins her and **Sam**.*

Kieran   Have you fallen out with me, Rosa?

Rosa   What do you think? I can't believe youse went with Jamesy.

Kieran   It wasn't like that. Jamesy's scary.

Rosa   So stand up to him?

Kieran   Jay did and he got battered.

Sam   People need to call Jamesy out. What he did to Jay was wrong.

Kieran   We didn't hit Jay.

Rosa   That's what Bo said. Did youse really try to sneak off?

Kieran *nods.*

Kieran   We always do that when Jamesy's acting the hard man but he saw us this time. He called us numbnuts for not joining in. I like Jay but I'm afraid of Jamesy.

A beat.

I don't want Jay to get hurt again. Will you tell him to be careful?

Sam   Is Jamesy planning something more?

Kieran *nods.*

Kieran   I dunno what it is.

Rosa   Does Bo know? Is he a part of this?

Kieran   Bo isn't like Jamesy.

Rosa   He's got a funny way of showing it.

Kieran   Sorry, Rosa.

*He returns to his mates. **Rosa** sits. **Sam** joins her.*

Sam   You ok, Rosa?

Rosa Me? I'm great. Pity I can't say the same for my so-called best mate.

Sam You don't want to be falling out with Bo over something Jamesy did.

Rosa Why not? I'm so disappointed in him.

Sam Yeah but he is your bestie. True friends stick together even if they're struggling to find the right answers and do the right thing.

She puts her arm around **Rosa** *and they lean into each other.*

Scene Thirteen: Communal Green Near a Housing Estate

Cast member takes centre stage with a sign that reads: 'Later The Same Day'.

Kieran You sure about this, Bo?

Bo No, but I don't know what else to do.

He opens his jacket and shows something to **Kieran**. *We don't see what it is.*

Bo It's ok if you don't want to come. I can go on my own.

Kieran No way. We're mates.

Bo Thanks, Kieran. We better head before Jamesy sees us.

Scene Fourteen: The Meadows, Colm's Shrine, Later that night

People are gathering for the vigil. **Rosa** *arrives with* **Sam**. **Maddie** *is filming kids as they leave trinkets and flowers by the stump. Some stay and some wave their goodbyes and head on.* **Jay** *thanks them for coming. There's a lovely peaceful and respectful vibe.*

Jay Thanks, everyone. There's a few more who said they're coming so we'll give it another ten minutes.

Bo *and* **Kieran** *arrive.*

Rosa Bo?

Jay You're not welcome.

Bo Hear me out, Jay.

Jay You've some nerve, I'll give you that.

Bo I know what it looked like the other day but I swear, on Colm's grave, that I didn't want to be there.

Kieran We're supposed to be with Jamesy now but we wanted to come here.

Jay To lead him straight to me?

Bo *reaches into his jacket pocket.* **Jay** *reacts.*

Matt Whoa! You got a knife?!

Bo *pulls his hand out. In it is a framed pic of Colm.*

Bo It's the only one of him on his own. It's my favourite. I thought it would be nice for the vigil. You can have it.

A beat.

Jay Why all the death stares every time you saw me?

Bo I thought you were giving them to me. I didn't know what I'd done wrong. I'm Jamesy's brother but I'm Colm's brother too and I know how he felt about you. Here.

He hands the pic to **Jay**. **Jay** *looks at it and smiles.*

Jay He was so handsome.

Bo It didn't feel right to bring one with Jamesy and me in it. Anyway, I'll be on my way.

Jay Wait, Bo. This is really thoughtful of you, thanks. (*Pause.*) I'm glad you're here.

A beat.

Rosa Me too.

Jay I was gonna say a few words. Would you like to as well?

Bo I think Colm would want it to be you. Thanks for asking me.

Matt Best get started; people will want to head on soon.

Maddie *rallies the troops.*

Maddie Hi, everyone. Thanks for waiting. Jay's gonna say a few words then we'll have a minute's silence. If you need to head on that's fine, we understand.

No one moves. **Jay** *is emotional.* **Maddie** *hugs him as he composes himself. A hush descends. Mostly everyone has their phone out, filming* **Jay** *as he speaks.*

Jay A lot of you are here because of what's happening to our Meadows and we want to thank you for sticking with the campaign. We'll keep on fighting.

There's a round of applause and some whoops. **Jay** *raises his hand. Hush descends again.*

You all know the other reason why I started the campaign and why you're at this vigil tonight. Exactly a year ago today my boyfriend Colm lost his life. These Meadows are – were – his favourite place, just like it is for most of us and our older brothers and sisters and probably most of our parents too. It's part of our rites of passage into adulthood but Colm never got that far. If we stop campaigning no one else will get to enjoy them. Colm left and took his life-light with him. This shrine ensured there was at least one chink of that light still shining.

There's gentle, respectful clapping. This is interrupted by **Jamesy** *and his gang. Some of the kids who came for the vigil scarper. Others are pushed out of the way by* **Jamesy**'s *gang.* **Jamesy** *gets right up into* **Bo**'s *face.* **Bo** *backs off, afraid.*

Jamesy   So this is where you got to.

He holds out his hand and **Dee** *hands him a can. He shakes it. Liquid sloshes inside.*

Jamesy   We're gonna have a wee bonfire to celebrate Colm.

He points at Colm's pic in **Jay**'s *hand.*

Jamesy   What are you doing with that?

He turns to **Bo**.

Jamesy   I was looking for that! You brought it here? For him?

He starts to push **Bo** *around.* **Rosa** *goes over to* **Bo**.

Rosa   Leave him alone. This isn't about you. Stop being a dick. Come on, Jay. Let's get Colm's flag up.

She and **Jay** *start to unfurl the LGBTQIA+ flag.* **Jamesy** *is furious. He grabs the flag and throws it to the ground. He turns his vitriol on* **Bo**.

Jamesy   You just gonna stand there? Help me here!

Bo *doesn't move.*

Jamesy *goes to the stump and stands over it.*

Jamesy   Shoulda done this ages ago, woulda stopped all this shite from happening.

He takes the cap off the container and sloshes the petrol all over the stump. The others rush forward to stop him but he holds up a lighter.

Jamesy   Youse stay where you are! Get back!

They retreat.

Jamesy   Bo, c'mere.

Kieran   Bo, don't.

Jamesy   You shut that stupid mouth of yours, Kieran. We talked about this, Bo, time to put family first. Make me proud to call you my brother.

He holds the lighter out for **Bo**. **Bo** *looks at the others then walks over to* **Jamesy**.

Rosa   Please, Bo, don't do this!

Bo *takes the lighter . . . and chucks it.*

Bo   There's only one brother I'm proud of and he's not here.

Colm's friends cheer and whoop. They gather round **Bo**, *slap him on the back.* **Rosa** *hugs him tight. (During the rest of this scene* **Jamesy**'s *gang will gradually step away from* **Jamesy** *until they've fully retreated. Colm's friends will gradually draw closer to* **Jamesy** *and he'll become aware of the shift in energy.)*

Jamesy *splutters, sensing the temperature shift.*

Jamesy This, this, this . . . is all your fault, Jay!

Jay What?

Jamesy *flusters, out of his depth and looking for any reason to blame* **Jay**.

Jamesy If he hadn't known you, he wouldn't have gotten into that taxi and he wouldn't have been in a car crash and he'd still be alive!

Jay And he'd still be gay.

Jamesy *is lost for words. He has no comeback.*

Bo Everyone here wants to celebrate Colm, someone who meant something to all of us, so what's your problem?

Jay We're gonna do what we came here to do. To show our love for the Meadows, for each other and for the Colm we knew and loved.

Bo And the Colm we'll never get to know and love.

Jay *turns to the others.*

Jay I'm gonna do all the things Colm wanted to do.

Matt Me too. He had so many plans.

Maddie To be a designer.

Jay An actor.

Bo A rock star.

Rosa *holds her hand out to* **Sam**. **Sam** *joins her.*

Rosa To dance on a podium in a gay bar.

Kieran With his top off!

Jay Flexing his pecs.

Matt The scrawny wee git.

They all laugh.

Bo Clubbing every night.

Maddie Not every night. He liked to study too!

More laughter. The friends encircle **Jamesy**. **Jamesy**'s *gang has fully retreated. He has no option but to listen to them.*

Jay All the things he loved to do and wanted to do, like kissing in public.

Rosa Marching at Pride all over the world.

Bo Breaking hearts.

Matt Falling in love.

Rosa Falling out of love.

Maddie Going to uni.

Jay All of us friends, sharing a house, having the best time together.

Bo Going to the shops, having a drink with mates. Doing everyday things just like the rest of us. Cos he was a bright shining star.

Jamesy *takes a few steps back and bumps into the stump. He sits on it, defeated.*

A beat. **Bo** *sits beside him.*

Bo You're not Da. Nobody wants you to be like him. You can be better than this. Can't you?

Scene Fifteen: The Meadows Shrine

Cast member takes centre stage with a sign that reads: 'ONE YEAR LATER'.

Maddie Look at that, rows and rows of houses.

Reema Yeah, nice houses. At last.

Matt Where we hung out is gone for ever.

Rosa Not really.

She points off to the right.

What about all those fields over there? They haven't been touched.

Maddie The Meadows are still here.

Jay The council promised. No more building on the green belt.

Matt That's your dad out of business, Clarke!

Clarke He'll find somewhere else to ruin.

Rosa We all won.

Jay It's good that the council respected the shrine.

Bo They're taking good care of it too. Even our Jamesy visits.

Matt Did he have a brain transplant?

Jay More like a heart transplant.

Bo *shrugs.*

Bo He doesn't talk to me any more but he's not bothering me either, which is something. He knows Da's wrong.

Jay Thanks for helping us get this plaque for the shrine, Bo.

Bo I know none of us will ever forget Colm, but it means other people won't either.

Jay Let's have a moment's silence for Colm.

Everyone bows their head. During the silence **Jamesy** *approaches. They watch as he puts his hand in his jacket . . . and pulls out a trinket. He places it on the shrine. He pays his respects then turns and leaves. As he passes the others he nods at them and they nod back. No words pass between them, but there is peace.*

Bo *watches as* **Jamesy** *disappears into the distance.*

Bo I won't give up on him.

End.

Character Plot

	1	2	3	4	5	6	7	8	9	9A	9B	10	11	12	13	14	15
Bo		✓		✓				✓		✓		✓	✓		✓	✓	✓
Kieran		✓		✓				✓		✓				✓	✓	✓	
Rosa		✓		✓	✓	✓	✓					✓		✓		✓	✓
Reema		✓		✓	✓	✓		✓									✓
Jay	✓	✓	✓	✓	✓		✓		✓		✓					✓	✓
Maddie	✓		✓	✓	✓			✓			✓					✓	✓
Clarke			✓	✓							✓						
Matt			✓	✓	✓		✓		✓		✓					✓	
Jamesy		✓						✓		✓				✓		✓	✓
Sam				✓	✓	✓			✓					✓		✓	
Dee		✓					✓			✓						✓	
Mox		✓					✓			✓						✓	
School kids				✓												✓	

More information about the characters and how much they speak

Bo – Significant dialogue
Kieran – Significant dialogue
Rosa – Significant dialogue
Reema – Significant dialogue
Jay – Significant dialogue and a monologue
Maddie – Significant dialogue
Clarke – Significant dialogue, has the option to be in fewer scenes
Matt – Significant dialogue
Jamesy – Significant dialogue
Sam – Significant dialogue
Dee – Minimal dialogue
Mox – Minimal dialogue
School kids – Minimal choral lines, could be shared between multiple people or reassigned amongst cast

Main Narrative Beats

1. Jay is at a shrine on the Meadows, it has been vandalised. On the green, Bo and Rosa are playing football, Bo is late to meet his brother.
2. Jay walks past the football, Bo and Jay nod. Bo thinks Jay has been giving him funny looks since Colm, Bo's brother, died. Jamesy arrives, Bo's friends don't like Jamesy, he's homophobic. Jamesy is angry with Bo.
3. The shrine has been vandalised again. Jay is tidying it up, he thinks Jamesy vadalised it. Jay's friends help to tidy it. New houses are going to be built on this land, Jay doesn't want to move the shrine, it's for his boyfriend Colm. Jay decides to start a campaign against the new houses.
4. At school Jay leads a protest against the new houses. Most people support the protest. Reema thinks the new houses are a good idea.
5. A few days later, the campaigners are at the shrine, Jay is being interviewed about Colm for the school news. Jay chats to some of Bo's friends, he thinks Bo has been vandalising the shrine.
6. Rosa and Reema argue. Reema doesn't see why the shrine being damaged is such a big deal. Rosa does, as an LGBTQ+ person. Reema leaves and Sam flirts with Rosa.
7. At the Meadows, the fences have been put up, construction on the new houses is beginning. Jay gets the others to film him, he calls people to come and protest, the video goes viral.
8. Jamesy watches Jay's interview. Jamesy is angry because Jay says Colm was gay. Jamesy and his friends make a plan for revenge.
9. The next day at school, Jay has been beaten up by Jamesy. Jay's friends are shocked, they're going to be Jay's bodyguards from now on.
10. On the green, Jamesy is showing off to his friends about what he has done to Jay. At school, Jay and friends see Clarke, whose dad is in charge of the building site. There are security guards coming. The friends plan a vigil for tonight.
11. On the green, Rosa speaks to Bo, Bo insists he wasn't involved in the attack. Bo sees Jamesy in the street, Bo tells Jamesy to leave Jay alone.
12. On the green, Rosa and Sam are flirting. Kieran arrives and tells them Jamesy has more plans. Later that day, Bo shows Kieran what he has planned.
13. That night, people are at the vigil on the Meadows. Bo arrives, Jay is suspicious, Bo brings a framed picture of Colm, Jay and Bo make peace.
14. Jay makes a speech remembering Colm, the Meadows were his favourite place. Jamesy turns up with a petrol canister, he's going to start a fire. Jay's friends get out an LGBTQIA+ flag, Jamesy grabs it and throws it to the ground.
15. Jamesy pours petrol on the tree stump shrine, he asks Bo to help him, Bo walks to Jamesy, takes the lighter and throws it away. Jamesy is defeated, Jay's friends want to live their best lives, like Colm would have done.
16. One year later, the new houses are built, but not on the Meadows, the shrine is still there. Jamesy arrives, he puts a trinket on the shrine and then leaves.

Normalised

BY AMANDA VERLAQUE

Notes on rehearsal and staging drawn from a workshop with the writer led by Rhiann Jeffrey held at the National Theatre, October 2024

How the writer came to write the play

I have a lot of young people around me, both in my family and friends. The world they are growing up in now is different to the one I grew up in. I came from a time when it was so much easier to live in the shadows. There are these warning signs in the world at the moment of us going backwards, there are terrible things being said and done in the world, and they are being normalised. People are getting away with doing morally wrong things and not being called out for it. The ideal time to start conversations around these things is with children when they are young so that we don't have these issues later on. I thought Connections was a good opportunity to explore that. I think it's better to be visible and have the conversation, than having to hide in the shadows. Allies are so important.

It's important not to exist in an echo chamber, the play is an opportunity to look for allies and to increase awareness. Yes, we are individual beings but we all need allies.

(Amanda Verlaque, 2024)

Introductions and icebreakers

Exercise: This is my story

Lead director Rhiann Jeffrey asked everyone to get into small groups and to share a story about their childhood with their group. They then had to choose one of the stories and perform it to the wider group as if it was their own story.

The wider group then had to guess whose story it was.

This exercise can be good for young people to identify what makes a convincing story; what are the telltale signs of truth?

Exercise: Strongly agree/disagree

Jeffrey assigned different areas of the room for 'strongly agree', 'not sure' and 'disagree'. She explained that she would make a series of statements/provocations to explore the themes in the play and everyone was to choose somewhere in the room to stand to show whether they strongly agree, disagree or weren't sure about the statement.

She made the point that it was okay if people changed their minds as the statements were discussed. For each provocation, Jeffrey asked everyone why they had chosen where they were.

The statements/provocations in the workshop were:

- Friendships are equally as important as family
- I loved being a teenager
- It's easier being a teenager now
- Cis males are the only people to develop toxic masculinity.
- Opinions should be accepted and respected even if you don't agree
- We should wear our sexuality on our sleeve

Jeffrey explained that this exercise can be a way to have discussions with your group about the themes of the play. You can start with lighter statements/provocations like 'Should pineapple be on pizza?'

To alleviate any tense feelings or heaviness that arose in the discussions, Jeffrey asked everyone to take a light walk around the room to shake it off before moving to the next provocation.

Exercise: Character work

Jeffrey asked the group to get into pairs and gave each pair a character to focus on for the following exercise.

The task was to create a character biography by answering the following questions:

Who is this character? Who are they as a person?

What is their personality like?

What do they want from the play?

What do the other characters think of them?

Below are the results of the exercise:

Jay

- Is lovely and very nice
- Has a lovely group of friends
- Is Jay just being indulgent? For example, not thinking about the family they might be destroying and just wanting the world to see him? Or are they just a young person grieving?
- Does Jay want the acceptance from Jamesy that they are allowed to grieve as well?
- Does Jay need to be male?

Verlaque's thoughts on Jay:

- Jay comes from a middle-class family. The family is neither particularly supportive or unsupportive. They want Jay to be a doctor but Jay wants to go to art school
- Jay spends a lot of time at Maddie's home because her family understands them

- Jay is grieving and does the things they do in the play because Colm's family denied him visibility in life, and they are denying him visibility in death
- Jay's parents know they are gay, but don't want to talk about it
- Jay needs validation from Jamesy's family but is not aware of that. They want Jamesy's family to accept that they were Colm's partner, that they were in a relationship
- Jay was born cis male and now identifies as non-binary and gay.

When casting, whatever feels believable and stays true to the heart of the story will be right, but as the character was born cis male and now identifies as non-binary and gay, that should be respected.

The queer joy comes through Reema and Sam's story, so keep that in mind when casting. Sexuality and gender are both really important elements of the play.

Bo

- Is in a sticky situation between his two brothers and dealing with grief on top of that. He doesn't have a space to share his feelings
- He hasn't had time to grieve properly because there is so much drama going on around his grief
- He's a bit lost
- Does he agree or disagree with the statement 'Friends are more important than family'?

Verlaque's thoughts on Bo:

- He is sensitive
- He lives in a house of fear; his dad is a bully and his mum is not there
- He grew up watching Colm getting tormented
- He wants out
- Rosa and Kieran are his safe place
- In five years' time Bo will be a lovely person who doesn't talk to his dad
- The family he wants is not at home; he knows the family he wants is the one he'll make
- Some people choose to hang out with the bully because if you are in the bully's circle, you are safe

Reema

- Best friends with Rosa
- She fancies Bo

- She is very confident; she's not afraid to give her opinion and it always comes from a factual place
- She has come from somewhere else
- She has obviously had experiences of living in not nice houses
- She is opinionated

Verlaque's thoughts on Reema:

- Reema's family has fled persecution from Syria
- She had a lovely life in Syria and now lives in not a very nice place
- She doesn't understand the significance of the Meadows because she's not from there, she wants better housing
- She is a bit catty and probably jealous of Rosa
- She doesn't like being told what to do
- She stands up for herself
- She doesn't understand her parents' relief at being alive as she remembers having her own room and having a nice life, and now they live in a shoddy place
- She would have compartmentalised the memories of fleeing Syria – the trauma of it is buried somewhere
- She can see how other people live in nicer houses
- She doesn't disagree with Jay but, to her, houses are more important

Clarke

- Mum went to university and dad is a self-made man. There are ambitions for all the children to go to university in the future
- They live in a middle-class area
- We meet him at a point of real turmoil; he knows what his dad is doing and he doesn't know how to tell Jay. He knows something the other characters don't know
- He wants everything to be okay with his dad and with his friends. But he finds it tricky because he has to support his dad (he might take over the company in the future)
- He is very loyal to his dad
- He accidentally tells his dad that there is a protest being planned by his friends, which brings the end of the Meadows closer, but then he makes it right by giving information to his friends

Verlaque's thoughts on Clarke:

- Clarke watches what is going on for a lot of the play

- He comes from a place of entitlement and he has a lot of confidence
- Five to ten years in the future he'll still be friends with Jay but won't be looking twice at the Bos and Rosas of the world
- He is in a family of friends who are grieving
- His story line brings up the question: what does ally-ship look like?
- In his backstory he and Maddie had a thing.

Rosa

- Embodies integrity
- She knows who she is and her place within the world
- She is supported by her family
- She makes a stand
- She is only seen as being on the other side because of her relationship with Bo
- She is the one that uses the word 'normalised'
- She is willing to put her relationship with Reema on the line to make a stand
- She will blaze a trail through her life.

Verlaque's thoughts on Rosa:

- She's the ballast Bo needs
- She's the girl we all wanted to be, cool but fun and decent.

Jamesy

- He is trying to protect the legacy of Colm, and that protection makes him a bully. It's part of his grief for the loss of his brother
- What is normalised from father to son?
- He is trying to get his dad's approval by emulating him; trying to be the son his dad wants.
- When does he realise that his friends are not his friends?
- Colm and Jamesy were identical twins.

Verlaque's thoughts on Jamesy:

- Jamesy hasn't even had a chance to think about his own sexuality because he has seen his dad bully Colm
- Some people become a bully trying to hide and push down who they are
- He operates through fear; that's how his dad keeps the household and so that's how he keeps his friends in line
- Jamesy hates anybody who is queer because he looks like his brother, and he is worried that people will think he is gay because his brother was

- The most attention Jamesy received from their dad was when the dad was making fun of Colm. His dad would turn to Jamesy after making a dig at Colm and Jamesy would say 'Ah, nice one, Da!' That's how Jamesy survived.

Kieran

- Is a very sensitive young guy who potentially could have special educational needs
- Is protected by Bo
- He is not going to do well at school.
- He worries about Bo, and he doesn't know how to express that because Jamesy is so dangerous
- He doesn't get jealous.

Verlaque's thoughts in Kieran:

- Kieran is a decent bloke who knows right from wrong.

Matt

- Is a decent bloke
- He instinctively knows to do the right thing
- He's like a big brother
- He's very empathetic and liberal
- He's not a comedic character
- In the future he will grow up to be the most gorgeous, wonderful man.

Verlaque's thoughts on Matt:

- You would want Matt on your side
- He's reliable.

Maddie

- Comes from a high-flying family
- She will always be someone's rock; at this stage in her life she's Jay's rock
- She and Jay will be friends for ever
- She's really cool.

Verlaque's thoughts on Maddie:

- Just like Rosa, Maddie is the type of girl from school that you'll always remember as being cool but friendly.

Dee and Mox

- Are yet to define themselves
- They think they are being seen in a group like Jamesy's; they think there is some sort of kudos and status in being seen as the one to be feared
- They're easily swayed
- They are in transient friendships.

Verlaque's thoughts on Dee and Mox:

- They think they are safe from being bullied if they hang out with the bully. Once Jamesy loses his power they will desert him.

Sam

- A go-getter
- In the future she will probably be presenting *Newsnight*!
- Will keep going to get what she wants
- Flirty and down to earth
- Has a lot of self-confidence herself.

Verlaque's thoughts on Sam:

- The perfect sparring partner for Rosa. She is a powerhouse!

Exercise: Busy bees (a good one to do after lunch)

Rhiann Jeffrey asked everyone to buzz around the room being bees. She explained that she would call out a letter and everyone had to create something beginning with that letter. The rules were that you can't make a person or a place and if there was more than one of the same thing (two tables, for example), the people creating those items were out. The people who were out became observers. When only two people are left, the observers vote on the most creative response to find the winner.

Exercise: The smartest person in the universe (AKA categories)

Jeffrey invited everyone to get into a circle and explained that she would state a category (e.g. colours) and one by one everyone should swap places with someone in the circle, saying something in that category. Make eye contact with the person you are walking towards. That person then has to say another thing from the category as they swap places. The game continues until someone cannot think of something and then the category is changed. Some of the categories offered were car brands, shoe brands, high-street shops, types of tea, sweets.

Exercise: Objects

Jeffrey gave everyone a random object and asked them to consider three ways that the object relates to something within the play. The object must stay as the object, it can't turn it into something else.

Some examples the group shared are:

Banana – fruity relationships, Jamesy goes bananas, the colour yellow representing hope for where the characters could go in the future.

Red marker pen – red symbolic of the anger and violence, as a prop to write placards for the protest, Jamesy using the marker to write homophobic graffiti, Jamesy's friends holding Jay down and writing homophobic slurs with the marker.

Glue stick – represents the bond that Jay and Colm have, the sticky situations that happen throughout the friendships when glue dries it doesn't always stay stuck, represents the building of the houses.

This exercise is good for peeling back the layers and looking at the different relationships within the play.

Exercise: Staging

Jeffrey asked everyone to get into small groups and gave them 20 minutes to come up with a set design for the show. She asked them to try to facilitate all the different spaces in the play and to think of the Meadows as another character. Each group was given a budget to work with (£0, £100, £1,000, £10,000).

The groups then shared back.

£0:

- The shrine as a permanent feature on the set
- Sneaking in a tree!
- Making the shrine out of a pile of folded clothes with pictures around (clothes that Colm would have worn)
- Using brown and green card to make the natural elements
- Creating the barriers and gates by using physical theatre
- Using school uniform as uniform and adjusting what items are worn or how they are worn for different parts of the play; for example, school shirt and tie when in school and no tie when out of school.

£100:

- A permanent fixture that gives a nod to each location with the shrine at the centre
- Artificial grass for green area
- School desks in a space to represent the school
- Markings on the floor to signify the river or basketball court
- Using lighting and sound effects to help to show the different locations.

£1,000:

- Raised slope of artificial grass leading up to the back of the stage
- Shrine at the top at the back of the stage
- Fencing wheeled on with gauze on
- A little platform at the top.

£10,000:

- A huge shrine that takes up a lot of the stage with a ladder going up to it – the shrine is on a mount; we see Jay climbing up the ladder representing the journey of his grief
- The shrine opens up and the areas roll out (e.g. the school)
- Transformation door to hide the Meadows
- Fly in the set pieces in the transitions.

Location

Jeffrey asked Verlaque about the actual place where the play is set. Verlaque explained that it is set in south Belfast. It's a mix of working- and middle-class areas, with some really old, terraced houses and newer more expensive houses. The Meadows is a space where a lot of people go for walks and the River Lagan cuts through it. It's beautiful and peaceful. People walk along the towpath. Young people go to the Meadows and woodlands when they're too young to go to the bars. A safe place to go where it doesn't matter where you come from and it's somewhere your parents can't find you. Police raids have happened in the past when they arrested teens for being drunk. The deeper you go into the Meadows the less you hear the traffic. The shrine is a field or two in – it's not miles away and there's trees there, some of which were destroyed by a storm. She imagines that on the shrine there are little lamp jars, photocopies of CD covers, part of a rainbow flag, a rainbow lanyard, mementos, a string of lights and if he supported a football team there might be a football scarf. The tree stump is big enough for two people to sit on comfortably but not three. Verlaque said that you could take the signs out (the ones that show the time stamps) as the play works without it; a way you could show the time shifts could be with the sounds of the construction workers, the houses being built taking over from the sounds of nature.

Question and answer with Amanda Verlaque and Rhiann Jeffrey
AV =Amanda Verlaque, RJ = Rhiann Jeffrey

Q: What does queerness mean to you?
AV: Authenticity.

Q: Can you tell us a bit more about Jamesy's gang – how did that come about?
AV: It grew organically really. At first he was on his own as a bully but I felt he needed people around him. I find the term 'gang' interesting as they are everywhere; it's technically the name for a group of people, like for a group of girls at school – they can be vicious or they can be brilliant.

Q: Why did you choose to use the word 'witch'?
AV: It's a softer word for bitch and because 'bitch' is normally associated with women.

Q: What elements do you hope to see in all the productions of the play?
AV: You have to be sympathetic to people. Finding a way to grieve and that it is okay to grieve. Having the courage of your convictions. The light at the end of the tunnel may not come from the people you live with, it can come from your friends. I hope to see passionate performances.

RJ: Performers understanding their characters and where their characters are coming from. All the nuances in the character work; like the subtle change, the chink of light in Jamesy at the end. The sense that it's not all sorted but his aggression has gone.

AV: Jamesy still has a long way to go by the end of the play. The watershed is when he gets challenged; if that moment hadn't happened he would have gone on being a bully. I felt a key moment for me was discovering if he had a chink of humanity.

Q: What are the most important beats that need to be hit?
AV: When Rosa and Bo are talking, and Bo is saying 'I swear, I didn't lift a finger' and Rosa says, 'Didn't lift a finger to stop Jamesy or help Jay?'. When Bo is talking to Jamesy. And the end when they say Colm didn't get to do all the things he wanted to do.

RJ: There are a lot of serious themes in the play but find the lightness, the queer joy, the camaraderie of being in a protest and the passion. There's opportunity for fun in the transitions.

AV: There's moments like when Maddie asks about pizzas, they're really serious things being discussed and someone is asking, 'Well, what are we going to do about food?' There are moments of lightness.

Q: What's more important to Jay, the shrine or the environment?
AV: Both of them. When you talk to young people it [the environment] is something they are really worried about. Jay really means it; this is for the shrine and for the environment.

Q: If every other prop I have is physical, is it okay to add the ball in instead of it being imaginary?
RJ: Just make sure you have a clear idea of the language of the props and make it consistent.

Q: How do you want the audience to feel?
AV: Hopeful and encouraged. Yes, it's set in Northern Ireland but it could be set anywhere because of the common denominators.

Q: You say you love Bo, but can you love Jamesy?
AV: I think I could come to love him. I feel sorry for him.

Peer exchange

The group shared some things that have worked well for them in the past:

- Treat your transitions as scenes in themselves
- A look between two characters can say a lot
- Don't leave the thing you're scared of until the end
- The character development exercises can bring up ideas for the transitions
- Making scene titles and putting them on the wall are useful for any visual learners
- The process of breaking a script down into units, objectives and actions is helpful.

From a workshop led by Rhiann Jeffrey
With notes by Brigitte Adela

Brain Play

by Chloë Lawrence-Taylor
and Paul Sirett

Chloë Lawrence-Taylor is a playwright from Oxfordshire. She is on attachment at the National Theatre Studio and is a member of the Royal Court Theatre's Long-Form Playwriting Group having previously taken part in their Intro Group (2022/2023). She has been commissioned by Women & Theatre in Birmingham and has worked with Clean Break Theatre Company as a Lead Artist. She is an alumnus of the Royal Court Theatre, the North Wall's Catalyst Residency, the Old Fire Station, Broken Silence Theatre and Pentabus' National Young Writers Programme. Lawrence-Taylor's play *When the Head Became a Cage, the Heart Took Flight* was longlisted for the RSC's 37 Plays in 2023, while her play *True Cry* was longlisted for the Bruntwood Prize in 2022. Her work includes *If We Ended This* at Camden People's Theatre; *Hereafter* for the North Wall; and a reading of *When the Head Became a Cage, the Heart Took Flight* for RADA.

Paul Sirett is an award-winning, Olivier-nominated playwright, dramaturg and musician. He has written over 25 stage plays and musicals which have been produced in the UK and around the world. Eleven of these were first produced at Theatre Royal Stratford East, most notably *The Big Life* (also West End). Other productions include *Rat Pack Confidential* at Nottingham Playhouse and in the West End; and *Reasons to Be Cheerful* for Graeae. He has also won awards for his radio plays and worked extensively as a dramaturg for companies including the Royal Shakespeare Company, Soho Theatre, Royal Court, National Theatre and West End and Broadway producers. His book *The Playwright's Manifesto* was published by Bloomsbury Methuen Drama in 2022. Paul Sirett has also toured and recorded extensively as a guitarist.

Characters

Mia *is 15 years old and in Year 11; a bookworm with a big appetite for fantasy fiction.*

Frankie *is 16 years old and in Year 11; Mia's closest friend and an incredibly gifted mathematician.*

Gee *is 13 and a half (the half is very important) and in Year 9; Mia's cousin, an only child, painfully shy and a brilliant dancer.*

Nish *is 15 years old and in Year 11; has five siblings, likes setting things on fire in Chemistry class, loves basketball and is always wearing PE kit.*

AJ *is 16 years old and in Year 11; lives next-door to Mia and her dad, wants to be a comedian, is always testing out new material on friends.*

In the script, we are specific in our use of pronouns; however, these can be changed dependent on casting. Any role can be played by any actor, and we encourage you to fit the character to the actor playing the role.

Puppet Characters

All adult characters in this play should be played by puppets. The characters should be physically represented by a specified item (or items) of clothing to be puppeteered by one (or more) performer(s) while another performer voices the character. Ideally, there will be three puppeteers plus one voicing performer for each character. For example, the character of **Tony** (**Mia**'s dad) can be represented by a dressing gown on a coat hanger which is held by Puppeteer One, the arms of which are manipulated for gestural purposes by Puppeteer Two, a pair of slippers that are manipulated by Puppeteer Three, and Tony's voice delivered by Puppeteer Four. Puppeteers might be dressed in black or neutral colours, but whatever they wear it is important they can be easily distinguished from the friends and the **Brain Chorus** (see below). If you would like to make puppets, this is fine. Our only stipulation is that the adult characters must be played by puppets.

The adult characters are:

Tony
Nurse
Consultant
Teacher
Professor Greco

Brain Chorus

The play has a chorus which can be comprised of any number of performers with the lines divided between them at the discretion of the creative team. You should feel free to experiment with choric techniques such as movement, unison speaking and the use of masks.

To distinguish the Brain Chorus from the friends and the puppeteers we suggest that as the brain is largely made up of grey and white matter that they should be dressed in either white or grey clothes. They pronounce all scientific, neurological and technical terms fluently and with ease.

The 'Song of the Neuroscientists' performed by the Brain Chorus in Scene Nine, can be chanted, or sung in any preferred style. We would like to invite the creative team and/or performers to write original music or create the chant for this song themselves, adapting or reconfiguring the lyrics as needed.

Set

The set design is at the discretion of the creative team.

Pronunciation Guide

Below is a list of medical terms used in the play with a phonetic pronunciation guide:

Amnesia: am-knee-zee-uh
Arachnoid: arack-noyd
Auditory: or-di-tory
Axons: ack-sonz
Binaural: bye-naw-rull
Callosum: kall-oh-sum
Cerebellum: serry-bell-um
Cerebral: serry-brall
Cerebrospinal: serry-bro-spy-nal
Cochlear: cock-lee-arr
Cognitive: cog-ni-tiv
Corpus: kaw-pus
Corti: kaw-tee
Cranial: kray-knee-ull
Delirium: dell-ear-ium
Dura mater: de-yur-ah may-tur
Encephalopathy: en-keff-al-oh-path-ee
Gyrus: jai-rus

Haemorrhage: hem-err-age
Hyperacusis: high-per-a-cue-sis
Lesions: Lee-zhunz
Meninges: meh-nin-gez
Myelination: my-ell-in-a-shun
Neuro: new-row
Neurology: new-row-lo-gee
Neuronal: new-row-nall
Neurons: new-rons
Occipital: okk-si-pital
Parietal: pah-riot-ull
Pia mater: pee-ah may-ter
Psychosis: sy-ko-sis
Scala tympani: skar-la tim-panny
Subarachnoid: sub-arack-noyd
Tinnitus: tinny-tus
Tonotopy: toe-not-oh-pee
Traumatic: traw-ma-tick
Vestibular: Vess-tee-bue-lar
Vestibulocochlear: vess-tee-bue-lo-cock-lee-arr

Prologue

The **Brain Chorus** *sit or stand at the edge of the performance area. They watch as* **Mia** *– in her bedroom, wearing a dressing gown – packs her school bag.*

Mia (*to herself*)   Ruler.
Calculator.
History textbook.
Purse.
Pencil for diagrams.
Green pen for corrections.
Two black pens for everything else.
Period pads.
Spare pants.
My annotated copy of *An Inspector Calls*.

She looks out at the audience.

(*To audience.*) It's hard to trust that I know what I'm doing because it's been a while since this felt . . . normal.
It's been a while since Sunday night meant getting up for school on Monday morning.
It's been a while since getting up and going to school was something I did at all.
I've repacked my bag at least half a dozen times.
I know that everything's in there.
But there's a not-quite-right feeling in the pit of my stomach.
It's a feeling I've not had so much lately.
Because I've been doing so much better.
That's what everyone's been saying.
That's why I'm going back to school.

She takes a deep breath.

Focus on five things you can see:
my bed,
my feet,
my desk,
my hand,
my blue curtains.

Focus on four things you can feel . . .

She touches her dressing gown, the carpet, her school bag, her hair.

Now, three things you can hear . . .

She listens for sounds.

And two things you can smell . . .

She sniffs.

And one thing you can taste . . .

She smacks her lips.

. . . ketchup!

There's a knock on her bedroom door.

You can come in, Dad.

Tony *puppet, physically represented by a dressing gown and a pair of slippers, enters.*

Tony Doing alright?

Mia Off to bed?

Tony I'll watch a bit more telly first.

Mia Sounds good.

Tony It's getting late.

Mia I'll be in bed soon.

Tony Sleep tight.

Mia See you in the morning.

Tony Night then.

Mia Dad?

Tony Yeah?

Mia Will you be alright on your own tomorrow?

Tony Course I will, Mimi.

Mia Okay . . . sleep tight.

Tony Don't let the bedbugs bite!

He leaves.

Mia (*to audience*) Strange, he looks almost completely normal, doesn't he?
You wouldn't know.
You couldn't guess.
But I still see the bruises.
And the neck brace.
There've been twenty-eight Fridays since the Friday it happened.
That's twenty-eight Fridays since the last day of my life that felt normal.

1. Friday Night

The **Brain Chorus** *continue to watch as* **Mia** *takes her dressing gown off – she is dressed for school.*

Mia (*to audience*)　Twenty-eight Fridays ago,
not a care in the world,
I'm walking home from school with my mates,
about to eat a fuck-tonne of pizza,
arm-in-arm with Frankie.

Frankie *appears.*

Mia (*to audience*)　My best and longest friend.
Not longest as in tallest.
But as in they've been my friend for a very long time.

Frankie (*to audience*)　Gifted mathematician.
Founder of the school's Pythagoras Club.
And bassist in a local up-and-coming folk-punk band called Not Your Theorem.

Mia (*to audience*)　And AJ.

AJ *appears.*

Mia (*to audience*)　He lives next-door.
He's properly funny.
He started doing stand-up comedy gigs when he was thirteen because his parents run a pub with a comedy club out the back.

AJ (*to audience – one of his routines*)　For work experience, I'd planned a week spent helping out at the local pet shop, but I got sent home after one day. Thing was, I trod on a tortoise and knocked over a tank of terrapins. It was a turtle disaster.

Mia　Ay, caramba!

AJ (*to audience*)　Just think of me as the 'younger, hotter, fresher, cheekier James Acaster'.

Mia (*to audience*)　And our friend Nish.

Nish *appears.*

Mia (*to audience*)　He's always in his PE kit and almost always in trouble.

Nish (*to audience*)　Thing about me is, I'm not 'disruptive', right, I'm UNDERSTIMULATED!

Mia (*to audience*)　In Year 8 he set fire to Lydia Stephens' pencil case in Chemistry.

Nish　It was an EXPERIMENT.

Mia (*to audience*)　And my little cousin Gee, who barely says a word but dances like a pro.

Gee *dances on stage – she's phenomenal!*

Mia (*to audience*)　I say she's my little cousin but she's not really 'little', she's thirteen.

Gee (*to audience – quietly but forcefully*)   And! A! Half!

Mia (*to audience*)   Every Friday is always the same.
The same routine.
My house.
My friends.
And pizza.

Mia, **AJ**, **Frankie**, **Gee** *and* **Nish** *lounge on the living-room floor at* **Mia**'s *house surrounded by pizza boxes.*

Nish   Can someone pass me a slice of the veggie BBQ one?

Mia   All gone.

Nish   No!

Mia   I thought you didn't like vegetables.

Nish   I don't. Any crusts?

AJ   I'm stuffed.

Mia   I know I'm being really brave but . . .

AJ/Nish/Frankie/Gee   MY TUMMY HURTS!

Mia (*to* **Frankie**)   Eeeurghh. Do my legs feel hairy?

Frankie *feels* **Mia**'s *legs.*

Frankie   You bet!

Mia   Shut up!

Nish *burps loudly into* **AJ**'s *face.* **AJ** *doesn't flinch. He sniffs.*

AJ   Hmmm, I would say that's the pepperoni, with a slight hint of . . . Red Bull?

Nish   Correct.

Mia   Ay, caramba!

Gee   You're disgusting.

Nish (*to* **Mia**)   When'll your dad be home?

Mia   Usual time . . . 10pm . . . ish.

Nish   He was early last week.

Mia   The singer had a cold.

Frankie   He knows I'm staying over, right?

Nish   Do you ever actually go home?

Frankie   Not if I can help it.

Sees a spot on **Mia**'s *face*

Frankie Oh! Hold on!

Frankie *leans in to squeeze it.*

Mia (*to audience while* **Frankie** *squeezes*) My dad works Friday nights.
He plays piano in the bar of a nice hotel in town.
He accompanies a jazz singer who does an Ella Fitzgerald act.

(*To* **Frankie**.) Got it?

Frankie Hold on.

Frankie *continues to squeeze.*

Mia (*to audience*) Way back in the day, he used to play piano for an Elton John tribute act.
So he's gone up in the world.

Frankie Done!

AJ Our very own Dr Pimple Popper!

Frankie Is that a blackhead I can see, AJ?

AJ Get off! Can we watch something funny tonight?

Frankie Depends on your definition of funny.

AJ . . . Me!

Mia (*to audience*) Every Friday night comes and goes just like this one: in a blur of dough balls and films and video games and piss-takes and arguments.
Then, one by one, everyone goes home . . . except Frankie.

AJ, **Gee**, *and* **Nish** *move to the edge of the space.*

Mia (*to audience*) Frankie's mum's just had a baby with a guy who looks a bit like a hairier Jason Momoa, so my place is a refuge.

Frankie (*to* **Mia**) I don't think she loves him as much as she thinks she does, I think it's all hormones.

Mia (*to audience*) Frankie and her mum don't get on.

to **Frankie**

(*To* **Frankie**.) They seem pretty loved-up.

Frankie That's because she's an idiot.

Mia (*to audience*) Case in point.

Frankie You know I've decided I never want kids.

Mia (*to audience*) I chat with Frankie as I tidy up and make everything perfect for when my dad gets home even though he's forever telling me I don't need to.
And then we pull the sofa bed out.

I never go to sleep before my dad gets home.
I always make sure to stay awake.
So we watch a couple of episodes of *Come Dine with Me* –
but it's getting late.
Frankie falls asleep.
My eyes close too.
Just for a few seconds.
Then, for a minute . . .
BUT ONLY A MINUTE, ONLY EVER A MINUTE, BEFORE . . .

Mia's *phone is vibrating.*

Frankie Mia! Your phone!

Mia *is suddenly wide awake.*

Frankie It's vibrating. Where is it?

Mia *finds her phone and answers the call.*

Mia Hello?

Nurse *puppet, represented by scrubs, crocs and a phone, appears.*

Nurse Who have I got there?

Mia Who's this?

Nurse I'm calling from St Jude's, from A&E, can I ask your name please?

Mia Mia.

Nurse Last name?

Mia Lee.

Nurse And are you related Anthony Lee?

Mia That's my dad.

Nurse How old are you?

Mia Fifteen.

Nurse And are there any adults with you?

Mia No.

Nurse Mia, your dad's been involved in an accident but we're taking good care of him. Is there a grown-up with you that can come to the hospital?

One by one, members of the **Brain Chorus** *slowly close in on* **Mia**. *Lines to be divided between them.*

Mia No.

Brain Chorus You never fall asleep.

Mia Is he alright?

Nurse Any other grown-ups with you? Your mum?

Brain Chorus No chance.

Mia My mum lives in Malaga – they aren't together.

Nurse Is there anyone that can bring you to the hospital, Mia?

Mia My uncle?

Nurse Okay, Mia, I can tell you and your uncle more when you get here.

Brain Chorus You fell asleep.

Nurse I'll let you contact your uncle and then I'll ring back in a bit to check in with you, okay?

Brain Chorus You caused this.

Nurse My name's Kay. Mia?

Mia Yes. Thank you.

The call ends. **Mia** *is stunned.*

Brain Chorus You fell asleep.

Mia I shouldn't have fallen asleep.

Frankie What's happened?

Mia That's why I always stay up until he gets home.

Frankie Mia?

Brain Chorus It's your fault.

Mia It's all my fault.

2. Hospital (1)

In this scene, **Mia** *and* **Frankie** *struggle to pronounce the technical terms they mention. They sit side-by-side. The* **Brain Chorus** *loiter around them.*

Mia (*to audience*) Frankie holds my hand tight and squeezes twice every so often and says stuff like:

Frankie I've only ever been to the maternity ward of a hospital before.

Beat.

No, wait, that's not true, I've been to A&E, too, but I don't really remember it because I was two when it happened – when I fell over in the library and impaled my skull on the sharp edge of a hardback book. That's the only time my mum says she's ever properly prayed.

Mia (*to* **Frankie**) Can you remember what the nurse said?

Frankie He was hit by a car.

Mia Not that, the . . . his head. It was a sub . . . arack . . . something.

Frankie They said it meant like a bleed on the brain.

Mia Can you google it?

Frankie Sure.

Mia Because I want to know exactly what it is. That way I can know what to expect.

Frankie *types into their phone.*

Frankie Where's your uncle?

Mia He's still on the phone to my nan – his mum – as in my mum's mum.

Frankie Will your mum come back here do you think?

Mia I don't know.

Frankie *scans their search results.*

Frankie Shit! 'Subarachnoid haemorrhage is the term that describes bleeding into the subarachnoid space which is the space between the arachnoid membrane and the pia mater.'

Mia 'Pia' . . . what?

Frankie Mate-er? Matt-er? I don't know.

Mia Arachnoid means spider, doesn't it?

Frankie Wiki says, 'The arachnoid mater is one of the three meninges.'

Mia What are the 'meninges'?

Frankie Meninges-meninges-meninges . . . 'the three membranes that line the skull'.

Mia Three?

Frankie 'The dua mater, arachnoid and pia mater.'

Mia The *what*?

Frankie 'The dua mater, arachnoid, and pia mater.'

Brain Chorus How are you going to remember all of that?

Mia I need to write it down. Have you got a pen?

Frankie *hands* **Mia** *a pen.*

Brain Chorus Quickly, Mia!

Mia What was it again? What was it?

Frankie Try to stay calm.

Mia I need to remember!

Frankie Alright! 'The dua mater, arachnoid and pia mater.'

Mia *writes on her hand.*

Brain Chorus Dua mater. Arachnoid. Pia mater.

Mia Dua mater. Arachnoid. Pia mater. Wait, what's the subarachnoid then?

Frankie That's the in-between bit, I think.

Mia In-between what? I don't understand!

Frankie '. . . the subarachnoid space which is the space between the arachnoid membrane and the pia mater.'

Mia And that's the bit that's filled with blood in my dad's head? The subarachnoid bit. Right? Yes?

Frankie Yes. I think so. Yes. 'The arachnoid space is a spiderweb-like structure . . .' There you go! '. . . a spiderweb-like structure filled with cere-bro-spinal fluid that cushions the brain.'

Mia A spiderweb thing filled with spinal fluid and blood?

Frankie Yes.

Brain Chorus Eeurghh!

Mia I feel sick.

Frankie Me too.

Mia No, I'm going to be –

Brain Chorus *scatter as* **Mia** *vomits.*

Frankie Woah.

Mia *puts her head between her knees.*

Frankie Do you feel any better?

Mia He's going to die, isn't he?

Frankie Should I get someone?

Mia Who?

Frankie Someone . . . anyone . . . who knows what the fuck is happening? Someone who can help?

Mia Yes, please.

Frankie *hands their hoodie to* **Mia**.

Frankie It's not totally clean. But it's cleaner than what you've got on.

Frankie *moves to the edge of the space.* **Mia** *buries her head in* **Frankie**'s *hoodie.*

3. Discharged

Mia (*to audience*) He fractures three ribs.
He splits his collar bone.
His eye socket cracks.
His neck breaks in two places.
And he has a massive bleed on the brain.
But he lives.
Miracle, right?
But that's just the start.
Because after a brief stay on the Brain Trauma Unit, he gets sent home to recover.

Mia *is joined by her friends at school.* **Brain Chorus** *loiter.*

AJ (*to* **Mia**) Isn't it a bit soon?

Mia (*to audience*) Is what AJ asks me at school the day after Dad comes home.

AJ I mean, it's good, it's just quick given the circumstances . . .

Frankie (*to* **AJ**) They wouldn't send him home if he wasn't alright.

Nish He can't be fully better though?

Mia He wanted to come home.

AJ And you have to look after him?

Mia Sort of. Yes. I need to message him.

She takes out her phone and starts typing a message.

Nish Can he walk?

Frankie You can't ask that!

AJ Why not?

Mia *sends her message.*

Mia He can move around a bit. But not much. And he has to wear a neck-collar-brace-thing.

AJ Must be shit to sneeze. Or have the hiccups.

Frankie 'Shit' in that he'd be in a massive amount of pain that you couldn't even comprehend.

Mia This thought keeps popping into my head of him . . . breaking his neck.

AJ I thought he'd already broken his neck?

Mia But if he falls over, he could break it again and make it worse.

Nish Can he have visitors?

AJ Can he go to the loo?

Frankie AJ!

AJ What?

Mia We don't have many people around to visit anyway.

Nish Me and my mum could come by – she mentioned it last night, like bringing food and stuff.

Mia We're fine.

Frankie And I plan on being around as much as possible so I can help.

Mia Thanks.

Gee My dad said he'd pick me up from yours tonight, he said he'd sort dinner.

Mia *gives* **Gee**'s *hand a squeeze.*

Frankie (*to* **Mia**) Are you okay?

Mia Just a bit tired. And I'm going to get a right bollocking from Mr Berry for not doing my homework.

Frankie Do you want to copy mine?

Mia You'd let me?

Frankie Sure.

Nish Can I?

Frankie No.

Mia *checks her phone to see if her dad has replied – nothing.*

Mia Sometimes he needs me around to help get him up or settled into a more comfy position.

Nish Can't they send someone?

Mia We don't qualify.

AJ Does this make you a young carer or something?

Frankie AJ!

Mia You know, I actually don't know.

Frankie But he won't always be like he is right now.

Gee *takes hold of* **Mia**'s *hand.*

Gee I'm going to help out.

Mia *checks her phone again.* **Brain Chorus** *start to close in.*

Frankie Everything alright?

Mia My dad hasn't replied.

AJ You only messaged him a minute ago.

Brain Chorus He's fallen out of bed.

Mia What if he's fallen out of bed?

Frankie He's probably just sleeping.

Brain Chorus He's hurt himself.

Mia He could have hurt himself.

Brain Chorus He's collapsed.

Mia What if he tried to go to the loo and collapsed?

Frankie He'll message you.

Brain Chorus Not if he can't get to his phone!

Mia He might have banged his head.

Frankie Stop.

Brain Chorus Go!

Mia I'm going.

Frankie Mia –

Brain Chorus Go now!

Mia I have to go!

She goes. The friends look at each other – they're worried about her. The **Brain Chorus** *follow* **Mia**.

4. Home (1)

Mia *and* **Gee** *in* **Mia***'s bedroom.* **Gee** *is doing homework,* **Mia** *is on her laptop.* **Brain Chorus** *are watching.*

Mia (*to audience*) Gee is the only one of them that I let in the house. It's sort of necessity. But it's also sort of a relief to have someone in the group who knows what my life looks like.

Gee For three marks, what are three causes of World War I?

Mia What have you got so far?

Gee Franz Ferdinand's assassination.

Mia Then put 'European expansionism' and 'conflicts over alliances'.

Gee What's the 'Blank Check Assurance'?

Mia Not important for a three-marker.

Gee   What are you doing?

Mia   Research.

Gee *goes back to her homework.*

Gee   How do you spell ex-pan-sion-ism?

Mia   Like it sounds.

Gee *writes it phonetically.*

Gee   What's that noise?

Mia *doesn't react.*

Gee   Mia?

Mia   How have you spelled 'expansionism'?

Gee   E-x-p-a-n-s . . . is that your dad . . . crying?

Mia   He does that sometimes now.

Gee   Is he okay?

Mia   Can you not tell anyone about this? Please?

Gee *nods and goes back to her homework.*

Mia (*to audience*)   And as far as I know, she never does.
And while she does her homework, I neglect mine.
Because instead of BBC Bitesize and Revision World I'm scrolling through WebMD –

Brain Chorus   Traumatic brain injury!

Mia   – the NHS website –

Brain Chorus   Post-traumatic stress disorder!

Mia   – Mayo Clinic –

Brain Chorus   Cognitive decline!

Mia   – Healthline –

Brain Chorus   Chronic traumatic encephalopathy!

Mia   and the *British Medical Journal* for proof that my dad will get better and be normal again.

5. Music

Mia *and* **Tony** *are sitting on the sofa eating crisps.* **Mia** *is reading a book. She puts it down.* **Brain Chorus** *look on.*

Mia (*to audience*) We take to eating crisps and meal-deal sandwiches and pretty much anything you can just add boiling water to.
Because my dad can't stand long enough to cook properly.
And the last time I tried to cook something I got so worried about giving him food poisoning, I threw it in the bin.

Tony Nice big crisp. Fold up a cheese slice. Another nice big crisp. You've got a sandwich. It's not haute cuisine but it's not bad!

Mia Dad?

Tony Love?

Mia Are you in a lot of pain?

Tony Not with all the drugs I'm on!

Mia AJ was asking when he might be able to come over for a piano lesson?

Tony Well, not for a while.

Mia If you're not in pain, then why do you cry so much?

Tony I don't cry.

Mia I hear you.

Tony Drop it.

Mia Why won't you leave the house?

No reply.

Why are you always telling me to keep the noise down?

No reply.

Why don't you play the piano?

No reply.

Let's listen to some music!

Tony Let's just clear up and head to our beds.

Mia Pick a record!

Tony Not now, Mia.

Mia I want you to have fun!

Tony Well, I want to go to bed.

Mia How about Duke Ellington? Full blast? Like you used to?

Tony No.

Mia Just while we tidy up?

Tony I said NO.

Mia   You used to be fun.

Tony   Upstairs. To bed. Now.

Mia   So this is when you choose to start parenting me?

Tony   I can't even look at you right now.

Mia   WHY DON'T YOU EVER DO ANYTHING YOU LIKE ANY MORE?

Tony   . . . Because I can't!

Mia   Why?

Tony   It's my ears! Nothing sounds right any more. The world's gone all . . . wonky . . . and I, I, I . . . don't . . . I'm scared . . .

He is broken and deflated.

Mia   I don't think you're trying as hard as you could be.

A horrible moment of silence.

Tony   Go upstairs.

Mia (*to audience*)   To date that's the worst thing I've ever said to him.
But it's really hard when you want someone to get better so much more than they seem to want that for themselves.

6. Deep-dive

Mia (*to audience*)   Why your hearing turns to mush, and music starts to sound 'wonky' after a brain injury becomes my new area of special interest. Because I think if I can understand it, then it can be fixed, right?

She consults her phone and makes copious notes, filling a folder, as the **Brain Chorus** *close in around her reciting her research. Lines to be divided between them.*

Brain Chorus

— The cerebral cortex is divided into two hemispheres
— Connected by the corpus callosum
— Each brain hemisphere has four sections called lobes
— The frontal lobes
— Parietal lobes
— Occipital
— And temporal
— Then then there is the cerebellum
— And the brain stem

- The auditory cortex of the human brain receives and processes the contents of sounds
- Voice
- And music
- A TBI
- A traumatic brain injury
- Can cause damage to the auditory cortex
- People who experience a TBI can be permanently affected by central auditory processing disorders
- Lesions in the brain can be the result of movement of the brain in the skull upon impact
- Tinnitus
- Distortions
- Hallucinations
- Delirium
- Confusion
- Post-traumatic amnesia
- Psychosis
- Inability to hear sound frequencies
- Damaged neurons
- Damaged temporal lobe
- The auditory cortex can be found in the temporal lobe
- More specifically, it is located on the superior temporal gyrus in the temporal lobe
- The cranial nerve 8 is fundamental to auditory processing
- Otherwise known as the vestibulocochlear nerve

Mia (*to audience*)   And the words get longer.

And the explanations get harder to understand because I've just about got my head around the idea that the mitochondria are the powerhouse of the cell, so I'm not really ready to be knee-deep in the biomedical literature available on PubMed!

She slams her folder shut and puts it in her school bag. **Brain Chorus** *back away to the edge of the space, watching her.*

7. School Library

Mia (*to audience*)   I stop going to lessons.
And I start hiding in the library or the loos or empty classrooms instead.
Because I can't sit still, and I can't concentrate –

Brain Chorus (*together*)   Subarachnoid haemorrhage!

Mia (*to audience*)   Because words that I don't understand –

Brain Chorus (*together*)   Meninges!

Mia (*to audience*)   Keep flashing up in my head and –

Brain Chorus (*together*)   Central nerve eight!

Mia (*to audience*)   Every time a word flashes it's a reminder that –

Brain Chorus (*together*)   Auditory cortex!

Mia (*to audience*)   It's a reminder that –

Brain Chorus (*together*)   Lesions in the brain!

Mia (*to audience*)   It's a reminder that I need to be doing all I can to make my dad better because this is really all my fault in the first place!

Teacher *puppet, represented by a blouse, lanyard and knee-length boots, enters.*

Teacher   Mia?

Brain Chorus (*together – in a whisper*)   Don't forget about the superior temporal gyrus!

Teacher   Mia?

Mia *tries to control her breathing.* **Brain Chorus** *close in on* **Mia**, *breathing erratically.*

Teacher   What are you doing here?

Mia *tries to control her breathing.*

Teacher   Shouldn't you be in class?

Mia *tries to control her breathing.*

Teacher   What's wrong?

Mia *tries to control her breathing.*

Teacher   Are you ill?

Brain Chorus   It's all your fault.

Mia   I caused it!

Teacher   Caused what?

Brain Chorus   You did it.

Mia   I did it! So I have to fix it!

Teacher   What are you talking about?

Brain Chorus   You fell asleep.

Mia   If I hadn't fallen asleep . . .

Teacher   What?

Mia *is struggling to catch her breath.*

Teacher   Mia? Breathe!

Mia   I can't!

Teacher   Come with me. Mia. Come on . . .

Teacher *strides off.* **Mia** *follows but turns back to us instead of exiting.*

Mia (*to audience*)   And it's obvious that Miss is worried I've gone mental because she frog-marches me to the school health centre like it's a Victorian asylum.
So after that Thursday, I stop going to school entirely.
I just refuse.
I don't care about my mocks.
Because when life as you know it is circling the drain what the fuck is the point of balancing equations?

8. Intervention

AJ's *house.*

Mia (*to audience*)   A week into my school boycott, AJ invites me over to his house where the others assemble like the Avengers.

AJ, **Frankie**, **Nish** *and* **Gee** *come centre-stage.* **Brain Chorus** *loiter.*

Frankie   We're worried.

Nish   Really worried.

AJ   I'm sorry I didn't tell you we'd all be here, I just didn't think you'd come if I did.

Frankie   Don't hate us.

Gee   Please.

Nish   Is it . . . your dad . . . is he . . . how are things?

Frankie   This isn't an intervention or anything.

AJ   It's just us asking you to start coming to school again.

Frankie   Because we miss you.

AJ   And we've got mocks.

Nish   And my mum says it's not actually legal for you to just stop going to school.

Gee Don't scare her.

Nish I'm not trying to.

Frankie We're just looking out for you.

Nish But my mum says your dad might end up going to court.

Mia At least it'd get him out the house.

AJ Is there anything we can do?

Nish Because we'll do it.

Gee We promise.

Frankie We want to help.

Mia I'm fine.

Frankie We know you. We know when you're not fine.

Gee Do you want to talk to my dad?

Mia No!

Frankie What can we do?

Pause.

Mia I've got to go.

Nish Don't storm out.

Mia Do you really want to help?

Frankie/AJ/Nish/Gee Yes!

Mia *takes out her folder and plonks it down in front of them.*

Gee What's that?

Mia My dad can't hear things right any more and he can't play his music and he can't leave the house and he can't stop crying so I need to fix it and to do that I need to understand about the auditory cortex and auditory distortions and this thing called hyperacusis so if you want to help me do that then you're welcome but if not just leave me alone . . .

Silence.

Nish Have you googled it?

Mia Right, I'm off!

Frankie Where?

Mia To talk to someone!

Gee Who?

Mia My dad won't go to his appointments at the hospital, so I'm going to go for him and talk to the consultant.

Nish Which hospital?

Mia St Jude's.

Nish We'll come with you.

AJ This doesn't feel right.

Frankie Is this the only thing you'll let us do?

Mia The number 33 bus leaves in 10 minutes and goes straight to the hospital from outside the newsagents. Are you coming?

She picks up her folder and clutches it tightly to her chest.

9. Hospital (2)

Mia (*to audience*) We go to the hospital.
All of us.
And we sit in the waiting room of the Neurology Clinic, and we wait.

They sit in the waiting room. **Brain Chorus** *loiter, perhaps as outpatients?*

Frankie (*to* **Mia**) I'd say they're running at least an hour late!

AJ (*to* **Nish**) I hate hospitals.

Mia I'm freaking out I'll forget something.

Gee Mia, you've got the memory of a dolphin, you'll be fine.

Nish Do dolphins have good memories?

AJ Dolphins have fin-tastic memories!

No one laughs.

AJ Ba-dum-tsssss!

Consultant *puppet, represented by a white lab coat and brogues, enters.*

Consultant Anthony Greg Lee?

They all look at **Mia**; *she stands.*

Consultant Mr Anthony Greg Lee?

Mia Yes.

Consultant Are you with Mr Lee?

Mia I'm here on his behalf.

Consultant You're his proxy?

Mia What?

Consultant Do you have written consent?

Mia I'm his daughter.

Consultant How old are you?

Mia Fifteen.

Consultant No. Sorry. That's not quite how this works . . .

Mia I've got some questions I'd like to ask, that's all . . .

Consultant I'm sorry. Tell him he needs to come in person.

Consultant *turns away.*

Mia He can't. He won't even leave the house.

Consultant I can arrange a telephone consultation.

Mia But he can't hear properly because of the accident, and he won't even pick up the phone when I call so there's absolutely no way he'll –

Consultant I'm sorry.

Frankie She's the one looking after him!

Consultant *is taken aback.*

Nish (*to* **Mia**) Get your folder out!

Mia *takes out her folder.*

Nish She's done bare research!

Mia Look-look-look! I know where the auditory cortex is and everything!

Consultant *doesn't know what to say!*

Mia And I read a paper in a medical journal by this professor at the Neuro-Audiology Research Centre in *[London or a nearby major city]* about the link between TBIs and APDs and potential therapies and treatments.

Consultant He'd need to speak to a specialist about that.

Mia BUT I DON'T KNOW WHAT TO DO AND IF HE CAN'T OR WON'T HELP HIMSELF THEN IT'S ME THAT HAS TO HELP HIM AND I CAN'T DO THAT ALONE!

Consultant I'm sorry, I really am. I'd love to help. But I can't talk to you without his permission and even then, you're too young.

Mia *throws her folder down and hundreds of A4 pages float down from above until she is partially buried beneath them. Then, music!* **Brain Chorus** *move in and start to swirl around* **Mia**.

Brain Chorus So, you want to know more about the auditory cortex?

Song of the Neuroscientists

*As **Brain Chorus** performs the song, they gradually pick up some of the pages that have fallen on **Mia** so that by the end of the song, when they move to the edge of the space, she is no longer buried. Lines to be distributed.*

Brain Chorus
   We are here to do our duty
   Yes, we are here to serve
   To explain the auditory cortex
   And the axons of the auditory nerve
   And the axons of the auditory nerve

   There's . . .
   Stimulus intensity
   Tonotopy
   And frequency
   Vestibular polarity
   And parity
   For clarity
   Binaural
   Sensitvity
   Disparity
   Is plain to see
   Neuronal
   Circularity
   Is fixed
   And regulatory

   Hair cells
   Have some dexterity
   And can be
   Excitatory
   Neuronal response properties
   Can be slowed down to some degree
   But damage
   Of severity
   Can upset
   Your reality
   And injure scala tympani
   But deafness
   Is a rarity

   The organ
   Of the corti, see

Is delicate
It's clear to me
The membrane
At low frequency
With apex wide can floppy be
Head injury
I guarantee
A problem that is auditory
And loud noise of intensity
Plays havoc with your
Cochleeeeee – arrrrrrr

Brain Chorus *moves to the edge of the space continuing to chant in a whisper . . .*

We are here to do our duty
Yes, we are here to serv
To explain the auditory cortex
And the myelination of the auditory nerve
And the myelination of the auditory nerve

AJ, **Frankie**, **Gee**, *and* **Nish** *gather around* **Mia** *and tidy up the last of the papers.*

10. Bus Stop

The friends wait at a bus stop.

Gee (*to* **Mia**)   I've not seen you like that for a looong time.

Nish *wraps* **Mia** *in an enormous hug.*

Nish   SQUEEEEEEEEZE!

The **Brain Chorus** *loiter.* **AJ** *steps away from the others – they look upset.* **Frankie** *sees this and crosses to them.*

Frankie (*to* **AJ**)   You okay?

AJ   Yeh.

Frankie   You don't have to be.

AJ   I'm fine.

Frankie *holds* **AJ**'s *hand.*

AJ   Is that what I look like? When I have them?

Frankie   Panic attacks? I've only ever seen you have one.

AJ   I guess. But that was a big one – the one I had before the gig – when you found me.

Frankie I don't think it matters what you look like when you're feeling that shit.

Nish (*announcing to the group*) Bus is delayed!

AJ (*to* **Frankie** – *referring to* **Mia**) I just want her to stop.

Gee I'm going to be so late to dance practice. I'm never late for dance practice!

Mia *takes out her phone to check something.*

Frankie (*to* **Mia**) Everything alright?

Mia Fine.

Nish What are you looking at?

Mia My Plan B, Plan C, Plan D and Plan E.

Nish *El classico.*

Mia Realistically, I have to talk to the professor who wrote that paper. That's what the consultant said.

Frankie I'm not sure he did . . .

Mia He told me I'd have to talk to a specialist! And this is *the* specialist: Professor Greco.

AJ Just because what they wrote made sense to you, doesn't mean it's what your dad's got.

Mia Just because you don't understand it, doesn't mean I'm wrong!

Nish Woah!

Frankie Where does this professor work?

Mia The Neuro-Audiology Research Centre.

Nish Where's that?

Mia It's right next to the Science Museum!

AJ As in the one in *[London or name of city]*?

Mia That's the one, let's go!

AJ As in *right now*?

Frankie We can't go *right now*.

Brain Chorus You can.

Mia Why not?

Frankie Because . . . well you're . . .

AJ   Because what if they're not even there?

Nish   And we go all that way for nothing?

Brain Chorus   Do something!

Mia   We can check! The phone number's here! Look!

She shows her phone.

Gee   Bus is due!

Mia   Frankie, can you call while I look up the journey?

Frankie   But I hate calling people.

Mia   Well . . . so do I!

Nish   Me too.

AJ   I'm not calling!

A stalemate!

Gee   Fine. I'll call.

Mia *shows* **Gee** *the number,* **Gee** *taps it into her phone and waits.*

Gee (*barely audible*)   Hello?

The others turn towards **Gee** *who clears her throat – they're impressed, but worried she'll clam up.* **Gee** *rolls her eyes and takes a deep breath.*

Gee   Hello . . . I'm calling because . . . is this Professor Greco?

She listens.

Gee   Thank you, very much . . . yes.

Gee *listens for a little longer.*

Gee   Oh I'm . . . no . . . yes . . . have a lovely day too.

The call ends – a huge relief for **Gee***!*

Gee   She's lecturing until 4 pm. But she'll be in her office after.

Mia   Then I'm going!

Frankie   So I guess I'm going too.

Nish   Bus is here.

Gee   Mimi, you know I can't come. My parents'd kill me.

AJ   I've got a stand-up gig tonight. I can't get stuck in *[London or name of city]*.

Nish   I'll come. But one of you has to lend me some dollar for the train.

Frankie   Done.

Mia   AJ, take Gee home. Gee, don't stress, and don't tell your parents anything.

Gee   I won't.

AJ   I don't think this is a good idea. Not after the day you've had already.

Mia   You're not coming, your opinion doesn't count.

AJ *is wounded.*

Mia   Frankie, Nish, let's go to the station.

AJ *and* **Gee** *move to the sides of the stage and watch their friends as their journey begins.*

11. Journey

Mia (*to audience*)   We *just* make the 14.37 train!

Brain Chorus *join them on the train.*

Mia (*to audience*)   And as we catch our breath, Frankie says:

Frankie   You were really horrible to AJ back there.

Mia *doesn't reply.*

Brain Chorus   Horrible people say horrible things.

Frankie   He's going through stuff too.

Mia *looks out of the window.*

Brain Chorus   You're a horrible person.

Frankie   I'm not saying it to upset you.

Brain Chorus   Why else would they say it?

Mia   If AJ's all you care about, why are you even here?

Frankie *looks out of the opposite window;* **Mia** *takes out her folder and studies.*

Nish   I told my mum we're revising together at the library, so if you could just . . . you know . . . say the same thing . . . that'd be sweeeeeeet.

Frankie *and* **Mia** *grunt 'yes' in response.*

Mia (*to audience*)   No one says anything until we've arrived.
Then, we're stood outside the station relying on Maps to tell us where to go.

Nish   It's basically straight once we're on that big road.

Frankie   27 minutes walking.

Mia (*to audience*)   The closer I get, the quicker I get –
and I'm practically running when we hit this big, huge road.
Nish keeps up because he's the fastest runner at school.
But Frankie falls behind.
And that pisses me off.
Really pisses me off.
And there's the perfect gap in traffic for me and Nish to cross the road but he pulls me back and says –

Nish   Wait for Frankie!

Mia   But –

Nish   Wait! For! Frankie!

Mia (*to audience*)   And, in that moment, every scrap of me wants every scrap of Frankie to hurt as much as I'm hurting.

Frankie *catches up.*

Frankie   Sorry . . .

Brain Chorus   Frankie's doing it on purpose.

Mia (*to* **Frankie**)   You're doing it on purpose.

Nish   What?

Mia (*to* **Frankie**)   You're doing it on purpose! Dragging your feet!

Frankie   I'm trying to keep up!

Mia   Well, don't! You don't need to. I don't need you here.

Nish   Be careful, Mi.

Frankie   Do you want me to go?

Brain Chorus   Yes.

Mia   You didn't even want to come!

Frankie   I want to look after you!

Mia   I don't need looking after!

Nish   Frankie probably meant like 'look out for . . .'

Mia/Frankie   SHUT UP, NISH.

Frankie   I'm doing everything I can.

Mia   Well, I'm sorry it's such HARD WORK.

Frankie   No, you're HARD WORK.

Mia   You have no idea what I'm going through.

Frankie We're going through it with you.

Mia This isn't about YOU!

Frankie We're worried about you.

Mia Nish, are *you* worried? About me?

Nish Honestly?

Mia/Frankie YES!

Nish Then . . . yeah.

Frankie See!

Mia Neither of you know what it's like to be *this* scared about someone you love.

Frankie That's not fair –

Mia You don't even know what it's like to be *close* to a parent.

This is the worst thing **Mia** *has ever said to* **Frankie***. A . . . long . . . pause.*

Frankie No. I don't.

Nish Christ, Mia.

Mia Go home, Frankie. Go watch AJ's show. Go find someone else to latch onto.

Frankie *is silent.*

Mia (*to* **Nish**) Are you coming?

Nish *looks at a broken* **Frankie***; there is something in the way* **Frankie** *looks at him that implores him to stay with* **Mia***.*

Nish Yeah, I'm coming.

He gives **Frankie** *an enormous hug.*

Mia Come on!

(*To audience.*) So the two of us dive through the traffic until we're standing at reception and Nish says:

Nish Hi there. Here to see my aunt – Prof. Greco – she said to go up to her office after she's done teaching at 4? Got a friend with me . . . careers chat stuff . . .

Mia (*to audience*) He's good at this.

Nish Cool, thanks, and can I just check how I get there? It's been ages! (**Nish** *listens attentively to the receptionist.*) First floor, second on the left! Thanks.

Mia (*to audience*) I knock on the door.

Nish I'll be just out here.

He moves to the side of the stage.

Mia (*to audience*) A voice from inside calls out:

Professor Greco Come in.

12. Professor Greco

Professor Greco *puppet, represented by low-heeled court shoes, a smart jumper/ cardigan and a pair of glasses.* **Brain Chorus** *loiter, or perhaps they* can *form the walls of the office?*

Professor Greco (*to* **Mia**) Just you?

Mia *doesn't know what to say.*

Professor Greco Reception called. Said my nephew and his friend were on their way up.

Mia Oh . . .

Professor Greco But I don't have a nephew.

Mia *mutters an inaudible apology.*

Professor Greco I am intrigued, though.

Mia It's a bit of a long story.

Professor Greco I'm Claire.

Mia It's Mia . . . Mia Lee.

Professor Greco Would you like to sit down, Mia?

Mia I read your paper.

Professor Greco Which one?

Mia The study about the man whose brain injury meant he couldn't recognise certain sounds like he used to – like strong accents, and music, and fast-talkers – you called it King-Kopetzky Syndrome.

Professor Greco Not that I came up with it!

Mia *takes out her folder.*

Professor Greco Bloody hell . . .

Mia This isn't just a . . . a special interest . . . or a hobby.

Professor Greco I'm not optimistic enough to assume it would be . . . given your . . . how old *are* you?

Mia Fifteen.

Professor Greco And what's brought you here?

Mia My dad. Not that he knows that I'm here . . . seeing you.

Professor Greco Where does he think you are?

Mia We don't really talk all that much any more. And I'm not sure he cares.

Professor Greco Time for the 'long story', I reckon?

Mia (*to audience*) So I tell her everything.
From start to finish.
She asks:

Professor Greco How long was he in hospital?

Mia (*to audience*) And:

Professor Greco So, will he not leave the house at all?

Mia (*to audience*) And a little bit later, she tells me:

Professor Greco I grew up with a Deaf mum and a hearing dad.

Mia (*to audience*) And I feel like I can share a lot with her.
So I tell her that she has to help me so that I can help my dad because it was all my fault in the first place.
(*To* **Professor Greco** – *fast.*) I never ever go to sleep before my dad gets home because it feels like inviting things to go wrong.

Professor Greco Are you getting any help? Talking to anyone?

Mia It's my dad that needs help.

Professor Greco But it sounds like things are quite hard for you, too, at the moment.

Mia (*to audience*) I skip over this detour into my messy head and ask:
(*To* **Professor Greco**.) What can you do for my dad? What treatment is there? Surgery? Hearing aids?

Professor Greco There's no one thing – there's no one answer – no one-size-fits-all kind of cure.

Silence.

Mia?

Mia But you have to be able to make him better? You can't just write about a problem and not be able to offer a solution!

Professor Greco It's not always about solutions. Or cures. It's about how we care.

Mia But no one cares!

Professor Greco I do. I just can't give you the answer you're looking for because life is far more complex than either of us would like it to be.

Mia *doesn't know what to say.*

Professor Greco Your research is tremendous. And so is your heart. And the questions you're asking are important and necessary and well beyond your years. But the brain is this beautiful, enigmatic thing that we're still only reaching the outskirts of in terms of our knowledge. That's why I adore it. It's like a planet. A whole universe. The truth is, I can only tell you what I think based on what you're telling me. And I believe that with time and the right care, your dad's standard of life could get better. But he needs to talk. And so do you. Not about your dad, but about *you*. Because the feelings you're having and the things you're doing – have to do – sound like they're making your life miserable. And you have to understand that the answers you get won't always sound like solutions. But that doesn't mean you should stop trying and wanting for better.

Mia *is silent.* **Brain Chorus** *slowly back away to the edge of the space.*

Professor Greco Does any of that make sense?

Mia Tell me what to do?

Professor Greco Go home. Talk to your dad. Tell him about all of this. I'm going to write down my email, and a list of places you can call when you need to talk to someone about what's going on in your head. We can't make better the things we don't know – or won't admit to ourselves, Mia.

Mia I don't like my head very much.

Professor Greco Tell me someone who does.

13. Return

Nish *reappears.* **Brain Chorus** *look on.*

Nish How did it go?

Mia I don't know.

Nish Can she help?

Mia I think we need lots of different kinds of help.

Nish Like?

Mia Can we not talk about it for a bit?

Nish *waits for more –* **Mia** *is silent.*

Nish Let's get you home.

Mia (*to audience*) On the train, Nish shows me frog memes and we do a quiz which tells you which kind of frog you'd be if you were a . . . well . . . a frog.

Nish Javan gliding tree frog!

Mia You're a really good friend, Nish.

Nish *shrugs.*

Mia I'm a really nasty person.

Nish I don't think that.

Mia Frankie and AJ do.

Nish You want to hear some of the stuff my sisters say to each other.

Mia Really?

Nish But they always forgive each other because they're really close.

Mia So what do I do?

Nish Apologise.

Mia *rests her head on* **Nish***'s shoulder.*

Mia Thank you.

Nish Any time.

14. Home (2)

Mia (*to audience*) I see Frankie sitting on the doorstep next to my dad's Elvis gnome.
It's like an accidental indie album cover.

Brain Chorus *slowly start to move in towards* **Mia.**

Mia (*to* **Frankie**) I'm sorry.

Frankie I know.

Silence.

Don't worry, I've not said anything to your dad. I just wanted to be here when you got back.

Mia Thanks. I met her . . . Professor Greco.

Frankie Nish told me.

Mia I thought he would've.

Frankie I don't want to talk to you for a bit.

Mia I don't like me very much either. Not when I lose it like that. I don't like losing control.

Frankie No one does.

Mia How long do you not want to talk to me for?

Frankie I don't know. Just a bit.

Silence.

Mia Do you want to come in with me?

Frankie Best not.

Mia *nods.*

Frankie Love you.

Mia *smiles.* **Brain Chorus** *slowly move back to the edge of the space.*

Mia Love you.

Frankie *leaves.*

Mia (*to audience*) Inside, my dad's on the sofa eating garlic bread.

Tony There's soup in the fridge. And more garlic bread.

Mia Dad, can we talk?

Tony You alright?

Mia Not really, no.

Tony What is it?

Mia What do you think?

Tony *is quiet.*

Mia I went to the hospital today.

Tony What for?

Mia To ask them what to do about you.

Tony Me?

Mia Yes. You had an appointment, but I knew you wouldn't go, so I went.

Tony And what did they say? Take him out and shoot him?

Mia *raises an eyebrow.*

Tony Sorry.

Mia They wouldn't tell me anything. So I went to *[insert city]* to find someone who would. A professor called –

Tony Today?!

Mia Yes.

Tony You went to *[insert city]* today?!

Mia . . . yeah.

Tony Mia! That's really not on, I need to know where you are in case something happens, and I need to –

Mia What? Come and get me? You can't leave the sofa!

Tony Watch yourself, Mimi.

Mia I'm scared, Dad. About you.

Tony We're alright.

Mia You can't leave the house or hear like you used to, and I feel so guilty and so afraid, and it's weird but I didn't realise what a fucking brilliant human you were until you couldn't . . . 'human' any more. Because you play music for a living, you raise me on your own, and you think cheese and crisps constitutes gastronomic experimentation. And I don't really know why you won't realise you're worth more than *this*.

Tony I'm just low, Mia.

Mia So you're going to hide from everyone and anyone who could help?

Tony I don't –

Mia As a parent, what would you say to me if I was in your position? If I'd nearly died, couldn't hear like I used to, was terrified, incapacitated and sick at the thought of leaving the house?

Tony . . . I'd say . . . that you need . . . that you should probably talk about that with a professional.

Mia Then that's what I'm saying to you as my parent. Because you need help. We need help. And it'd be reckless not to ask for it.

Tony Okay.

Mia What?

Tony Don't say 'what' say 'pardon'.

Mia *smiles.*

Tony Don't think I'm not fuming you went off travelling about the country today.

Mia *stops smiling.*

Tony Did he talk to you, the professor?

Mia She!

Tony Sorry, did *she* talk to you?

Mia Yes. She was impressed with how much I knew.

Tony What's her thing? What'd she say?

Mia That you'd probably need to see lots of different specialists.

Tony Right.

Mia And that no doctor can treat something they don't know needs treating.

Tony She single?

Mia Dad!
(*To audience.*) That night he makes me laugh – proper belly laughs – for the first time in a very long time.
And he swears on his collection of jazz records that he'll make himself a telephone appointment – and send an email to my school counsellor.
And he does.
And I do see the school counsellor.
And they refer me to a special service for young people.
And I take some time off school to focus on my own brain before I start the year again.
Meanwhile, Dad tries going outside.
And he makes appointments that lead to brain scans that lead to doctors thinking there might be an operation that could improve his hearing just a little bit.
They say it might get better all by itself anyway.
Which would be brilliant.
And we cope.
In our way.
And my friends . . .

15. Pizza Night

Mia (*to the audience*) My friends . . .
Last Friday we got together for our first pizza night in twenty-eight Fridays . . .

Nish, Frankie, AJ and **Gee** *join* **Mia** *with several empty pizza boxes.* **Brain Chorus** *watch them.*

Nish More?

Gee All gone.

AJ If you like, I can give you a pizz-a my mind! Ba-dum-tssss!

Frankie Your material's getting worse, AJ.

Nish Have you got any new stuff?

AJ I'm actually thinking of packing it in.

Nish No you aren't!

Mia No!

Frankie You can't do that!

Gee Please don't.

Nish Do something for us now.

AJ I haven't got anything.

Nish Then make something up.

AJ Not gonna happen!

Nish AJ! AJ!

The others join in.

Nish, Mia, Frankie, Gee AJ! AJ! AJ!

AJ Alright! Alright! This is something that . . . like . . . I'm not really sure what it is yet . . . it's not funny-funny, it's . . . I don't know what it is, but here goes . . .
Hi!
Hello!
It's me!
Again!
Absolute delight to be back here.
At Mia's.
Scranning pizza.
Anyway . . .
Tonight I'd like to talk about something called . . . TUMMY ACHE SURVIVORS.
Seen the memes?
My personal favourite is the guy at a party wearing the party hat holding a little cup thinking:
'They don't know how much my tummy hurts cause I'm being so brave about it.'
And it's become a bit of a thing with my friends.
Wherever we are, whatever we're doing, one of us might say:
'I know I'm being really brave but . . .'

All MY TUMMY HURTS!

AJ Because we're all tummy ache survivors here, aren't we?
We're all unsung heroes
And the older I get the more I realise that life is just pretending your tummy doesn't hurt.
But pretending something away doesn't make it go away.
And we don't have to be okay.
And that's beautiful.
I think.
So I dedicate this to my friends –
to my loose-bowelled, warm-hearted, fellow tummy ache survivors!

The friends clap and cheer and hug. And perhaps the **Brain Chorus** *do too?*

Epilogue

Mia *puts on her dressing gown. We have returned to where we left* **Mia** *at the start of the play with the* **Brain Chorus** *on the edge of the space.* **Mia** *looks at her bag, then at the audience.*

Mia (*to audience*)   My dad went for a CT scan yesterday.
I don't go with him to the hospital any more.
He says I have to trust him.
And apparently there's some things I don't *need* to know.

The **Brain Chorus** *slowly gathers around* **Mia** *until they are standing in a semi-circle behind her – this is solidarity!*

Mia (*to the audience*)   I think I have a funny brain.

Brain Chorus   Always have.

Brain Chorus   Always will.

Mia   But the good thing is that the thoughts I don't like come less frequently now.
And they have a bit less power than they did.
And being in-the-moment doesn't feel like such a battle.
And that leaves room in my brain for the things that I actually like.

Brain Chorus   Friends.

Brain Chorus   Reading.

Brain Chorus   Pizza.

Mia *turns to the* **Brain Chorus** *and for the first time they acknowledge each other.* **Mia** *turns back to the audience.*

Mia   Being alright is quite hard sometimes.
But I have a good feeling that we're going to be alright.

Brain Chorus   We'll be alright.

Mia *glances back at the* **Brain Chorus** *again. She turns back to the audience. She smiles.*

Mia   Yes.
We're going to be alright.

End.

Character Plot

	Prologue	1. Friday Night	2. Hospital (1)	3. Discharged	4. Home (1)	5. Music	6. Deep-dive	7. School Library	8. Intervention	9. Hospital (2)	10. Bus Stop	11. Journey	12. Professor Greco	13. Return	14. Home (2)	15. Pizza Night	Epilogue
Mia	✓	✓	✓	✓	✓	✓	✓	✓	✓	✓	✓	✓	✓	✓	✓	✓	✓
Frankie		✓	✓	✓					✓	✓	✓	✓			✓	✓	
Gee		✓		✓	✓				✓	✓	✓					✓	
Nish				✓					✓	✓	✓	✓		✓		✓	
AJ		✓		✓					✓	✓	✓					✓	
Tony	✓					✓								✓			
Nurse		✓															
Consultant										✓							
Teacher								✓									
Professor Greco												✓	✓				
Brain Chorus	✓	✓	✓	✓	✓	✓	✓	✓	✓	✓	✓	✓	✓	✓	✓	✓	✓

More information about the characters and how much they speak

Mia – In every scene, significant dialogue, multiple monologues and scenes where she acts opposite various puppets
Frankie – Significant dialogue
Gee – Significant dialogue
Nish – Significant dialogue
AJ – Significant dialogue with one long monologue

Adult characters are played by puppets (see notes at start of play for information and suggested approach)
Tony – Significant dialogue
Nurse – Dialogue in one scene
Consultant – Dialogue in one scene
Teacher – Dialogue in one scene
Professor Greco – Dialogue in one scene and medium-length monologue

Brain Chorus – Can be played by any number of people, two long monologues/songs with lots of scientific words in them

Main Narrative Beats

1. Mia is getting ready to go back to school after a long time, her dad Tony pops in to say goodnight. Mia realises it's been 28 weeks since the accident.
2. It's Friday night, 28 weeks ago. Mia is hanging out with her friends, they make jokes and eat pizza while her dad is out at work. The friends leave and Mia falls asleep, her friend Frankie is sleeping over.
3. The phone rings. A nurse tells Mia that her dad has been in an accident, she needs to come to the hospital. The Brain Chorus tell Mia it's all her fault. At the hospital Mia is trying to understand all the medical information. Tony has been hit by a car, he has a brain injury, and lots of broken bones.
4. When Tony comes home from hospital Mia is looking after him, her friends are worried about her, she is worried about her dad.
5. At home Mia is with her cousin Gee, doing homework. Mia is researching her dad's brain injury.
6. Mia and Tony sit on the sofa eating crisps. Mia asks Tony why he's not leaving the house, or listening to music. Tony explains his ears don't work the same any more and he's scared.
7. Mia is researching brain injuries and hearing. The Brain Chorus whoosh around reciting the research.
8. At school Mia is hiding in the library, a teacher wants to know why. Mia can't breathe, she thinks the accident is all her fault.
9. At AJ's house the friendship group ask Mia to start coming to school again. Mia tells them about her research, she's going to go to the hospital and speak to the doctor. The group decide to go with her.
10. At the hospital, Mia wants to speak to the consultant, she has questions, Tony isn't there so they say no. The Brain Chorus sing about the auditory cortex.
11. At the bus stop, Mia's friends are worried about her. Mia is going to the university to speak to a professor. Mia has been unkind to her friends.
12. Nish and Mia meet Professor Greco, Mia shares all her research. Professor Greco is kind but says that Mia needs some help and support for herself, and needs to talk to her dad.
13. On the way home Mia realises how nasty she's been to her friends. Nish tells her to apologise and it will all be fine.
14. At home, Mia finally tells Tony everything she's been doing, she tells him all her worries. Tony and Mia make a plan to get them both the support they need.
15. After 28 weeks, it's pizza night, the friends hang out and eat, AJ tries out his stand-up comedy.
16. Mia talks to the audience. Her dad is attending his hospital appointments, and Mia is not having such a tough time with her brain, they are both going to be all right.

Brain Play

BY CHLOË LAWRENCE-TAYLOR AND PAUL SIRETT

Notes on rehearsal and staging drawn from a workshop with the writers, led by Freyja Winterson held at the National Theatre, October 2024

How the writers came to write the play

I was a new writer, and had read previous NT Connections plays while at school. Paul Sirett taught me while I was an MA student, and I had been exploring ideas for a play for young people. As he mentored me, we realised that there could be one play from a few possible ideas that we had individually been working on.

I have experience of obsessions and compulsions stretching from childhood into adulthood and, the longer I've been working with young people in primary and secondary schools, the more I've been driven to write theatre for young people that feels relevant to their own experiences of and navigation of mental health. It became really important to explore early intervention for young people, to discuss all of these things that come up in this play.

(Chloë Lawrence-Taylor)

We were essentially talking about ideas around mental health. My experience specifically was, well I'm not Tony, but there is Tony in me – I had an accident, bashed my head and I've now got funny hearing. While recovering from that accident I became agoraphobic and found it really difficult to leave home. And playing music, which I often did, became difficult for me.

(Paul Sirett)

Warm-ups and introductions

Game: Bunny (a passing the 'energy' game)

Lead director Freyja Winterson said she enjoys starting rehearsals with circle games like this one, and repeating throughout rehearsals:

1. One person starts with the 'energy'. Holding their fingers like bunny ears, they say 'bunny bunny' before passing 'bunny bunny' to someone else in the circle, using the bunny ears to point to that person. You receive the energy by saying 'bunny bunny' and making bunny ears.
2. Underscore this by creating a rhythm with the rest of the people in the circle: 'ooh aah' with soft tapping on thighs on 'ooh' and a clap on 'aah'.
3. Two people either side of the person with the bunny do 'choppy choppy' as if chopping down the bunny person like a tree while saying 'choppy choppy, choppy choppy'.

4. Don't fight the urge to get faster – let it speed up!

Game: Hemispheres

In this play, there is a lot of brain-based science. There is a creative challenge about how to share this science in a way that engages the young people.

Everyone stands in a big circle, with two different zones inside the circle: one for the **left** and one for the **right** brain hemisphere. When a word is called out, go to whichever side you think the word belongs in. You then have ten seconds to make a still image of that word as a group.

- Spoken language (correct hemisphere: Left)
- Hearing (correct hemisphere: Right)
- Creativity (correct hemisphere: Right)
- Number skills (correct hemisphere: Left)
- Spatial orientation/awareness (correct hemisphere: Right)

Approaching the play

Winterson invited participants to think about the themes of this play.

The group came up with the following themes:

- Relationships/friendships
- Being a young carer
- Single parenthood (particularly fatherhood)
- Value of talking
- Superstitions/obsessive behaviours/'magical thinking' (from Lawrence-Taylor: 'Magical thinking brings together superstitions and OCD behaviour')
- Loss of control
- Survivor's guilt
- Power dynamics (adults and institutions)
- Medical systems (and its failures)
- Perceptions of adults from a child's perspective
- Neglect
- Inside v outside (including the brain)
- Negative thought patterns

Exercise: Provocations

In groups of six, discuss the following provocations:

- A fantastic production of *Brain Play* looks like . . .
- An amazing process feels like . . .
- The key challenges are . . .

Character work

Exercise: Character study

Small groups were given one of the five main characters: Mia, Frankie, Gee, Nish, AJ.

1. Identify from the text all of the **facts** about that character (e.g. If they say they are going off to do their history homework, then it is a fact that they study history), and list it down on a big piece of paper.
2. With a different colour pen, identify things that you can **infer** or make an **educated guess** at that aren't in the script (e.g. What does this character's bedroom look like? What do they carry in their school bag? What's their favourite meal?)

This can take a lot of time, so here are some quick alternatives to not have to spend a whole session:

- Choose a different character each week for the whole group to explore – everyone says something they remember about the character
- Hot-seating in the rehearsal process
- Give the young people key pages/sections or lines from which to identify facts or educated guesses
- You as director could write a little three-line character bio to give to the young people

    1. In your group create a single still image of that character's life, with one person playing the character (can be a mixture of facts and guesses)
    2. Share back in a 'Carousel Performance' of images: when a character's name is called out, that group comes into the middle of the circle and presents the still image, but plan it: for example, if there is a chair, who brings that in? Hold the image for five seconds and then leave the space. Music can be played during this sharing, to elevate the showings

Text work

How can you help young people understand what is happening so that the storytelling is clear?

Uniting a script

Units of action: a new 'paragraph', a new event that happens.

In professional productions, uniting can take days, or even weeks, sitting around a table discussing the text. With young people this can be heavy going, so how can you make this kind of work accessible and fun?

Exercise: Identifying units

In groups of five or six, allocate one person for each character and one person as a 'director'. Using Scene eight 'Intervention', from the play:

1. Decide who is playing which character and read the scene
2. Ask 'What happens in this scene?' in its simplest terms. E.g. 'The friends confront Mia'
3. (This can be done as a whole group or in the smaller groups.) Read again, but every time you think there is a unit change for the scene (*not* for individual characters, think about the overall storytelling), clap or tap the floor and say 'Unit'. There will inevitably be disagreements! It is about exploring the units. When there is a disagreement, discuss together and come to an agreement about whether it is a unit change or not, and if you need to tweak where the unit changes. Mark the unit changes in your script (in whatever way works for you – a line, an asterisk, etc.).

Observations: negotiating and compromising are good: it forces you to justify your thoughts. It is not about a right or wrong answer, it's about really understanding what happens in the scene. Also, it is useful to unit the section for yourself first, before doing this exercise with your students or young people, so that you already have a sense of what you believe the units are.

1. Once the units have been identified, *name* the units
   - They can't have fancy language – they need to be simple
   - The titles need to contain **active verbs**

The participants came up with the following units:

Unit 1: Mia sets the scene

Unit 2: The friends worry

Unit 3: The group hassle Mia

Unit 4: The friends bombard Mia with help

Unit 5: Mia relents

Unit 6: Mia explodes

Unit 7: Nish fails to help

Unit 8: Mia leads the way

Observation: the more dramatic *the verbs are, the easier it will be for the young people to explore physically.*

1. When the unit title is called out, as an individual (and not in the smaller groups of five or six) make a still image with your body that represents that title and hold it until the next unit title is called. Don't return to your own body between

unit titles. It doesn't need to be 'dance-y' or beautiful. If there is more than one character in the title, choose which character you are portraying

2. Repeat the process and this time add a sound to your physical gesture (make it vocal, not a slap or clap)
3. Return to the group you initially read the scene with, and repeat unit six (body and sound together) with the 'director' reading out the unit titles. Only play the character you are reading. Remember not to drop the physical body between titles
4. Repeat the exercise and now replace the sound with a word or improvised phrase. Try to keep it within the world of the play – resist the urge to be funny, and instead embrace being earnest.

What can you do if you have a large group or other actors who are not in that particular scene you are working with?

1. Bring together two smaller groups into one larger group
2. Identify your character or director partner
3. Now when the director(s) read(s) the unit titles out, one of the character pairs will be the physical pose, and their partner will read the lines of the actual scene. The aim is to separate the text from the physicality.

It will probably be messy and chaotic at times (and the flow of the scene will be interrupted by the unit titles), but this can be a great way to explore the uniting exercise with more people than are actually in the scene.

Taking the exercise to the next level

1. Return to your original small groups of five or six
2. Perform the scene while building on the physicality you have previously found. Again, the text will be interrupted by the director reading out the unit titles
3. Try not to worry about where the audience is
4. As a director, resist the urge to stage the performance. Allow the actors to explore the space
5. Share back to the larger group.

Reflections from the participants:

- Freeze-framing the units makes them dynamic
- Makes the individual characterisation very clear, especially in a group scene
- Useful for groups with low literacy levels – physicality is the drive
- Gives agency to the students

If you want to add a transition at the end of the scene, you could try adding an extra unit: Unit 9 (a non-verbal unit). Maybe connect this to one of the themes you have identified.

De-roling from out of a character

De-roling can be crucial at the end of a rehearsal. Decide on a specific practice for your room: for example, you may decide that personal stories are not part of rehearsals – identify the clear distinction between fiction and reality. Be clear that although your group may connect with the characters, rehearsals might not be the space to unload personal experiences with mental health. Plan your rehearsals to enable getting in and out of character. A 'ritual' to finish the day can often help.

Exercise: Character shake-off

1. Ground your feet, like a tree
2. Deep breath in and out
3. Imagine there is a big rain cloud above you and gently use your fingertips rapidly tapping on your head and down your body to mimic gentle rain falling. 'Brush' your body down as the rain washes everything away, leaving it in the rehearsal room.

Puppetry

Game: Getting ready for puppetry

- Walk around the room
- Pick someone in the room and think about being their shadow. You don't necessarily have to be directly right behind them
- Choose someone else and shadow them
- Walk around the room and explore the differences of slow and fast pace
- Imagine having a snow fight with everyone else in the room. Explore having a **slow** snow fight. Now a **fast** snow fight
- In groups of two or three people, make a triangle with your bodies. Remember how and with whom you made the triangle
- On your own, imagine walking through sticky mud
- In groups of five or six make a hexagon – six-sided shape. Remember how and with whom you made the triangle
- Walk around the space and when 'triangle' or 'hexagon' is called, replicate the shape with those specific partners
- As a whole group make a star shape.

Game: Each person randomly chooses an item of clothing/pair of shoes. Get into groups of about seven or eight people.

- Make and imagine, using every person in your group and each item (the items of clothing do not need to represent their actual nature: shoes do not need to be used as shoes!)

- A pizza
- Someone waiting for a bus
- A brain

Exercise: Creating characters through items

Each group is given one of the adult characters from the play.

- Discuss what you know about that character (facts as well as educated guesses)
- Think about how you might want to divide the group – puppeteers, voice, director, etc.
- Choose the clothing to represent this character
- Create the character as a still image. And then explore how these characters:
  - Breathe
  - Sit
  - Eat
  - Stand
  - Walk
  - Sleep
  - Connect
  - Speak
- Start to work out how your character interacts with actual human beings (so someone will have to be Mia) and read the scene this character is in
- Continue staging the scene. Think about where the audience is. Additional points to consider when creating the puppet character is where they sit on the following spectrums:

  Reality
  Real person <—> Completely unrealistic

  Formation
  Arrives fully formed <—> Created/taken apart on stage

  Size
  Human sized <—> Cartoon/caricature size

  Present the scenes to the rest of the group.

Responses from participants about things that worked:

- feet – subtle fidgeting
- glasses moving while speaking
- enough to get the character but allowing the focus to be on Mia
- flourishing/slightly magical exit of clothes
- props (doctor's folder, coffee cups)

- head tilt as shown through glasses
- the clothing items that are *not* used as much as the ones that are
- the gradual build of the character, showing shoes first
- breathing (use of shoulders to show this)
- actor's direct eye contact with the puppet
- using the whole body to move, rather than isolated arms
- clear actions in conjunction with the text
- deliberate choice of clothing (dressing gown for Tony)
- using coat hangers to help with manipulation of boots
- stereotypical personal items (lanyard, cup, etc.)
- height difference between the character and Mia
- movement of hands
- giving the puppet moments to shine
- momentary disassembly of the character didn't negatively affect the story
- human character/puppet character interaction (shaking hands)
- removing the glasses didn't lose the head
- the voice not needing to be physically connected to the puppet.

Observations: each group used glasses to denote the head, but it is unlikely that every single adult character will be able to wear glasses, so think about a range of items. Also, explore the emotions or feelings that specific clothes arouse in us (e.g. dressing gowns are 'familiar' and 'cosy'). Things such as rods can be used to help puppetry, but also simplicity can be just as effective. Swapping in/out can help people observe and see what they are creating.

Brain Chorus

One of the big challenges of the Brain Chorus is that there is a lot of language and specifically a lot of *scientific* language.

Exercise: Brain jargon tongue twisters

Get into four large groups and turn some of the medical jargon from the Brain Chorus song into a tongue twister. Say it together as a group.

Observation: tongue twisters are a great way to make the language less scary.

Discuss among your group all of the possible answers to the following provocations about the Brain Chorus:

- It feels like . . .
- It looks like . . .

- It sounds like . . .
- It is in the genre of . . .

Responses from participants:

Feels like:

- Intrusive
- Oppressive
- Threatening
- Varied (like '*Inside Out*')
- Social embarrassment

– Anxiety
– Always correct
– Ominous
– Like a bad friend

Looks like:

- Are they uniform or varied?
- Grey, mottled
- Monochromatic
- Mirror-masked

– Beehive
– Linked like neurons
– Tin-foil helmets, tacky sci-fi
– Like a cult

Genres:

- Horror
- Pixar
- Psychological theatre
- Circus

– Gangster
– Greek theatre
– Barbershop quartet
– Musical theatre

Sounds like:

- Echo
- Unison
- Processed sound

– White noise
– Distorted

Exercise: Brain Chorus styles

Split into groups to explore the Brain Chorus in the following styles to show back:

- In song
- Not sung – *spoken*
- Only two actors: Mia and a single Brain Chorus member
- Wild card ×2 – making bold choices (based on the four provocations)

Observations: all of the above exercises help give you a way to create material. Make something, even if you don't like it, and then you have something concrete to work from. It's easier to make decisions from 'something' than from 'nothing'. The more you just go for it with the Brain Chorus, the more interesting it is to watch.

Question and answer with Chloë Lawrence-Taylor and Paul Sirett

CLT = Chloë Lawrence-Taylor, PS = Paul Sirett

Q: What message do you want people to take from this play?
CLT: Whatever it means to them. There is no one single message. There's a lot about how we look after each other. There will be a lot for caregivers and guardians to learn about how young people look after each other. That urge to care. It's not only about what young people learn while doing it, but also what they want to tell their caregivers and parents.

PS: Brains are very interesting. This is a 'by stealth' way to get people to engage with the human brain. I'm particularly interested in the voice we all have in our head – 'consciousness', whatever you want to call it, that's sometimes like a bad friend. Confronting what that voice is and putting it together with science, with brain function. Because a lot of brain study comes from exploring brain injury. Only when a particular part of the brain becomes damaged do we learn things about it.

Q: There are bold theatrical choices (puppetry, chorus work, etc.), where did these come from?
CLT: The puppetry came from my time working with students and young people who love being on stage and are very creative, but who don't feel able to speak on stage or have difficulty learning lines. I've worked with some brilliant non-verbal young actors and have seen puppetry bring out something very special in them. The aim was always to get as many people involved as possible in this play.

PS: I love theatre, and theatrical things. I adore puppetry. Chlöe and I were thinking about how to do the adults and thought it would be good fun to do them as puppets. Chlöe came up with the idea to use clothes and shoes and manipulate them, and we workshopped the idea in Oxford and it really worked. With the Brain Chorus, we just wanted to represent literally what happens in the brain, to show Mia's brain on stage.

Q: Where does 'Ay caramba' come from (it's not language some students use)?
CLT: It's a catchphrase from *The Simpsons*. Maybe let the students use their own equivalent to help them find the intention of how to say it.

Q: Is there a reason we don't meet the Brain Chorus until after the accident happens? And is there a reason the Brain Chorus seem to be the negative thoughts and when Mia directly speaks to the audience it is more positive?
CLT: Partly practicality – setting up the five friends and their relationships. The Prologue is her *after* having had support, it's different from the Mia who is having the bad thoughts.

PS: The Brain Chorus is triggered by events. They are like a hornets' nest that has been stirred up in her mind. The journey she goes on means that the voices become friendlier again, she has learned to live with her thoughts.

Q: Can you cast two people as Mia? It's a significant part for a single actor.
CLT: Where possible stick to one Mia and prioritise the clarity of storytelling. There are creative solutions, writing diaries, etc. that could mean the Mia actor doesn't need to learn all of these lines off by heart.

Q: Is there room to remove the swearing?
PS: If it's a deal-breaker, it can be cut.

CLT: It's a question about what your students are comfortable with. They can replace with something they are more comfortable with. 'Mental' in the context of the play is intentionally derogatory. It's a comment on how Mia feels about herself through how other people might describe her.

Q: Is Nish intentionally a troublemaker? Or just doesn't know how to help?
CLT: That might be for the actor to decide what feels right.

Q: Why is Nish 'under-stimulated'?
PS: I think that's up to you and the actor.

CLT: That line is a direct quote from a child I work with. Sometimes it's just a word that kids have picked up! You could say it in any way: it could be a useful justification. It could also be genuine. It's open to whoever plays that part.

Q: Does Tony's agoraphobia stem from his auditory loss or his PTSD?
PS: The auditory aspect compounds the rest, but it's not the main thing. Stepping outside the front door has nearly killed him, so he's decided 'I'm not doing that again', and then that's compounded by the loss of hearing.

Q: How did you see the Brain Chorus when you wrote it?
CLT: I don't write like that. I don't see it when I write – I just heard voices. Paul, did you?

PS: I see everything when I write! For me, they represent the white matter and the grey matter of the brain and connect through synapses that don't quite touch. They've always kind of been the neuronal part of the brain. I see people in grey tops and white trousers. But that's just me. There are so many ways of doing it. One of the most exciting things is seeing how you are going to solve that riddle.

CLT: And Paul and I don't always agree! It is open.

Q: Where did the tummy metaphor come from at the end?
CLT: It comes from a meme – a meme of a party where someone is complaining about their tummy hurting!

Q: Why are the adults puppets?
CLT: I sometimes feel an aversion to seeing children playing adults on stage. Partly it came from that, and also a desire for clarity of storytelling – sometimes group ages can range from thirteen to nineteen. But also we wanted it to be as fun as possible. We wanted to give as much opportunity as possible. And also for young people that like being on stage but don't necessarily want to speak.

PS: It was also a way of showing the gulf between the young people and the older people, a way of showing the older people as slightly alien to the young people.

Q: Is there something you would feel disappointed to see, or not see, in a production?
PS: I'd be disappointed if you didn't grab it by the scruff of the neck and squeeze every bit of joy you can out of it. Don't apologise for the song. Don't apologise for the

puppetry. Embrace it all and have fun! Especially as it's a difficult story. The more energy and fun you bring the better. We need to realise how complex the lives of these young people are. I'd like to come out with a smile on my face.

CLT: No, there's nothing prescriptive. I want to be surprised by whatever the young people dig deep into.

From a workshop led by Freyja Winterson
With notes by Luke Kernaghan

Saba's Swim

by Danusia Samal

Danusia Samal is an actor, writer and jazz singer from London. In 2018 she won the Theatre503 International Playwriting Award for *Out of Sorts*, which was later shortlisted for the George Devine Award. Her garage musical *Bangers* (in which she also performed) sold out at Soho Theatre and the Edinburgh Fringe. She is also a climate campaigner, founding the Green Rider to cut film and TV pollution. Writing for theatre includes *Cinderella* at Brixton House; *Bangers* for Soho Theatre, Cardboard Citizens and Paines Plough; *The Keyworker Cycles* at the Almeida; *Out of Sorts* at Theatre503; and *Busking It* for Shoreditch Town Hall and High Tide. Screenwriting includes *Doing It* for ZDF; *Virdee* for the BBC; *Gangs of London* (seasons two and three) for Sky; and *Bodies* for Netflix.

Characters

Saba *16 The glue holding the friendship group together, until she disappeared seven months ago. Saba used to be 'normal' – she liked cats, dancing in her room and sending memes to her friends. Until the dream came. Now she can't stop seeing pain all around her. Saba blames the adults for lying to them all. She's determined to take action.*

Bea *16 Saba's best friend since they were four. Bea's become the leader of the group since Saba left, but she feels totally lost without her. She has a difficult home life that she keeps secret. But since Bea found love, the world seems a bit brighter.*

Obie *16 Obie knows what he wants, and he works hard to achieve it. He can't wait to leave secondary school and start his new life. Obie resents Saba for leaving him to the mercy of the school bullies. But he also really misses her.*

Jay *16 Jay has always wanted to be famous, and that's what she throws all her energy into. A natural performer with a flair for the dramatic, Jay wears her heart on her sleeve. Sensitive, emotional and keen to prove to everyone how important the 'arts' are.*

Carla *16 Carla's grown up in privilege, and she's a bit embarrassed about it. She tries to pass on her good fortune to her friends as much as possible. She's kind-hearted and loyal, but a bit clueless about how the world works.*

Dean *16 Dean's charismatic, popular, funny. People dismiss him as the class clown, but he's also very loving and protective. Dean used to be in love with Saba, but she ghosted him. Now he's found love with Bea, he's not planning to let that go. As the only one in the group having to repeat his GCSEs, Dean is scared of being left behind.*

Walid *16 Dean's best friend. Walid's been in the UK for three years. His family came here as refugees. The horrors Walid's seen have left their mark on him, but he's determined to build a new life. He's intelligent, popular and funny, but also has a very vulnerable side.*

Thor *16 Thor is a careful observer of humans and how they behave. They're thoughtful, principled and intelligent. People are often surprised by Thor and Dean's friendship, but they understand each other. Thor doesn't speak much, but when they do, you're gonna want to listen.*

Notes

This is *your* play. If any slang or phrases feel unnatural to where you're from, feel free to adapt them! Just make sure the new line has a similar meaning.
Genders and pronouns in the text are suggestions only. Please use what feels comfortable for you and fits your group.
Dialogue in *italics* means the word is being stressed.
A slash (/) in dialogue marks where the next character should interrupt.
A dash (–) at the end of a line means a character is being interrupted or cut off.

The Dream

Bea, **Jay**, **Obie** and **Carla** *on stage, wearing prom outfits.* **Saba** *stands apart from them in normal clothes. The rush of waves.* **Saba** *addresses the audience.*

Saba I have this dream. I'm standing on a beach. Pink-blue sky, far as I can see. I breathe it in.

She breathes. **Bea** *speaks to the audience.*

Bea What to say about Saba? There isn't really – there's nothing that's gonna make you go: 'Ohhhhh, *that's* why it happened . . .' She's my best friend. Was. Is. *Is.*

Saba I walk towards the water. My feet sink into the sand. I think: 'This whole ocean belongs to me. I'm going to swim wherever I want.'

Jay Saba . . . well she's funny, like fun to be around. Likes attention – I mean we all do. Maybe she liked it more than other people but not in, like, a weird way . . .

Saba I step into the water. It's perfect.

Jay We'd always compete for the lead role in school shows. I normally got them. We used to . . . used to laugh about that. But maybe she didn't find it that / funny . . .

Obie I don't really like talking about people behind their backs. Even if you're saying nice things.

Jay Maybe it hurt her feelings.

Obie I think it just opens the door for you to start saying nasty things.

Carla Saba was kind of the glue holding our group together. We make less sense without her.

A sound like the rush of waves, made up of hundreds of whispered voices.

The water's at my chest now. I get ready to dive in: one, two, three!
. . . But something's dragging me back.
A woman. Holding my wrist. She's also trying to swim. But she's got her tiny baby on her back. And she's bleeding. The water around her is pink.
The baby is too weak to cry. It looks like it could break in my arms.
I dream this every night.

Lights change. A school bell rings. The friends get into a line. Nervous, apprehensive. **Saba** *is calming everyone down.*

Carla Oh my God, I can't remember any of the periodic table. My dad is going to kill me!

Saba Take deep breaths, it'll come back to you.

Saba *takes* **Carla**'s *hand.* **Carla** *breathes, slowly calming down. Beside them,* **Jay** *paces.*

Jay I just think it's backward to take away our phones. Like, in real life if I wanna know something, I'm gonna Google it, so why make me sit in a dusty room trying to remember something I'm never going to need?

Obie It's essential chemistry.

Jay Essential for you!

Saba I'm sure everyone's gonna be fine. And even if we don't pass, we have options. We're the lucky ones.

Bea Speak for yourself.

Saba (*putting an arm around* **Bea**) We *all* have options, OK? BFF promise.

Bea *nods, reassured. The bell sounds again. The friends line up, as if heading into the exam hall.*

Bea GCSE Mocks. Combined Science. Exam Paper 1. We sit down at 100-year-old desks in the Joseph Wilton Auditorium.

Jay You'd think they'd buy new desks.

Obie The auditorium was built in 1901, but got a refurb last year.
. . . Paid for by Carla's dad.

They all look at **Carla***. She doesn't notice.*

Carla Everything seems normal. Students whispering, teachers warning us about cheating . . .

Bea The timer starts . . .

Obie Those of us who revised pray we remember it all . . .

Jay Those of us who didn't pray for miracle . . .

They look to **Saba** *for her cue. But* **Saba** *just turns, leaves the space. A moment . . .*

Bea And Saba . . .
Well, she just, stands up. Walks out. And she doesn't come back.

Obie Not after the exam when we call her.

Bea Not the next day when we show up at her house.

Carla Not when we message her every day for the next few weeks.

Bea She just . . . disappears. And she doesn't tell anyone why.

Obie It's not like her. It confuses us. Maybe there's been a mistake? But as days become weeks . . .

Jay Weeks become months . . .

Bea And nothing we try works, we start to wonder:

Everyone Was it something we did?

Carla Jay says it was Obie who put too much pressure on Saba.

Jay (*to* **Obie**) Always forcing her to study – like that's the only way to make something of yourself!

Bea Obie has other ideas . . .

Obie (*to* **Jay**) It's you who made her feel like a loser for not having as many followers as you!

Obie *and* **Jay** *glare at each other.*

Carla Jay on one side, Obie on the other. We're forced to pick.

Bea I think Obie's a bit patronising . . .

Carla I think Jay's a bit shallow . . .

Carla & Bea But I try not to get involved.

Bea And after seven long months without her . . . our group just kind of . . . splits.

They leave one by one. **Saba** *takes the space.*

Saba In the dream, the woman with the baby begs me: 'Take him, please, it's the only way he'll survive.'
And I pause. For a moment. But then I think:
'How can I carry on swimming if I have a dying baby on my back?'
So move away. I kick my legs, I splash. Another wave is coming. It gets taller and taller as it rushes towards me. I get ready to be carried over it . . . freedom!
And then I see them.
Their faces in the sea foam. Thousands of people. There's faces I recognise – family, friends. Faces I don't. They're screaming, begging, calling out . . . too many to ignore. The wave is coming, closer and closer. Their suffering is coming. They are going to drown me. I open my mouth, to beg them to stop. But I choke, swallow seawater. And it tastes like. It tastes like . . .
Iron. Like blood.
The wave breaks over my head. A thousand screams.
I am sinking. Sinking under it all.
And that's when I know. I can't carry on swimming.
Because everything has changed.

A pause. A buzzing. Lights flicker, then: black.

Freedom

Bea (*off*) And then there was light!

A click, then light floods the stage. We're in a classroom. **Bea** *and* **Jay** *enter, cautious. They relax when they realise the coast is clear. From somewhere nearby, we can hear the sound of a party in full swing.*

Saba *watches them from the shadows.* **Jay** *waits a moment, then:*

Jay So? Can I see it now?

Bea *hesitates. They're interrupted by the sound of* **Obie** *and* **Carla** *bickering off stage:*

Obie (*off*) Carla, this area's off limits! What you playing at?!

Carla (*off*) I'll explain in a minute . . . Just in here . . .

Carla *enters, dragging* **Obie** *with her. He doesn't notice the others yet. Thinking they're alone, he's suddenly nervous:*

Obie Carla . . . I know it's prom night, and like, I'd be the luckiest guy in the world if something happened between us, but we're friends, and I don't –

Carla Eugh. Obie. No!

She spins him round. **Obie** *is less than pleased to see* **Bea** *and* **Jay**.

Obie What's going on?

Bea Obie. Thanks for coming. I know things haven't been great between us –

Obie Understatement of the year!

Bea But this is important. We think Saba's contacted us.

Obie *freezes. Wtf.* **Bea** *pulls out a small envelope – her name scrawled across the front.*

Bea I was dancing earlier, I felt something brush against me. And when I looked down . . . this was pinned to my dress.

She carefully takes the letter out of its envelope and reads. As she does, **Saba** *steps into the light.* **Bea**'s *voice slowly morphs into hers:*

Bea 'To Bea, Jay, Carla and Obie: Congratulations! You made it. You finished your five-year sentence at Cawdor Secondary!
. . . I'm sorry I'm not celebrating with you. I know you've probably been worried, blaming yourselves. Please don't. What happened to me / is difficult to explain . . .'

Saba Is difficult to explain to people who are still swimming. I couldn't drag you down with me! But I also couldn't pretend.
So I did the only thing I could. I went away. Spent time thinking about the things I've seen. About what I could *do* about them. And I think I know now. I'd like a chance to show you all. If you want to. If you're ready.

Obie What is she on about? She hates swimming, we all do –

Jay Shh!

Saba I've left some clues around Cawdor High. Things I hope will help you understand where my head was at then. And where it's at now. So if you want to find me . . .

Saba & Bea Follow the clues, that's where I'll be. Love Saba.

A beat, then:

Obie It's a prank. That could literally be from anyone.

Jay It's *her* handwriting, genius.

Obie As if you'd know what Saba's handwriting looks like! You don't even know your own!

Jay What's that supposed to mean?

Obie It means I can't remember the last time I saw you pick up a pen and write something.

Jay Screw you, you stuck-up –

*A fight might kick off, but **Bea** intervenes.*

Bea Guys! Can we focus? We've been waiting for this for months. An answer to what happened to our friend!

Obie Is she still our friend?

They all stare at him, stunned.

Obie Cos a friend doesn't disappear with no explanation. Or block you. Or keep you awake night after night wondering if it's something *you* did.

Jay How can you be so cold? What if she's been lying in bed, sick, for the last seven months? She's finally got the strength to pick up a pen –

Obie If Saba wanted to contact us she would've. Sorry, but I'm out.

*He starts to go, **Bea** grabs his hand. Raw:*

Bea All those nights lying awake, didn't you ever think: 'I miss her so much. I'd give anything to speak to her and find out what happened'?
. . . 'Cause I did.

Jay Me too.

Carla And me!

*A beat. **Bea** holds **Obie**'s wrist tight, looking him in the eye. Eventually **Obie** also nods.*

Bea Good. Then let's put it to a vote. If you want to find Saba tonight, raise your hands.

*They all do. Except **Obie**. **Bea** takes charge.*

Bea Good. Let's split up, cover more ground. Obie, you stay here and keep watch.

Obie I told you, I'm out.

Jay You can't be 'out'. Democracy has spoken.

Obie Since when are we a democracy?

Jay (*losing patience*) Argh! Just be a good friend, Obie! FOR ONCE!

Jay *storms off.* **Carla** *and* **Bea** *follow.* **Obie** *is left alone.* **Saba** *watches him, folding a piece of paper. It grows darker.*

The Uninvited Guests

Scared, **Obie** *mocks* **Jay** *to cheer himself up.*

Obie 'Argh! Be a good friend, Obie – for once!'
I love how I'm the bad guy! *I'm* the one who's been bullied every day since Saba left. *I'm* the one who took care of Carla when Bea and Jay started leaving her out – even though hanging with the poshest girl in school is like having *another* target on my back . . .
(*He groans in frustration.*) It's always me! Man, I just wanted *one night* without drama!

Saba *throws the paper aeroplane she's been folding at* **Obie**. *He turns round.* **Saba** *hides.*

Obie Who did that? Who's there? Hello?
. . . Saba?

He notices the paper aeroplane on the ground, picks it up nervously. He reads aloud.

Obie 'Doctor Obie knows what he wants to be . . .
And that's an impressive thing . . .'

He finishes reading in silence. Whatever's written there clearly upsets him.

Obie Wow. Really nice! Why don't you come out and say that to my face?

There's a silence. No one seems to be there. **Obie** *tuts, crumples the paper and starts to go –*

As three figures in hoodies jump out at him! They drag **Obie** *to the ground. He yells and fights back, but they soon have him pinned to the floor.* **Obie** *struggles and screams.*

Attacker One OK, OK calm down!

The first attacker pulls off his hood, revealing himself: **Dean**. **Dean**'s *friends* **Walid** *and* **Thor** *also pull off their hoods.* **Obie** *seethes.*

Dean Gotchaaaaa! We had you shook, innit?

Obie No . . .

Dean (*picking up the crumpled paper*) What's this?

Obie (*trying to snatch it back*) Give it back!

Dean *dodges* **Obie**, *waving the paper.*

Dean Little love note, is it? Didn't know you were such a player, Obie! That why you surround yourself with girls all the time? Who is it? Carla? Jay? Bea?

There's an edge of jealousy as **Dean** *tries to read the note and work out who it's from. Furious,* **Obie** *attacks* **Dean**, *wrestling the paper from his grip.* **Thor** *and* **Walid** *try to drag them apart as* **Bea**, **Carla** *and* **Jay** *enter.*

Bea Obie! Are you OK? We heard shouting . . .

She trails off when she sees **Dean** *and* **Obie** *tangled up together.* **Dean** *is suddenly shy.*

Dean Sorry. Sorry, Bea. Just lads being lads, innit.
(*Correcting himself.*) Lads in like a, gender neutral way, obviously.

Bea . . . Right. Why are you lot up here? Prom is downstairs.

Dean Well, I was . . . Looking for you.

The rest of the group roll their eyes. **Bea** *clocks it, uncomfortable. She notices the paper in* **Obie**'s *hand, changes subject.*

Bea What's that?

Obie It's mine.

Bea Can I see it?

Obie No.

Bea *approaches.* **Obie** *is about to rip the letter up, but* **Dean** *snatches it and hands it to* **Bea**. **Bea** *reads aloud:*

Bea 'Doctor Obie knows what he wants to be . . .
And that's an impressive thing . . .
Always swore that we would leave this school
Free adults, prepped for our swim
But your dream's a drop in the ocean, Doc
These hands will ne'er be clean
More wounds to patch than you'll ever heal
So give up, write a new scene!'

Jay (*grabbing the note*) 'These hands will ne'er be clean' – that's the Scottish play!

Dean What Scottish play?

Jay Shakespeare. The one we can't say.

Dean That's a weird name for a play.

Jay It's about guilt. Doing something evil and not being able to wash it away. Maybe Saba's trying to say one of us has, like, wronged her?

Bea *looks uncomfortable.* **Jay** *looks at* **Obie**.

Obie Why are you staring at me for? Go find a mirror!

Jay *ignores him, reading over the letter.*

Jay This is probably our first clue . . .

Obie It's not Shakespeare and it's not a clue. It's a letter to *me*. Give it back.

Jay (*ignoring him*) Leave this with me, guys, I played Sherlock Holmes in drama camp. I can work this out!

Dean Work what out? What's going on with Saba?

Carla We think she pinned a note to Bea's dress earlier. And now there's this letter to Obie –

Obie *elbows* **Carla** *to shut her up.*

Dean Wait – Saba's here tonight? I heard she'd gone to rehab!

Bea Who said that?!

Dean (*glancing at his friends*) I dunno. Lots of people?

Walid I heard she went to live in America. And Thor told us they saw Saba dancing down the marshes at midnight.

Thor *nods solemnly.*

Bea Well, none of that is true.

Obie How do you know? It's not like she told us anything.

Jay Could you all shut up for a second? I'm trying to think! 'More wounds to patch . . .' I'm thinking plasters, bandages . . .

Walid A first-aid box.

Carla There's one in the staffroom!

Jay Yes! Then we have 'free adults, prepped for our swim' – what could that mean?

Dean She can't mean a pool. We don't have one at Cawdor High.

They look at him like 'duh'. **Obie** *has a thought.*

Obie Hang on – do you think she's talking about . . .

Bea When Mr Wilde took everyone to the leisure centre for a swimming / lesson?

Jay But we all hid in the locker rooms? You're a genius, Bea!

Obie*'s a bit put out.* **Jay** *doesn't care.*

Jay Right! Then we've got 'throw it out . . .'

Dean School bins!

Jay (*with surprise*) Thank you, Dean.

Dean Not just a pretty face, innit? I can help you guys, if you like . . . Me and the mandem.

Obie *signals an obvious 'No' to* **Jay***.*

Jay That would be great, Dean.

Walid*,* **Thor** *and* **Obie** *are all a bit put out by this. But* **Dean** *puffs his chest proudly.*

Jay OK. Carla and Thor – staffroom. Bea and Dean – locker rooms, and Walid and Obie . . . BINS.

Obie (*under his breath*) I knew it.

They move off, on a mission. **Saba** *enters, holding a tray. She watches them go. Blackout.*

Carla and Thor 1

Saba *lays out a kettle, mugs, instant coffee, sugar and milk. She places a first-aid kit on the floor – and now we're in the staffroom.* **Saba** *hears a voice from off and slips away just as* **Carla** *enters.* **Carla** *heads for the mugs, studying them.* **Thor** *starts searching the first-aid kit methodically, laying each item out.*

Carla 'Sex Bomb' – bet this one belongs to Ms Thompson.
Can't get over how many coffees adults drink in a day, can you? My mum has, like, six. I can't imagine *ever* liking coffee. Except maybe salted caramel frappes.
Do you like coffee, Thor?

Thor *looks at* **Carla***. The silence stretches.* **Carla** *covers her embarrassment.*

Carla It's weird being in the staffroom without the teachers here. Feel like I'm looking through my parents' underwear drawer!

Thor *is grossed out.* **Carla** *backtracks.*

Carla Not that I do that, I just . . . You found anything yet?
(**Thor** *shakes their head.*) I mean how would we even know what was a clue? A plaster could mean – 'I want to heal the wounds', a pair of scissors could be 'I want to cut ties' . . . I don't really know what Saba would choose. Maybe that's cos I don't know *her*? We hung out every day for nearly five years, but when she walked out of that exam hall, I couldn't even *begin* to tell you what was going through her head, you see?

Does **Thor** *see? They certainly don't say.*

Carla The way we all became friends, it was just a thing that *happened*. Then it just . . . stuck. Like you, Walid and Dean. You've got nothing in common, but you're mates, right?

Thor *shrugs.* **Carla** *waits for more. It doesn't come. She hovers, awkward.* **Saba** *sneaks in behind them with a tray that holds a kettle, instant coffee, sugar and milk.*

She slips away just as **Carla** *turns to see the tray. Relieved to have a task, she starts to prepare a coffee.*

Carla Are you not speaking to me cos of the things you've heard about my father? Because, I know people say he sent me to this school as a publicity stunt, to win votes, but it was *me* that wanted to come here. And you know, he's actually donated loads of money to Cawdor High? It would be, like, shut down if it wasn't for him!

Thor *just looks at her, a half smile.*

Carla Not that I'm saying you have to be grateful, and obviously if you don't want to talk to me you don't have to . . . it's just . . . this search is gonna be a lot harder if we're not, like, communicating, you know?

She holds out the mug to **Thor**.

Carla I made you a coffee?

Thor *takes the coffee and sips. They begin to choke and cough.*

Carla Are you OK? Did I put too much sugar in? Thor? Thor!

Carla *tries to do the Heimlich manoeuvre. She doesn't know how. She rushes to the medical box, searching for something that will help, making a total mess of everything* **Thor** *has carefully laid out. She finds a box holding cough medicine, rips it open to see:*

Carla I found something!

She holds up the bottle. There is writing on it. She's so pleased with herself she completely forgets **Thor**'*s choking fit.* **Thor** *swigs coffee to clear their throat, coughs, as* **Carla** *reads aloud:*

Carla 'Ask us to *examine* the world
But refuse to let us see
These aren't tests, they are a *mock*ery
Between the line's the real message you need . . .'
What is that supposed to –

But **Thor**'*s understood something. They head off with purpose.*

Carla Wait, where are you going?

Dean and Bea 1

Carla *follows* **Thor** *off.* **Saba** *sets up the space – as the girls' changing rooms. As* **Bea** *and* **Dean** *enter, she quickly hides something, then ducks out of sight.* **Dean** *is mesmerised by the room.*

Dean Woah. To think of all the girls that have changed in here over the years . . .

Bea Dean!

Dean No, I just mean – it's so different. It actually smells clean in here!

Bea Surely the boys' changing room isn't *that* bad?

Dean Everything is sticky and the whole place reeks of piss and Lynx.

Bea shudders. **Dean** *takes her hand.*

Bea Dean . . .

Dean But there's no one here, and you look so beautiful . . .

Bea (*moving away*) We need to focus. Tonight is about Saba.

Dean (*mumbling*) When's it not?

Bea What was that?

Dean Nothing . . .

Bea Something happened to her. Something massive. And instead of being a good friend –

Dean What more could you have done? She didn't wanna talk to you!

Bea I could have not got together with the guy she liked!

They've clearly had this argument before.

Dean For the last time! Saba never told me she liked me. She never told *you*.

Bea Didn't need to. A friend just knows . . .

Dean (*snapping*) No! A friend doesn't 'just know'. You can't read someone's mind, Bea!
(*Softer now.*) I love you. And we're happy, right?
(*She nods.*) So why feel guilty about that?

He hugs her. She slowly relaxes. **Saba** *watches them from the shadows.*

Bea I just miss her so much. I can't understand why she didn't talk to me.

Dean Well, you'll get to ask her soon!
(*He shudders.*) Not gonna lie, it is freaking me out a bit though.

Bea What is?

Dean That she could be watching us right now. She coulda been watching us for months. Sneaking around, playing pranks . . .

Bea *stares at him, lightbulb moment. She heads over to some lockers.*

Dean What are you doing?

Bea It wasn't just that swimming lesson with Mr Wilde. The five of us often hung out here. We'd smuggle Obie in, keep games and snacks in my locker . . .

Dean Sick, you got snacks, I'm starving –

Bea *finds her locker, twiddles the padlock.*

Bea Few weeks after Saba left, our Jenga went missing. Then my multi-pack of Skittles. Then Cards Against Humanity. Only us five have the code. Jay blamed Obie. Obie blamed Jay. I thought it was Carla. But maybe it wasn't any of them. Maybe it was *her.*

She gets the locker open. It's empty, except for a gift bag. **Bea** *takes it out, reads the tag.*

Bea 'For Dean . . . from Saba.' What the hell is this?

Dean *looks caught out. Lights fade . . .*

Obie and Walid 1

As **Saba** *wheels on some bins in another part of the space. She leaves as* **Obie** *is marched on by* **Jay** *and* **Walid**. **Jay** *shoves* **Obie** *towards a bin.*

Jay You're gonna search these for clues. And if you try to leave, Walid will stop you.

Obie Why aren't *you* going through bins?

Jay Cos *my* job is to go back into the party and gather witness statements.

Obie That isn't fair!

Jay What's not fair is you withholding vital evidence and jeopardising our investigation.

Obie It's not an investigation and you're not Sherlock Holmes! It's Saba making idiots of us, and you lot all falling for it!

Jay Saba's not like that.

Obie How do you know? You haven't seen her in seven months!

Jay Obie. All you have to do is say sorry.

Obie NO!

Jay Fine. Walid, he's all yours.

She storms off, **Obie** *yells after her, angry.*

Obie You know, I've wanted to be a doctor my whole life. Saba called that dream 'a drop in the ocean' – pointless. That's what she chose to say to me after seven MONTHS of silence. *That's* the friend you're looking for!

No response. **Walid** *and* **Obie** *stand in silence.* **Obie** *feels awkward after his outburst. For something to do, goes to the bin, hand over his nose as he reluctantly rummages. From inside the school we can hear the prom still going.* **Walid** *takes a packet of cigarettes out of his pocket.* **Obie** *stares.*

Walid This is why people bully you. Stop staring.

Obie I just don't get why you'd do that.

Walid It keeps my hands busy.

Obie But what about cancer? Lung failure? Asthma, infertility, bad teeth – what?

Walid *is laughing at* **Obie**. *Can't help it.*

Obie What's funny?

Walid (*doing an impression of* **Obie**) 'What about getting hit by a car the next time you cross the street? What about choking on a piece of popcorn? What about getting swallowed by a whale?'

Obie I'm just saying it's a shame. That you've let Dean influence you –

Walid How do you know it's not *me* influencing him?

Obie Because. He's *Dean*, and you're –

Walid What?! Too weak to know my own mind?

Obie No, I just mean –

Walid You know I used to be like you. I nagged my aunties and uncles whenever they smoked: 'That stuff will kill you. Don't you want to live till you're one hundred?!'
(*Matter of fact.*) Then one day bombing started. Some of my family were killed by explosions. Some by dirty water. Some by sickness that would've been healed if the hospital was still standing.
Things don't happen as you expect. So why worry about a cigarette?

Obie *is silent – he has no answer to this.* **Walid** *takes out his cigarette.*

Walid You should focus on finding your friend instead.

Obie Saba's not my friend any more. You heard what she wrote about me.

A beat as he searches for the right words.

Walid It wasn't about *you*. She was saying: 'There is more pain in the world than you can ever heal. Let's try building a world with *less pain* instead.'
Like all the doctors in my city, standing outside a bombed hospital. Maybe it wasn't more doctors we needed, but less bombs?

A pause as **Obie** *takes that in – impressed by how* **Walid**'s *mind works.* **Walid** *goes to light his cigarette. On impulse,* **Obie** *grabs it and chucks it to the ground, grinding it under his foot.*

Walid What the –?

Obie (*doing an impression of* **Walid**) 'That stuff will kill you. Don't you want to live till you're one hundred?!'

Walid (*laughing*) Fine! But give me something else to do. My hands need to be busy.

Obie notices Walid's hands are shaking, a nervous tic he can't control. He digs a packet of crisps from his pocket and offers it to Walid.

Walid   Like these are any better for you than cigarettes!

Obie   At least they're tastier.

Walid   Fair enough.

He takes some crisps. They eat together.

Obie   You really think that's what Saba meant?

Walid   Maybe.

Obie   I just thought she was trying to get our attention.

Walid   Sometimes when people ask for attention, it's because they need it.

Obie   I just wish she'd said something before.

Walid   Maybe she was scared.

Obie   Saba? No way!

Walid   Everyone's scared sometimes.

Obie   Even you?

Walid   *Especially* me.
(*Beat, then.*) . . . Like how I treated you this year. That was fear.

Obie   What are you talking about?

Walid   I watched people make fun of you. I joined in. I was scared if it wasn't you, it would be me. I owe you an apology.

It's painful for Obie, but he tries to be casual.

Obie   It's cool, man. It was a joke.

Walid   A joke should not hurt that much though. I'm sorry.

Obie   I . . . Thank you.

Walid   Friends?

Obie   School's over – it's probably a bit late for that.

Walid   I don't think so. We have our whole lives ahead of us, right?

They share a smile – a promise in it. As Obie heads back to the bins . . .

Dean and Bea 2

We come back to Dean, and a stressed Bea.

Bea   Why is it addressed to you?

Dean I dunno.

Bea *I'm* the one who – I'm her oldest friend!
(*With sudden fear.*) Don't open it.

Dean I thought you wanted to know what she has to say.

Bea What if it changes everything?

Dean Nothing will change how I feel about you. So don't worry, OK?

Bea *is doubtful, but nods.* **Dean** *opens the bag. Inside it is a toy teddy bear with a heart on its tummy.* **Dean** *squeezes it. An instrumental of a cheesy love song [company's choice!] plays.*

Saba *appears on stage. Her voice comes out of the teddy bear. This can either be a recording or* **Dean** *and* **Bea** *acting as if this is happening.*

Saba Hello, Dean. Sorry about the music. Asked the man in the shop, but they didn't have any teddy bears that played Drill *[or whatever music the company thinks* **Dean** *likes]*.
I wanted to say congratulations to you and Bea. Finding love's a big deal at our age. I'm jealous! Not in like a: 'YOU'RE MINE' way . . . I had my chance, and I blew it, right?

Bea (*turning to* **Dean**)   WHAT?

Saba I've just never trusted love. I wish I did. Maybe it would've helped me forget all those screaming faces. Maybe back when you said those three words to me, I should've said them too, and everything would be OK now.
But we can't change the past, only the future. So meet me where it happened. I want to ask you and Bea a question. This time it'll be up to *you* to answer.

Saba *goes. An awkward silence.* **Bea**'s *world is rocked. She manages to speak.*

Bea You . . . said you loved her?

Dean It was years ago . . .

Bea What happened?

Dean Nothing. I never got an answer. So after a while I just . . . stopped.

Bea You don't just stop loving someone!

Dean Of course you do.

Bea So, what, you'll stop loving me too?

Dean No! That's different . . .

Bea Why?

He can't answer. **Bea** *makes a decision.*

Bea Right. I need to speak to Saba. Where did it happen?

Dean What?

Bea Where did you tell her you loved her?

Dean It was Year 8. Just after morning assembly. Outside Wilton Auditorium.

Bea *processes that. Then heads off.*

Dean Bea, wait!

*He follows **Bea** off, calling after her.*

Carla and Thor 2

Thor *and* **Carla** *enter, rifling through exam papers.* **Thor** *still carrying their coffee.*

Carla Haha! Look, I just found Dean's maths paper – let's see all the questions he got wrong . . .

Thor *slaps the exam paper out of her hand.*

Carla What? It's only mocks, we already know he failed the real ones!

She laughs. **Thor** *doesn't.* **Thor** *shoves another exam paper at* **Carla**, *pointing to the name at the front.* **Carla** *reads.*

Carla 'Saba Carlisle – Combined Science. Exam Paper 1.'
Oh wow. This is it. This is the mock paper she walked out of.

Thor *nods.* **Carla** *hesitates, then carefully opens the exam paper. On the first page, she reads:*

Carla 'Why I'm not doing this exam – by Saba Carlisle:
What's the point of GCSEs – if there's no clean air to breathe?
What's the point of English lit, when armies bomb people to shit?
What's the point of grades, reports, merits, what's the point of staying here
When I could come back in a few months, with a much better idea?'

A beat as **Carla** *works it out. She turns to* **Thor**.

Carla Thor, drink your coffee. We've got somewhere to be.

She exits with purpose. **Thor** *swigs their coffee and follows.*

Obie and Walid 2

Now it's just **Obie** *and* **Walid**. **Obie** *is rooting through recycling bins,* **Walid** *organising things they've found into neat piles.* **Obie** *pulls out a ripped-up maths book.*

Obie Remember this one?

Walid Ugh, algebra, throw it away.

Obie   You're good at algebra!

Walid   Doesn't mean I like it.

Obie *puts the book aside. A beat, as he builds up the courage to broach this:*

Obie   You know, I heard Mr Reynolds telling you to apply to Ravensbourne College. That's where I'm going next year.

Walid   I can't afford it.

Obie   Nobody can – except Carla. I got a scholarship, you probably still have time to apply –

Walid   I mean I can't afford to not work. I will be starting an apprenticeship in construction.

Obie *stares at* **Walid** *in shock.* **Walid** *catches him. Embarrassed,* **Obie** *goes back to searching the bins. He finds something. Takes a moment to realise what it is. Yells out and holds up –*

Obie   The Scottish play! It's Saba's copy. Her name's on the front!

Walid   Go through it! There might be a clue.

Obie *(flicking through)*   Where's that line about blood on hands . . . I bet Jay made it up . . .

Walid   Your hands are bleeding.

Obie   No, that's not it.

Walid   No, your hands are bleeding.

Obie *looks down, noticing the cut.*

Obie   Oh! It's just a paper cut.

He carries on rifling through the play. But **Walid** *is concerned. He pulls a wipe from his pocket, takes* **Obie**'s *hand.* **Obie** *is embarrassed and tries to wave it off, but* **Walid** *calmly begins cleaning the cut. A tender moment between them. As* **Walid** *pulls out a plaster:*

Obie   You just carry those around?

Walid   My little sister falls over a lot.
(*He puts on the plaster carefully.*) You're staring at me again.

Obie   No, I'm not.

Walid   Yes, you are. You're staring like you feel sorry for me.

Obie   No, not *sorry* for you, I just . . . Do you remember when we performed this play to the whole school?

Walid   Year 9, yes. I had just arrived in the UK.

Obie Yeah, and Ms Hamish said the way to understand Shakespeare is not just read it but *feel* it, like a heartbeat, and you . . . You played Macbeth but you didn't really speak English yet so you did it in your own language and . . . and everyone went silent when you spoke. Because even though it wasn't English, we understood what you were saying. You felt it like a heartbeat and so did we.
(*He means this.*) You've always been special, Walid. You could choose any future you wanted.

Walid And I am choosing construction.

He takes the play from **Obie**, *flicking through it.*

Walid I've seen so much get torn down. I want to rebuild. There's power in that. More power than pretending to say the words of a 500-year-old bald English man.

Obie Pretending?

Walid I wasn't saying the words from the play. I was just talking. Enjoying that you all had to listen – for once.

Obie But . . . You can't rewrite Shakespeare!

Walid You sound like Jay.

Obie YOU CAN'T!

Walid Oh, really? Your friend Saba doesn't think so. Listen to this:
(*Reads from the book, Shakespeare style.*) 'Two lies were told,
As happy prologues to the swelling act
Of growing to a teen.
Teachers well-intentioned soliciting
Did not mean ill, but did not do good: why,
Why did they promise happiness and success,
When they know the brutal truth? A cursed Year 7 of Cawdor . . .'

He stops. **Obie** *grabs the book from him.*

Walid I remember that speech. Macbeth is trying to decide if his life should stay the same, or if it should change forever.

Obie I thought you didn't say the lines from the play.

Walid I did my own version. Looks like Saba has too. So, what does *this* one mean?

A beat. **Obie** *thinks.*

Obie 'A cursed year 7' . . . I think it means I know where she is.

He exits, **Walid** *follows. The space goes dark.*

Wilton Hall

We hear footsteps in the darkness.

Jay Hello? Saba?

A spotlight suddenly appears on **Jay**. *She shields her eyes. Tries to make a joke of it.*

Jay Good one! I guess I *have* always loved the spotlight.
(*Beat, then.*) I knew you'd be here. I kind of knew from the second we read Obie's letter.
. . . I haven't told the others. I thought you might just want to talk. One on one. I know what it feels like to want to get away from your life for a bit. It's what I do when I get on stage – become someone else. Only time I feel at peace.

A silence. **Jay** *waits. Then from the darkness,* **Saba** *emerges. They lock eyes.*

Jay Hi, Saba. How are you?

Saba *hesitates, about to speak, when:*

Obie (*off*) There she is!

The moment is broken as the rest of the group enter. They all speak loudly, interrupting each other. It's overwhelming:

Carla We found you! I can't believe / it!

Dean Like catching a Pokémon shiny!

Walid No one plays Pokémon any more, / Dean.

Obie What was with that letter you sent / me?

Jay Obie's just upset that I solved the clues.

Obie No, I'm not! And no, you / didn't!

Carla Sabs, that poem in your exam paper was so weird!
(**Thor** *shoots* **Carla** *a look.*) I mean – Thor made me read it!

Bea *reaches* **Saba**. *She doesn't say anything. Just pulls* **Saba** *into a huge hug.* **Saba**'*s taken aback for a moment. Then she reciprocates.*

Bea I've missed you so much.

Saba I've missed you, too.

Bea We were so happy when we read your note. Things haven't been the same without you. But if you needed to talk to us, why didn't you just call?

A beat. **Saba** *looks around, to see if someone's going to jump in. But they're finally quiet.*

Saba I needed to check. If you were ready to listen.

Jay We're all ears, Sab.

They all show agreement. **Saba** *hesitates, takes a deep breath. Then:*

Saba I can't swim any more.

They look at her blankly. Look at each other. Finally . . .

Dean . . . Maybe you shouldn't have skipped that swimming class then?

Obie Oh my God, why are you so THICK?!

Dean Don't call me thick!

Obie She doesn't mean actual swimming! It's a metaphor! Right, Saba?

A beat. She is seeing it as she speaks it.

Saba It's what I see in my dream. An ocean ahead of me, a voice telling me to swim. And I know I'm supposed to. Everyone else does. But the things that happen in the dream – they change how I see stuff in the day. Like, I watch the news and recognise people. The dad buried under rubble. The children running from bombs. The woman with the sleeping bag who lives behind Argos. I *know* them. I look in their eyes every night as this wave of . . . of everything, of all their pain . . . crashes over me.
I tried going doctor. They said I was just stressed about by GCSEs. I searched: 'What do I do about all the bad things that are happening?' There was a protest in town. I went, stood with the shouting people, felt better for a bit. But nothing actually *changed*. I thought I was crazy, cos you all seemed fine. But then I realised – no. It's what they're teaching us that's crazy. To keep swimming like nothing's wrong, telling ourselves we're kind, caring people when just a little way away, a *person*, people like *us*, are drowning.
(*To* **Obie**, **Jay**, **Bea** *and* **Carla** *in turn.*) And becoming a doctor, a celebrity, or falling in love, or making Mummy and Daddy proud – it's not gonna stop that happening. We *have* to do something bigger.

An awkward silence. **Carla** *ventures first.*

Carla So, you left school . . . because of a dream?

Saba Because I couldn't stay here, knowing nothing they've taught us to care about matters.

Everyone's confused and concerned. **Jay** *tries to be helpful and lighten the mood.*

Jay I mean, I get it, babe. Cawdor High hasn't prepared us for real life! We're *all* scared about what's coming next . . .

Obie Yeah, but that doesn't mean we give up on the future! Look at Walid!

They all look at **Walid**. *He is uncomfortable.*

Obie He saw his home destroyed. He lost all hope. But now he's found his calling!

Walid I'm just doing a construction apprenticeship . . .

Obie Because there's power in rebuilding! You could come back, Sab, redo the exams you missed –

Jay Here he goes with the exams . . .

Obie (*snapping at* **Jay**) They literally shape the. Rest. Of. Your. Life.

Dean I'll be retaking my mine too, / Sab!

Bea (*shooting him a look*) But the most important thing is your health. If you're feeling depressed . . .

Carla You can always donate money somewhere. That's what my dad –

Saba Oh my GOD! YOU'RE DOING IT AGAIN! YOU'RE NOT LISTENING!

Her outburst stops everyone in their tracks. **Saba** *sighs. Gentler now:*

You know, I tried to talk to you – before I walked out that day. I tried so many times. You all brushed it off, changed subject, made a joke. That's why I did all this. Poems, letters, clues. To get you to pay attention. To get you to understand what I'm feeling, why I left, and why I'm asking you now: Will you help me burn this all down?

A beat, then:

Jay I'm sorry, burn what down?

Saba This building – the Joseph Wilton Auditorium.
(*Off their stunned silence.*) Cos this is where the adults lied to us. Assemblies telling us we can achieve anything if we work hard, pointless talent shows, meaningless exams . . . By destroying it we tell them – we know. We know you've been distracting us from the things that matter, and we're not going to let you do it any more! So who's with me?!

A beat. Then they all whoop and cheer. All except **Jay** *and* **Walid**.

Dean Hell, yeah! Burn it to a crisp!

Carla Go on, Saba!

Bea You show them!

Obie Screw this school and screw Wilton Auditorium!

Jay *cuts the celebrations short, serious.*

Jay I'm sorry, but has everyone gone mad? You can't burn down a theatre!

Saba Why not?

Jay Because . . . theatres are expression, and art, and –

Saba We didn't do art here, Jay. We did *Bugsy Malone*. *[or another show your group did!]*

Jay This is about me getting picked for the leads, isn't it? Tallulah to your Dancer Number 3. Lady Macbeth to your spear carrier. The day you walked out, we'd just got cast for the second-term show. I was Juliet, you were sweeping the stage –

Saba Don't be silly. I don't care about that stuff.

Jay Then why destroy the thing I love?

Saba   Because it's not all about you, Jay. There's bigger dramas out there in the world.

Jay   Of course there is! There's always a bigger drama happening somewhere. Doesn't mean the little ones aren't important. If you burn this building down, nobody out there's gonna suffer any less. But the people that love this theatre will be gutted.

Obie   No one loves it but you, Jay.

Jay   That's not true.

Dean   I hate it.

Bea   Me too.

Carla   And me.

Jay   Seriously?

They all nod. **Jay** *is horrified.*

Jay   Uncultured trash, the lot of you! I'm gonna go tell Ms Hamish.

Bea   Good luck finding her. Last I saw, she was pretty drunk.

Jay   Mr Reynolds then.

Dean   He's getting busy with Mr Green.

Jay   Ms Ravens?

They all shake their heads.

Obie   Oh no. Looks like this building will be burnt to a crisp before you can find anyone!

A beat. **Jay** *hovers, unsure what to do, then runs out yelling:*

Jay   Ms Hamish! Ms Hamish!

Her shouts are heard off stage. **Saba** *turns to the rest of the room.*

Saba   OK, where were we?

A beat, then everyone breaks into laughter.

Dean   That was brilliant!

Obie   You properly got her.

Bea   'Ms Hamish, Ms Hamish!'

Carla   Good one, Sab. So funny!

Saba *looks at them all, surprised.*

Saba   It's not a joke. I've been gathering wood all day. There's a big pile in the other room.
(*She gets out her phone.*) I also wrote this. To post after the fire starts. What do you think?

She passes her phone to **Obie**. **Bea** *peers over his shoulder. The others join, one by one, their horror rising as they read what's on the screen.*

Dean Shit. You're for real?

Saba Never been realer.

Beat. Then **Walid** *begins to hyperventilate.*

Walid I can't . . . I can't . . . no!

He's panicking. **Dean***'s by his side instantly.*

Dean It's OK, it's OK, bro, I'm here.

Walid My hands . . . please, something for my hands . . .

His hands are shaking uncontrollably. **Dean** *roots into his jacket pocket and pulls out the love-heart teddy. He gives it to* **Walid**, *who strokes its fur, his hands and breath slowly settling.* **Saba** *observes their tender friendship – it's obvious she yearns for that too.*

Dean You're OK, bro. You're OK.

Walid I can smell it. The smoke . . .

Dean There's no smoke, I promise. You're OK.

Walid The fire mustn't start. Once fires start, they don't stop.

Dean Mate, I'm doing my retakes in here next year! I won't let her burn it down. Go outside, get some air. I'll be right out.

As **Walid** *leaves,* **Dean** *rounds on* **Saba.**

Dean What are you playing at?!

Saba (*genuine*) I'm sorry. I should've realised it'd be hard for Walid. Probably best he sits this one out.

Dean 'Sits this one out'? Can you hear yourself? You're talking about arson!

Saba So? I've seen you set a school bin on fire just to make us laugh.

Dean Yeah, and I've regretted it!

Saba What?

Dean Don't get me wrong, I hate this school. They've done nothing but make me feel stupid since the day I got here. But I spent five years messing about, and the only person who lost out is me. You're all going off to live your lives, and I'm stuck here another year.

Saba This isn't messing about. It's a statement –

Dean Of what? That you need help?

Saba That we're standing together. Starting a small blaze to spark real change.

. . . I don't get why you're all just standing there. Ms Hamish could be along any minute.
(*They don't move.*) Fine. I'll get the wood myself.

She heads for the door. **Dean** *gets in her way. She tries to push past, he grabs her hand.*

Saba Let me go.

Dean No.

Saba I said. Let. Me. Go.

Dean I can't.

Saba Well, that's *always* been your problem, hasn't it?

A charged moment between them. **Bea** *doesn't like it. She intervenes.*

Bea Leave her alone, Dean.

Dean But –

Bea YOU'RE NOT HELPING!

Her anger surprises **Dean**. *He lets* **Saba** *go. Tuts as he moves to the door.*

Dean Fine. But I'm not giving this attention-seeker any more of my time. You coming, Bea?

Bea *stays put.* **Dean** *waits. Then leaves, gutted.* **Bea** *takes a deep breath. This is hard.*

Bea I'm sorry. About Dean, that I didn't tell you . . .

Saba You don't have to say sorry. All that matters is you're both happy.

Bea (*closer, quieter*) You should've called me. Told me how bad you felt. I'd have dropped everything. I'd have come over, I'd have *listened.*

Saba Really?

Bea Of course. That's what best friends are for.
(*With a smile.*) BFF promise, right?

Carla What's the BFF promise? I didn't know we had a BFF promise!

Bea It's just me and Saba, actually.

Carla Oh.

Saba It's a no-questions-asked promise made to your best friend when they most need it. Unbreakable.

Bea We came up with it when we were four.

Saba Bea often needed the promises more than I did. Though I could do with one now.

Beat. **Bea** *grows nervous.*

Bea Now? You mean . . .

Saba Yeah. BFF promise me you'll help burn this building to the ground.

Bea I meant it . . . more like a metaphor? BFF was a kids' game, Sab, not real –

Saba (*hurt*) Not real? Then why did you make me lie for you for six years?

Bea *looks at the others, frightened.*

Bea I . . . I didn't.

Obie What are you talking about?

Saba I can't tell you, obviously. It's Bea's secret. The BFF promise.

Bea I'm not burning down Wilton Hall, Sab.

Saba Why?

Bea It's a *crime*. I'd be arrested. And you know that would kill my mum.

Saba I think she'd be proud of the difference you'd made!

Bea (*snapping*) What difference? People call what *you* do activism, cos your parents have good jobs and you live in a big house with solar panels. I'd just be another troublemaker in my family!

Saba That's not true. If you just stopped / swimming for a second –

Bea Of course it's true! You say you've had your 'eyes opened', but you don't see the real world, Saba – you never have!

This comment really gets to **Saba**. *She snaps:*

Saba At least I get the bigger picture, instead of spending all my time worrying what people think of me and my criminal dad!

It just comes out. She regrets it straightaway. A beat. **Bea** *is shocked.* **Saba** *backtracks.*

Saba Bea, I'm sorry. I didn't mean to –

Bea *turns to face the rest of the group, defiant.*

Bea OK, fine. When we were ten, I asked Saba to tell everyone my dad worked in Dubai. He doesn't. He's in prison. I go to see him on weekends. When he went in, my mum fell apart. I had to take care of *her*. Make sure I never put a foot wrong. I used to be ashamed. Now I'm just proud of how far I've come. How far my mum has. (*To* **Saba**.) There. I don't owe you anything now.

She heads for the door. Then turns back:

Bea You know, all these months I've felt guilty. For not being there for you. But while you've been home, worrying about *all* the suffering people in the world, did you ever think about us? Your actual friends?

She exits. It cuts **Saba** *deep. She yells out.*

Saba It's cool, go have fun with your boyfriend! We don't need you anyway!

She turns to the remaining three – a concerned **Obie**, *a nervous* **Carla** *and a silent* **Thor** *– and begins to give them tasks.*

Saba OK. We don't have much time. Thor, can you help me bring the wood in here? And Carla, start barricading the main door and windows? Obie, you can go through the props store and see if there's anything flammable. Jay's Tallulah costume will be a good start.

They nod and jump to work. **Carla** *exits. We hear doors and windows lock.* **Thor** *exits and we hear the sound of wood being dragged from across the floor.* **Saba**'s *about to go too when she realises . . .* **Obie** *is not moving. She stops.*

Saba No way. I thought you of all people would get it.

Obie It's prom night, Sab. There's people who've had a shit year, who just wanna dance and celebrate. How are they gonna feel when they see this building up in flames?

Saba They're gonna understand we did it for them.

Obie By ruining their special night?

Saba (*frustrated*) Prom doesn't *matter.*

Carla *re-enters, eavesdropping.*

Obie Maybe it *does*. You're right, the world's messed up, shouldn't we grab all the joy we can?

Carla You know, my dad says the same thing: 'Keep yourself happy, or you won't know how to make others happy . . .'

Obie That's not really what I meant, Carla. Your dad's not like Saba.

Carla Yes, he is. He cares about the world, too, he gives to lots of charities –

Saba To buy their silence.

Carla What?

Saba Oh, come on, you must know. Your father's a criminal. Only difference between him and Bea's dad is yours will never get caught.

Carla But . . . but . . . you came to the opening of this hall . . . you all said it was cool . . .

Saba Cos the rest of the school was making fun of you, we didn't want you to be upset.

Carla Is that true, Obie?

Obie (*gentle*) Carla. Your dad named this building after himself. Not, like: Mary Seacole Hall or even the Carla Auditorium . . . but *Joseph Wilton Hall*. Who does that?

Carla *falls silent, thinking about that.* **Saba** *turns to* **Obie**.

Saba   If you're gonna stay here, I need you to pick a side.

Obie   I pick yours.
But I want to offer you a different option.

Saba   What's that?

Obie *takes out his phone. Presses play. Music rings out. It's a song they both love, and it clearly has an effect on* **Saba**. **Obie** *starts to dance – silly, fun. Inviting the girls to join him. His playfulness is infectious.* **Carla** *joins in.* **Saba**'*s feet start tapping. Her shoulders relax. Soon all three of them are spinning around the room, letting go, enjoying themselves . . . Until . . .*

Suddenly, there is banging on the door. The lock rattles. They freeze. A voice from off stage.

Ms Hamish (V/O)   Saba? This is Ms Hamish. Are you in there? Jay told me something rather concerning, and I'd like you to open this door . . .

Saba *covers* **Obie**'*s mouth, gestures to* **Carla** *to stay quiet. We hear* **Ms Hamish** *talk to someone:*

Ms Hamish (V/O)   What do we do? I mean she has other students in there. (*louder*)   Saba, if you do not unlock this door, I am going to have to alert the authorities. We take threats like this very seriously. I'm giving you till the count of five – one . . . two . . .

Obie *and* **Carla** *look to* **Saba**. *She stays still.*

Ms Hamish (V/O)   three . . . four . . . five. OK, Saba. I'm afraid you leave me no choice. I'm calling the police.

The sound of **Ms Hamish** *walking away. For the first time, we see* **Saba** *have second thoughts.*

Obie   It's not too late. Come to prom with me. Forget about all this. There's gotta be other ways to make the world better.

Saba   What, like being a doctor?

Obie   Or something else. You've got your whole life to find out.

Saba *hesitates.* **Obie** *sees his chance:*

Obie   Things will look different in the morning. I promise. Just come to the party. Please.

Beat. **Saba** *shakes her head.* **Obie** *is gutted.*

Obie   OK. I'll be in there if you change your mind. I hope you do.

He comes forward to hug **Saba**. *She steps away from him. It hurts them both.* **Obie** *heads for the door.* **Carla** *blocks it. Looks at* **Saba**.

Saba It's OK. Let him.

Carla *follows* **Obie** *out. We hear the door unlock and lock again.* **Saba** *stands alone, taking deep breaths. She looks ready to break.* **Carla** *returns.*

Carla It's OK, we'll get this done between us. I learned how to light fires in Girl Guides.

Saba Why are you helping me, Carla?

Carla What?

Saba Is it a rebellion against your dad? A bit of fun before you go off to sixth form? Are you a secret arsonist?

Carla I'm helping you because you asked.

Saba That's it?

Carla I don't really get why you're doing it. But you're my friend, I wanna make you happy. Plus, if it all burns down, my dad will just pay for a new building. He'll tell the school it was an accident, we won't get in trouble, and soon everyone will forget it ever happened.

She means to cheer **Saba** *up. But for* **Saba***, it's a punch in the gut. Realising how quickly her BIG ACTION could be forgotten.*

Saba *flops to the ground. Curls up into a ball.*

Carla Are you OK?

Saba You should go, Carla.

Carla But I thought you wanted –

Saba Not like this.

Carla Do you want me to call my dad now and explain?

Saba JUST GO!

A beat. Then **Carla** *heads off, confused as hell. The door unlocks again.* **Saba** *stays curled up.* **Thor** *re-enters from the back with firewood. Seeing* **Saba** *on the floor,* **Thor** *stops.*

Saba Carla and Obie are gone. You may as well leave too. Door's open. (**Thor** *doesn't move.*) Did you get that?! I said you can go.

A pause. **Thor** *puts the wood down. Lies down beside* **Saba** *and curls up into a ball, just like her.* **Thor** *takes a deep breath, and then:*

Thor I also have a dream about swimming, you know.

Saba *turns to look at* **Thor***, stunned.*

Thor Mine is a bit different. In mine, people are not begging for help. They're asking me to *show them* how to swim. And once I show one person, that person shows another. And another. And another. And pretty soon nobody needs me at all.

But dreams mean different things to different people, so.

A silence, then:

Saba I've felt so alone. I didn't know there were others.

Thor There's probably way more of us than we think. All looking for each other.

Saba But what do we *do* about it?

Thor Lots of different things, I guess. Depending what the dream means to us. . . . Would you like a hug?

Saba *nods.* **Thor** *embraces her. It's obvious* **Saba** *really needs it. After a moment:*

Saba That's the most I've ever heard you speak.

Thor I prefer doing it when there's something to say.
Shall we go for a walk, just us? And talk some more?

Saba *thinks about it, then:*

Saba Yeah. That'd be nice. Let me clean up here and I'll meet you outside.

Thor *smiles, exits.*

Saba *is alone for a moment, thinking. She stacks some chairs, heads for the door . . .*

The sound of waves. Or is it human voices?

She turns back. Listens for a moment. She's torn. A police siren starts in the distance.

Saba makes a decision. She heads for the pile of wood. Takes out a box of matches . . .

Blackout.

Epilogue

Bea, Jay, Obie *and* **Carla**, *back in the positions they were at the top of the play. But now* **Walid, Thor** *and* **Dean** *are with them.*

Bea What to say about Saba? There isn't really – there's nothing that's gonna make you go: 'Ohhhhh, *that's* why it happened . . .' She's my best friend. Was. Is. *Is.*

Jay She liked attention – I mean we all do. Maybe she liked it more than other people but not in, like, a weird way . . .

Obie I don't really like talking about people behind their backs. Even if you're saying nice things. I think it just opens the door for you to start saying nasty things. . . . Like how people are saying Saba was a sociopath. That she tried to trap Thor inside.

Walid There's people saying they saw her, running away from the building as it collapsed . . .

Dean Some who swear she stayed in there, dancing . . . but the flames didn't hurt her . . .

Bea Which is stupid.

Obie Nobody ever found Saba. Not the police, not the school, not the fire brigade.

Jay Took them three hours to put the blaze out. Apparently, the materials used for Wilton Auditorium were very flammable.

Carla As my dad said in his interview, it was a freak accident.

Bea We miss Saba every day . . .

Dean We wish we could have convinced her not to do it.

Jay But we hope wherever she is, she's OK.

Carla And my dad would like me to share that when it's rebuilt Wilton Auditorium will be renamed: the Saba Carlisle Theatre.

They all get ready to leave. **Thor** *speaks up.*

Thor Actually, I'd like to say something.
I'd like to read the statement Saba wrote. The one she was going to post after the fire started.
(*They read from their phone.*) 'Some of you might think what I did today was crazy. Some of you might think it was stupid. My hope is that it gets us talking. Questioning. Cos we're not just vanity projects for self-centred politicians. We don't have to believe the lies told to us by our teachers, parents and peers. We don't have to accept fake friends, or fake promises that everything is going to be OK. Lots of bad things have happened, are happening, *will* happen. And we've got a lot to do if we wanna fix it. We've got to be brave, and generous, and smart. We've got to work together. That's what the fire today was about. About starting a fire in you. Because I believe we can do this. We can find a new way.
And if you want to keep swimming, that's up to you . . .'

Thor *looks out at the audience.* **Saba** *is standing at the back of the auditorium. They speak this line at the same time:*

Saba and Thor 'Just don't ever let them put that fire out.'

End.

Character Plot

	1 The Dream	2 Freedom	3 The Uninvited Guests	4 Carla and Thor 1	5 Dean and Bea 1	6 Obie and Walid 1	7 Dean and Bea 2	8 Carla and Thor 2	9 Obie and Walid 2	10 Wilton Hall	11 Epilogue
Saba	✓	✓	✓	✓	✓	☐	✓	☐	☐	✓	✓
Bea	✓	✓	✓	☐	✓	☐	✓	☐	☐	✓	✓
Obie	✓	✓	✓	☐	☐	✓	☐	☐	✓	✓	✓
Jay	✓	✓	✓	☐	☐	✓	☐	☐	☐	✓	✓
Carla	✓	✓	✓	✓	☐	☐	☐	✓	☐	✓	✓
Dean	☐	☐	✓	☐	✓	☐	✓	☐	☐	✓	✓
Walid	☐	☐	✓	☐	☐	✓	☐	☐	✓	✓	✓
Thor	☐	☐	✓	✓	☐	☐	☐	✓	☐	✓	✓
(Ms Hamish)	☐	☐	☐	☐	☐	☐	☐	☐	☐	✓	☐

More information about the characters and how much they speak

Saba – Significant dialogue, multiple monologues and significant time on stage watching and not speaking
Bea – Significant dialogue
Obie – Significant dialogue
Jay – Significant dialogue
Carla – Significant dialogue
Dean – Significant dialogue
Walid – Significant dialogue
Thor – Doesn't speak for the vast majority of the play, some dialogue and a medium-length monologue
Ms Hamish – optional character (can be a voice-over), a couple of lines

Main Narrative Beats

1. Saba explains her dream, she is swimming among drowning people. Saba's friends talk about Saba, about the day she left, it was during GCSE Mocks, she never came back.
2. The friendship group are in a classroom, it's Prom Night. Bea tells them that Saba's contacted them, she found a note pinned to her dress. Saba has left clues around the school for them to find her, the group split up and start searching.
3. Obie is frustrated by the search for Saba. Saba throws a paper aeroplane at him, on it is a secret message. Some attackers jump on Obie, it's Dean, Walid and Thor. The commotion brings everyone out to them. The clue from the paper aeroplane suggests they should go to various spots around the school to search for more clues. Dean, Walid and Thor agree to help.
4. Carla and Thor are in the staffroom, Thor doesn't say anything. Carla makes Thor a coffee. Thor drinks some coffee and starts to choke, Carla runs to the first-aid box and finds another clue.
5. Dean and Bea are in the changing rooms, they're a couple. They argue about Saba liking Dean, Bea really misses Saba, Bea realises where the clue is, in her locker.
6. Outside, Obie, Jay and Walid are searching in the bins. Jay is acting like a detective. Obie is upset about Saba's note, Obie nags Walid about smoking. Walid grew up in a war zone, the cigarettes help him. Walid and Obie chat, Walid is sorry he never helped when Obie was being bullied.
7. Dean and Bea have found a note, it's addressed to Dean. Bea is upset, in the note Saba reveals that Dean said 'I love you' to her, Bea storms off.
8. Thor and Carla are searching through exam papers, they find Saba's paper from the day she left. Obie and Walid are looking through the bins, Obie finds a copy of *Macbeth* with a message from Saba. Obie realises where Saba is.
9. In the school theatre Jay calls out to Saba. The others all arrive, they've missed her so much. There is a moment of joyful reunion.
10. Saba tells them she can't swim any more. She explains her dream, she needs to do something big. The group don't really get it.
11. Saba is frustrated, she explains she's going to burn down the school theatre. The group whoop and cheer, Jay panics and storms off to find a teacher.
12. The group all laugh, they think Saba has played a joke. Saba is not joking. Walid starts to panic, Dean tries to convince Saba, he grabs her, Bea is furious.
13. Bea reminds Saba of the BFF promise. Saba has been keeping Bea's secret for six years, Saba wants Bea to help with the fire, Bea refuses, Saba tells Bea's secret.

14. Bea explains her dad doesn't live in another country, he is in prison. Bea leaves. Saba starts piling up firewood. A teacher knocks at the door, if Saba doesn't unlock the door then the teacher will call the police.
15. Obie tries to convince Saba to join him at the prom. They dance together. But Saba is determined to carry on with her plan. Obie leaves. Carla says she will stay and help Saba, mainly because her dad can easily rebuild the auditorium. Saba realises her big plan won't work, tells Carla to leave.
16. Thor finds Saba curled up on the floor. Thor tells Saba they have the same dream, but in theirs, they help drowning people swim. Thor and Saba decide to go for a walk together. Thor leaves, Saba takes out a box of matches.
17. Everyone except Saba is where? They are reflecting on Saba and what happened in the fire. No one ever found Saba, the theatre will be rebuilt. Thor reads Saba's note to them all, right at the end we hear Saba's voice.

Saba's Swim

BY DANUSIA SAMAL

Notes on rehearsal and staging drawn from a workshop with the writer led by Guy Jones held at the National Theatre, October 2024.

How the writer came to write the play

I didn't get to do Connections plays as a young person, but I came across them when I was applying to drama schools as an actor. I think there's a real lack of fully rounded young characters in modern drama. So, in the Connections programme there's a real legacy and some of Britain's best playwrights have written for Connections. I can be guilty of being London-centric, but I've enjoyed touring the UK as an actor and getting to know different places, so it feels like a huge responsibility for me to write something that will resonate across the UK with lots of different groups of young people.

Initially the play I wrote was far too adult. It started from an idea about 'frenemies'; friendships we have as young people which can be a bit toxic. This led me to exploring the transition from being a teenager to becoming a fully functioning adult, which I am very interested in. This moment, when you realise that everything in the world is messed up, yet everyone else is carrying on as if nothing's wrong. That became the story of Saba, this one night, a group of kids and their friend having disappeared.

Then there's the theme of finding your voice, making yourself heard, trying to make a change. On a personal level, I'm fascinated by what we can do to be useful in society. I sometimes wonder whether being an actor or writer is useful. As a young person, you're still forming your opinions. The world isn't making you get a job or a mortgage yet, so there's space to explore them, but you don't have the confidence or platforms to voice them yet.

(Danusia Samal, 2024)

Approaching the play

Lead director Guy Jones asked everyone to walk around the space and explore it. Then to:

- Stand near something that you're curious about
- Find something else that you're curious about
- Go to somewhere in the space that makes you feel powerful
- Go to somewhere in the space that makes you feel safe
- Find a partner and stand opposite them. Find something that you have in common with that person

- Find someone new and discuss the best piece of live performance you've ever seen
- Find someone new and discuss inventing a new rule for your school or youth theatre
- Find someone new and discuss something that you have sacrificed in your life
- Find someone new and discuss something that you want to change about the world, that you think is worth fighting for.

This exercise began as an icebreaker, but guided participants to begin discussing the themes of the play and their personal responses to it.

Key question

Plays often ask a key question. There are many options for this play. It could be: 'If you want to create change in the world, do you exploit the system or bulldoze it to start a new one?'
You should explore the question you think the play is asking with your group.

Directorial vision

Jones asked the group to think of their 'dream version' of the play, and to express their fears or worries about it, their 'nightmare version'.

Nightmare version

Some examples of 'nightmares' shared by the group:

- Feeling a lack of confidence, and the pressure of directing, comparing yourself to others
- The young people don't enjoy the experience
- The young people find it hard to step out of the confines of naturalism.

Dream version

Some examples of 'dreams' shared by the group:

- That all young people connect with the material on a deep level, and that it ignites a passion in them
- The company feels a sense of pride when the play is done
- That all young people have ownership of the work. It feels like theirs, not like they've been told what to do. They discover things in it that the practitioners weren't thinking of.

Jones reflected that all these fears and aspirations were valid. Feelings of imposter syndrome or a lack of confidence are the most significant part of being a director, they just need to be managed.

With regards to budget, the classiest idea should be valued over the most expensive idea. Your set could just be one chair if the concept is cohesive and helps to illuminate the play. Young people might need a variety of access points to explore the material and its relevance to their lives; trust that you know your group better than anyone and will help them to discover the themes.

Production concepts

The group watched a short extract of Julie Taymor's TED Talk 'Life on the Creative Edge', which describes a process for creating ideographs to 'distil the concept for a production'.

An ideograph in this context relates to a Japanese brush painting, which uses three brush strokes to create the impression of a larger story.

Jones said this was not about reducing or diminishing the art, but about finding spirituality in the lack of resources. For example, when he directed a play about alcoholism, his concept began with a circle of chairs, reminiscent of an AA meeting. In collaboration with his designer, they released themselves from the constraints of having to literally represent the locations referenced in the play, and this very grounded concept was paired with a more cosmic idea of two planets revolving around each other. In the production, the different technical elements all supported this image. For example, the lighting began in a wide circle, and by the end of the play shrank down to just a small circle with one person revolving around on their own.

Creating an ideograph enables your group to ask:

- What is the question at the heart of the play?
- How can I distil this into one image?

Creating an ideograph

Jones took the group through a process for creating their own ideographs. They began by creating a series of lists about the play. They were encouraged to reference key moments or lines from the piece as they worked, or any questions that arose.

Lists

Lists created by the group included:

1. All the locations
2. All the offstage locations (anywhere else the characters have touched or been during the play)
3. Sounds
4. Stories
5. Questions
6. Feelings

7. Things about the prom
8. Judgements
9. Clothes
10. Colours

Expressing themes in contradiction with one another can be a useful tool for exploring a play's content. For example:

1. Heart vs head
2. Present vs future
3. Happy vs sad
4. Still vs movement
5. The individual vs the group

The process for creating these lists is similar to 'The Morning Pages', a free writing exercise from the book *The Artist's Way* by Julia Cameron. The aim is to write freely and impulsively, without judgement or critique of your work.

Drawing moments

Once the group had completed their lists, they looked in detail at two consecutive scenes from the play. Jones asked them to draw the central dramatic event from each scene, as if they were creating a mini flip book.

Distilling the ideograph

The group were encouraged to look again at everything they had drawn out of the play in the last two exercises, and to reduce all their ideas down to an ideograph.

The group shared some of the ideographs they created, and what the process of 'boiling down the play' had done. Ideas included:

- **A rope.** Because of the sense of push and pull and tug of war in the play. A rope can represent the tension between people, and the ties that bind the group. A rope can also be shaken, like Walid, or like the sea in which Saba swims. Ropes could even be piled up to make the pyre at the end
- **A piece of paper.** Because of the notes left for the others by Saba, the paper aeroplanes, the *Macbeth* book. Paper is also very present in schools, and a very green material – you could recycle your whole set
- **A matchstick.** Because of Saba's threat to burn the theatre down. A match can also represent a fiery conflict or ideas that spark from one other
- **A plaster.** Because of the plaster's literal use in the scene with Walid and Obie, but also to visualise the covering up of the cracks in relationships, the cracks in global systems, and the moments when the cracks become too big for the plaster

- **A platform.** Because of the absence of Saba, but the significance of her voice throughout the play; in letter form or heard through the teddy bear, for example. This made the group think of 'Speakers' Corner'. There is an interesting tension in the fact that Saba's very absence creates noise in the play.

Characters and characterisation

Participants got into eight groups and were each assigned a character from the play. The task was to make two lists:

- A list of everything a character says about themselves
- A list of everything that other characters say about them.

Here are some examples of the group's discoveries for each character in the play:

Saba

- Doesn't seem to comprehend the consequences of her actions
- Can only articulate the first step on the journey towards change
- Makes big statements like 'I never trusted love' – could she be depressed?
- Has an angry, impulsive and rebellious side to her
- Exams feel like a large pressure on her
- When she speaks about herself, usually says 'we' to include the rest of the group – is she switched on to the way her friends see her?
- The others often talk about her in positive terms – she's the 'glue holding our group together'
- As the play goes on their views become more negative – 'you don't see the real world'. Perhaps this is a sense of affection turning to anger and loss at their being abandoned
- We don't know definitively what happens to her after she burns down the theatre.

Bea

- Has been in relationships since she was five. When relationships ended, she went straight into another one
- Needs someone else to hold on to, a lack of independence or her own identity
- Dad is in prison
- Mum is ill
- Says Saba 'is/was' her best friend – is she unsure of where she stands?
- Defines herself by the people she associates with

- Is going out of her way to be good
- Her comments about herself are often in relation to others in the group
- Has moments of strength – she refuses to burn down the theatre.

Jay

- Mentions the plays she has been in a lot
- Acting is escapism for her, her comfortable place is to be on stage
- Is looking forward and can see adulthood coming towards her
- Is conscious of herself and her feelings, escapes her worries by being on stage.

Obie

- Doesn't feel seen, like his voice is heard
- Wants to be part of something – 'There's gotta be other ways to make the world better'
- Doesn't want to be seen negatively – 'I love how I'm the bad guy!'
- He talks about the future a lot, his plans
- Awkward in his skin
- Others perceive him as patronising.

Walid

- Dean's best friend
- A refugee
- Very intelligent and popular
- Shaky hands (could this be PTSD?)
- Very funny, but very vulnerable, has come from a war zone
- Played Macbeth in the school play, spoke his native language
- Interested in construction, linked to the act of rebuilding which his home country really needs
- Status in the group seems fluid
- Apologetic, empathetic towards others, especially Saba
- Family circumstances could make going to university difficult
- Puts on a persona to cover himself sometimes; for example, joining in with bullying Obie.

Carla

- Family is rich, her dad in particular
- Looks up to her dad but is embarrassed by her privilege too
- Says her dad sent her to the school as a 'publicity stunt' but that she 'wants to be there'
- Makes contradictory statements – she says she 'misses Saba' but later says she 'barely knew her'
- Parrots her dad's opinions – is she scared to have her own?
- Often agrees with whoever said the last thing in the room – is she a people pleaser?
- Changes to fit the situation she's in
- We don't know what her dad's job is; this could be interesting to explore.

Dean

- References food a lot – hungry?
- In a relationship with Bea but used to like Saba
- Likes Pokémon cards, despite being an older teenager
- Young at heart, playful.

Thor

- Doesn't talk much, but is always watching and reacting
- Tidy – sorting everything into piles
- Defends Dean when Carla makes fun of him
- Is recognised as they/them by the group
- Has the same dream as Saba, but theirs is more positive
- Only speaks when they feel like they have something to say.

Staging

The challenges: The group explored staging a few scenes from the play and then discussed the staging challenges they had faced. Questions included:

- **Who are the characters talking to in scene one and the epilogue?** Is it to each other, or the audience, or both? Could the characters be in separate rooms trying to articulate to an adult what happened?

Jones suggested that the first five minutes of a show should teach the audience how to watch it, and establish the rules. The clear transition the group found between the opening monologues into the first scene was helpful in establishing this. Making a clear decision about who you are talking to and who the audience are is vital in these scenes. Are the audience other students in the school, or teachers, parents? The simpler and bolder the better – halfway houses don't work.

Samal added:

> The first scene aims to set up that the friends are very honest and grounded, and that Saba is on another plane. You need to establish this in scene one. Scene one and the epilogue mirror each other, but you could explore how to stage them differently. Is there something interesting about hearing the same words but in a different context at the end of the show? Like a memorial assembly? Or something else?

- **The presence of Saba as a 'ghost'.** For example, one group found the tea tray appearing to be a challenge in scene four. They found it hard to understand what Saba's intention was at this point.

Samal said the original idea was that Saba could become a sort of 'stage manager', moving in and providing props to help the characters find the clues:

> As this convention isn't consistently there throughout the play, you may want her to be really present in your production but unseen by the other characters throughout – to make sense of the convention that she's seen but not there. Another option is to integrate Saba into your transitional language. Do we see her set the clues for the next scene to be found by the next group of characters? In this scene with the tea tray, if it's challenging to make it work, you could have her bring in something else which would make Thor cough.

- **The use of heightened, symbolic language.** This convention appears early in the play, in Saba's first monologue about the dream. The group thought this could be good for getting their ensemble involved early but may be harder to stage early in the process, before the group has settled on the physical language of the play.

Give yourself permission to explore and try different things when staging scenes for the first time. The group can always say 'we think it's this, but we might change our minds'. Adjusting your rehearsal schedule to tackle challenging ensemble scenes later in the process could be another option.

Exercises for use in rehearsals

Jones led a series of warm-up exercises with the group.

- **Transforming the circle:** Stand in a circle, then turn the circle into a square, a triangle, a pentagon
- **Zip, zap, boing:** Many will have played variations of this game, here is just one of them:

    1. 'Zip' goes quickly around the circle from person to person with hands together
    2. A 'boing' (hands in the air) reverses the direction of the zip

3. 'Zap' (two hands together, pointing at someone) sends the energy across the circle
4. 'Catch' and 'roll'. You can catch a 'zip', then mime rolling it under the feet of the participants around the circle. They then jump over it, whilst saying 'jump'. At any point a participant can 'catch' it again, saying 'catch, aha!' then start off a new 'zip'.

Question and answer with Danusia Samal

Q: How did the theme of swimming and water come about?
A: Swimming felt like a good metaphor for living for me. The ocean is the huge amount of stuff going on in the world and what's asked of you is to keep swimming through it. There are storms and massive waves sometimes, murky stuff beneath you that you ignore and dark stuff grabbing at your legs. This hits for me as an adult grappling with life. When I began the play, the first thing I wrote was Saba's dream, and this was a physical representation of the thing she couldn't get away from. I hope the imagery brings the idea to life in a visual way for your company.

Q: What led you to set the piece at a school prom?
A: A school prom is the moment for young people when you're pushed out of school and have to become an adult. I also liked the idea of there being a party, and the school becoming a different space to its usual context. A school at night still has the ghosts of what happened in the day, like when someone shouted at you in the science lab.

Q: Why did you choose to include the mystery elements of the play?
A: It felt like a useful vehicle to explore these ideas. There are some technical requirements which the device serves. Each character needs to explore their individual relationship with Saba, and to themes of the play more widely. Creating private spaces within the school helps them to do this. I also thought it could help directors to introduce more actors into the staging of the play, as the ensemble can help create the changing spaces around them.

Part of the mission of dramaturgy is to work out what the engine that drives the play forwards is. The mystery of the play makes it more dynamic as the audience are active alongside the characters who are trying to solve it. All the characters have 'skin in the game', so it matters to everyone what happens.

Q: Why all the references to the Scottish play?
A: My nephew is doing his GCSEs at the moment. I'm fascinated by the fact that I was once an expert on this play too, and the amount of stuff that you learn at school that you leave behind and don't think of again as an adult. I liked the idea that the characters of the play are all experts in *Macbeth* because they're studying it. The play is full of themes of darkness, ambition and being haunted by visions that stop you being able to function. However, I offer this as something for you as directors – if you like, you can change the references in the play to another text your participants are studying at the time. If it's big and epic and you feel it would be fun for your young people to reference, then go for it.

Q: Our young people were fascinated by the darker themes in the piece. Was your earlier draft even darker?

A: It was initially much more of a revenge story, like *Cruel Intentions*, but as I wrote and developed the play with Ola [Animashawun, Connections dramaturg], I realised the themes that were the most important to me were the most interesting to include for an audience.

Q: How anarchic is Saba? Is the intention of the play to encourage young people to burn down the system?
A: No, I'm not suggesting burning everything down is the solution, but it can feel like this for young people – that's where Saba is. If it feels safe for your group, this could be an interesting theme to pull apart with teenagers. As I developed the play through workshops in a school, the students thought that burning the theatre down was a weird choice. None of them thought it was a good idea. However, as we explored her motivations, they recognised that Saba felt frustrated and unheard. That she wanted to be noticed, and to make a statement. It's not my intention to lay out political arguments in the play, the characters all approach the themes from different angles. It's about igniting something in yourself rather than burning down your school.

Jones added that all the characters have a valid take on the problem. The skill for you and your cast is to make the audience fall in love with each of their points of view. Some characters are harder to love than others, but it's the purpose of the endeavour.

Q: What's the significance of the burning down of the theatre?
A: I think my industry, the theatre, can be a bit self-important sometimes, thinking it can change the world. So, I thought it could be interesting to have Saba say 'We didn't do art here, Jay. We did *Bugsy Malone*.' Please feel free to change this reference if you've done a recent production at your school which you'd like to include!

Q: Does Saba have a fear of falling in love?
A: I'm not sure. That's for you to explore. I think that she wonders that if she had been able to fall in love, it would perhaps have dulled the pain. On the one hand this is a seductive idea, on the other it could be a bad thing because it would dull her senses as to the problems of the world around her.

Q: What sparked the idea of Saba and Bea's 'BFF promise'?
A: I was interested in the loyalty that existed between those two friends. They're not always nice to each other in the piece, so it became a way of expressing it, that they have had this love for each other for a very long time. Of course, then one of them tries to use it in a manipulative way, as a bargaining tool, which is interesting.

Q: Can we use the rehearsal process to explore our young people's thoughts about the world?
A: I'd encourage you to make your rehearsal process about exploring the things your young people fear, what they worry or care about. Enable them to get up and say things without worrying if they make sense or come out right. I'd love the play to help them feel safe about voicing their concerns, but also for them to think about what action they should take – how to ignite their own passion and fire, especially if they think Saba's solution is terrible. I remember having thoughts and ideas as a young person but not feeling able to say them. There's a cognitive dissonance you experience at this age. People say 'your future is important so don't focus on the future of the world, focus on

your exams' – that doesn't make sense to me. It's the scale of huge problems and the small problems too. As an adult, the small problems become your life, but as a teenager there is more space to grapple with the big problems. This play could be an opportunity for them to set them free.

Jones added that the condition of being young is a condition of being able to see the world purely. This is the only time you can articulate your response to it freshly, because you've just learned it. You haven't become tired of the problems of the world yet.

Q: Why is Thor mostly silent in the play?
A: There's something interesting about mostly silent characters. What are they thinking all the time? Thor chooses to resolve things quietly within themselves before speaking, as a contrast to the way Saba approaches things.

Q: I'm interested in the amount of time Saba is missing and if she is a missing teenager. If she's been missing for seven months, the group would really feel it, it's a major trauma for them? Is she missing presumed dead?
A: I think she's missing in the sense that she's missing for them. Decide with your group where you think she is – is she staying out of town with relatives, or is she staying at home due to her mental health? I don't think she's missing in the sense that the police would be involved.

Jones added that creating a timeline which begins before the play, at a point to be decided by the group is a useful exercise. Decide on key events that are mentioned in the text, including offstage action.

Q: There's loads of subtextual stuff in the script which is interesting and fun. How do you feel about us staging movement-based moments which haven't been written in the transitions?
A: A transition needs to propel the play into the next moment of action. If you want to embellish one of the relationships, or have Saba deliver other props into the scenes then go for it, it could be interesting and fun.

Q: My company is smaller than the cast, would you have any suggestions for merging characters?
A: It's difficult. Carla and Jay could possibly merge as one character but it would be a complex edit. You could look to do something with Thor as they are silent through most of the play. Could Thor be an audience member who is given the speech to read at the end? Could Saba be a video projection, as if she's on a FaceTime call? Or if you have a large cast, could she be played by an ensemble?

Q: My company is larger than eight people, what are the opportunities for ensemble work?
A: The play is set at a prom. Can you use the rest of your company to show us what that looks like, is there music, dancing, fights? Another option is to talk to the young people you're working with about the things they are afraid of or worried about and build in transitions where other cast members can express these thoughts, perhaps like the platform ideograph.

Q: Is Obie written as a gay character?
A: I've left the play open enough that students can interpret it. There's a version where he and Walid fall in love, and another version where he is really in love with Saba, plus many, many other versions you could explore.

Q: What nationality is Walid?
A: I haven't said where Walid or his family are from in the text. I did this intentionally because I wrote another play in this way and people fed back to me that they thought they were a Syrian or an Iranian family. It was nice for them to find that connection. On a practical level of course, it keeps the play open for groups to consider the casting of this role. Sadly, there are a lot of conflicts in the world, so Walid's experience could be relatable to many. Saba talks about global conflicts, but I wanted to have a character who had been touched by it, who had experienced that trauma. There is no need for the character to have an accent from anywhere, as they've been in the UK for three years. Unless the student you cast is from somewhere specific and can relate to that or would like to personalise the role.

Q: Can we change the names of the characters?
A: You could change the names if you want to, apart from Saba as it is her story. If an actor feels more connected to a particular name, then why not change it?

Q: Can we change some of the references in the script or adapt slang to fit with the way our young people speak?
A: Yes to changing specific references (e.g. Pokémon cards) and swearing if necessary. And do change slang to fit with the vernacular in your part of the UK. With someone like Dean, it would be great to hear all the 'localisms' come through for your area. If you can see young people struggling to connect to the words, then explore these options.

Q: Should we cast young people who are close in type to the characters? Or allow them to adapt the roles to suit them more closely?
A: I think the most exciting rehearsal processes (as an actor) are when you find a character that's so different from you, but then find points of connection. You won't get exact matches with actors, but if there's something fundamental that that person can connect to then aim for that. The exact identity of the characters is less important. The thing about working with a script is that if it's not your words it's safer. The script should keep people safe. It might feel too much for some young people to say something from their own experience, but maybe it would be empowering, if they wanted to in some circumstances. There's a speech on page 194 about Saba's dream. If it's useful or interesting to your group, you could insert some of the things your group thinks or sees in your area that they are concerned about. There are important boundaries there to protect the integrity of the story, but Saba's sense of injustice is both big and small, and reflecting that through the thoughts of your participants could be really meaningful.

Suggested references

Julie Taymor's TED Talk 'Life on the Creative Edge', which describes a process for creating ideographs to 'distil the concept for your production':

https://www.ted.com/talks/julie_taymor_spider_man_the_lion_king_and_life_on_the_creative_edge?subtitle=en

Bewildered, a novel by Richard Powers about the relationship between a father and his neurodiverse son in a near-future world where environmental collapse is accelerating.

'The Morning Pages' a free writing exercise from the book *The Artist's Way* by Julia Cameron.

From a workshop led by Guy Jones
With notes by Tristan Jackson-Pate

No Regrets
by Gary McNair

Gary McNair is a writer-performer based in Glasgow. His work has been translated into several languages and been performed around the world. He is a mainstay of the Edinburgh Fringe where his last seven shows have sold out and he has won the Scotsman Fringe First Award three times. He is an Associate Artist at both the Traverse Theatre in Edinburgh and the Tron in Glasgow. Recent works include *Dear Billy* for National Theatre of Scotland; *Nae Expectations* and *The Alchemist* at Tron; *Jekyll and Hyde* at Reading Rep and Lyceum, Edinburgh; *Black Diamond and Blue Brazil* at Lyceum, Edinburgh; *Square Go* (co-authored by Kieran Hurley) at Paines Plough; *McGonagall's Chronicles* at Òran Mór; *Locker Room Talk/Letters to Morrissey/Donald Robertson Is Not a Standup Comedian* at Traverse; and *A Gambler's Guide to Dying* for Show and Tell and Traverse.

Notes from the author

These scenes are all based on or taken directly from conversations I've had with people over the last few years on the subject of regret. In some of the scenes, it is obvious what the regret in question is and who holds the regret. In some it is not so obvious. In some it is deliberately ambiguous. When playing with the scenes, have fun exploring the idea of where the regret may be held. Sometimes it might be possible that all parties involved have regret. You don't have to make it obvious to us the audience but do make a choice. There is no right or wrong. If in doubt, explore more. The more you explore perspectives, the more depth you will find and the more we, the audience, will be invited to look inward at ourselves and our own lives.

Similarly, the locations and characters are deliberately not set in stone. There are hints as to where they might be taking place, what is going on and who is involved, but I have deliberately held back on sharing specifics of who these people are, what they are doing and where they are doing it. Though some names are used in the text in mid-conversation these are not significant. The characters (apart from in Big Leap 1, 2, 3) are not recurring. But should you find it useful to find links and connections between the scenes, then follow your heart. Have fun making it and sharing with us a world that you want us to see.

I do think it will be worth considering how you make it clear to an audience that each scene is different and new. Whether that is a big reset on stage, or through clear performance choices, the audience will come on the journey if we can make the vignette nature of the play clear in your own wonderful style.

A note on scenes: They are in a particular order for the build of the play. I believe it works. However, if during the process of rehearsing it, you have a eureka moment and it requires you to shift a few scenes, or play the whole thing backwards, then by all means go for it. It's important you have fun.

The scenes have been written as monologues, dialogues and multi-role scenes. But this is just a guide. Have fun with it. Perhaps the dialogues are played by one actor, perhaps the monologues are performed by multiple actors. I don't mind, whatever helps you explore the text and convert the heart you find in it. Did I say, have fun? I did, but it bears repeating.

When sentences begin or end with a solidus, it indicates the overlapping of speech.

Words in brackets are not designed to be read, they are either information or sometimes what the character is thinking but choosing not – or not getting the chance – to say.

Sentences that don't end or end with no punctuation can be whatever you want; a drifting off, a distraction, deep consternation or

Oh, and *have fun*.

Intro Montage

— Oh, that's a good one, let me see ... Oh I've got lots. *Loooots*. Too many. Oh yeah.

*

— Crikey, how long have you got?

*

— Well. ... yes, unfortunately I probably do have quite a lot of those. But then I guess we all do I suppose ... well, maybe some have more than others. Maybe I have more than most, yeah ... Maybe.

*

— Oh, no, ah couldn't tell you that. No, that'd be a confession! No ... no, I'll live with that till I die. But yeah, there's ... yeah. Oh yeah, so many things.

*

— I don't think I ... well, lots of little things, I guess. But I don't think I ... maybe I'm quite lucky in that respect, that I can't think of one big thing that I regret. No. Mind you I don't feel that lucky.

*

— Regrets are like your cousins. They're never very far from you and when they are with you, they are, at best, annoying and, at worst, something that can drain you of all your desire for life.

*

— I had the chance to go to the 1966 World Cup final. Got offered a ticket. And a lift. Said 'no'. Said 'there's no way we're winning that'. Let that sink in.

*

— Well, where do I start? I've lived a long life and well ... I've had a long time to chew over those moments, those, let's say, harder-to-look-back-on moments. I'm sure everyone has them. I've just had such a long time to think about them.

*

— I regret stopping to talk to *you*, I'm gonna miss my bus.

Choices

— come on come on come on come on come on, we've gotta go, you gotta just do it

= Ok. Okay. Right. Right okay. Okay. Right. Right, I'm ready. I'm ready. Right /

— / Come on!

= Oh, I don't know!

− It's simple.

= Simple?!

− Come on. Strawberry or pineapple. Strawberry. Or pineapple . . . Pineapple or strawberry /

= / Don't confuse me.

− Confuse you?! I'm just /

= / Well don't. I'm /

− / Come on, it's hardly high-stakes stuff. Just pick one and leave. Or better still, let's just leave

= Oh, come on, what are you doing to me?!

− No, *you* come on, we need to go. And you don't actually *need* either and this is causing you so much pain.

= Causing *you* pain, more like

− No . . . Look, why don't you just get both?

= No!

− Why not? You're good for it

= Believe it or not, the 95p expenditure is not the issue here.

− So, just get both then

= No.

− Why not?

= A whole host of reasons

− . . .

= Putting aside the blood sugar spike that two of these would create, I mean one is bad enough, but we need to have some fun, don't we? It's more that they're completely uncomplementary flavours. There's no balance.

− Ok, well . . . get them *both* now, but make your mind up later in the heat of the moment. Eat one on instinct. Just open the box and just . . . [*wolfing food noise*]

= I'm not an animal. I *can* decide *now*. Your suggestion is just kicking the can down the road. That's just delaying the decision to later

− but / (it gets us out of here)

= / And what do I do with the other one? Throw it away? Honestly, I just think you're not thinking this through

Someone new enters.

There is a social dance of 'oh, are you queueing?' between them and the new person.

− Oh, it's fine, on you go, yeah, yeah, I think we'll be here a while

\+ Right, cheers
Ok. (*Scans.*)
Hi, can I get four pineapple, please?

= Oh, but that means . . . /

± / Sorry, there's only three left

\+ Sure, that'll be fine, I'll take that strawberry one as well then, someone can get a wee surprise.

Big Leap 1

− I absolutely can!

\+ You cannot

− Of course I can, it's easy.

\+ There is no way you can make that jump.

− watch me

\+ Mate, you'll die

− shut up!

\+ well, maybe not *die*. But, also . . . maybe. Mate, I really don't think / (you should)

− / I could clear that in my sleep

\+ yeah, cause you'd be dreaming! In reality there is no way /

− / come on, get out my way. Here we go . . . 3, 2, 1.

\+ Mate. Please . . . PLEASE don't try it. I'm really worried.

− For real?

\+ For real

− Ok, I won't.

Adventurous

− Ok. Let me see . . . I'll have . . . the squid. Thanks.

Rain

− Does it look like rain?
+ What?
− Outside. Does it look like rain outside?
+ I don't know
− well can you check?
+ can you?
− no, or I wouldn't be / (asking you)
+ / fine. No.
− no, it doesn't look like rain? Or no, you won't check?
+ it's not raining
− that's not what I'm asking
+ What?!
− I want to know if it looks like it *will* rain. Not if it's raining now.
+ I don't know
− well, do you think it might?
+ I don't . . . how am I meant to know?
− well, look
+ how in the hell am I meant to know what *might* be? I can't see the future
− Well . . . I don't know, is it bright? Really bright? Cloudy? Dark clouds on the horizon?
+ It's . . . daytime . . . it's not raining now. A couple of clouds
− What kind of clouds?
+ I don't know, cloud clouds
− Are they dark? How dark? Are they moving fast?
+ They're clouds. I really can't go much beyond that.
− OK, well thanks for the help
+ why can't *you* just look?
− I'm in a rush
+ And how has this helped with that?

− Exactly what I was wondering

+ Right don't get all /

− / I just want to know if I should take an umbrella

+ how do I know?

− DO YOU THINK IT'S GOING TO RAIN?

+ I. DON'T. KNOW

− OK. (*Deep breath.*) Would you take a brolly?

+ no

− ok

+ But I never take a brolly

− right . . .

+ If I take one, it never rains. And then, because it's not raining, I forget I have it, so I leave it wherever I am and then I don't have one for when I need one

− So, you should always take one with you

+ How?

− Then it will never rain . . .?

+ That's not what I /

− / I don't want to be humphing one around but it's very important I look my best today. I don't want to get soaked if I can avoid it. I want to look smart, there's a lot riding on this.

+ I say . . . leave it. Looks fine

− you sure?

+ yeah

− . . . yeah?

+ yeah

− ok

+ ok.

Weddings Are Fun, Right?

− Hey, listen, my cousin is getting married next weekend. And I wondered if you'd be up for . . . if you'd like to . . . you know, come with?

+ Eh . . . yeah. Sure. Sounds like fun.

Late

− we're gonna be late. We're gonna / miss it!

+ / sorry! I just need to grab one more thing

Vote

− You are, aren't you? You're actually going to vote 'Leave'?

+ Yes

− Why?

+ I just think we need to . . . take back control

− what does that even mean?

+ Well, we can . . . take back control.

− oh thanks, that's much clearer, control of what?

+ Well, we can make our own laws

− We already do make / (our own laws)

+ / Yeah but. But no, but, but

− But what?

+ But

− . . .

+ I just think we could spend more money on the NHS

− And you believe that will happen?

+ Well, they're saying that's what they'll do. And I just think . . . why would they say that if . . . It just feels like the right thing to do.

Why Not?

= Black 23!

− Holy shit! I'm . . . (rich) . . . that's . . . Holy shit!

+ No way! That's like (*Internally calculates, but gives up at the scale of the amount and disbelief.*) Holy SHIT!

− I know!

+ Like so much

− Like . . . *so* much!

+ Let's go celebrate!

- YES!
+ Come on (*Goes to leave.*)
- Hold on, hold on, hold on . . . One more!

Shop

- Here, I'm going to the shops, you want anything?
+ Nah, it's all right, thanks
- (*Leaves.*)
+ Actually! (*Sigh.*)

Nothing

- And there's nothing I can do to change your mind?
+ Nope
- A salary review?
+ No
- A change of department
+ No
- something to make it more exciting?
+ Nope. Nothing you can offer will be more exciting than where I'm going I've started a band. And we're gonna make it.
So you can stick your salary review and your change of department. All your departments. Stick 'em all. I'm out.
See ya!
(*Makes parting gesture to suit.*)

Do You Ever Feel Any of That?

*(*The lines that appear in brackets are examples that you can use but can be replaced with small everyday regrets from the group.*)

I feel like anything can lead to regret.
It can with me anyway.

Like, I should genuinely have like no complaints.
But, like . . . is *anyone like* that?
Or is *everyone* wondering around thinking ('oh I wish I hadn't said that thing, I wish I'd gone to college, I shouldn't have bought that car, I should have stayed friends with so and so, I've settled too early, I don't make enough time for my parents, I should have learned a language') * I should have tried harder at things I should have . . .

You know?

Or is it just me?
Ah don't get me wrong, I am . . . '*alright*'. I just . . . there's just so much that . . .

I don't know, it's probably just that my dad or my teachers always telling me I was doing the wrong thing. But. I don't know. I just. I wonder, you know, like what it would be like to not regret every little thing.

Even now, I'm like, 'my God, shut up and stop talking', like . . . I'm regretting saying all *this* because I'm like 'ah, you're so needy, this is stupid, just get on' but also I . . . *don't* regret it because, like, I don't actually ever get the chance to talk about this sort of stuff very often.
You know?
I normally just push it down. Or suffer through it.
And that's . . . (no good)

Maybe we all just need to look each other in the eye more and say: *'it's alright, you're alright, we're all alright'* You know? And then maybe we'd all start to believe it? And we might start to feel . . . alright? Maybe I just need to tell myself that until I believe it and then I might not regret so much.

But I won't. 'Cause I don't really (know how to do that)
How *do* people . . . Like, *who* helps with that sort of . . . like, do *you* ever feel any of that? Do you?

Mini-montage 1

Window

− Oh, come on, they'll find it funny

+ Are you sure?

− Of course. Who *wouldn't* find this funny?!

*

Drink 1

− We're gonna go for a quick one after work, wanna come with?

− Great idea.

*

Insurance

− Ok and would you like to add Fully Covered Insurance Plan to cover you for any bumps, scrapes or mishaps for the length of the hire?

− How much is that?

− Our Fully Covered Insurance Plan is only £3.95 per day. For three days, that's . . . £11.85

− No, thanks

− It covers you for literally any damage

*

Drink 2

− Let's just stay for one more

− Ah go on then!

Big Move

− Mum. Dad. I'm moving to London!

Big Step

− Honey, let's get a dog!

Kids

− I think we should have kids

All or Nothing

− This is it. You'll remember this day. You will. You'll remember this day for the rest of your life. This is the day you get your record contract.

+ Are you . . . (for real?)

− Congratulations! You legend. You genius. You . . . you . . . I knew you'd make it. You're original. You're inspiring. You're a real . . . voice!

+ I can't . . . I can't believe. I need to tell the others. We need to celebr /

− / well . . .

+ Well what? Do they already know? The crafty devils

− No.

\+   oh, you want to tell them together? Ok, I like that.

\−   No, listen, it's just you.

\+   I don't understand

\−   They just want you

\+   but . . . Crazy Motorcycle Helmet isn't just me

\−   they don't want Crazy Motorcycle Helmet.

\+   . . . but . . . Jean and Pat, they write the songs

\−   It's not about . . . the songs . . . the songs are . . . shite. It's *you* we want. Not them. Not their songs. We'll get you songs. Lots of songs. We'll team you with writers. Band mates. Good ones. Really good ones. You could be the next . . . Robbie Williams!*

\+   I . . . (don't think I necessarily want that)

\−   Listen, this is your chance, this doesn't come along more than once.

\+   nope, it's all of us or nothing

\−   it's a half-million-pound contract

\+   oh God. . . . No. We'll do it together! Sorry.

(**It was Robbie Williams that was told to me when I spoke to this person, but you can replace the name with a pop star of your choosing.*)

It'll Be Fine

\−   The electrics need doing in here

\−   Ok. I'll have a look at it

\−   Sorry, you'll *what*?

\−   I'll take a look at it.

\−   That's what I was worried you'd said

\−   How hard can it be?

\−   Extremely. It needs a professional

\−   Based on what?

\−   Based on . . . you absolutely don't know what you're doing and /

\−   / Away. It's simple circuitry

\−   Please don't

\−   It'll be fine!

−   *Please* don't

−   It'll be *fine*.

Flatmate

−   I know Terry seems nice, but his job doesn't sound too secure. What happens if, in a few months, he can't get rent together? We could all be thrown out. Whereas Robin seems like a safer bet.

+   Robin seems pretty weird

−   well, yeah maybe, but has a more stable job than Terry /

+   Terry likes the same things as us. We could actually all have a nice time together. Robin had a fishing rod.

−   Nothing wrong with that.

+   I don't think he was going, or has ever *gone*, fishing. I think it's just his 'thing' that he does

−   He could have been taking it round to a friend or selling it on Gumtree

+   But there you go, the very fact we don't know shows we were too afraid to ask him about it, which shows we shouldn't be living with him

−   I wasn't afraid to ask, it just . . . would have been rude, is all

+   It was an interview. He was literally here to be asked questions. By us.

−   Well, you didn't ask him!

+   Yes. Because *I* was scared!

−   So we're not going to have a reliable wage earner take the room in our flat because he may or may not fish?

+   No. And that 'may not' is doing a lot of heavy lifting there.

−   I think you're just too focused on the fishing rod

+   If anything, I don't think you're focused enough on the fishing rod. And it wasn't just the fishing rod. There was more. There was a definite . . . vibe.

−   A vibe?

+   Yeah. A vibe. A vibe that I would find pretty hard to explain without the fishing rod, but much easier with it.

−   Right. Vibes aside. Let's get practical. Pragmatic. Let's get sensible. Robin can definitely pay rent.

+   So can Terry.

−   For now.

+ Yeah, but that's all we've got to think about. He's got a deposit and first month down.

− And after that?

+ Who knows? Do *you* know what happens after that? No. Life is a mystery.

− It's a cycle. You picked last time. You picked Dennis because he had a PlayStation.

+ Dennis was lovely.

− Yes, and how long did he last?

+ Three months

− And what did I say?

+ 'he wouldn't last the year'

− Exactly. And now we have to replace him. We need to be more sensible.

+ So, that's it, is it? Dennis has ruined lovely people for us for ever now, has he? 'I'm sorry, Terry, you seem like a really lovely person, but the thing is, we've lived with lovely people before and while it was, and I cannot stress this enough, lovely, it didn't really work out, so we're going to go in another direction. Sorry'

− You're being reductive but . . . you know what I mean.

+ Terry likes baking. Robin probably /

− / I don't really want to go through all this again in a few months' time. We need security. Long term.

+ So, what, we've just to accept the inevitable that we're going to have to live with a weird guy eventually, so we may as well bite the bullet and do it now?

− No. Just. Well. Maybe.

+ Terry. Likes. Baking!

− It's Robin

+ I don't want to live with that man and his . . . vibes.

− It's my turn. It's the sensible thing to do.

+ Put the phone down. Please. Put it down. Now. Please.

− Hi, Robin, great news.

Wish I'd Said 'No'

− Hi, I was wondering, you look really pretty by the way, if you wouldn't like to join me at the cinema on Friday night, to see a film? I don't mind which film, you can

choose, but I've already seen most of them, and most of the others I've heard aren't very good and I know what happens in the rest. I *have* heard good things about one of them but again, I don't mind, it would be your choice. I'd just be happy to go with you. Like really happy. Like, oh my God, what is going on, happy. Will you? Would you? Can you? (please?)
Don't worry if / It's ok if you / if you don't / I won't, you know, mind / I just /

\+   Erm . . . eh. . . . I . . . eh . . . Yeah. I. Yeah . . . I. Yeah. Sure. Sure I . . . Yeah

Wish I'd Said 'Yes'

\−   Hey, listen, I know we don't really know each other that well but we seem to get on and we have a laugh and we share some of the same, you know, interests and, you know, your favourite book series is *Sally Lockhart** and that's my favourite too, and basically I was just hoping . . . wondering, really . . . if . . . would you like to maybe come to the cinema with me on Thursday to see the opening of the *Golden Compass***?

\−   I'm sorry I just . . . I don't think I can. You're nice and I like our chats, but I don't think we'd be suited for each other long term.

*,** (*These were the names given to me when told the story, but you can replace them with books and connected movies of your choosing.*)

How Hot?

\−   How hot do you want it?

\−   Erm, well I don't . . . erm . . . what are the options?

\−   So, there's fire,

\−   Crikey

\−   Extra fire,

\−   Oh, oh my, they're going up!

\−   Mega flame.

\−   well, that doesn't sound

\−   Or incineration!

\−   Incineration?!

\−   Right you are!

\−   No I /

\−   What?

\−   Eh . . . nothing

− there you go. 12 quid please.
− Thank you. Thanks.

Decision Time

− You're taking Physics?
+ Yeah
− What?
+ What's wrong with that?
− That means you can't take Biology
+ Yeah, but I don't need Biology, I'll need Physics
− But then we won't be doing it together
+ Well . . . why don't *you* take Physics?
− I'm no good at numbers. And I want to work at the zoo.
+ Well . . . I
− Oh, you've said yourself already that you don't know what it is you want to do
+ Well, I don't want to work at the zoo. I like Physics. It's fun.
− More fun than being in the same class for one more year?!
+ well, no, but I'm good at it and I might do something with it at uni. Okay, I don't know what job I'd do with it but, I really do like it and maybe I'd work that out /
− / You really don't sound too sure. Come on, let's stay together, you can make your mind up later.
+ I don't know.
− Classic you: 'I don't know'. Come on!
+ Ah, ok.
− Yeah? Biology? Together?
+ Sure, why not.
− Yas! This'll be great.

Bystander Guilt

− Hey, how's it going?
− Not great, actually
− Shit. What's wrong?

— Well, I was just. I was on my way home and I. There was this. Boy? Man? Young ... man. Like a young man. But a kid, really. Like /

— / Are you alright?

— I think so, yeah

— Shit, what happened? Did he (hurt you?)

— Oh, no, nothing like that. He was, *they* were. I don't know if he was running away from them, if he *knew* them or . . . He was . . . They caught him. Caught up with him. And they just. They were laying into him. And he was . . . He was trying to get . . . They couldn't really get a grip of him. I think maybe something had happened before. Like earlier. But he was. They really . . . They . . . It looked sore. Like, bad. He got up. And they seemed to stop. I don't know if they were worried people were watching or what. But they. Headed off. And he seemed to . . . He just sort of limped off in the other direction. He looked really badly hurt.

— Shit!

— I know, right. It was. I'm still. Shaking

— Did you do anything?

— No, I . . . (Fuck I never even thought of that, oh my God, who the hell do I think I am?)
No. I didn't.

One Small Job

— Three grand /

— / Three grand?

— Three grand.

— Just to take a trip?

— Yeah. Well . . .

— well?

— To make a . . . delivery

— What am I delivering?

— A car

— Great! . . . is there anything wrong with the car?

— no

— is it . . . it's not . . . stolen, is it?

— no no no

- Ok. So just the car?
- well
- Ok, there's that word again. So is there . . . there's . . . something in the car?
- look we're paying you three grand to drive a car outside of town, what do you think?
- Ok. Well, what's in it?
- I really wouldn't ask that if I were you
- ok, so, just drive the car?
- just drive the car.
- three grand?
- three grand
- one time thing
- well

Let's Go

- Come on. Let's go. Quickly
- We can't.
- Stop it!
- We can't, you're so pissed
- I know what I'm doing
- But that's not the point
- Look. I can close my eyes and touch my nose. I can drive
- That is not enough proof
- That is literally the test
- That is not the . . . I am not having this discussion. I'm not letting you drive.
- Well, get in or out, I don't care, I'm driving.
- My God, just, I'll get us a taxi
- Thanks but I'm not worried about the twenty quid
- You're not worried about anything
- No. You're too worried. Just think, right, either way I'm going. And if you leave me, if you walk home, you're gonna be so worried, wondering all night if something terrible has happened to me. That'll be torture. So, don't torture yourself like that.

And I am going, so if you want to save yourself that torture, you may as well get in. Come on!

– Fine.

Multiverse

The multiverse. You know the multiverse, yeah? No? Well, it's this thing. Well, a theory. I like it. I like theories. Well, the good ones. And this is a good one. Because basically it says that every time a decision needs to be made, you actually make every possible choice. Just in different universes. So, yeah, *you* only make one. But . . . *other* yous see that everything that *could* happen *does* happen . . . just in other universes – and so whenever I feel I've made the wrong choice, I like to try and remember that I've actually also made the right one somewhere else in an another universe and so I'll try to be happy for me in that reality. And then I think about all the other universes where I've definitely made a worse decision and I feel really glad I'm not me in that reality. And that stops me worrying about whether it matters if I'm right or wrong, or what. You get me? So, anyway, tell me a bit about you, do you have a favourite theory?
No?
Okay . . . Do you have any cats?

Something New

– what are you looking for today?

+ I don't know. Something new.

– Ok. Have you anything in mind?

+ Well I was . . . I don't really (know) . . . I've just looked the same my whole life. I've just always looked the same. You know. And I don't want to look back at photos and never be able to tell what age I am other than by the fact that I'm getting a bit heavier in the chin and a bit sadder round the eyes. I want something bold, you know, something I could look back on and go 'my God, I can't believe I did that!'

– Like, you want it to be bad? Why would you want to (have a bad haircut)

+ I don't want to look bad. No. I want to look bold even though I might look back on it and think it's awful.

– Well, if you're looking back on it and can see it's terrible, chances are other people can see it's terrible now.

+ No. You can be bold and outrageous and awful only upon reflection. You know like . . . the eighties. You know how I looked in the eighties? This!

– It's a classic look

\+   I should have got a mullet like all my pals. I should get a mullet now!

\-   eh . . . they're not really in

\+   exactly! Bold

\-   And with the curls, its not really /

\+   Do it! Mullet me, my friend!

Yeah, in Just a Minute

\-   Dad. Can you play with us?

\+   yeah, yeah absolutely

\-   Dad.

\+   Yeah, pal.

\-   Can you play with us?

\+   yeah, pal. Of course I can

\-   But you're not playing with us?

\+   I am. I will just give me a minute

. . .

\-   You're not playing with us

\+   I am, I said I would, I just need a little minute

\-   But you're on your phone.

\+   I know I know, I just have to . . .

\-   Dad!

\+   Sorry, I'll just be two minutes. Why don't you start playing with something and I'll come join you?

\-   you will join us this time

\+   Yeah. Yeah I will. I just . . . just in a minute.

Big Leap 2

It feels important that, however you decide to do it, it is made clear that this is following on immediately from Big Leap 1.

\+   I can't believe you were actually thinking about jumping that. I'm so glad you /

\-   / Yeah, *about that* . . . you see, the thing is, I actually just really . . . *don't* think it's actually that big a jump. So I think, I think . . . actually, sorry but yeah, yeah I actually am just going to go for it.

− Oh come on now! You said you weren't going to do this! This is /

− I know, I know, but listen. I actually just think I momentarily let you get to me. A jump like this is all about confidence. And I feel confident as long as I don't listen to you.

\+ Confidence is just one part! It's also got a lot to do with ability. And physics!

− Oh try and be a little more positive.
This is exciting. I might never get a chance to jump this again

− You might never get a chance to do anything again if you do this!

\+ Oh come on, that's not helping my confidence.

Or Else

− Give me your wallet

\+ No

− Give me your wal / hold on! What the hell do you mean, 'No?!'

\+ I don't know. I just. I don't want you getting my . . . no. It's mine

− Give me your fucking wallet or you are getting stabbed,

\+ I'm not gonna . . . it's mine, I worked hard for i / t AAAAAHHH! Fuckin' hell! Aaaaaah! Help. That man stabbed me and he has my wallet!

Angst?

− Mum, I hate you!

Trust Me

− You alright?

\+ Yeah, fine.

− You sure, you don't seem yourself

\+ ach, yeah, it's just . . . nothing.

− Ah go on. What's the matter? You can tell me.

\+ Well it's, erm . . . nah, look, it's fine, I don't /

− / Listen, you can trust me

\+ I honestly can't tell anyone

− But I'm not anyone. I won't tell a soul. It really looks like you need to talk to someone.

\+   Yeah but

−   I promise.

\+   Right well . . . if you promise you promise.

−   I promise I promise. Come on. You trust me, yeah?

\+   Yeah, I do. Ok, so . . .

Value

−   Guess what?

\+   What?

−   Good guess! Ha!

\+   Who says 'ha'?

−   Me, I thought my joke was funny.

\+   Then laugh.

−   ok . . . ha!

\+   that wasn't /

−   / Never mind, just . . . guess what

\+   What?

−   You know that, that thing you got me, that USB thing, the digi bank thing, e money whatyamacallit?

\+   Bitcoin?

−   Yes.

\+   Yes?

−   Well . . . It turns out . . . That was worth quite the pretty penny.

\+   yes . . . ?

−   10,000 pennies. To be precise!

\+   you fucking . . . what?!

−   I know, I know it was a gift but I literally wasn't using it and I was able to buy . . . this! (*Presents something worth around £100.*)

\+   Ten thousand . . . PENNIES?!

−   Yeah, I'm daft / /

\+   // You're telling me!

−   / just a fun way of saying it. Because when you think about it. A hundred pounds is way more pennies than you'd think.

+   Yeah. So's a bitcoin!

−   I know, right? A hundred pounds! And I'll be honest, when you got us those I thought this was going to be another one of those, ye know, here's a donation in your name to blah, I got you shares in de blah

+   Apple! I got you shares in Apple! You have those right?!

−   No. But I do have a new telly, so . . .

+   I cant. I just can't with you.

−   What?!

Need Change

I don't know what I'm doing. I need a change. I have spent the last seventeen years in the same place, working for the same people. I thought I was getting something in exchange. Satisfaction or something. But all I'm really doing is running down the clock and trying to avoid the reality that one day I'm going to die. And if I keep doing that I'm not living. And you know what scares the shit out of me even more? I'm not going to do anything about it. I know I won't. I know I'll wait. I know I'll wait for things to be worse, hoping for the moment where I *have* to change. Like I get fired or the company goes bust or something. And I know that if that moment doesn't come soon then I'll be too tired and too sad to do anything about it when it does. I could, I probably *should,* just walk out that door, sell everything I have worth selling, burn the rest, and go live in a yurt near some hills. But I won't. I know I won't. I'll walk back in there, back through that door and go back to it, hoping I can just get through long enough for me to get my shit together before these thoughts return. Anyway, sorry, I'll have a six-piece nuggets and a diet Sprite.

In on the Ground

−   And the best thing is . . . we can be making profit by the end of the year. A good profit. For *us*. Not for this place. Not for this lot. For *us*!

+   I don't know. It sounds /

−   / We do all the actual work for them and get nothing for it.

+   They pay us well.

−   Nowhere near what they pay themselves.

+   But it's their business

−   *We're* their business!

+   Yeah but it was *their* idea.

− *Coding* was their idea?! They came up with *coding*, did they?

\+ Well /

− / They don't even code!

\+ Well /

− / So really their idea was 'exploit some coders'

\+ But they set it up. Made the contacts.

− And now . . . *we* have all the connections.

\+ Offices, how would we afford offices?

− We pay for *these* offices already.

\+ No we don't. They pay for the offices

− Yeah but we literally generate all the income. Look, right now we *are* this whole organisation. The four of us. We run every aspect of what makes this place money. They literally contribute nothing to the working, the running, the income generation. Yet they skim off all the fat. So, yeah, we pay for the offices. And once you take off all the money they take for nothing, we could actually get offices that aren't shit!

\+ But we . . .

− Look, it's happening. They only risk is that maybe some of the clients won't come. But the big ones will. I've spoken to them. They trust us. We do the work.

\+ And what if it doesn't work?

− Well, it least we'd have tried.

\+ I . . . can't take that kind of risk, I've got /

− / It's more of a risk for you to stay here when the rest of us leave

\+ I'm sorry, I just . . . Sorry, I can't

Come With

− You should come with me. Don't you think it would be amazing

\+ I do. It would be . . . yeah. It's just . . . timing.

− When would ever be a better time?

\+ I don't know. But with Mum and . . . well, she . . . what if she needs someone?

− What if she doesn't? This is your life.

\+ But she's getting older. What if she needs looking after?

− What if she has fifteen great years and gets hit by a bus?

\+ That's awful!

− OK, sorry. But my point is she won't need looking after in that scenario. Unless the bus doesn't kill her I guess.

+ My God. Honestly?!

− Sorry. Look, if something like that happens you can come home

+ and you?

− Well, yeah, I could totally come home too.
Think of the change of pace, the culture, the [*makes noise exemplifying inability to convey the joy and satisfaction*] of it all.

+ Yeah I know. I'd love it. I really would. I just . . . timing

− Are you going to have the fight, the spirit to make something like this happen in fifteen years time?

+ No. You're probably right.

− Then come on then. Come with me.

+ It's just not who I am

− But it could be . . .

+ I know. But . . . sorry.

Tell Him

− I've had enough. I'm going to go and tell him exactly what I think of him.

+ I'm not sure it's a great idea /

− It's happening

+ I think he's having a hard time, mate, maybe give him space?

− Space? No chance. He's let us down for the last time. I'm sick of it. I've had enough.

I Stabbed a Guy

I stabbed a guy once. So, obviously, as you can imagine, I have a lot of regret around that. Yeah . . . I regret getting caught! No. No, sorry, I seriously do regret it. Almost every minute of every day actually. Sorry, I've never actually made a joke about it before, I don't know where that came from. No, yeah I'm glad I got caught. Absolutely. Wasn't thrilled about it at the time. But then I wasn't in a good place was I? But no, yeah, yeah, sorry agin for the joke, I wasn't really . . . thinking. I've made peace with it all in a way, but I still wish I hadn't. I always will. I think about the guy, what fear he must have felt at the time and afterward and how I did that to him, how I inflicted that on him and . . . yeah, it lays heavy on me. Like a toad in the hole. Sorry. Again, I've never joked about this before, I don't know where this is coming from. It really must sound like I'm being frivolous. I'm not. I think it's just maybe the embarrassment. I'm really remorseful. like I get on with my day but it's there, ye know, I did this *thing*, and so I'm busy getting on and then it comes up and so I get embarrassed so I try to say something funny and it doesn't help but it's a nervous thing. So, let me be clear, explicitly so – If you're thinking about stabbing someone, don't. Seriously. Right. Mind you, folk said that to me before I stabbed someone and, well, you know . . . so I don't know how much that'll help but, there you go.

Teach Us Something

−   Ok, class, who can tell me the prime minister at the start of World War Two? Charlie, you don't normally have an answer, this should be interesting

+   Tony Blair?

−   Wow, Charlie, that's really amazing, I didn't actually know that myself. Would you like to come up and tell us anything else? Like how Harry Styles invented the pencil? Or when camels took over the Spanish government

+   Sorry, sir. I just got a little confused /

−   / Confused? No, no, come on up, Charlie, take my chair. we'll swap. I can't wait to discover what else we can learn.

+   Sir, I'd rather not, if you don't mind

−   Oh come on, don't get shy. We've all got so much to learn. Teach us something. Go on

+   Can I sit down?

−   Aye, you can sit down. Maybe read a book while you're at it.

Over

−   What's wrong?

+   It's over!

−   What's over?

+   All of it. It's all over.

−   What is? What's over?

+   My LIFE!

−   How?

+   I asked her out and she said no.

−   Oh it'll be ok. You'll bounce back.

+   No! It's not ok. It'll never be ok! You don't understaaaaand!

−   Look I'm sure /

+   / Ooooooooveeeeer!

Potential

−   So, what course are you looking at for next year? I think you should start making a list, if you haven't already, and then I can help you find universities that have a suitable course

+   None.

−   Oh, well, not to worry, it is early days yet, still plenty of time. You just tell me which subjects you think you'd like to carry on studying and we can identify some course for you to consider

+   I'm not looking at any courses for next year

−   Alright. So . . . this year, it's quite soon but if you're prepared, I have no doubt you can get all the grades you need this year to go after the / summer

+   / no, I'm not looking at any courses at all.

−   Well, why don't we start now, you tell me anything that takes your interest and /

+   / None of it.

−   You're an extremely bright student and I really think you could, with your talents, gain access to many exciting courses at any number of excellent university courses

+   Thanks, I just, erm . . . don't really think it's for me

First Impressions

Good morning students, I am Mr Head Teacher your new Brian. Thompson. Mr Brian . . . Thompson your new, Teacher head.
I'll be, I am, you are, I can't. Things will be excellent, You will achieve. Future. Times of hard work. Success. Mr Thompson!

Pretty Sure

−   Oh, look a shortcut!

Trial

−   Ok, that's all very clear. I tell you what, why don't I sign you up for a free month. So, that's absolutely free. Won't be a penny to pay. Nothing. For the whole month, and then you can cancel at any time you like?

— Yeah sure ok, on you go
— Marvellous

Mini-montage 2

Too Late

— Please make sure you don't / ahhhh (it's too late) / . . . touch that
— Sorry

Before You Go

— You sure you don't want to go to the bathroom before we go?
— No, I'll be okay.

That's Entertainment

— Yeah, definitely, I'd erm . . . *love* to come see your play.

Pre-emptive Regret

If there's one thing I wish I could get rid of, it wouldn't just be the regret, it would be the fact that I worry so much about the fact I might regret something that, most of the time, I end up not doing anything at all.

I heard this thing recently, a famous person on one of these podcast things, she said, and I think it's an old adage, maybe a Buddhist thing or something, one of them that are into relaxing and breathing and being kind, or more . . . mindful. She said: 'If I worry about it and then it happens, then I've suffered twice.' And I did find that kind of comforting, it was like a lightbulb going off, you know, or should the lightbulb go on? You know what I mean, it was like pchhhh [**makes explosion sound**] it made so much sense. I thought 'yeah, stop the worrying, no regrets, they don't work'. Right.
And it did bring me comfort.
But like, that was like six months ago I heard that quote and I haven't actually done anything useful with it. I haven't changed. I regret regret too.

I used to think I would stop with this cycle of worry and regret one day. But I'm fifteen now and so I kind of think – well . . . well, I'm probably not going to change now, am I?

Rest and Be Happy

— There's only a couple more weeks like this and then things should calm down

– I reckon, though, that what you need to do, more than anything else, is to take a rest

– Yeah I know but, like, but there's lots to do

– I don't doubt it but you'll do them better if you take a rest, gather yourself /

– / Ha. When?! There isn't time. I'm swimming, barely swimming, *drowning* in stuff as it is. If I stop for a bit, I'll just be further under and then it will make things worse

– Or, you'll take a short rest and . . . look. Look out there right now. See that man?

– What man?

– Him there

– That doesn't (help) . . . there are many men out there

– The one with the boxes

– Right, that's more helpful, ok, what about him?

– Ok, what's his problem?

– Wouldn't be my place to (say) . . . needs a haircut? Maybe have a shave?

– I don't mean . . . not with his physical appearance, I mean with . . . why's he struggling?

– Well, he's carrying a load of boxes for a start

– Yeah but what's making that harder?
Look at his feet.

– He's shuffling?

– He's shuffling

– Ok?

– Well, why's he shuffling?

– Boxes are heavy

– I've no doubt they are. But look closely

– For someone who knows I'm stressed about time you sure are taking up quite a lot of it on a riddle about a man with some boxes. I /

– / His laces. Look at his laces.

– . . . they're undone.

– Yes. Exactly. Now, no doubt the boxes are heavy. No doubt the task is tiring. But there is no doubt that the task is made harder and is being prolonged by the fact that he's trying to keep his shoes from falling off whilst he walks. Now. He would undoubtedly get to his destination quicker if he stopped for a second, put the boxes down, tied his laces and got going again. So why doesn't he?

— he probably doesn't think he has the time.

— Ah ha!

— Ah ha what?

— There you go. Your work is the boxes, you're tired body and mind is the untied lace and you don't think you have time to stop and do it but you know you will be better for it.

— Ok. . . . But look at him now! What's happening?

— Well . . .

— No, go on. He's delivered his boxes. And now he's tying his laces and skipping off to his next challenge. So *actually* /

— / Please take a rest

— I will. When I'm finished.

— But what if you don't get a moment when you feel like you're 'finished'?

— Then I'll sleep when I'm dead. Love you, byeeee, Gotta go.

Cab

— Ok, I'd better go, I've got way too early a start for it to be / bloody hell how is that the time?!

— My God I can't

— Good time I suppose

— Yeah it was

— Ok then I'll see you in a couple of days

— would you get a cab

— ach it's only 20 minutes, by the time one gets here it'll be

— yeah but it's just . . . it's awful dark and it's just so late

— I've been out in the dark before

— I know it's just

— And I'll get home quicker if I

— I just worry

— I'll be fine. I get around my life just fine the rest of the time. Don't worry.

- I know, I just
- It's fine. I'll see you soon.
- ok

No More Chances

- This is it. You've run out of chances.
+ Bit I . . . please, it wasn't /
- / No, save it. I've had enough. I've run out of options. I have tried and I've tried. I can't take any more of it. You're no child of mine
You're out.
+ But I . . . I . . . promise . . . I /
- / I've heard it. Heard it all. My heart is broken but I am done. I'm done with you. You can find somewhere else. You're old enough. I can't help you any more.
+ Please. *Please!*
- I'm sorry. No.

It's Too Much

- I just don't think I can go in. I want to. I do. But I just /
= / look, I get you. But what you have here is an opportunity to say . . . well, not goodbye, or well, maybe, if that's what you want but well, for you to say anything actually.
-
= It doesn't have to be . . . sad. It can be . . . hopeful. If you want.
- That's the thing though, I just don't think I can do hopeful. And that's what she'll want. That's what she deserves I just don't think I can.
= Yes. she's in there now. Just her. She has no expectations from you other than to be you. And spend a moment with her. Just a moment. No pressure. Just a few minutes. The most normal thing in the world.
- But it's not normal. If it was normal, we'd be having a cup of tea and a Blue Riband, if it was normal, she'd ask me how I was doing. If it was normal, I'd say 'see you tomorrow' and I'd mean it. But I can't say that because I can't mean it because I know I / (won't see her tomorrow)
= That's a lot to hold. And it's true. This will be goodbye whether you say it or not. No one is asking you to not feel your feelings but I think you'll feel warmer about the whole thing once you get in there and you make that connection. You can even pretend

it's normal with her. But you can't pretend it's not happening by leaving. By not engaging. I can't tell you it will feel good to go in there. You certainly won't cure her. This is it. It will only last a moment and then you can grieve. You can grieve straight away. But then you'll heal. If you don't go in, you'll grieve twice as long because you will regret it. You go in and you'll play it over in your mind in the quiet moments, when you look to remember her. You stay out here, you go home and you will play it over and over again, for the rest of your life. I'll be right here when you come back out

– I'm sorry. But I can't. It's too much. I just. I'm sorry.

Just One More

I *want* to give up. I do. I really do, I want to. And I *will*. I *will*. I want to. My God I want to. But if I could just . . . Look, just one. Just for . . . I know. I know I've been good. And I will be. Again. Soon. Tomorrow. I just need this . . . This *one*. Just for now. Then . . . Then I'll get everything sorted and I'll . . . Just this one. Please.

Extra-vigilant

– Now, he's putting a lot of things in his mouth at the moment. you've really got to watch him

– I will

– Like a hawk / because

– / I will

– You have to be really vigilant because it's what he's doing at the moment

– Don't worry

– Once or twice I've had to take things out of his mouth I didn't even see him put in there

– That's very normal with kids his

– Promise me you'll be extra-vigilant

– Yes

– Promise?

– Promise

You'll Have Time

– . . . When you say it's bad, how bad is it?

– well, it's not good . . . But

– Sorry

— It's not not *your* fault

— I know. It's just . . . what are they saying is . . . When does it . . . Will they . . . I'm sorry

— It is what it is. There's no point in /

— I'll come home

— you can't do that you've got your /

— / never mind all that. I want to . . . *see* you

— I'm not going anywhere

— yeah but still . . . I /

— / you've got important things to do there

— yeah but I'll catch up, they'll understand

— I'm fine. Listen to me. You'll be back at Christmas right?

— yeah but

— that gives us both something to look forward to

— yeah but /

— I'm already looking forward to it. Aren't you?

— yeah. But /

— so thats that. we'll keep on keeping on until Christmas. Perfect.

— But what if /

— / Perfect. Ok. Christmas?

— . . . ok. Love you.

— That's right well get a big tree. I'll see you then

— Ok. I'll see you then. Love you.

— Love you.

— See you then

— See you then

I'm Grateful for It

You know, I don't know what other people have said but . . . I like regret.
Don't get the wrong, it's not that I go around doing things I'll regret.
No, I don't mean it like that.
What I *mean* is like . . . I'm grateful.
Yeah. That's more accurate. I'm grateful for regret. I think we all should be.

The way I see it is – regret is our way of telling ourselves – 'I didn't get this right, here'. And that might not feel good. But if you can properly recognise it when it happens. If you can separate it from the anger, the sadness or the shame, you get a chance to ask yourself 'Ok, what am I going to do about this?'. Like, how can I learn from this? How can I put this right?
You know?

And yeah. That doesn't feel good. But sometimes the most important stuff doesn't.

Life's a balance. If you try to make it that you just feel good all the time, and believe me I've tried, you'll just end up . . . look, if you ignore regret, because you don't like it or whatever, then you'll not learn from it and you can end up making the same mistakes over and over again. And what will that lead to? More regret. Exactly.
And so, yeah, I am. I'm grateful.

Closing Montage

—   I didn't call when I said I would

*

—   I just wasn't paying attention

*

—   It was just this little moment of weakness

*

—   I just flipped

*

—   I lost control

*

—   I ignored the signs

*

—   I didn't enjoy my youth when I had the chance

*

—   I didn't see that I still had time to turn it around

*

—   I grew up too quick

*

−   I've spent so much of my life worried about what's to come that I've never really taken the chance to appreciate what I have now.

*

−   I get too cut up on things from the past. I hang on to them. Little things. They fester and I ruminate on them and should just let them go. I know, but . . .

*

−   I think about it every . . . single . . . day of my life.

*

−   Oh where do I even start

Big Leap 3

Again, it is important that it is made clear that this is following on immediately from Big Leap 2.

−   So I'm affecting your confidence am I? Ok. Well, maybe your confidence would take a real knock if you actually saw how dangerous this was

\+   What are you (talking about)?

−   I'll show you

\+   What?

−   Yeah, I'll show you, will I? I'll do the jump and you'll see how likely it is you'd make it, yeah?

\+   Absolutely no

−   Oh, it's different when you're the one that has to watch someone do something completely stupid.

\+   No, it's just . . . I don't think you'd make it.

−   I know I wouldn't. That's the point.

\+   No, but you see, I think I would.

−   You wouldn't. No one could. But I tell you what, I'd get further than you.

\+   No way!

−   I would!

\+   You just absolutely would not

−   Fine then

\+   Fine then

− Okay then.

\+ Okay . . .

(Both) One . . . two . . . three (*They both jump.*) Bloody hell!

Forgive Yourself

I regret not forgiving myself sooner for the stuff I regret. Now I live by this: Put right what can be put right and try to forgive yourself for what you can forgive yourself for. I regret not finding that idea sooner. In fact, no, hold on . . . no, that's . . . I don't. I'm good. It's all good.

End.

Character Plots

Below are three different character plots for No Regrets *by Gary McNair, one for eight actors, one for 15 and one for 30. For each plot each actor has been given a number, and then detailed is which scenes they are in.*

These are a guide – use them as much as is useful, and feel free to change it around. Gary says the only characters which should repeat are the ones from Big Leap 1; other than that you can play around with it as much as you like.

If you want to make your own version, there is a blank list of the scenes at the bottom of this page, try to vary how you give out the numbers so you don't get the same pairs over and over again (unless that's what you would like!).

Noted here are which scenes are big monologues.

Character plot for eight actors

Intro Montage – Actors 1–8
Choices – 1, 2, 3, 4
Big Leap 1 – 5, 6
Adventurous – 7
Rain – 8, 1
Weddings Are Fun, Right? – 3, 5
Late – 7, 2
Vote – 4, 6
Why Not? – 8, 1, 5
Shop – 2, 3
Nothing – 4, 7
Do You Ever Feel Any of That? (big monologue) – 5
Mini-montage 1
   Window – 6, 7
   Drink 1 – 8, 9
   Insurance – 1, 2
   Drink 2 – 3, 4
   Big Move – 6
   Big Step – 7
   Kids – 8
All or Nothing – 1, 3
It'll Be Fine – 2, 4
Flatmate – 5, 7
Wish I'd Said 'No' – 6, 8
Wish I'd Said 'Yes' – 1, 4
How Hot? – 2, 5
Decision Time – 3, 6
Bystander Guilt – 7, 8
One Small Job – 1, 4

Let's Go – 2, 5
Multiverse (medium-length monologue) – 3
Something New – 6, 7
Yeah, in Just a Minute – 8, 1
Big Leap 2 – 5, 6
Or Else – 2, 7
Angst? – 3
Trust Me – 4, 6
Value – 1, 5
Need Change (medium-length monologue) – 2
In on the Ground 3, 7
Come With – 4, 8
Tell Him – 5, 2
I Stabbed a Guy (medium-length monologue) – 1
Teach Us Something – 3, 4
Over – 5, 6
Potential – 7, 8
First Impressions – 1
Pretty Sure – 2
Trial – 3, 4
Mini-montage 2
   Too Late – 5, 6
   Before You Go – 7, 8
   That's Entertainment – 1, 2
Pre-emptive Regret (medium-length monologue) – 4
Rest and Be Happy – 3, 5
Cab – 4, 6
No More Chances – 7, 1
It's Too Much – 8, 2
Just One More – 3
Extra-vigilant – 4, 5
You'll Have Time – 6, 8
I'm Grateful for It (long monologue) – 7
Closing Montage – 1, 2, 3, 4, 5, 6, 8
Big Leap 3 – 5, 6
Forgive Yourself – 8

Character plot for 15 actors

Intro Montage – Actors 1–9
Choices – 10, 11, 12
Big Leap 1 – 13, 14
Adventurous – 15
Rain – 1, 2

Weddings Are Fun, Right? – 3, 4
Late – 5, 6
Vote – 7, 8
Why Not? – 9, 10, 1
Shop – 11, 12
Nothing – 13, 14
Do You Ever Feel Any of That? (big monologue) – 15
Mini-montage 1
    Window – 1, 3
    Drink 1 – 5, 7
    Insurance – 9, 11
    Drink 2 – 13, 14
    Big Move – 2
    Big Step – 4
    Kids – 6
All or Nothing – 8, 9
It'll Be Fine – 10, 11
Flatmate – 12, 13
Wish I'd Said 'No' – 14, 15
Wish I'd Said 'Yes' – 1, 4
How Hot? – 2, 5
Decision Time – 3, 6
Bystander Guilt – 7, 10
One Small Job – 8, 11
Let's Go – 9, 12
Multiverse (medium-length monologue) – 13
Something New – 3, 1
Yeah, in Just a Minute – 15, 2
Big Leap 2 – 13, 14
Or Else – 4, 8
Angst? – 5
Trust Me – 6, 9
Value – 10, 12
Need Change (medium-length monologue) – 11
In on the Ground – 13, 15
Come With – 1, 5
Tell Him – 2, 6
I Stabbed a Guy (medium-length monologue) – 14
Teach Us Something – 3, 7
Over – 4, 8
Potential – 9, 13
First Impressions – 10
Pretty Sure – 11
Trial – 12, 14
Mini-montage 2

Too Late – 15, 8
Before You Go – 1, 9
That's Entertainment – 2
Pre-emptive Regret (medium-length monologue) – 6
Rest and Be Happy – 3, 10
Cab – 4, 11
No More Chances – 5, 12
It's Too Much – 6, 13
Just One More – 7
Extra-vigilant – 8, 14
You'll Have Time – 9, 15
I'm Grateful for It (long monologue) – 1
Closing Montage – whole company excluding 13 and 14
Big Leap 3 – 13, 14
Forgive Yourself – 7

Character plot for 30 actors

Intro Montage – Actors 1–9
Choices – 10, 11, 12
Big Leap 1 – 13, 14
Adventurous – 15
Rain – 16, 17
Weddings Are Fun, Right? – 18, 19
Late – 20, 21
Vote – 22, 23
Why Not? – 24, 25, 26
Shop – 27, 28
Nothing – 29, 30
Do You Ever Feel Any of That? (big monologue) – 1
Mini-montage 1
    Window – 1, 2
    Drink 1 – 3, 4
    Insurance – 5, 6
    Drink 2 – 7, 8
    Big Move – 9
    Big Step – 10
    Kids – 11
All or Nothing – 12, 13
It'll Be Fine – 14, 15
Flatmate – 16, 18
Wish I'd Said 'No' – 17, 19
Wish I'd Said 'Yes' – 20, 22
How Hot? – 21, 23
Decision Time – 24, 26

Bystander Guilt – 25, 27
One Small Job – 28, 30
Let's Go – 29, 1
Multiverse (medium-length monologue) – 2
Something New – 3, 5
Yeah, in Just a Minute – 4, 6
Big Leap 2 – 13, 14
Or Else – 7, 9
Angst? – 8
Trust Me – 10, 12
Value – 11, 13
Need Change (medium-length monologue) – 4
In on the Ground – 15, 17
Come With – 14, 16
Tell Him – 18, 20
I Stabbed a Guy (medium-length monologue) – 19
Teach Us Something – 21, 22
Over – 23, 24
Potential – 25, 27
First Impressions – 26
Pretty Sure – 29
Trial – 28, 30
Mini-montage 2
   Too Late – 1, 4
   Before You Go – 2, 5
   That's Entertainment – 3, 6
Preemptive Regret (medium-length monologue) – 7
Rest and Be Happy – 8, 11
Cab – 9, 12
No More Chances – 10, 13
It's Too Much – 14, 17
Just One More – 15
Extra-vigilant – 16, 19
You'll Have Time – 18, 21
I'm Grateful for It (long monologue) – 20
Closing Montage – 22, 23, 24, 25, 25, 27, 28, 29, 1, 2, 3, 4, 5
Big Leap 3 – 13, 14
Forgive Yourself – 6

Blank scene list

Intro Montage
Choices
Big Leap 1
Adventurous

Rain
Weddings Are Fun, Right?
Late
Vote
Why Not?
Shop
Nothing
Do You Ever Feel Any of That? (big monologue)
Mini-montage 1
    Window
    Drink 1
    Insurance
    Drink 2
    Big Move
    Big Step
    Kids
All or Nothing
It'll Be Fine
Flatmate
Wish I'd Said 'No'
Wish I'd Said 'Yes'
How Hot?
Decision Time
Bystander Guilt
One Small Job
Let's Go
Multiverse (medium-length monologue)
Something New
Yeah, in Just a Minute
Big Leap 2
Or Else
Angst?
Trust Me
Value
Need Change (medium-length monologue)
In on the Ground
Come With
Tell Him
I Stabbed a Guy (medium-length monologue)
Teach Us Something
Over
Potential
First Impressions
Pretty Sure
Trial
Mini-montage 2

Too Late
  Before You Go
  That's Entertainment
Pre-emptive Regret (medium-length monologue)
Rest and Be Happy
Cab
No More Chances
It's Too Much
Just One More
Extra-vigilant
You'll Have Time
I'm Grateful for It (long monologue)
Closing montage
Big Leap 3
Forgive Yourself

Main Narrative Beats

1. Various people share their regrets. Some people are trying to decide what ice-cream to buy. Someone is thinking about doing a big jump. Someone chooses to eat squid. Someone thinks it won't rain.
2. Someone invites someone else to a wedding. Someone is going to be late. Someone is going to vote 'leave'. Someone keeps gambling. Someone doesn't ask for anything from the shops.
3. Someone leaves their job. Someone wonders if others feel regrets like they do. There is a montage of regrets – doing something by a window, going for a drink, getting insurance, going for a drink, moving, getting a dog, having kids.
4. Someone turns down a record contract. Someone doesn't call an electrician. Some people debate who should be their next flatmate. Someone asks someone out, they say yes, they say no. Someone orders a spicy meal.
5. Someone takes Physics not Biology. Someone didn't help someone who was being attacked. Someone agrees to deliver something. Someone drink drives. Someone thinks about the multiverse, and all the choices they make in this world and other worlds.
6. Someone gets a mullet haircut. A dad is on his phone instead of playing with his kids. Someone is still thinking about making a big leap, their friend tries to persuade them not to.
7. Someone steals someone's wallet and then stabs them. Someone shouts at their mum. Someone wants someone else to trust them. Someone cashed in their bitcoin. Someone regrets staying in the same place for seventeen years.
8. Some people plan to start their own business. Someone invites someone else to come with them. Someone invites someone else for a drink. Someone wants to go and tell someone else exactly what they think about them.
9. Someone remembers when they stabbed someone else. A teacher asks a question and gets a silly answer, they are unkind to the student. Someone explains how they asked someone out, and were refused.
10. A teacher suggests that a student could do well, the student decides to leave. A new head teacher introduces himself, his words get muddled. Someone takes a shortcut.
11. Someone signs up for a free trial. A montage of regrets – someone touches something they shouldn't, someone doesn't go to the bathroom, someone agrees to see a play.
12. Someone wishes they could stop worrying about regretting things. Someone tries to convince someone else to take a rest. Someone decides to walk home at night. A parent cuts off a child. Someone decides not to say goodbye. Someone doesn't give something up.

13. Someone asks someone else to watch their kid in case they put something in their mouth. Someone decides not to come home until Christmas. Someone explains how much they love regret.
14. There is a montage of various people sharing their regrets.
15. The person who wants to do the big jump is ready, the other person has been trying to convince them for ages. They decide to jump together.
16. Someone regrets not forgiving themselves.

No Regrets

BY GARY MCNAIR

Notes on rehearsal and staging, drawn from a workshop with the writer led by Finn den Hertog with movement director Vicki Manderson held at the National Theatre, October 2024

How the writer came to write the play

There's a responsibility in writing for Connections – you're inviting the imaginations of young people to come together and create something that can be shared. My starting point was wanting a positive play; a play that was not only about the very idea of positivity but that was in and of itself relentlessly positive. The fact that I've ended up writing a play about regret perhaps shows that this may have been an impossible dream.

Around the same time, a few people had randomly suggested to me that I might quite like to read *Buckets* by Adam Barnard. I loved its fractured structure; it put me in mind of one of my favourite plays, *Constellations* by Nick Payne. While reading it I got rather excited about writing in a fractured form when I came across a collection of interviews I had conducted a while ago where people always ended up talking about regrets. I'm a naturally curious person and noticed that when I was chatting to people, it would often drift towards talking about regret because people open up about it. Somehow with this piece we've inherently ended up back in a positive place.

I found that when a conversation happened naturally, we'd always segue into regrets and that subject. For example, if you're talking to someone who is 98, all you have to do is let them talk and you'll hear so many life stories.

You could describe this as verbatim in that it stems from real conversations and real people's words, but I would describe the piece as 'loose verbatim'. 'Verbatim' is a Latin word meaning 'an exact copy'. In theatre it means real text, not imagined text. Some people are very strict about this definition, so what is spoken on stage must be exactly the same as the recording. But some people are looser with that meaning.

In *Locker Room Talk* – a previous play of mine – the cast had an earpiece and repeated the words of the recordings exactly. But although it's strict verbatim, there is of course still a level of artifice. The original tapes were hundreds of hours-long, so in order to make it fit an hour-long show you have to edit in order for the real words to leave the audience with a certain feeling and create a certain arc.

With this piece, some of the scenes are exactly what people said to me from start to finish but some are edited down and turned into duologues and whatnot.

You could also describe this play as interview-based. It's capturing the essence of what happened with as many words as you need to capture that. In theatre we're playing with truth and lies all the time. When we step on stage, we are not the people that we say we are. We are not in fair Verona, despite it being where we chose to lay our scene. It's the same with verbatim – although it comes from a true source it's still dealing with artifice. This play is telling a story that has been inspired by real life.

(Gary McNair, 2024)

Introductions and icebreakers

Exercise: Speed introductions

Participants were given five minutes to walk around the room and introduce themselves to as many people as possible with their name and a fact or piece of information.

Exercise: Regrets

Split into small groups.

Each person takes a piece of paper and writes down one regret they have. It can be big or small, but they must be comfortable with someone else reading it out loud. Once done, fold the paper and make a pile of regrets in the middle of the small group.

Now everyone breaks apart, finds a new group and a new pile of papers. Each person takes one and reads them out loud to their group.

Choose a favourite regret.

Nominate one person to read it aloud to the wider group.

Movement workshop with Vicki Manderson

This workshop was led by movement director Vicki Manderson and was based around different moments in the script that she felt could offer movement opportunities.

She led a number of devising tasks with the participants as if they were a group of young people.

Exercise: Warm-up

- Gentle shake out of the body
- Rub down the body – starting with hands, creating heat.
  - Arms, shoulders, torso, ribcage, lower back, legs, lower legs, hold your knees and give them some warmth. Hold onto your feet, push them down and connect to the ground. As you roll up, give yourself an energising tap all over the body. Release sound with an *'ahhhhh'* as you do this.
- Head and neck
  - Head facing down, hands interlocked behind your neck. With a soft jaw, give yourself a gentle neck massage. Then raise your head and tap all over your head. Now move this onto your face (as if you are splashing water on it).

- Gentle shake out again.
- Raise your shoulders up to your ears, then release and bend knees with a sigh.
- Lift your arms towards the ceiling and flop down.
- Bent over, hands to the ground, gently sway side to side.
- Push down into your feet and gently roll up, your head being the last thing to come up.
- Ankle/balance exercise:
  - Roll your left ankle round and step that foot forward into a stretch, front leg bent. Now step forward onto that front foot and see if you can balance. Roll your ankle in the balance and shake your leg out.
  - Put your weight on both feet. Feel the difference between the one you've just moved and the one you're about to move. Name the differences in your head.
  - Now repeat the movement on the other side.

Exercise: Fill the space

Walk around the space. If you see any spaces, fill them. The aim is to balance the space with people. Lift your eye-line as you walk so you are making eye contact with others as you move. Check that you're not moving in a circle all the time.

Exercise: Instructions

While the group are walking round the room, instructions are called out that mean the following actions:

'Centre' – move into the centre and have a point of contact with a hand on someone's shoulder. Lift your eyes so you see everyone

'Clear' – move to the side of the space as quickly as you can

'Swap' – try and end at the opposite side of the space at the same time as everyone else

'Person' – find someone and give them a hug (this is person one)

'Music' – stand and point at where the music is coming from in the space. Make this a strong gesture

Exercise: Based on 'adventurous'

Instruction one:
In small groups, devise a scene that shows one person on a journey, with the rest of the group creating three obstacles for that person to overcome.

After a few minutes of devising:

Instruction two:
This sequence should feel epic. The sequence should flow from one to the next, no stopping and starting. Think about how you can make it epic – what does this mean for physicality? Breath? Sound? Movement quality?

Instruction three:
Join with another group, choose one person to lead and teach both groups what you have made to create one group with six obstacles.

Instruction four:
Run through your sequence and at the end read the line on p. 226: 'Ok. Let me see... I'll have ... the squid. Thanks.'

Reflections

Manderson suggested that she would then spend some time making it more dynamic, probably making it shorter, focusing it. She would probably place a waiter at the end with a menu, making sure the focus is always on that.

This text is exciting as there are lots of options for physicality – particularly with the short scenes.

What works well with young people is giving clear tasks, knowing there are different steps that you will add on. It's building blocks, so nothing ever feels too big. You can add and add, so there's always somewhere to go.

Sometimes it's useful to not always give the actors all the information. If you tell them everything then their creativity can be narrowed because they're thinking about the end game. Which, in this scene, is that one line. Whereas if you start with more of an open book then there are more possibilities. What you make might not always work for that scene, but it's material that you might then use elsewhere.

Exercise: Opening and closing montage

With these scenes you get a big, long list of regrets. It made Manderson think: 'What does regret feel like in the body?'

Manderson wondered if the show could be bookended with some physicality. She invited the groups to create a short solo for the start and the end based around **regret**.

Instructions

Find a space and close your eyes. This is just for you, so think of it as quite a private exercise for now.

Hands by your side. Feet shoulder width apart. Take a couple of breaths into your body.

Manderson gave the group four words. With each of these, they spent some time exploring what they felt like as a movement.

> **Word one:** Friction
> **Word two:** Hollow
> **Word three:** Contortion
> **Word four:** Blank

Place your hand where you feel that word in your body. From that place, is there a movement that might happen that represents the word to you? How do you bring the internal feeling into an external movement?

Once you have a movement, you can start to become more familiar with it. How would you describe it? How would you teach it to someone? Start to get it into your body, what this movement is to you.

Once you have done the exercise for the first two words, try joining the movements together.

Then repeat the exercise for the third word and once you have created that, try adding it onto your sequence. Think about how dynamic the changes are, how do they flow from one into another. Is it sharp? Fluid? Sustained?

Once you have a movement for all four words, add all the movements together:

Friction/Hollow/Contortion/Blank

They can be in any order you like, just let them connect.

Now explore them at 150 per cent. What does this do to your breath? Your movement?

Now go back to 100 per cent (or the 'normal' version). What does that feel like?

Now take it to 50 per cent – how does this feel? The intention is still there, you are just shrinking the material.

What happens if it's 20 per cent of what you originally made?

In small groups

Teach the rest of your group your favourite movement. Now you all have some shared movements, and you are going to slot those into your own routine.

The result is an individual piece of movement that has points of similarity with the other individual movements around.

Reflections

- Creating movement through building blocks works well and is a helpful way in
- It's a good way of including everyone in the group – movement won't be affected by people with louder voices overtaking because it's an individual exercise
- It's helpful not knowing where the exercise is heading. It takes away the pressure of 'what are we trying to do with it?'
- People with a dance background can feel pressure to be very accurate, but using words to inspire the movement means that pressure of accuracy is less
- Young people can assume that if they aren't a 'dancer' then there's no way they will achieve a 'movement piece' but this unlocks a way in
- Placing the movement in the body gives specificity to how you move which is useful

- Scaling up and down helps in exploring the movements
- Idea – you could use the titles of the scenes to inform the movement.

Manderson reflected on the following:

- Movement can be really exposing, and making people feel comfortable is important. Starting with something that is very personal and private can help – there's no pressure to show and perform
- Learning each other's movements and incorporating them gives you a palette of movement, which means moments of recognition can start happening. You can then say: 'Let's make everyone's fourth movement the same.' This starts connecting a piece that was previously individual
- When I approach a text like this I'm asking, 'What allows me to move'. E.g. with actioning a text, it's looking for words that allow you to affect someone through the body
- Building a palette of movement can help you inform characters, gestures and movements that you can bring to other scenes through the play.

Exercise: First impressions

Instructions

In pairs, create six movements that are focused around 'preening yourself'. You'll both be doing it in unison.

Do one version which is calm – as if you have been meditating for 40 minutes – and one version where you are panicking.

Split the group in half, to become an audience and performers.

A volunteer stands at the front as the Head Teacher. They perform their meditative sequence once, and then begin to read **First Impressions**. The rest of the performers do their meditative sequence behind the Head Teacher until the text begins and then they immediately start their panicked sequence.

Manderson reflected that on having created this initial sequence, she would then play with the dynamics of it. She might squeeze the group really close together so you have Head Teacher at the front and everyone else fanning out like a triangle. She would also play with how it ends; there's a lot of fun to be had.

It can be helpful to think about what you might want to see, then work out how to achieve that – Manderson often knows the essence of what she wants to make and then there is a process of discovery to find what that looks like.

Reflections

- A reference to Disney's *Inside Out* is helpful as a way of thinking about this. What's going on inside vs outside.
- Great to see the contrast between the calm and the panic.

Text workshop with Finn den Hertog

This workshop was led by lead director Finn den Hertog. It looked at the delivery of the text and explored different ways to approach a piece that is a specific genre and style.

Exercise: Looking at verbatim text

Instructions

Record a minute-long voice note about what you did at lunchtime. This should be a stream of consciousness, and no stopping and re-recording – just enjoy it as it comes.

Get into pairs and swap recordings. Listen to the recording you have been given and try to re-create what you hear. You can make notes, however, if it helps you embody the recording.

Perform the recording back to your partner.

Reflections

- You might have different accents but can still have the same speech pattern
- The text becomes more interesting when embodied by someone else; they bring something new to it, even though they are re-creating the original
- Re-telling the story brings new images to life and reminds you that there is a real story being told
- The TV show *Creature Comforts* is raised as a reference point, where the people involved aren't doing impressions and there is creativity found in how we are seeing real speech being shown.

McNair reflected that he likes to try to capture real speech as much as possible by including speech patterns in the writing; for example, when people start sentences again. In a regular play the speech is very thought out, and often very lean, which isn't actually how people speak.

An exercise you could do is record a monologue as you walk somewhere. If you head home and type it up there will be something there that will be interesting.

You'll see lots of the text is written like verse. Look for the places where someone is communicating without talking – are there big pauses where someone is gesturing or searching for the words?

On accents – you want to find a truth in the verbatim. Accents often get in the way of truth. You're always better to find an equivalence within yourself, find the cadence without going for the accent. Look at speech patterns, speed and intention to find the way of delivering a line, rather than just copying how people sound.

Den Hertog reflected that there is a temptation to lean into the comic and do an impersonation. With work like this there does need to be some safeguarding around making sure young people aren't being mocked or laughed at for the way they speak. However, this can be a good exercise for young people to show how to do real speech and what that feels like.

The offer with this text is that it has been taken from someone who is much older, but put that into the voice of a young person and there is a disconnect between the content and the vessel. That juxtaposition creates something joyous.

Another exercise to explore could be getting your group to record someone who is different (e.g. a teacher, parent, aunt, uncle). Someone who speaks differently to the young person. Then asking them to re-create it and see how that disconnect sits and what it reveals.

Exercise: Intro Montage

Instructions

In small groups, read the lines one by one.

Read the lines again, each person re-creating the line the person before them has read, in the same way they read it, before reading their own line.

Reflections

- It frees you from what the line is trying to say
- Normally you are thinking about what they are doing with the line, but this approach removes the 'subtext' and just looks at the musicality of the person's voice. It's an interesting backwards approach
- At times it feels overstimulating trying to read and listen, but then the rhythms settle in. You hear the pauses that they are bringing
- When you are hearing your line re-created it lets you hear what sounds real and what doesn't
- I found myself clinging onto one thing, or a word (e.g. 'bouncy') and then found that that informed my physicality while speaking
- It would be nice to get young people to use this exercise to play. Perhaps it could work once the script has been learnt to highlight if people are getting stuck in certain rhythms of speech
- If people are used to working in a musical theatre style, then they might be used to a certain way of speaking and delivering text – very heightened. This way of working will hopefully help challenge that and improve script reading
- Parroting is something that young people are very good at. This type of script could be pitched as copying and then we are adding the layers
- TikTok generation – means there is lots of experience in copying, repeating, mouthing along to audio. How does this inform this process?
- Different ways of reading punctuation – what do people think the ellipses mean?

McNair encouraged groups to interpret the script however you want. Interpret the punctuation how it makes sense to you.

You'll all have different amounts of time in working on this script. If you have lots of time you may want to take time on the punctuation.

One thing to watch out for is young people adding lines to the text to make it seem 'more real'. E.g. 'I mean' / 'like' / 'well'. It's a good challenge for them to stick to the text on the page, don't add things, but find how they can make that line come to life as it is.

An alternative approach to the naturalism of verbatim

Exercise: Duologue / Dialogue

Instructions

In small groups, choose a scene that has more than one character. Read through the scene you have chosen.

Looking at the text, make some decisions as a group about the characters, the location, the situation. What is the regret in this scene? What can you layer on top of the text?

Have a go at staging the scene.

Reflections

- Loads of great ideas pop up.
- Great to see you can add extras e.g additional characters or splitting the scenes
- It's a great offer to the young people to get invested in the script, find what makes them excited and gets them involved. But within that, also finding the moments of emotional truth
- Noticing lots of multifaceted regret. There are regrets now and regrets in the future. There's a complexity that feels exciting
- The regret depends on who's saying it. The way the regret lands also depends on the choices you make
- It's nice to have the option of the other flatmates that have been discussed onstage ('Flatmate'). It's exciting to think about what additions can help bring the text to life on stage.

There are so many options throughout the text and so many ways of realising it (e.g. 'Rest and Be Happy' feels like it could be a conversation someone is having by themselves).

Keeping large groups present in the duologue-style scenes is important. Think about how to keep them involved so it isn't just duologue after duologue. Keep it dynamic.

Exercise: Multiverse

Instruction

Five volunteers in the middle of the space. Read through the monologue one line at a time. All join in on the line: 'But . . . other yous see that everything that could happen does happen . . . just in other universes –'

Repeat the exercise, but this time moving around the space talking to the audience, sitting beside them.

Den Hertog's reading of the play has this scene of the multiverse right at the core of it. It's about all these people experiencing a multitude of regrets, and this scene sits in the centre of that. There are many exciting gestures to be found; the potentials are endless for what people could be doing.

Exercise: Closing Montage

Building an idea of what the closing monologue could look like, Den Hertog asked for 13 volunteers to come into the space, and to think about their solo movements from the earlier movement workshop.

Version one:
One by one people read one line from the closing monologue into a microphone. When they finish, start their calm solo movement sequence in the space. The music underneath is gentle, sombre.

Version two:
Everyone is seated in chairs in the space. They repeat the earlier exercise, reading the lines into the microphone one by one but this time journeying around the chairs and giving a more positive reading of the lines. When they return to the chairs and start the movements there is also more energy. The music underneath is more positive and upbeat.

Question and answer with Gary McNair and Finn den Hertog

GM = Gary McNair, FDH = Finn den Hertog

Q: What's the offer for a group of young people – how might they connect the idea of 'regret'?
GM: When thinking about regrets during the making of this play, I was surprised by how often young people would speak in a regretful way. Sometimes talking as if they'd already blown it, just because they didn't have their lives together at such a young age. I think maybe regret and anxiety are interlinked – but I am not a scientist. This piece tries to reflect the subject on a wide range of ages. But I think when performed by younger people it will hopefully have a louder resonance. Perhaps the idea of younger people looking at why older people regret certain things may make space for us to ask, 'Why are we spending time and energy regretting things now?'. Perhaps it will help put some regrets in perspective. It is exciting to explore how this play speaks to your group of young people.

Q: Can we use the recordings? If we wanted to play them to the audience and then hear the characters say the words for example?
GM: This comes back to the ideas around truth / lies / artifice. On one hand it sounds exciting but perhaps it becomes limiting. Might it pull the audience out of the journey you're taking them in if they're thinking 'Was that recording real?' Does it matter? What does it add? Have fun is what I'd say. There's no right or wrong answer.

Q: I'm thinking about an anthology series where there's different stories pieced together with an overarching theme. Would you describe this as that?
GM: I'd totally accept it as a description. But it's not necessarily how I'd describe it as from the get-go. I like to think that it has to describe it as an album – you know how a good, classic album like R.E.M.'s *Reckoning* or Joni Mitchell's *Blue* have a real sense of an arc to them. They don't have a narrative as such, but they take you on a journey. It might be useful to look for the musicality of the piece, so that you're left with an overarching tone. Whatever way you want to see it, whatever allows you to unlock it will be the best way for you.

Q: How do you structure a piece like this? From so many interviews.
GM: For me, it starts with making it too long. That way you've got as much variation in it as possible. You'll have repeated ideas in there but they can come out later. Then I like to share it someone I trust, someone who you don't mind seeing a big, possibly messy draft full of ideas, Ola [Animashawun] from Connections was great for this and immensely valuable. We then did a read-through with a group in Glasgow which was useful. It's a long process, you have to build it, then step away, then come back to it and see what works. It's only when you step away from it for a few months that you can tell what's there and what's missing. Then you can edit, cut, move things around – following your gut to discover what makes sense where. It's like building a huge jigsaw. It starts as a big mess, but then corners come in and it starts to have edges. Then you realise that perhaps there's a main feature that you're finding pieces for, and then all the other elements slowly come together.

Q: Are there any visual images you latched onto while writing, or that you want to draw people's attention to?
GM: I can see all the scenes in my head but that's just my version which would probably be quite static. Do whatever's not in my head, whatever's in yours will be better!

FDH: A useful thing to do with your groups as you start reading the script is to ask, 'What does this play make you think of?'. You could ask: 'What music does the group associate with this text?'. This is a collage piece. A montage. It's not a traditional play with scenes that feed into one another, it's a series of vignettes. It's an offer to you as artists and your participants to generate your work yourselves.

The author's note at the start of the play is a useful reminder of what Gary thinks is important to consider when approaching the play. But mostly, have fun.

Q: There are lots of titles across the piece. What are the ways that we might share them? E.g spoken/sound cues/placards? Should we share them?
GM: There's lots of options. Personally I see them as a guide for the reader, to spark your imagination and worry that sharing them could potentially limit the range of how you play with them. But of course if you think there's something to be gained by using the titles then by all means go for it. You can change them too. If you want to use the titles but some don't quite work for you, then change them. I'm not precious about things. I really don't mind – have fun! You don't need to honour every word, every comma. Use them, enjoy them. When I'm in the rehearsal room I love changing things if instinctively something isn't quite working for an audience. So, if you come across

that then do change it. If there's a word that is particularly Scottish, for example, and your group isn't Scottish, I would say, firstly, take the invitation to bring a new word into your lexicon. But if it's tripping you up and it isn't sitting right then change it. Have fun with it. But do follow the intention. E.g. if it's a fun word that isn't working for your group, find your version of a fun alternative. Don't feel that the words are in the way of delivering the truth of the piece.

Q: What was the significance of the big leap and it being repeated three times across the piece?
GM: It's not necessarily significant, it's just that, as a scene, it's got a tension that holds well and so by spreading it out the audience get a chance to guess where the regret may come from: Is someone going to go splat at some point? It was a suggestion that came from the read through in Glasgow and I really liked it. I also think that it does something interesting to the structure; by returning to a scene several times it takes us back to earlier in the play, to when we last saw them and reminds us how far we've come. And how you show them returning, I think, offers a fun staging problem. Do the characters always enter the same way? Are they permanently on stage throughout the piece? It's an invitation.

FDH: There are other sections that I feel could be linked together, e.g. Bystander Guilt and Or Else about the mugging – potentially connected; Wish I'd Said 'Yes' and Wish I'd Said 'No'. It's an interesting opportunity to go through the script (either by yourself or with your group) and look at what sections go together.

GM: This has landed in the right structure, for me, to see the arc of the piece but if you think scenes could be more impactful if shifted around, then go for it. Have fun.

Q: Is there a significance to the + and – etc. at the start?
GM: It's a small system to say this could be someone different. A previous draft had '–' for each line, but even I got lost when reading it back. So it's just a system for saying 'this is a different person'.

Q: In the scene 'Choices' there's a + and – making '±'. Does it mean it is two people speaking at the same time or is it a new person?
GM: It's a new person. In my head it's the person behind the counter.

Q: There are moments within the text that we want to turn into musical numbers. If we do that, how do you feel about us repeating certain lines?
GM: Very, very happy. Have fun. If you're making a musical and not having fun, that would be so unfair! Go for it!

Q: Did you interview people with a set of questions or was it just: 'Do you have any regrets?'
GM: The opening was always a variation on: 'I'm speaking to people about regret, do you have any thoughts on that?'. Sometimes all you'd say is: 'I'm talking about regret' – and someone would just bounce off that and speak for ages.

Something to consider with this would be particularly when you're looking at sections like the 'Opening Montage', for example, to think about what the characters want. Interview work creates a bit of a unique context for characters' wants because they've been stopped from doing teething they wanted to do to talk to me. They didn't leave the house with a desire to talk to me about regret, they're getting on with all the normal stuff of life (e.g. going shopping) and so the tone of their answer may well come from the fact that they want to carry on with that activity, that they are trying not to forget their to-do list or that they are very pleased to have a break from the activity they were doing in order to have a chat.

I think it was Ira Glass that said the magic happens when people forget the microphone is there – and he's right, there's always a moment where that happens. It's not to say the characters are necessarily all in a hurry, but it's important that they're not coming into this world ready to say their answer like they've prepared. They've all been stopped and asked a question, caught off guard.

FDH: It could be interesting in that montage to have someone dressed as the interviewer dashing around getting answers in the montage. How does that impact the way people give their response?

Q: What do you want an audience to take away?
GM: I want them to feel that they've had a ruddy good time. To laugh, perchance to cry. Beyond that, I think it's best that I don't say specifics, I don't want to give you things to aim for. I want you to take the offer and make what feels right for you.

Q: Was there anything you wanted to keep to the end? A punch, a realisation, or something that the audience should specifically experience towards the end?
GM: There's not a right or wrong answer but it's about tuning into the piece and finding where the peak is and how you need to find it. You might hone in on a tiny detail that I haven't looked at and make it really resonate. Trust your gut.

FDH: My advice for you as leaders of your group, is to make those decisions about what you want to focus on before you go into it. Otherwise, you could get overwhelmed by choice.

So many of you have come up and spoken about your ideas, you've clearly got loads of inspiration. Go with your instincts and don't second guess yourself. You're never wrong, your multiverse is the right one for you to be living in.

Q: When you were writing this did you find that regret lives in the past or the present?
GM: That's a great question. I think that question should be your central question of the play as you work through it with your group. I'll tell you my thoughts after. It's such a good question I won't answer it!

Q: Talking about scene structure – could these scenes run side by side?
GM: Yes. Run with it. If that intrigues you, follow that. Not everyone would be interested in doing that so I wouldn't say everyone should do it, but you should follow your instincts. You might lose some words, but you'll gain some art.

Q: I get overwhelmed by the possibilities, and currently don't have a gut feeling about where to go. How would you approach narrowing the options down?
FDH: I would do too much and then pull away. Do all the ideas and then work out what is too much. If I was approaching this play, I would look for running themes and start taking it from there. Maybe cast certain actors in similar scenes so they all have a similar tone.

GM: I know this feeling, I knew I could do 'too much' with this show because I knew I could send this messy bunch of ideas to Ola [Animashawun, Connections dramaturg] who would interrogate it. So, I would say: use the trusted people around you. Ask them to come and watch bits, or bounce ideas off them, and it will help you find your truth.

FDH: Give yourself a set of parameters to work within. Freedom through restriction. For example: Are all the scenes done with just three chairs? Or are you using microphones? Give yourself a palette to work from. Your palette will help you distil what you can make and what you can achieve.

Q: How important is it for you that the audience knows that this is based on the words of real people?
GM: I'm open to people's thoughts on this. If there's a strong need for the audience to know, then it can happen. I've tried to structure the play in a way that the audience will know. There are clearly older voices in the piece (e.g. the reference to having a ticket to the 1966 World Cup final) so I hope it's clear there's an element of reality to the text.

Music used in the movement workshop

- *Ash Grey and the Gull Glides On* – Andrew Wasylyk and Tommy Perman
- *Canto Ostinato* – Simeon ten Holt and Erik Hall
- Kiasmos
- Ólfur Arnalds
- Janus Rasmussen
- Colleen
- Hybrid
- Erland Cooper
- René Aubry
- Pina Bausch soundtrack
- Henri Texier
- Young Fathers

From a workshop led by Finn den Hertog and Vicki Manderson
With notes by Jessica Daniels

Jane Bodie is a playwright, screenwriter and teacher. Her plays, including *Lamb, Music, This Years' Ashes, A Single Act, Ride* and *Fourplay*, have been performed worldwide. In 2020 she was shortlisted for the Women's Playwriting Award and won the Victorian Premier's Literary Award in 2006 for *A Single Act*. Her writing for TV and radio includes *The Secret Life of Us* and *No Angels*. Her short film *Alice*, directed by Garth Davis, was selected for screening at Cannes Film Festival. Jane Bodie worked at the Royal Court Theatre and Royal Central School of Speech and Drama as a tutor. She was Head of Playwriting at NIDA in Australia from 2009 to 2012 and Associate Artist at the Griffin Theatre, Sydney. She has written extensively with communities and worked as a dramaturg on many standout productions, including *Rice* by Michelle Lee.

Characters

Willow – *female, 14*
Taylor – *female, 14 (turning 15)*
Nat – *gemale, 15*
Amy – *female, 14*
Adele – *female, 14*
Rowan – *male, 14*
Olive – *can be male or female, or non-binary, 15*
Laurel – *can be male or female, 14*
Luke – *male, 15*
Ash – *male, 16*

Notes

/ denotes a line that is interrupted and the point of interruption (so an overlap).
No punctuation at the end of a line is a cut-off, sometimes of one's own thought.
A bracketed word is the word that is meant to be there, but isn't spoken out loud.
A beat is slightly shorter than a pause, the length of a breath, or two.
A pause is a pause.

The set can be as much or as little as the director and cast sees fit – there's nothing that has to be there and the actors can create each space and what's in it in their own way. But the tree should be somehow represented, built or somehow visualised there, so we know that it's a tree, a big old one, that can be climbed – an elm if possible.

I've taken the liberty of choosing/suggesting two songs for the play, for scene changes, or between scenes and sometimes running into or during a silent scene. The music is by The Roches and is to establish mood, tone and atmosphere. This music is a suggestion only, so feel free to choose an alternative that you feel sets the right tone, mood and pace. In order to use The Roches' songs, you will need to secure the necessary permission from the Performing Rights Society (PRS). You are of course welcome to choose other songs in your production or rights-free music instead if you encounter issues sourcing permissions for these songs.

There is a little bit of swearing in the script. Please feel free to omit the swear words in text, if you feel you need to – each line will work without.

1. The Elm Tree

A large, majestic elm tree at the back of the stage – a sense it's high up, watching over us. It moves in the breeze, in ripple-like waves.

Silhouetted at the start, light slowly falls on it, illuminating it.

Then something drops from its leaves, branches – it's **Willow**, *dressed in black jeans and an earth-coloured T-shirt.*

She lands on the ground, a natural – touches the tree, as if speaking/communing with it.

Lights and tree fade out.

2. Flyover – over a Motorway

Taylor, **Amy**, **Rowan**, **Nat** *and* **Adele** *sit on the flyover, looking down. They hang their legs over the edge through the railings/bars – only just about still small enough to fit in.* **Taylor** *holds a pack of Tic Tacs in one hand, mobile in the other. All hold phones.* **Taylor** *chucks a Tic Tac below. They watch it fall.*

Taylor (*as she chucks*)   Goodbye never-ending revision for taster MOCKS!

Passes Tic Tac box to **Amy** *beside her.*

Amy (*chucks Tic Tac*)   Arrivaderch uncontrollable mono brow!

Adele   *Ahh*, I like your furry facial hair.

Amy (*outraged*)   I wasn't talking about me. Just . . . *in general*, obvs.

Passes to **Rowan**.

Rowan (*chucks Tic Tac*)   Sy-o-nara the school uniform trouser re-style, which is now a universally unflattering (*does finger quotes*) *slack*.

Adele (*staring ahead*)   Try wearing a kilt Monday to Friday.

Nat *grabs Tic-Tacs.*

Nat (*chucks Tic Tac*)   So long *way* below minimum wage babysitting for my hypo brother, and school catering enforced high-calorie snacks.

Taylor   You don't get two.

Nat   / But

Taylor (*not looking at her*)   Nobody gets two at once Nat, that's the rules.

Nat, *proper annoyed, passes Tic Tacs to* **Adele**, *who's eating Hula Hoops.*

Adele (*chucks with force*)   Asta La Vista the untimely and uncalled for discontinuation of Marmite-flavour crisps!

All look at **Adele**, *slightly disgusted.*

What? There's a public outcry and an online support group, so . . .

Tic Tacs are passed back along line to **Taylor**, *a smooth routine.*

Taylor (*chucks Tic Tac, violently*)   Laters so last season loser Luke!

Nat   Okay, so . . . are you like officially finished with Luke, *again*?

Taylor *pretends she hasn't heard.*

Rowan   He's dead to her. He who shall not be named. So, he's dead to us.

Adele   And, is Ash like . . . totally way better?

Taylor *holds up screen saver on her phone, a pic of* **Ash**.

Rowan (*to picture*)   Stun.

Amy   Slay.

Taylor   And, he's sixteen, nearly, he's getting a car. Will be. One day. We're talking serious upgrade.

Adele *nods, not getting it, then looks philosophical.*

Adele   Did Tic Tacs exist before TikTok?

No one answers – all stare below.
Hey, can we make wishes too? Like, that we all stay like this, BFFs, forever.

Amy   Like that's ever *not* gonna be the case.

Adele (*looks down*)   Y-es, I got a windscreen!

Amy   This, *us,* is totally for forever.

Adele   OMG, is that a . . . person down there! Walking on the motorway. Look. (*Points.*) They look . . . like an ant.

Taylor   Be that *new girl*, totally the type to walk on a motorway, for *fun*.

All laugh. **Adele** *suddenly screams, flicks off an ant, dramatically.*

Adele   S'alright, it was, literally, like (*flicks it off, making sure*) an ant.

All squeal, full-blown overreaction. They swing legs.
(*Thoughtful.*) Can ants fly?

Rowan   The flying ones can.

Adele *shudders.*

Nat   So, is the new motorway gonna go under the old one?

Adele   Like a taco?

Taylor   No. It's going to go over it, twice. Like a double front handspring.

Adele   Or, a burrito?

Nat   My dad says smart motorways bring in money to places, by increasing ... capacity on roads, and that they make them way safer.

Amy   So, he read the leaflet?

Taylor   Yeah, he *wrote* the leaflet.

Taylor/Amy *high five.*

Nat (*defensive*)   My dad *contributed* to the smart motorway campaign, yes.

Adele   My mum said smart motorways are more dangerous than the old motorways, cos people still drive on them thinking there's a hard shoulder, so then they drive up the wrong way and collide with oncoming traffic, get crushed like ... (*enjoying this*) *Coke cans.*

All stare – unnerved.
She read the other leaflet, the (*does quotation marks*) Green one.
They handed them out at her Slimming World.

Nat   And that's totally eco-warrior fake news.

Taylor   Depends on your perspective. Where you are, on the road.
Coming in, or ... *going out.*
Me, I'm taking the exit.
She gets up. All copy her, except **Adele**.

Adele (*spits out Tic Tac, with force*)   Goodbye endless procrastination caused by everyone constantly telling us this is supposed to be the best time of our LIFE!

She stares where it falls – till she can't see it.
Are Tic Tacs biodegradable?

Now seeing everyone's up, she climbs out, stands – all are taking selfies in unison.

Adele   This break is supposed to be used for some digital downtime.

Rowan   Well, we're in *nature*.

Nat   Soon to have a new smart motorway slap bang in the middle of it.

Taylor   Still just be a big fucking road, that comes in, and then goes out.

All start walking off the bridge in single file; the girls adjust their skirts, pull/roll them down, so they're no longer hitched, mini-style. We hear a truck shudder below.

Amy (*to* **Taylor**)   You see that new girl at assembly this morning?

Taylor   I *smelt* her, three rows back.

All laugh.
Like proper ... off-milk, cheap *skanky* deodorant and dandruff.

Rowan   She didn't even have a phone.

All stop walking – WTF!

Amy Yeh, when we had to save those numbers, for the anti-bullying campaign, she . . . *freakazoid*, wrote them in a book, with like . . . *a pen.*

Nat *And*, she signed up for the free school lunches.

Amy *mimes gagging.*

Taylor Someone should tell her there's no such thing as a free lunch.

Adele (*not getting it*) No, they are free.

They keep walking.
What does dandruff smell like?

Beat.

Taylor Loneliness.

Taylor *poses, takes selfie, all crowd in,* **Nat** *at the edge. All apply lip balm in unison.*
Rowan *stares down at the road, sadly, then runs to catch up, as lights fade.*

3. Willow's Bedroom

Willow's *sitting on her bedroom floor, surrounded by branches, with yellowing leaves falling off. She's studying them, drawing in a notebook. There's no sign of a laptop, or a phone. But there's an old record player.*

She picks up a large (human-like) branch. Makes it face her, as if talking to it.

Willow (*moves branch*) Knock-knock.

She pretends to ignore it.

(*Playing her mum, as the tree, moves it when it's speaking and uses a different grown-up voice.*) Will?
. . . Willow? I don't want to interrupt. If you're having a private
(*As herself, interrupting, quietly.*) Then . . . *don't.*
(*Beat – as her mum.*) Thought you might like a snack. To keep you going.
(*As herself.*) I'm alright.

A moment.
(*As her mum.*) You writing in your diary?
(*As herself, corrects.*) It's a *journal.*

A moment.
(*As her mum.*) I'm making your favourite tonight, Will. Shepherd's pie. With sustainably bought beef, as it's a special occasion.
(*A beat – as herself.*) It's cottage pie. If it's beef. Shepherd is lamb, hence, the shepherd.
(*As her mum.*) I'll put a bit of cheese on the top, so it melts, how you like.
(*As herself, interrupting, means this.*) Thanks. Thanks, Mum.

She goes to put the branch down, then.
(Back as her mum.) How was your . . . first day today?
(As herself, quietly.) . . . Fine.
(As her mum.) You make some new . . . pals?

She puts branch down, sighs.
(Quietly to herself now.) Probably take a bit of time, to settle in.

She looks at dead leaves. Picks up a leaf, studies, smells it, writes in her book.

We hear a door slam, loud, as if downstairs, keys chucked on a table, then silence.

*We hear a fridge door, sound of a wine bottle opened, with a cork, a TV going on, loud. Then a voice (***Willow's** **Mum***) calls up from down below.*

Willow's Mum (*off*) Will! You better not have brought any more of those dead twigs into the house!

Willow *sighs, carefully places the leaf in between the pages of the book, gently closes it. She goes to the record player, puts the needle on a record.*

Music (suggestion: 'Runs in the Family' by The Roches) begins to play – plays over the following scene.

4. The Tree

Willow *is at the tree, which has dropped more leaves.*

She is gathering them, putting them in her rucksack. She pours some water around it from a small flask, takes out a trowel, kneels, begins to dig a trench around it.

She walks into next scene, as the song comes to an end/fades out.

5. School – Gym Class and Presentation

NB: The **Teacher** *for this can be played by an actor (***Luke***) or we can just hear their voice, recorded, as if standing at the side, shouting instructions/blowing whistle.*

There's a large vaulting horse on stage with a mat beside it.

Amy, **Nat**, **Adele**, **Rowan** *and* **Taylor** *are dressed in smart red tight-fitting polo shirts/black tracksuits.* **Olive** *and* **Laurel** *wear ill-fitting faded t-shirts and baggy tracksuits, and stand separately from others.*

Willow *sits on her own, in large, oversized t-shirt and shorts.*

Teacher   You should be warming up!

Taylor, **Amy**, **Nat** *and* **Adele** *on cue begin applying* lip balm, *highlighter and curling their eyelashes with curlers.* **Rowan** *stretches, like a dancer.* **Willow** *doesn't move – stares at floor, face covered by her hair, clutches her drink flask.*

Amy (*motioning to* **Willow**)   Obvs didn't get the memo about JD Sports having a sale on.

Taylor   Na, you gotta admire her courage, coming out wearing that ensemble, in public.

They laugh. Whistle blows. They jog in a circle, chucking a football between them, **Adele**, **Olive**, **Laurel**, **Rowan** *at the back.* **Willow** *doesn't move.*

Teacher   Willow! Care to join!

Taylor (*to mates*)   Yeah, think she's already joined, like *an in-bred cult.*

They laugh, **Willow** *gets up, her flask open and spilling liquid on herself.*

Rowan   Where there's a Will, there's an *uh oh.*

They laugh. She picks up flask, shakes it and puts it in her bag. She's now wet.

Nat   Ohmygod looks like she's pissed herself!

They laugh.

Adele   Maybe she's like a Jehovah's Witness, who don't do technology.

Nat   They do technology, just not blood transfusions.

Rowan   Or, zips.

Willow *starts reluctantly jogging.*

Amy   Looks like she could do with the exercise.

Taylor   Bless. (*Mock caring.*) It's like she's in TikTok (*mimes*) sloooow mo.

Adele   Miss Faikus says we have to, like, include her in our activities.

Willow *makes a weird sound – an inaudible 'Get off!'* **Taylor** *suddenly chucks the ball at* **Willow**. *It hits her, hard. She doesn't react. The whistle blows, loud.*

Taylor   I was just including Willow in our activities, SIR!

Adele *stops, whistle blows.*

Adele (*to teacher*)   Sir, I've already done the morning mile today!

Whistle blows, louder
And I've got my period. And it's really heavy, so . . .

Whistle blows. **Laurel** *puffs on an inhaler, keeps jogging.*

Nat   So, scale from one to ten, how advanced is this . . . *move*?

Taylor (*corrects*)   Uh, it's a *movement*, and its official DV

Amy (*proudly explains meaning*)   Difficulty value

Taylor   Is a combined total of eight elements, including the dismount. Consisting of a front handspring salto forward, into a double somersault

Amy   Which is basically . . .

Taylor   . . . A Produnova.

Amy   One of *the* most *dangerous* moves.

Taylor   Yeh, for some people.

Rowan   For some people, putting one foot in front of the other's dangerous.

They look to **Willow***, who's now jogging with her shoelaces undone.*

Taylor   But not if you've got the physique, and you're in *peak condition.*

Nat   I thought Ash was coming.

Taylor   You're crowding me, Nat, can I have a bit of sp-ace.

She extends an arm, to mime some space between her and **Nat***.*
And (*she looks around*) he'll be here.

She looks again, expectantly, looking for **Ash***, as* **Teacher** *blows whistle, all stop.*

Teacher (*announces*)   Now we're lucky today to be getting a sneak preview, ahead of the end of year gymnastics contest, from one of our own homebred champions, in the making.

Amy   That's you, babes!

Taylor   Fact.

She beams. **Nat***,* **Amy***,* **Rowan** *and* **Adele** *get out phones.*

Teacher (*re phones*)   Away!

Taylor *walks with supreme confidence into position, a run-up to the mat and horse. She removes her polo shirt and joggers, to reveal a bright shiny new leotard.* **Amy** *runs and takes her clothes from her, a willing assistant.*

Somebody enters, **Taylor** *turns, looks over, excited, but her face falls seeing* **Luke***.*

Nat   At least your ex turned up (*does a pleased little wave to* **Luke***, who looks around, checks she means him, then waves back*). He must have got the memo.

Taylor (*glaring at* **Luke**)   There wasn't a memo.

Amy   Ash must just be held up, baybz.

Taylor *nods, unconvinced, looks at the door for a moment, then turning a big bright professional smile back on, she opens her arms wide, balletic, professional, strong – the start of the routine.*

The air's electric, breaths held, phones up, ready.

Teacher   I said, phones away, NOW!

All reluctantly put phones away (but not entirely, still clutching them below).

Taylor *stares, starts a run-up to the bench, as all hold their phones, low, filming.*

*As **Ash** coolly slips into the room, with a swagger, and as **Taylor** starts the run-up to the bench, he executes a very loud wolf whistle. She turns to him, distracted, thrown – launching off the floor at the same time.*
Blackout.

In darkness we hear a combination of crunching bones, breaking glass, flesh on metal, then a stunned silence – then a blood-curdling scream of agony – **Taylor***'s.*

6. The Tree, Silhouetted

It blows in a strong wind, as a large branch falls from it, crashes to the ground.

Music plays and into the next scene.

7. The Tree – Early Morning

Willow, *at the tree, stares at the fallen branch.*

She tries to pick it up, but it's too heavy. She strokes it, lovingly, whispers to it. She climbs the tree, with ease. Once up, she takes a small set of scissors from her pocket, clips off leaves, pockets them, leans back, held by the tree, in this moment, safe.

Song ends/fades out.

8. School Playground/Halls

*All characters, except for **Taylor** and **Willow** are in the playground on phones.*

They hold their phones at an angle (the angle they were when the accident happened) to see the footage, as shot.

We hear the sound, multiple times, over and over – the moment of the disaster, from their phones, as they watch, glued, covering open mouths, trying not to laugh.

Willow *enters, sees the group, nobody registers her – she finds a corner, takes out a leaf.*

On phones, **Luke**, *then* **Nat** *begin to laugh. Then they're all laughing, cruelly.*

Willow *stops, assuming that they're laughing at her, well used to this – then she sees they still haven't noticed her, still on their phones – she's invisible, walks away.*

9. Taylor's Bedroom

Music blasts from a phone (cast to choose song – they may sing along in moments).

Taylor's in bed, her leg suspended in the air in a comically large plaster-cast, which has already been signed, has stickers, kisses and glitter on it (it's pimped). There's a bunch of flowers on a bedside table in a vase, a few cuddly toys and a floating balloon, that says 'FEEL MUCH BETTER SOON'.

Amy, **Rowan**, **Adele** *and* **Nat** *gather round the bed – an entourage, taking shots of* **Taylor** *on phones,* **Amy** *fanning her with a get-well card.* **Taylor** *doesn't look sick, is loving attention, poses for snaps, in between dialogue.*

Amy   Oh my God, how do you still look so f-ing good though?

Rowan (*looking at shot on phone*)   And that's *without* a filter.

Adele   Yeah, you're, like, glowing, Tay.

Taylor   Mum's been making me *a lot* of soup, and I'm doing seated weights.

Nat   Just, flat *on your back*?

Adele (*really curious*)   What kind of soup?

Taylor   The *soupy* kind. I hate soup. And I'm on a *lot* of meds.

Adele   What . . . / kind

Taylor (*annoyed*)   The *painkilling* kind.

Amy   Because yeah, like, a full-on ankle sprain.

Rowan   A full-on *traumatic* ankle sprain.

Taylor   In two places.

Adele (*gets close to her, to look*)   Are there two places on an ankle?

Taylor (*to* **Adele**)   *Careful*! It's a delicate hydraulic system.

Nat (*to huge leg in cast, in a cute voice*)   For your delicate lickle ankle.
So, how long they saying it's gonna take, to fully heal?

All on **Taylor** *– who suddenly looks vulnerable.*

Taylor (*nervous*)   So, has anyone, at school, said anything about it . . . the

All (*shaking heads in unison*)   No.

All pocket their phones, quick smart, in unison.

Amy   Everyone's just like really sorry, for what happened to you.

Nat   And that it means you no longer qualify for this year's team.

Tries to look sorry – fails.

Taylor   Because it wasn't my fault. It was totally a health and safety issue.

Amy   Totally.

Nat Yeah, cos like, we know you *meant* to do the flip, then land on your feet, *upright*, not like land on your bent splayed out ankle with your legs . . . akimbo. Didn't know you were that flexible.

She breathes in, as in, painful, ouch – as do others, remembering, **Taylor** *glares.*

Nat I mean, you got distracted, obvs, / by

Taylor (*defiant*) No! The *mat* hadn't been positioned properly.

Amy Yeah (*To* **Nat**.) the mat wasn't positioned properly.

Taylor So I . . . took off, launched, at a faulty angle, so my landing was . . . off.

Nat (*not as quiet as she meant*) You're telling me.

All breathe in, in unison.

Rowan (*reassuring*) You could probably, like, totally sue, baybz.

Taylor (*stares off*) I'd been training for . . . for twelve months. Five four-hour practice sessions a week, three low-impact cardio seshes, five lean high-protein shakes.

Trying not to cry.
I was so ready, in peak prime condition, everything was . . . perfect.

Amy We're so sorry, Tay.

Looks at others, who all nod, silenced and trying to look sorry, really hard.

Adele Though, to be fair, on the clip, on You (Tube).

All the girls glare at her to shut up.

Taylor What . . . *clip*? What are you

Rowan We just watched some clips, of like, similar . . . routines, so we could fully get what you (*corrects*) what . . . went wrong.

Adele With the mat.

A moment.

Taylor I need LIP BALM!

Amy *gets hers out, holds it out to* **Taylor**, *who can't reach.* **Adele** *looks at hers*

Adele Oh, mine's medicated, so . . .

Amy *puts lip balm on* **Taylor**, *and fans her furiously.* **Taylor** *breathes, slowly.*

Taylor Who wants a fresh juice?

Nat We wouldn't wanna put your mum out.

Taylor Mum's enjoying playing nurse and having me immobile.

Nat But, don't worry, Tay, I promised her I'd keep you up to date with *all* the taster mock preparation homework, every last bit.

Taylor (*ignores her*)   I'll text the order, she'll bring it up.

All put hands up for juice.
(*Sends text.*) And now I've got Disney Plus *and* Hulu.

Taylor's *phone buzzes, she checks.*

Taylor   Mum says she'll bring up some snacks. Salty, and sweet.

Adele   Your mum's so cool.

Taylor   Then thought maybe we could all, like, watch something.

Amy   OMG, this is, like, more fun than summer hols, an Amazon discount code and a new girl pissing herself.

All huddle round **Taylor**'s *bed,* **Nat** *last –* **Taylor** *reclines, Queen of Sheba like.*

Do we see the tree shaking in a spring breeze?

10. Taylor's Bedroom

Taylor *is still in bed, now looks flatter, bored, paler. Her flowers are wilting.* **Amy** *and* **Adele** *stand at the end of her bed. A moment of stilted silence.*

Amy   Everyone, like, totally sends their love.

Pause.
There's just like a lot going on at the moment, in the lead-up to

Amy *stops herself.*

Adele (*dreamy*)   I love this time before summer, air's all heavy with . . . fluffy pollen-y like . . . (*can't think of another word*) fluff, long hot days and . . . possibil . . . it

She sees **Amy**'s *glaring, stops.*

Taylor (*bit desperate*)   Wanna stream something?

Amy   Your mum said you're now on limited screen time and socials.

Taylor *suddenly looks very tired.*

Adele   You should rest. We'll . . . (*motions to go*)

Taylor (*desperate and loud*)   No don't GO!

A moment, they don't know what to say.

Amy   We'll . . . come round Friday.

Adele   Friday's the debrief for the 'accepting diversity picnic'.

Amy   Thought that was Thursday.

Adele No, that's the pre-debrief, to confirm numbers, faith snack preferences and any newly developed life-threatening allergies.

A lull, nobody says anything. Blackout.

11. The Tree

Willow *sits alone, leaning up against the tree. After a moment.*

Willow I'm Willow.
Which isn't even . . . ironic.
You don't have to tell me your name.
But I thought maybe we could . . . hang out, for a bit. Totally fine if you don't want to talk, or. I get that too, sometimes.
A lot.

Beat.

But . . . sometimes it's good to, you know, do that, with somebody else.
Actually, not sure you get . . . irony.
But, even trees, old wise one's like you, must get lonely, sometimes.

She sits there, in the quiet.

12 Taylor's Bedroom

Ash *stands at the end of* **Taylor***'s bed, holding a balloon that says 'HOPE YOU FEEL MUCH BETTER SOON', stares at the one that she's already got.*

With difficulty, **Taylor** *leans, grabs old balloon, squeezes for dear life until it pops, loudly. Beat.*

Taylor Thanks for coming.
Finally.

Ash Life's been, like, hectic.

Taylor Not here it hasn't.
I must look totally *awful*.

Ash You look sick.

Taylor (*scared*) Like, in a good way?

Beat – he doesn't know what to say.

Ash (*moves closer, beat*) Can I . . . touch you?

Taylor No one else has, for days. Except Mum, when she gave me a bed bath.

She shudders. He's freaked out.
You know, I'm still fully functional, from the ankle up.

He doesn't move, is scared.
Ash, I'm not dying.

Ash   That's what my grandad said. When he was, like, proper dying.

She pats bed. He steps closer, leans on the bed, puts hand on something, jumps back.

Ash   Shit! That like a . . . a . . . compulsory bag?

Taylor (*laughing*)   A . . . *what?*

Ash   One of them bags you like . . . wee in, or. . . . *you know*, when you can't

She pulls out the lump; it's a family-size pack of Hula Hoops from under her sheet.

Taylor   Hula Hoop?
They're not . . . mine, they're for guests.

He shakes his head, a beat.

Ash   This is, like, weird.

Taylor   Can you help me, Ash?

He looks scared.
To scratch, my itch.

She goes to pull the sheet back, but he speaks, stopping her.

Ash   Got something in your hair, some kinda . . . *flaky*

She touches hair, mortified.
And there's a . . . weird smell in here.

Taylor   Of . . . what?

His phone buzzes loudly and which they both clearly hear.

Ash   Smells like when my grandad died and my nan kept his clothes in her bed, for weeks, till we found them and had to throw them out.
Then we found out she'd been ringing the speaking clock, twelve times a day, just so she could hear another person's voice.

His phone buzzes. This time he checks it. Pockets it. Looks at her.

Taylor   Ash, it wasn't your fault.

Ash (*no idea*)   What?

Taylor   This (*tries to motion to her leg, move it, can't*) me, like *this*.

Ash   Yeah. I still got a suspension though.

Taylor (*getting cross*)   So what, now you want an apology?

He looks at her – sees he's not going to get one.

Ash   Hoping at least it means I get to, like, miss out on sitting my GCSEs.

298   Jane Bodie

Taylor   No that's . . . you'll still have to sit them.

A moment.

Ash   Guess you're gonna miss the end-of-term concert, dance thing.

Taylor (*lying*)   I wasn't really into that, so

Ash   I just go to see people like have their dreams shattered. And for the leotards.

He grins. She winces, in pain; if he sees, he wishes he hadn't. A beat.
(*Meaning plaster cast.*) That thing is massive.
Anyway, you should probably, you know, rest

Taylor   What else am I GONNA DO!

A heavy pause.

Ash   I gotta go.

A moment. He puts the balloon on the table, looks at her, then leaves.

She picks up her phone, scrolls, it's not helping. She stares ahead, sad. She tries to itch her leg, can't reach. She yells, frustrated, chucks her phone; it falls on the floor, out of reach. She stuffs a huge handful of Hula Hoops in her mouth. Lights fade.

13. Taylor's Bedroom

The flowers in the vase have died, the balloon's sagging. **Taylor** *seems smaller, paler, her hair a damp hot mess.* **Amy** *stands by her bed. Pause.*

Amy   Want me to . . . tidy up your hair, baybz?
Looking a bit

Amy *pulls a disgusted face, can't help it.*

Taylor (*calls out*)   Mum, MUM! My meds are wearing off!

Blackout.

14. Taylor's Bedroom

The vase on the bedside table's empty, the balloon is deflated. **Taylor** *looks sick, starved of daylight, bored to death. Phone's in her hand, but it's silent and she's not looking at it.* **Willow** *stands at her door, wearing a small grubby backpack.*

Willow   Your mum said to come up.

Taylor *looks at her, doesn't move.*
(*In case she's forgotten.*) I'm . . . Willow.
I'm at your . . . I live just . . . it's a few miles away. Three, three and a half

Taylor (*horrified*)   You *walked* three miles here?

Willow And a half. This is en route.

Taylor To what?

Willow To where I was going.

Silence. **Willow** *looks over at the deflated balloon, now sinking. Moves so she can read it; its letters are crumpled, have run together, so it now reads.*

Willow Looks like . . . FOMO. Well (*cocks head to read*) . . . FE . . . MO.

She turns to **Taylor**, *takes a Tupperware box out of her bag.*
I brought soup. My mum's. Well, technically Tesco's, but

She holds it out. **Taylor** *doesn't move,* **Willow** *then realises she can't. She puts her bag down, takes out an elm branch, puts it on the floor. She goes over to* **Taylor**, *hands her the Tupperware box.* **Taylor** *stares at it, opens lid, picks something out.*

Taylor (*freaked*) That a . . . *leaf*?

Willow It'll be . . . broccoli, or

She steps forward.
Actually that is a leaf.

She takes the leaf from her and pockets it.
Got opened a bit, the container, in my bag.

Taylor Which is, *full of leaves*?

Willow It's okay, it's waterproof (*holds up bag, water drips from it*). It was.

She picks up the branch, sees the empty vase, puts it in it.

Taylor *What* is that?

Willow Ulmus Procera. (*Explains.*) English Elm. You can tell by the double serrated leaf margins.

She steps closer, touches a leaf, demonstrating, impressed. **Taylor** *doesn't look.*
Willow Where it connects to the stem, it's asymmetrical.

She stops, **Taylor** *still isn't looking.*
Willow Each bud has these reddish hairs, see, just above the leaf scar.

Taylor *turns, looks at the branch.*

Elms get a really rough deal. I mean aside from Dutch elm disease, which wiped out twenty million of them, they're often linked with melancholy, and death.

Before a horrified **Taylor** *can ask.*
Willow Which is probably because they drop their dead branches, without warning, big ones. And they're also the preferred choice, of wood

Taylor For . . . what?

Willow Coffins.

Taylor *stares at it.*

Willow But I think they're . . . beautiful.
When they flower, between February and March, the flowers are this dark pinkish red, and they hang, like . . . rubies.   They used to be really common in England, but now, they're rare.

Taylor (*freaked*)   Did you . . . cut it off?

Willow   It fell, off the tree at the top of the hill.

No recognition from **Taylor**.
Willow The hill, across from the . . .

Taylor *shakes head – nope, still not getting it.*

Willow You can see it from the road, up where the path ends. The hedgerow thins out and if you climb through it, the woodland starts.

Taylor   How near to Hogwarts are we talking?

Beat.

Willow   It's dying.

Taylor's *phone rings, she jumps. She answers it, relieved.*

Amy (*on phone/loud speaker*)   What you up to, babe?

Taylor   Just back from a run, and about to do some kick boxing.

Amy   Lols.

Taylor (*beat*)   Thought you were . . . visiting today

Amy   Dance routine practice took longer than we (*She stops herself.*) We weren't gonna go ahead with it, Tay, but we decided, as a group

Taylor   Without me? Because that's *not* the group. The *group's* all of / us

Amy   We've been working on it all year, Tay . . . and we can't just put everything on hold, because

Taylor   I'm ON HOLD!

Tries to calm down.
It's been two weeks. And most of the moves in the routine are mine.

Amy   I know. (*Chipper.*) So, we were thinking it could be, like . . . a tribute.

Taylor   I'm not fucking DEAD!

Willow   Do you want me to . . . (*Motions she'll leave.*)

Amy (*overhearing*)   Who's that? In your room, who's there?

Taylor   . . . No one.

Amy   I totally just heard another voice, Tay, in your room, a girl's voice.

Taylor   It's no one. There's no one here. I'm, like, literally, alone.

Willow *leaves.* **Taylor** *doesn't notice.*

Amy (*calls out*)   Ash, wanna say hello to Tay? She's, like, semi-naked!

Taylor (*smiling*)   Shut up.

A moment. **Taylor** *smiles, waits for* **Ash** *to come to the phone.*

Amy (*to* **Taylor**)   He must have been in a hurry.

Taylor   What did he (say?)

Amy (*aiming for hopeful*)   He did like a little wave.

Taylor   A . . . hello wave, or a, *I'm not talking to her*, wave?

Amy   Hard to tell. It was very little. Hey . . . (*Caring.*) You okay, baybz?

Taylor   I . . . I'm in a lot of pain, Ames, I'm really bored and you know, this is actually really *fucking*

Amy (*cuts her off*)   Totally, hundred per cent, gotta go, call you tomoz.

Taylor   When are you (coming)?

But **Amy**'*s hung up.*

Taylor   She hung up (*As if to* **Willow**.) She never hangs up first.

Sees **Willow**'*s gone. She looks sad. Grabs phone, no calls, she dials a number.* (*On phone.*) Hey, Ash, it's me. Your (*stops herself saying girlfriend*) Haven't heard from you for . . . I sent you a . . . not sure if you . . . where you've . . . I'm still here . . . I miss you, so . . . call me, yeah?

Tries to keep desperation out of her voice, doesn't manage. She hangs up. She leans with effort, grabs the branch, as **Willow** *enters with a jug. A moment, caught out.*

Taylor (*holding branch*)   I've got this full-on itch, under my cast, I can't . . . reach it and . . . If I don't itch it, I'm gonna fucking scream.

Willow *calmly takes branch from her, puts it in the vase and pours water onto it.*
Taylor   Thought you said it was dead.

Willow   I said it was dying. Not the same thing.

Taylor   I can totally see why people link them with misery and death.

Willow (*corrects*)   Melancholy.

Taylor   So, thanks anyway, for bringing round a piece of dying, but not quite yet dead tree, it's really brightened my day, given me a *boost*, and this (*motions space between them*) has been totes real.

Willow   I wrote a poem about it, the tree.

Taylor Yeah, not reading the room.

Beat.

Willow It's dying because of the new motorway.

They can live up to a hundred years, but this one's . . . the leaves should be green. I can't prove it, but developments like that, when they're rushed through . . . because chemical waste devastates woodlands, effects the nature around it, even changes the composition of the flora

Taylor Whoa, margarine's proper under threat too?

Willow The *ground flora.* Toxic waste causes a loss of micro-organisms, so it changes the soil, which affects how much water gets to the roots

Taylor You know, we were wrong about you. Like, we knew you were a weird, emo slash ewok hybrid, but we thought you were quiet.

Willow Who's we?

Looks around room.
Looks like you're on your own, to me.

Touché. **Taylor** *tries to itch her leg, can't.*

Taylor Why are you here? I mean, other than to deliver the weird . . . *soup*?

Willow I was following the ley line. From where the new road starts and the tree ends, and it, it led me here. Did you know that your house is right on the centre of a ley line?

Taylor I do now.

Pause – her mask drops for a moment.

The doctor said I could take up to eight weeks to heal. That's if . . . it's a straightforward break. He told Mum I'm not healing as well as I should be, not for a healthy young girl. I wasn't supposed to hear that, but his whisper was really fucking loud.
I'm getting this full-on allergic rash. I've eaten all the Hula Hoops and it was a family pack. And I really need to go to the toilet.

Beat – **Willow** *rummages in her bag.*
Does it smell in here?

Willow Not to me.

She wipes her nose with an earthy hand.

Taylor Maybe not the ideal person to ask.

Willow *walks to* **Taylor***, takes a knitting needle out of her bag, points it at her.*

Taylor Don't shoot! (*Grins, despite herself.*) I've only got one leg.

Willow For the other one. The one with the itch.

Taylor *grabs the needle, sticks it down her cast, scratches, hell for leather, a look of ecstasy on her face. She gets a message, grabs and reads it. Puts it down.*

Taylor My dad. Telling me to stop treating my mum like a slave. Says that's his job. LOL.
Does your dad think he's a comedian?

Willow My dad's dead.

Pause – then **Taylor** *can't help but scratch.*

Taylor I'm sorry.
That I said you weren't here before.
But you take a photo of me doing this and I'll kill you, with this weird arse branch.

Willow I don't have a phone.

Taylor *stops scratching.*
Willow And I don't like emo.

Willow *smiles, for the first time.*
See you tomorrow.

Before **Taylor** *can protest,* **Willow** *leaves.* **Taylor** *sits a moment, then sticks the needle down her cast, begins to scratch again, closes her eyes, in bliss. Lights fade. Music plays into next scene/can be music for next scene, or taken over by . . .*

5. School Playground

Dance routine music blares out of one of the girls' phones – cast to choose the song.

Amy*,* **Nat** *and* **Adele** *are working on their dance routine (it's good) but they're out of sync.* **Rowan** *stands at the front – makes a square with a hand – vogueing.*

Rowan Smashing it, bitches! Now, imagine you've got a grapefruit between those tight buns, and you're giving it a . . . *squeeze.*

They continue, trying this with varying degrees of success. On the other side of the playground (world apart) **Olive** *and* **Laurel** *sit on a bench, or floor, laptops open, facing each other, earphones in – playing a war game.*

Adele*'s behind,* **Nat***'s ahead and* **Amy***'s right in the middle.*

Rowan/Laurel/Olive (*in unison*) Killing it!

Nat (*stops*) We're . . . totally out of sync.

Rowan You're totally in sync. You're like, N Sync, literally.

Nat We're supposed to each have, like, a special moment.

Rowan You'll get your moment, baybz.

Nat Yeah, I had mine. But Adele was still *mid* her moment.

Adele Maybe you could stop calling us bitches, I feel objectified.

Rowan What about *bi-atches?*

Adele *thinks on this, hard.*

Amy Maybe we all need an *actual* moment.

Rowan Ho-kay. (*Clipper boards hands.*) Take five . . . *ladies.*

Nat (*to* **Rowan**) Erm, I thought I was choreographing this.

Rowan I'm on big vision, you're totally the CEO of moves.

Amy To be fair, a lot of the moves are still Tay's.

Nat Do they have to be though?

A shocked intake of breath from the others.
Like, I mean, I totally get it's like awful that she's missing out, hundred per cent traj and that, but, like, she's not here, so . . .

Laurel (*mid-game, screams*) Wither and DIE weakened EARTHLING!

Group ignore them.

Nat It blatantly works as a three-piece.

Looks to **Rowan** *for back-up.*

Rowan Destiny's Child *look out*!

Nat Like, sometimes it's good for things to . . . you know, change . . . evolve. And because everybody should get to shine in a, like, democracy.
And 'cause, you know, why does Taylor always get the first Tic Tac?

Amy So, I can have the second one?

Rowan I think that was rhetorical.

Adele I *really* miss her.

Nat (*to* **Adele**) Do you want the opening slut-drop solo or not?

Adele *walks up front – ready to shine.*

Rowan Remember embodying this year's theme in every move, *If you can't tweet something nice, then the only thing to follow is your heart!*

Luke *enters, bored, approaches* **Laurel** *and* **Olive**. **Olive** *has their hand down their pants – unself-consciously – it's a security thing.*

Luke What you doing?

Olive *takes earphones out.*
Luke Get your hand out your pants, Harry Potter.

Olive You say that like it's an insult.

Luke   And it's like you want someone to hit you.

Laurel   Their protective shield's currently active, so

Olive   And I'm disadvantaged.

Luke   Ah, *come on*, don't play that fuc–

Olive   No, I'm . . . playing, with a disadvantage (*motions screen*) by choice.

Laurel   Otherwise they always win.

Olive (*it's no fun*)   Always.

Luke   Is anyone really ever a true winner though, bruv, in *Minecraft*?

Olive   Oh it's Blade Guard Vectures.

Laurel   Vectures of the First Company, of the knights of ancient Terran . . .

Luke   Yeah, you're hurting my head.

Ash *sidles up, a battle mood, postures.*

Ash   Yo, Luke.

Luke *turns, they both untuck their shirts, in unison, a battle move.*
Ash   Why don't you pick on someone your own size?

Luke *untucks his shirt even more – it's war.*

Luke   Cos I'm the biggest guy in school.

Ash   Not what I heard. Not where it counts.

Luke   Yeah, well, Taylor never complained. And you know what they say, it's the motion of the ocean, not the size of the boat.

Ash   You kiss your mother with that mouth?

Luke   No, but I kiss yours (*Steps closer, alpha.*) every night, just before I . . .

Olive (*mid-game/yells*)   Time to face the futility of your feeble ego-driven attempt at a misguided COUNTER-ATTACK!

Distracted by this, **Ash** *and* **Luke** *look over to* **Laurel/Olive** *a moment, distastefully, as if they're aliens. Then* **Luke** *looks back at* **Ash** *and backs off.*

Luke   Actually, I don't wanna do this.

Ash   Na (*steps back*), me neither.

Luke   This whole like . . . *Alpha Nemesis* thing.

Ash   I don't even know what that means. Literally.

He doesn't.

Luke   I think we can be better than this.

Ash Yeah. (*Thinks.*) Than what?

Luke (*gives up*) I'm tucking this in.

He tucks his shirt in, game over, **Ash** *relieved now does the same.*
Luke Thought you'd been suspended anyway.

Ash *looks self-conscious*

Ash I got . . . bored, on my own.

Luke *nods, amused.*

Luke So, your *girlfriend's* got over a thousand views on TikTok

Both suck in breath – ouch.
Someone added some tunes. Quite catchy, actually.

Ash She's not my . . . we're, like, taking an official break. Because she's

Luke . . . Broken?

Ash (*guilty beat*) I mean, she was always, like, high maintenance

Luke Fact.

Ash But in like a good way.
Now, she's just . . .

Luke . . . . Got one leg?

Ash Na. She's like . . . sad. Needy. (*He shudders.*) I dunno what to . . . say.

Luke Still, guess she got her wish. Cos Tay always said she'd be famous.

Looks at **Ash**.
Luke You told her though, right? That you and her are . . .

Ash I left her *on read* for almost a week.

Luke *sucks in breath – nasty.* **Willow** *enters the playground, unseen.*

Luke Like on read, not *unread?*

Willow *wants to avoid them, but they're walking in her direction, can't escape.*

Ash So she knows she's been seen, but not 'seen'. So yeah / she knows.

Luke (*in unison with* **Ash**) / She knows.

They high five, as they collide with **Willow**, *but they don't see her, as she walks through them, under the arch of their arms, unseen and beyond. Nobody sees her.*

As **Luke** *and* **Ash** *pass the dancers,* **Ash** *and* **Nat** *lock eyes,* **Nat** *poses, hotly, badly.*

Luke (*to* **Rowan**) Dude, why do you, like, hang out with girls?

Rowan (*shrugs*) Same reason as you.
Because they're more mature and better company.

Ash *and* **Luke** *look totally blank, as a bell rings, to signal end of break. All begin to leave, except for* **Laurel** *and* **Olive***, still engrossed in their game. The battle ends.*

Olive (*taking earphones out, crestfallen*)   Sometimes wiping out an entire civilisation in a lunchbreak feels like a hollow victory.

Olive *looks sad.* **Laurel** *reaches into their bag, takes out an energy bar, which they hold out to* **Olive***.*

Laurel   Peace? In the temporary form of half a muesli bar.

Olive (*sighs*)   If only life were that simple, compadre.

But **Olive** *smiles and takes it. As* **Willow** *checks out the playground and sees it's safe (only* **Laurel/Olive***), she picks up some litter, bags it, walks past* **Laurel** *and* **Olive***, dribbling a trail of earth from the bottom of her backpack = and singing to herself.*

Laurel *and* **Olive** *watch her – as if she's their new leader, they're in love – as she exits. They look at each other and then, grabbing their stuff, they follow her.*

16. Taylor's Bedroom

Taylor *is in bed, looks brighter, sitting up a bit more and isn't on her phone. The room's now full of branches and bits of colourful plants, in cups, glasses, on surfaces and some on the wall, stuck in picture frames – a growing arboretum, it's alive, with life.* **Willow** *tends to the plants, seems at home.*

Taylor   So, what exactly is a lie line?

Willow   Ley line.

Taylor   S'what I said.

She's waiting, **Willow** *looks at her, sees she actually wants to know.*

Willow   It's a . . . straight line, alignment, drawn between . . . significant historical structures, or . . . landmarks. And, some people think

She   People, like you?

She grins.

Willow   They believe that . . . ancient societies deliberately built . . . structures on . . . along them, that they . . . represent ancient trade routes, and . . .

Stops, then:
A line of . . . earth energy.

Taylor (*snorts*)   For what, like alien spacecraft?

Willow (*beat*)   Yeah. (*Beat.*) Like that.

Taylor (*having fun now*)   And so, what's significant about this house then, I mean, other than it's where my entire life went to shit and you decided singing to yourself in public is acceptable behaviour?

Willow If you're really interested, look it up on your *phone.*

Taylor Where is my . . . (*Looks around bed.*) It's being weird.

She means quiet.
Must be the (*spooky voice*) *ley lines.*
Hey, you think one day plants, not dead ones obviously, might get cool?

Willow (*turns/hurt, for plants*) Plants *are* . . . cool, they're *more than*

Taylor You know, like Ed Sheeran, making being ginger cool and / that

Willow Who's Ed Sheeran?

Taylor What the . . . okay, so this is why you don't have any friends, Willow.

Willow (*a hurt beat*) Knowing the . . . latest . . . *TikTok sensation*

Taylor Steady on, Instagirl

Willow You think knowing that . . . *stuff* makes you cool?

Taylor I think knowing where the local ley lines run doesn't.

Beat.

Willow How do you know I don't have any friends?

Taylor . . . Wild guess.

Willow Friends are over rated.

Taylor What, like phones?

Willow They're a . . . a distraction, from what's important.

Taylor How do you know what's important, know *anything*, without a / phone?

Willow Books!
They're these things, tablets, made of paper, and they have words printed on them, literally.

Taylor *Hey*, you made a joke Willow, ok not a massively funny one, / but

Willow Nature, and *my eyes*. By . . . looking, observing . . . waiting, I see, know, what's important. What matters.

Taylor Won't your mum get you one, a phone?
You can get them proper cheap these days, online.
Wait, you haven't got a laptop either, have you?

A moment. **Willow**, *hurt, goes to leave, gets to the door and then turns. Beat.*

Willow I thought we were . . . becoming friends.

Taylor No, you're just the only person that's still coming to see me.

Willow And why is that, do you think, Taylor?

Beat.

Taylor Because of you, Willow.
They're not coming, messaging, because now they think . . . *associate* me . . . they think I'm like you.

With your weird . . . talking to yourself, writing poems that don't rhyme, and your half-dead bits of mele-fucking-choly tree that you carry round, as if that's somehow normal, Willow! It's . . . saving the planet, helping ANYONE!
This, *you* . . . are not normal, Willow!

Willow What's . . . normal?

A moment between them.
And it is helping. You sat up today, there's colour in your cheeks, and your mum said that the doctor thinks you're making progress.

Taylor (*a scared child beat*) Did she . . . really say that?

Willow No, not exactly, but you did sit up / Tay

Taylor And why do you keep chatting to my mum anyway, like she's your, go talk to your *own*

Willow And you know, you haven't mentioned your rash today, not / once

Taylor And what, you think that's . . . that I'm getting *better* because of us being *friends*, this room being full of bits of some old dead tree!

Willow It's not DEAD!

Pause.

Taylor Maybe in an ideal world, Willow, I'd look back on this time, use it, as a break, from the pressures we're all under, every day, to be special, cool . . . *the best*. Use this time, to . . . *grow*.

She is getting emotional, pushes it down.

And in an ideal world, being alone, *lonely* (*dirty word*) wouldn't have its own . . . smell, something that makes people take a step back, they don't know why, but they know it's a disease, and they don't want to catch it.
And maybe, in that place, I'd actually like my own company, Willow, and we'd be friends. But that's not where we live.

Beat. **Willow** *walks over to the branch by* **Taylor's** *bed, touches it.*

Willow A lot of animals, like people, prefer to be in groups, herds, packs. But there are some that prefer solitude. The platypus, the koala

Taylor These all . . . like Australian animals by any

Willow Marine turtles, blue whales, polar bears, orangutans and giant pandas, all isolate, by choice. Some actually live longer as a result, like the black-browed albatross and Hanoi, the giant tortoise

Taylor You know, Willow, quoting weird arse . . . facts about useless shit / (stuff) isn't actually having a conversation.

Willow's It's better than lying to yourself!
People aren't *not* coming round, or calling you, Taylor, because I'm here with you. Because how would they even know that?

Taylor Yeah, yeah well you said your dad was DEAD!

A moment. She's sorry, too late. **Willow** *begins to snap off the dead buds and leaves.*

Willow But it doesn't mean those species live a sad, lonely life.
In fact, they're . . . tranquil, they don't have to compete, they're calm, independent, they're self-sufficient.

Buds and leaves gone, she now starts pulling the branch apart.

Take the lionfish, which is a fish, not a lion, it has no choice to be anything other than a solitary marine animal. It's actually a very beautiful, fascinating fish, but nobody sees, notices that. Because . . .

She's demolishing what's left of the branch.

Taylor / Willow

Willow Because its dorsal fins are full of *deadly venom*, which is a way of protecting themselves. They've adapted, learned, not to come out, they've perfected the art, of, of staying hidden.

Taylor STOP!

The branch is in pieces on the floor, bits still broken in her hands, **Willow** *looks down.*

Taylor If being lonely is so great, Willow, why do you keep coming here?

Willow Because you keep letting me.

Longish pause.
Mum bought me a phone, on special offer. It's in the kitchen drawer, by the matches.

She bins what's left of the branches, looks at **Taylor**.
I got bullied, at my last school, online, and on my phone, and at my school before that. And at the one before

Taylor I get it.

Willow There are worse things than loneliness, Taylor.

Taylor (*beat*) Like . . . *what* though?

Willow Hunger . . . famine . . . environmental destruction, war. Death.
Though they now say that loneliness is likely to increase your risk of premature death by 26 per cent.
That it's worse than smoking fifteen cigarettes a day, and obesity.

Taylor   For someone who doesn't have a phone you know a lot of shit.

Beat.

Willow   This room does smell.

Taylor (*freaked out, shifts*)   Of . . . what?

Willow *puts her backpack on and turns to leave.*
Taylor Where you going?
Willow? . . . Will . . . Where you. . . . where could you possibly have to . . .

Willow *exits.* **Taylor** *looks at the space she's made, doesn't look at her phone.*

17. The Tree

As **Willow** *climbs down from the tree, she sees that* **Olive** *is standing at the bottom of it.* **Willow** *wipes her face, she's been crying.*

Then **Laurel** *comes up the path, carrying a shovel.* **Laurel** *holds out the shovel to* **Willow**, *who doesn't take it.* **Olive** *takes some shears out of their bag,* **Laurel** *begins to dig at the trench, as* **Olive** *picks up the increasing dead leaves, and* **Willow** *watches, not speaking, her tears drying.*

18. School – Dance Night

The girls are ready, dressed in their Strictly *finest for their dance, all glittered up.*

Rowan   Okay . . . *group huddle.*

Opens his arms. The girls huddle around him.

You know 'grown-ups' (*does quotation marks*) call this era we're in a 'period of mourning', because they think it's a time, of us, saying goodbye, to our (*quotation marks*) 'childhoods'. A time of . . . uncertainty, where we're left staring into a vast, unknown, and terrifying future.

Girls are starting to look a bit confused, all look at each other.

But that's because they don't understand, us, or now. They're limiting us, seeing us as types, 'labels', but we are *more than that*, we are so much more. We are not just . . . like, kids constantly on socials . . . or . . . like . . . one who's always replacement comfort eating. Or . . . one who's only ever gonna feel confident enough to be second place, ever.

Or, the one that only got a shot at any real power, when the true leader was incapacitated, due to breaking a vital body part. Or . . . the one that's . . .

Nat   Okay, we get the general drift. Can we . . .

She motions towards the stage, wanting to go there, now, they all do.

Rowan (*lost in his speech/moment*) . . . Whose sexuality is beyond ambiguous, fully decided yet. Even to them.

Back on them now.
Tonight we, you, are going to confront those labels, subvert and cast them off, like unwanted outgrown skins.

Like . . . glorious butterflies, emerging from our innocent years of . . . repressed slumber, *we* are going to burst out, smash their limits, and bravely fucking brilliantly SHINE!

Beat, **Amy** *snaps moment,* **Adele** *eats a handful of Haribos from her pocket.*
Rowan Now, go out there and smash it, bitches!
Ladies . . .
(*Corrects.*) Women.

We hear a drum roll, announcement, or the intro to their dance song, as girls exit, full of adrenalin, ready for their moment and starting their moves, beaming. . .

19. Taylor's Room

Willow's *standing at the door.* **Taylor**'s *sitting up properly in bed. A pause.*

Willow I didn't go to the dance thing.

Beat.

Taylor Thanks.

Willow Oh, I didn't . . . *not* go in protest.
My mum thought that maybe we should have an evening together, that night, just us . . . and I hate dance, and I

Taylor Maybe quit, while you're ahead.

Beat.

Willow I heard it was a disaster.

Taylor How d'you hear that, carrier pigeon?

Willow Adele OD'd on Haribos, slut-dropped too early, while Nat was attempting a samba point double shimmy cross, and Adele elbowed her in the face. Twice.
My mum told me. And it's all over school.

Taylor Bet you've seen the YouTube clip too by now, of my spectacular

Willow (*shakes head*) Nope.

Taylor Yeah, well you're the only one that hasn't.
Ash dumped me. Well, left me *on read* for over a month, so

Willow *nods, not getting it.*

Willow Your mum called my mum, must have got the number from school.

Taylor *nods.*
Willow She said it's been eight weeks.

Taylor Longest eight weeks of my life.

Willow Thanks.

She almost smiles, she made a joke.
She also said it was probably time I got rid of some of these.

Motions to branches.

Taylor (*sarcastic as fuck*) You *think*?

Willow (*comes into room*) And as my project is complete.

Taylor . . . What?

Willow There's eight different species of plants in here.

She looks around the room, pleased.
In Chinese culture the number 8 is seen as lucky, and of course 8 is also seen as the most healing number, according to numerology.

Taylor *looks around at the full room, impressed and also realising that she no longer notices them, she's got used to having them around.*
And, as you're going for your X-ray tomorrow.
And, it's your birthday.

Taylor *looks at her, vulnerable.*

Taylor I used to love summer, the run-up to it. The end of a school year, another step towards being . . . adult, being able to finally . . . do stuff.
Fifteen's supposed to be the best year of your life, Willow.
If this is it, I'm gonna quit now, stay in my room forever, lights off, emo style.

Willow I think you're pigeon holing and stereotyping emos, limiting their

Taylor Happy FUCKING birthday, Taylor!

Willow And now you're talking to yourself.

Beat.

Taylor I'm frightened.

Willow *sees she is, comes into room, stands by bed, looks solemn (bit too solemn).*

Willow (*reciting poem*)
 You let me crawl up into your arms

  Where I feel safe, hold me

  Make patterns of dappled light, on my face

>
> And let me believe, just for a moment
>
> That the turning away, the yellowing of your leaves
>
> Is just you taking a break, after all these years
>
> You're tired
> Of standing strong, facing the weather

Beat.

> But that you're not going, you're not leaving us
> Not forever.

Taylor   That is truly depressing, Will. Though to be fair, it rhymed, in parts.

Willow   My dad left us.
We moved here because he was going to work on the new motorway, a new start, for all of us. But then he, he left my mum.
He left us.

A moment.

Taylor   I'm glad you came. That you came back, Will.

Another moment.

Willow   Your mum said maybe I could, *we* could try and see if you could get up, stretch your legs. Maybe get some fresh air.

She grins.

20. The Tree – Dusk

Willow, **Olive** *and* **Laurel** *are wheeling* **Taylor** *up the path to the elm in an old wheelbarrow.* **Willow** *pushes the barrow.*

Taylor (*not loving this*)   You told mum you had a proper, like, wheelchair!

Laurel   You're sitting up.

Olive   And you're technically on wheels.

Taylor *turns to* **Olive**, *as if noticing them and* **Laurel** *for the first time.*

Taylor (*to* **Olive**)   When did you suddenly get a set of balls?

Olive   Technically? In the womb. Testes form, if they're going to

Taylor *goes to speak, doesn't get a chance.*

Laurel   To become balls, that is.

Taylor's *now open-mouthed.*

Olive   . . . At around six to seven weeks after conception. Though all humans actually begin development from the same starting point.

Laurel Because testes and ovaries originate from the same gonadal primordium, and don't start to differ from each other, officially, until about eleven weeks. So, until then, they, we . . .

Olive Are all the same.

Olive *and* **Laurel** *smile, a double act.* **Taylor** *stares at them.*

Taylor Starting to see why you three formed a close-knit 'group'.

Olive (*politely holds out hand;* **Taylor** *doesn't shake it*) I'm Olive.

Laurel (*with a little wave*) Laurel.

Willow I met them, here at the tree.

Taylor Came out of the woodwork, literally.

Laurel You mean metaphorically.

Olive We're both at your school.

Taylor (*doesn't recognise them*) Yeah, but . . . not, not in the same

Laurel And in your year

Olive Both of us.

Laurel In your class.

Olive I usually sit next to you. Literally.

Taylor *thinks on this, and that she's never noticed them, but then she sees that they've arrived at the tree. She looks up – it's beautiful, she's overwhelmed.*

Taylor So . . . what do we do now?

Willow We hang out.

Taylor Right. With, *a tree?*

They nod, go about their business, digging and checking leaves, perhaps watering.

Taylor (*shouts*) Wait, can I see my house from up here?

She tries to look, holds up her phone, looks at it.

Willow There's no signal here.

Taylor'*s about to protest, but then sees something coming up the hill, frowns.*

Taylor Shit! (*Tries to move.*) Get me . . . Oi, woodcraft folk, get me fucking up!

They up-tip the wheelbarrow, **Taylor** *wriggles out. Using her arms, she manages to get on her feet. Cast heavy, she limps awkwardly to hide around the tree, as* **Amy**, **Adele**, **Nat** *and* **Rowan** *appear – standing at the bottom of the path, looking up.* **Nat** *sports a juicy black eye.* **Taylor**'*s badly hidden.*

Amy (*butter wouldn't melt*) Hey, Tay.

Taylor *doesn't move.*

Amy Good to see you, like, up and about.

Rowan We went round to yours.

Amy As it's almost your birthday

Adele Thought you might want some . . . company.

Amy But your mum said you'd gone for a walk.

Rowan Not *a walk*, obvs.

Nat With some new *friends.*

A moment – **Taylor** *sees she can't hide. She comes out for all to see and leans on the tree – so it holds her up.*

Taylor Yeah, thought it was . . . probably time I . . . stretched my legs.

Nat Your *leg.*

A stand-off – West Side Story. Two worlds face each other. All stand their ground.

Rowan We didn't correct her, your mum, what she said.

Adele Cos your mum's really cool.

Nat About these . . . guys, being your *friends.*

Nobody moves.

Adele (*means this*) It's good to see you looking better, Tay.

Taylor *self-consciously touches her hair, uncombed.*

Amy We're going to Maccas tomorrow night, by the new motorway.

Rowan Thought we might catch a movie after. Something . . . escapist.

Amy Wanted to see if you wanted to join us, the *group*? See whether you're, like, *in.*

Nat Or . . . *out*?

A moment. All wait.

Taylor I'm . . .
I'm in. Yeah. I'm . . . a hundred per cent

Rowan Probably couldn't bring the wheelbarrow.

They laugh.

Amy And you'll have to leave the tree huggers behind.

Nat Maccas don't serve animals. Not live ones.

They laugh, louder.

Amy Be good to, you know, finally get things back to, like, normal.

Taylor *sees* **Willow**'s *looking at her. They advance and then stop in a line. Beat.*

Taylor (*half to self*) What's . . . normal?

Amy (*with a laugh*) . . . What?

Taylor (*beat*) Do you know where the term tree hugger comes from?

Olive *goes to speak,* **Taylor** *hushes them. They're all checking phones for answer.*
Taylor There's no signal up here.

All *look offended.*

Nat It's, like, a proper weirdo, who gets off hugging, *touching* like trees.

Taylor W*here*, I said.

No one speaks, **Laurel** *is about to,* **Taylor** *motions for them to shut it.*
Taylor Willow?

Willow *doesn't move.*
Taylor Tell them.

Looks at **Willow** *– imploring. A moment.* **Willow** *is tight-lipped.*
Taylor *Please*, Will.

Beat.

Willow The word, term, *tree hugger* was . . . first used in 1730, when a woman started a protest, in Northern India, against . . . deforestation, by the army. She did it, by hugging a tree, holding on to it and refusing to move, to protect the forest, the trees. And then, 294 men and 69 women, all Hindus, all joined her / and

Taylor *motions for her to stop – that's enough.*

Amy So, what, you care about like weirdos and weird nature shit now?

Taylor I had a lot of time on my hands lately. Time to think. Time alone. Then, then . . . I wasn't alone any more.

Nat *swats a fly.*
Taylor What happened to your eye, Nat? Overdo the eyelash curlers?

Olive *suddenly laughs out loud.*

Nat (*flustered, she retaliates*) Ash says hello. Actually, he doesn't.

Taylor Yeah, well tell him . . . actually don't tell him anything, not from me. I see now my upgrade wanted a downgrade.

Nat, *offended, goes to advance on* **Taylor**, *thinks against it,* **Taylor** *prepares to stand up to her, nearly falls, topples, ends up hugging the tree.* **Amy**, **Adele**, **Rowan** *and* **Nat** *hold up their phones to film it.*

Taylor What . . . you gonna film this, and put it up on YouTube?

Yes, they are – **Adele** *is about to say yes, but is interrupted by* **Taylor** *continuing.*

Taylor Then what, you gonna watch it over and over, alone in your room, instead of maybe actually getting out and *getting a life*!

Adele (*freaking*) What is that like . . . humming, *buzzing* sound?

Willow Nature.

They listen, sounds of nature, crickets before rain, birds, bees, and getting louder.

Nat (*afraid*) It's . . . getting louder.

Laurel (*grins*) That happens.

Willow It's getting dark.

Taylor And, you should know, that this tree is totes brimming, alive, with . . . *millions* of flying, furry, really hungry *bugs*.

The group look scared, buzzing gets louder, on cue. **Nat** *tries to move, is stuck.*

Nat Ohmygod what is that!

Pulls out her new shoe, which is covered in something dark and sticky.

Rowan Nature, and shit.

Adele Literally.

Nat This place is . . . freaky . . . it's not even like on my Maps! I'm DONE!

She starts to retreat, a moment, then the others follow, down the hill. **Adele** *can't help but do a little wave goodbye, as they leave. Perhaps* **Rowan** *smiles at* **Olive**.

Adele (*as they exit*) Can we . . . get an Uber?

They've gone.

Laurel Well, they seemed nice.

Taylor Shut up.

Taylor, *unable to stand any more, falls against the tree. She slowly spreads her arms out, around the tree, for support.* **Willow** *joins her on the other side, spreads her arms, their hands are almost touching.*

Taylor Oh my God, I can hear her, like . . . breathing.

Laurel (*wheezily sucking on inhaler*) No, that's me.

Taylor Wait, are trees like . . . girls, or boys?

Olive English elms are hermaphrodites. (*Explains.*) Intersex.

Taylor They're *what*?

Olive Both male and female reproductive parts are contained within them, within the same flower.

Olive *grins proudly,* **Laurel** *looks impressed,* **Taylor** *doesn't know what to say.*

Taylor (*leaning in to tree*)   It's . . . warm. Makes me feel all . . . (*Hasn't words.*)

Laurel   Hugging trees actually increases your levels of oxytocin, the happy hormone, along with serotonin and

Taylor   Can humans get Dutch elm disease?

Willow *laughs, shakes head,* **Laurel** *climbs the tree, swings,* **Olive** *clears leaves, digs at the earth, perhaps throws leaves at* **Taylor***, who looks up and suddenly laughs.*

Taylor   . . . Dappled light.

They both look up, close eyes, dappled. **Taylor** *opens hers.*

Taylor   Does it wash out my skin tone?

Willow, **Olive** *and* **Laurel** *laugh, then* **Taylor** *smiles, seeing the joke. Then she looks up, and suddenly looks serious.*

Taylor   Is it really . . . dying?

Laurel   We don't know.

Taylor (*pointing*)   Hey, look! It's . . . budding, up there!

Willow   Some things . . . bloom, suddenly, once, before they die.

Taylor   Good to know.

Beat.
How long do I have to stand here?

Willow   Long as you want.

Olive   There are no rules.

Taylor   Actually, not sure I can move.

Beat.
At some point I'll totally need to go to the toilet.

They all stand there, as the sun starts to set.
Might just stay here, for a bit.
'Hammond Song' by The Roches begins to play/or music of your choice.

Willow   Don't worry, it'll hold you up.

Beat.

Taylor   For how long?

Olive   Wait.

Laurel   Just . . .

Beat.

Willow   . . . Wait.
Listen.

Pause.
And, see.

She smiles. As all of them stand there, enjoying the beauty, as the sun sets around and on them, and nature serenades them – this moment.

End.

Character Plot

	1	2	3	4	5	6	7	8	9	10	11	12	13	14	15	16	17	18	19	20
Willow	✓		✓	✓	✓		✓	✓			✓			✓		✓	✓		✓	✓
Taylor		✓			✓				✓	✓		✓	✓	✓		✓			✓	✓
Nat		✓					✓	✓							✓		✓			✓
Amy		✓			✓		✓	✓	✓			✓	✓	✓			✓			✓
Adele		✓			✓		✓	✓	✓					✓			✓			✓
Rowan		✓			✓		✓	✓						✓			✓			✓
Olive					✓		✓								✓		✓			✓
Laurel					✓		✓							✓		✓				✓
Luke				✓			✓							✓						
Ash				✓			✓					✓			✓					
(Teacher)					✓															

More information about the characters and how much they speak

Willow – Significant dialogue, solo scenes and a poem
Taylor – Significant dialogue, spends much of the play in bed with a broken leg
Nat – Significant dialogue in a group
Amy – Significant dialogue in a group
Adele – Significant dialogue in a group
Rowan – Significant dialogue and a long monologue
Olive – Some dialogue
Laurel – Some dialogue
Luke – Smaller part, can be doubled with Teacher if necessary
Ash – Smaller part with some key scenes with significant dialogue

Main Narrative Beats

1. Willow sits in the tree. A group of girls sit on the motorway flyover, they are saying goodbye to exams and being teenagers. They discuss the new motorway being built.
2. In Willow's bedroom, she uses a branch and pretends it's her mum. The branch mum is kind and supportive.
3. At school, the girls are in PE, they have been told to include Willow. Taylor does a gymnastics routine and it goes horribly wrong, everybody sees. The video travels around the whole school.
4. Taylor is in bed, her ankle is sprained, the girls are visiting, they are going to keep her up to date with school, no one tells Taylor about the video.
5. Time has passed, Taylor is in bed, Amy and Adele visit, they don't know what to say to each other. In the tree, Willow talks to the tree, she asks it to be her friend.
6. Ash, Taylor's boyfriend visits. He's scared, this reminds him of when his grandad died. Ash leaves, Taylor is frustrated.
7. Time has passed, Amy visits Taylor, Taylor still ill, Amy pulls a face.
8. Time has passed, Willow visits Taylor. Willow has brought soup and tree branches. Amy rings Taylor, the group are going to do the dance competition without her. Taylor calls Ash, he's not replying to messages.
9. Willow tells Taylor that the elm tree is dying because of the new motorway. Willow found Taylor because her house is on a ley line, they chat. Willow announces she'll come back tomorrow.
10. At school the girls are practising the dance routine. Ash squares up to Luke, they talk about the video of Taylor. Ash says he's broken up with her, he's left her 'on read'.
11. Willow is at Taylor's house again, Willow has filled the bedroom with tree branches. Taylor tells Willow that the others won't visit because she's associated with Willow and Willow is weird. Willow tells Taylor she was bullied in her old school.
12. At the elm tree. Willow is visited by Olive and Laurel. At the school dance, Rowan is giving the girls a pep talk ahead of their routine.
13. Willow didn't go to the dance, she is visiting Taylor. The girls messed up the routine and it's gone viral. Taylor's birthday is tomorrow and she has her X-ray to see if she's recovered, Willow shares a poem and suggest that they get some fresh air.
14. Willow has brought Taylor to the tree in a wheelbarrow with Olive and Laurel, they hang out by the tree,

15. The girls arrive, they want to know if Taylor still wants to be in their group. Taylor gets Willow to tell the girls about being a tree hugger, she scares the dance girls off by talking about bugs and insects and they leave.
16. Taylor hugs the tree. Olive tells her that elms are hermaphrodites. The group stand with the tree, the tree is growing small buds, maybe it isn't dying after all.

The Company of Trees

BY JANE BODIE

Notes on rehearsal and staging, drawn from a workshop with the writer led by Natalie Abrahami held at the National Theatre, October 2024

Introductions

Lead director Natalie Abrahami asked everyone to introduce themselves with the following:

- Name and pronouns.
- What does the room need to know about you to make your best work?
- What do you need from the room?
- What can you offer to the room?

This gives everyone the opportunity to discuss anything that may be making them feel anxious about their engagement in the process. Even if you are working with a group that you feel know each other well, or that you know well, it gives a space for new things to arise that may be in response to the context of the play.

Provide an opportunity for those who may not want to address things within the group to talk to you at another time.

Code of conduct

Ask everyone to list three things they would like from your rehearsal room. This could be in small groups or individually.

Then come together as a whole group to share and vote for what things should appear in your room's code of conduct. These should be things everyone can agree on.

Examples could be:

- Be present, open and willing to share
- Respond to the point not the person in discussions
- Meet line learning deadlines
- Bring water
- No phones

It is also an opportunity for you to consider things that may be challenging within the play and how they might be mirrored in the room both positively and negatively. In foreseeing these issues, you can ensure that they are part of the code.

These can be on display in your rehearsal room and referred back to.

Approaching the play

Exercise: Leaves and logos

Abrahami provided a sheet from **gowildeducation.co.uk**

One half of the page had a selection of logos and on the other side had tree leaves. The names of the leaves and logos were removed from the document. The group had to identify as many of each as they could.

This really brought attention to the room's lack of knowledge about nature as opposed to their ease at naming the businesses attached to the logos.

You could make your own version of this that includes all the plants/trees named in the play. You could also perhaps swap out the brand symbols for emojis.

Exercise: Biscuits or crisps

Abrahami asked the group binary questions. One end (or corner) of the room represented one answer and the opposite corner the other answer. The group demonstrated their preference by moving to one location or the other.

- ← Biscuits or Crisps →
- ← Train or Plane →
- ← Walk or Cycle →
- ← Town or Countryside →
- ← School Lunch or Packed Lunch →
- ← Smartphone or Books →
- ← Individual or Follower →

Start with general questions and then build to the themes of the play. They can initially respond as themselves and then as their characters. You can then open this up to the group to add their own.

Start with simple things that don't need emotional investment for people to answer, before building to more in-depth questions. Avoid anyone feeling exposed in their responses.

Exercise: Character horseshoe

You could do this on the first day based on people's first instincts about character – no one is being held to their choices. You could return to the activity later in the process.

Stand in a horseshoe shape. The horseshoe represents a scale of one to ten, with one end being one (the least) and the other end being ten (the most). Do the exercise as your character.

Stand along the horseshoe scale depending on how your character responds to the question.

> How much do you like school uniform?
>
> How strongly do you feel about rates of babysitting pay?
>
> How much do you experience climate anxiety?
>
> How important is fashion to you?
>
> How important is family to you?
>
> Do you have a good relationship with animals?
>
> How positive are your relationships with adults in your life?

As with the earlier exercise, start with easier questions so no one feels too exposed to begin with and you can build to the more emotionally engaged questions.

Begin to observe patterns – who is next to whom? Are you always opposite someone?

If you do this at the start of your process it could be useful for everyone to wear character labels so it is really clear who is who.

You could ask your group to answer these questions from different sections of the play – does their character make a large journey about any issues? What stays the same for them from beginning to end?

Writer Jane Bodie discussed how it was important to her that every character has a journey over the length of the play and that they each have their moment. This exercise may help actors discover their journey.

You could also revisit this activity as everyone learns more about their characters.

Exercise: Character analysis

Abrahami introduced the group to Stanislavski's three questions to begin to analyse the information about character in the play text.

> What do they say about themselves?
>
> What do they say about others?
>
> What do others say about them?

In keeping with the underlying topic of the piece she also suggested an additional question:

> What do they say about the environment?

Go through the play and collate this information to give you an overview of each character over the whole piece. You could include stage directions if they give an indication of character – how someone walks for example.

What information does it give you? Does their opinion of themselves change? Does their opinion of others change? Has their approach to the environment shifted?

Example: Ash

(From the workshop participants)

What Ash says about himself:

> Life's been, like, hectic.
>
> I still got a suspension though.
>
> Hoping at least it means I get to, like, miss out on sitting my GCSEs.
>
> I got . . . bored, on my own.

What Ash says about others:

> You look sick. (To Taylor)
>
> That's what my grandad said. When he was, like, proper dying. (About his grandad)
>
> Got something in your hair, some kinda . . . flaky. And there's a . . . weird smell in here. (To Taylor)
>
> I just go to see people, like, have their dreams shattered. And for the leotards. (About the dance)
>
> Why don't you pick on someone your own size? (To Luke)
>
> She's like . . . sad. Needy (About Taylor)

What others say about Ash:

> Ash must just be held up, baybz.
>
> Ash coolly slips into the room, with a swagger. (stage direction)
>
> Ash, it wasn't your fault.
>
> He must have been in a hurry.
>
> I miss you, so . . . call me, yeah

Bodie suggested other things that could be useful to look for in the text.

The defining line – what is one line that each character says that shows who they are in the play?

You could also look for any lies they tell. What does this say about them? Why might they lie?

Exercise: First five minutes of the day

Instructions:
Sit or lie down in the space with your eyes closed.

Think of the first five minutes of your character's day on the first day of the play.
Think about your sleep.
What woke you up? Do you remember a dream? Did you sleep well? How do you feel?

As your character becomes more aware, engage with all the senses.
What can you hear? What does your bed feel like? Are you hungry? What are you wearing? How clean are your sheets? Who cleans your sheets? Is there a breeze from the window? What does your room smell of?

When you open your eyes, what does your room look like? Is it tidy? Who decorated your room? Is it your taste? What is the energy of the room? What can you see from the window? Are there photos in your room? Who are they of?

Think of the people in your life at home and when you get to school – who are you looking forward to seeing today? Who are you not?

In your room, picture a sacred object – an object that is important to you. Once you know what it is imagine holding it – what does it feel like? What is its significance to you? Put it away somewhere safe in your room.

Slowly start to get up – how does your body feel? How do you approach the world physically?

Start to move around the space – where in your body does the character lead from? Does their nose enter a space? Does their chest? What is your tempo? Are you late? Are you keen to go?

Stand still and do a task – how does your character engage with this task? It could be brushing your teeth, packing your school bag, etc.

Continue to move around the space – explore how your character differs in private and in public. Their internal life and their external life. Which settings make your character feel most comfortable?

As you're moving around, you can start to acknowledge others in the space. How do you feel about them or engage with them?

Following this activity, share what each character's **sacred object** was.
The workshop participants chose the following objects for these characters:

Taylor – a teddy bear from her dad

Olive – a silver necklace

Willow – her diary or journal

Amy – a second-place trophy as motivation for winning

These might be props or personal items you would like the character to have in the scenes.

You may want to ask the actor playing Willow to make her own journal as Willow as part of her character development, so she has an attachment to it.

An extension of this exercise can be to write in character the answers to these following statements:

Life is . . .
People are . . .
Boys are . . .
Girls are . . .
I am . . .

Example from the workshop participants:

Taylor

Life is dramatic
People are selfish
Boys are a distraction
Girls are jealous of my dance moves
I am central to my group

These questions could be answered for characters at different stages of the play.

Taylor might not say she's central to her group at the middle of the play.

Abrahami mentioned that as a director, no matter how much prep you do, you are always going to be taken by surprise by other people's offers about their characters. These activities allow you an insight into the choices being made by your actors. If it is a choice you don't understand you can interrogate it further – where in the text did they find this idea from? How does that understanding of the character change if you do this activity at different stages of the process?

Exercise: Character improvisations – expanding the world

What goes on in the characters' lives outside of the scenes of the play?

Set up an improvisation that explores an element of a character's life, that occurs prior to the beginning of the play's action, that may give an insight into their responses in the play.

For example, you may want to explore Willow and her mum's relationship before her dad left. Or what happened when Taylor and Luke broke up. Or when Willow first discussed their gender identity with their parents.

Once you have chosen the event be specific about the context:

Where are they?

Who are they with?

What is the time of day?

What is the time of year?

What is the weather?

You can then use other actors to populate and improvise the scene, so one person will play their character while the others may play additional roles that aren't in the play to facilitate the scene.

This gives you an opportunity to work on the characters and any significant experiences before you get to the text.

Production

Design parameters

Create a document listing where the scenes take place and any props or costumes that are mentioned.

This will show you where you need to put your energy set wise – for example only one scene happens at the bridge but multiple scenes happen in Taylor's bedroom.

For example:

Scene nine

Taylor's bedroom

Props: mobile phones (five), Taylor's bed, bunch of flowers in vase, beds table, cuddly toys, balloon, get well card, lip balm

Costume: plaster-cast

It doesn't mean that you have to have all of these items but that you know what has been suggested and can make choices from there. Some of these items may be in multiple scenes. Can some set items be used for multiple scenes – is Taylor's bed made up of staging blocks that are used in a different way in other locations?

You could have this as part of a broader spreadsheet document that breaks the play down page by page. This can list which characters are in each scene which will help you in planning your rehearsal schedule. It could also include when music is listed or time of day that may help when designing your lighting.

The tree

The group created two trees from items available in the rehearsal room: paper, chairs, a music stand, tables, a speaker on a stand.

In 15 minutes and with these limited resources the group were able to make two distinctly different trees.

There was a lot of anxiety about creating a tree for the production – especially when the dream version and the budget don't always align.

Bodie writes in the script that this play would work with no set but somehow a tree needs to be represented.

This can be achieved with very little – people, chairs, newspaper, lighting. In an ideal world, Willow would be able to climb it and jump out of it, but this doesn't need to be literal and obviously needs to be safe.

Any tree is ok – Bodie is really interested in things being created through very simple means.

Suggestions from participants included:

> *Shadow or silhouettes* – using objects or people behind a gauze to create the impression of the tree. References for this: X factor group Attraction; artwork of Tim Nobel and Sue Webster.
>
> *Projection* – showing the tree changing through the piece. Using stage blocks that the image can also be projected onto for Willow to climb.
>
> Keep it within the language of your production – perhaps whatever makes the tree is also in the show as props, or all of your props are made out of similar materials as the tree.

The environment

With the play having an environmental theme, the group discussed how to make the process environmentally conscious.

Design: One of the issues that arises in theatre is not planning ahead and then buying items from places like Amazon or fast-fashion retailers. Try to plan ahead to give yourself the best opportunity to make environmentally conscious decisions. It may take more time to find an item in a charity shop so plan ahead. See what is available for you to re-use what you already have.

Think of it from cradle to cradle – something that gets used in the show that can have another life after the show.

Traffic light all items:

> RED – bought from a fast online retailer and thrown away at the end of the show. Single use.

AMBER – if buying new it has another life after the show.

GREEN – it was found and has already had a life and is reused following the show.

If your initial idea is a red idea, can you think of a way of getting the same result (or better) with an Amber or Green idea?

In the rehearsal room:

Engage your company with the environmental theme.

- Learn more about a tree, perhaps the ones that represent their character or who their characters are named after. Get into nature.
- Reduce printing – asking everyone to take responsibility for their scripts.
- Your group could come up with environment-saving tips and ideas for the process – perhaps including them within your code of conduct.
- If there is anything already in place at school or within your organisation, how can you engage with that? Elect a green captain who could communicate with any procedures or societies that are already in place. If there aren't any, could your group begin one?
- Everyone could chart their day and find ways that they could affect change within that – how do you travel to the rehearsal? Could you bring lunch in a lunchbox rather than buying packaged items?
- Is your rehearsal space set up with the environment in mind – recycling bins; a space for reusable water bottles?

You can be environmentally conscious at all points of the process.

Music

The group listened to the music that Bodie suggests for the play:

The Roches – 'Runs in the Family' and 'Hammond Song'

For Bodie, music transitions are very much about setting the mood for the end of the last scene and what the scene then goes into.

For example, 'Hammond Song' is supposed to bring a sense of togetherness, and the opening of it sounds like nature somehow.

Bodie had originally chosen music for every scene change and sees songs in moments when she is writing. She doesn't want to be controlling and invites directors to have their own take on it. You could play the songs to your cast and see how they feel about them and whether they connect to them. What songs would they choose that have the same impact or are thematically linked?

If using contemporary music, it is better that your group chooses it rather than an adult having a sense of what is cool – like language, music can age quickly.

The text – rhythm, punctuation and humour

Bodie talked about how her plays are very rhythm specific. The beats and pauses are important.

A beat is a breath. A pause is something longer – they belong to you to decide how long this needs to be depending on the circumstances. The beats and pauses can be as important as the words in the delivery of the play. An ellipsis is used when someone doesn't know what to say, or has run out of steam, or changes their mind halfway. These are often harder to achieve but give them a try.

When it comes to humour, it is good for your actors to know it is a joke but not treat it like a joke – flat delivery often works best.

A lot of Taylor and Willow's banter is funny but may not obviously be so. The jokes aren't necessarily meant to make the other characters in the scene laugh but are for the audience. They can be quite tough on the people they are aimed at.

Deliver the truth of the line and the humour will come. Observe and try the punctuation. Honour what is written and that will assist with the delivery.

Observe how the delivery of the text supports the story – Taylor and Willow begin to speak more like each other by the end of the play; as they get to like each other more they mirror each other. Bodie has made their language very different at the beginning and by the end they are speaking in a similar way. You could find ways to support this in the staging.

Be aware that it might be tough for your companies as they are having to learn the beats as well as the words. Encourage them to stick with the script to get the full impact of the text – avoiding paraphrasing or ad libs as much as possible.

Check out

Abrahami spoke about the practice of leaving five minutes at the end of your rehearsal to check out. It is an opportunity for the group to bring up any feelings arising from the rehearsal – the process or the content – and release any anxiety.

This can take many forms and doesn't need to be full sentences: You could check out with three words or a feeling for example.

This can lead to practical solutions – for example, you could invite everyone to have a dance at the end of each rehearsal to shake off the issues being explored through the content of the production.

Question and answer with Jane Bodie

Q: What to do if we don't have the right gender mix for the ten characters in the play?
A: Depending on which character, changing the gender has different impacts. For example, changing the gender of Luke to female would open up questions about Taylor, potentially making an issue about something that isn't part of the play as written. Rowan on the other hand may be easier to change to being a female character. Be aware how one change may have ripples across all the other characters. The preference would be for the company to play the genders as written.

Q: How did you see Olive when you were writing them?
A: Bodie saw Olive as a non-binary character and throughout the development process was fortunate to have non-binary actors explore the character. You can respond to the actors you have in your process and whether someone associates with the character – you could have someone who is not a non-binary actor play the role. Bodie wanted to ensure that if there was someone who is non-binary that they felt included in the play.

Q: If we have students who are less mature or unable to deal with the language in the play, are we able to soften or alter some of the words?
A: In an earlier draft the play was crueller and had more swearing – which felt more reflective of the environment that was being created. That is the way these young people shame or bully each other. Bodie wanted to represent it that way, as at the end of the play those on the receiving end are the victors and not the victims. Having been bullied herself and witnessing the bullying of others, she wanted the language to have an edge to it. However, Bodie totally understands that this language may be triggering for some and has pulled it back from the original draft, leaving more mild language in. You are welcome to take out the swearing, just ensure the replacement you choose maintains the sense and intention. You could invite your company to choose any replacement words, so they can own them and so they make sense for the room as a shared language.

Q: Are we able to work around the physical moment of hands down the trousers if we have participants that would not be able to manage this section?
A: Bodie would rather take this section out than have it rewritten. It is important to still have the characters facing off against each other. The moment, if tricky or too explicit, can be achieved by the actors untucking their shirts dramatically, then tucking them back in when they've decided the fight is over – this moment is about boys playing up to expectations of masculinity and bravado and, in a way, the sillier it is (they barely believe in it themselves after all) the more fun and showy it can be – the shirt pulling-out should do!

Q: Where is the play set? Do you want the cast to have specific accents?
A: Bodie would love groups to use their own accents. If there are words that don't fit with your regional vernacular, there can be variations as long as they have the same intention. If there are words that actors are struggling with, then allow your actor to say it how it works for them. It is good practice to avoid letting your company paraphrase or change the writing. References are designed to not be too vernacular laden, but there

may be things that don't work for your specific region – for example, Scotland doesn't have smart motorways. You can find a reference that is relevant to you that has the same impact.

Q: Why are some of the characters named after trees?
A: Bodie wanted to include some tree names and discussed how there could be some character development in exploring which characters know where their names come from and which don't.

Q: There are some scenes that show the passing of time and the transitions require some development of the scene and costume setting. Should we avoid long blackouts?
A: You can find a language for these moments so that you aren't trying to disguise them. Perhaps characters that have an association with particular items can bring them in. You could heighten it and add music, a clock ticking, etc. You could use some of the props that are already in use – perhaps Taylor could eat Hula Hoops while everything changes around her, or be lit up by her phone screen as things change. You should never apologise for what you are doing onstage.

Bodie writes 'blackout' sometimes to give the intention of the energy of the change, but you don't necessarily need to go for a literal blackout.

Q: How do we go about staging Taylor's accident?
A: You can decide the language of this – if your room can't get to a full blackout, then the stage directions as given may not have the same impact in your setting. You could go into slow motion or use lighting or have the moment of the event shielded by everyone filming. The cast could facilitate Taylor's lift in a more stylised way.

Q: The section of Willow speaking to Tree Mother could be difficult for a young actor – how might we approach this?
A: At this moment Willow is enacting a conversation as she would like it to be. It is ok if it isn't perfect when she acts as her mum, as Willow is not necessarily a great actor. Make sure your actor has an understanding of who they are being when, which will make it clear to your audience – a shift in physicality for the two voices could also help.

Q: In Rowan's monologue on page 313, who is he talking to in the second section? Is this direct address?
A: This sounds like a lovely choice. Whether direct to the audience or he goes into his own world, he really stops talking to the other characters in the scene. The period of coming out of being a teenager into an adult is now quite a dark period and though Rowan is not speaking *to* all of them he is speaking *for* all of them.

From a workshop led by Natalie Abrahami
With notes by Leigh Toney

Their Name is Joy

by May Sumbwanyambe

May Sumbwanyambe is an academic, radio dramatist and award-winning playwright from Edinburgh. Previous plays include *Enough of Him* for the National Theatre of Scotland and Pitlochry (2023 Best New Play at the UK Theatre Awards and Best Production at the Critics' Awards for Theatre in Scotland); *Ghost Light* for Edinburgh International Festival and National Theatre of Scotland; *Joseph Knight* for the BBC and National Theatre of Scotland; and *After Independence* for the Arcola and Papatango. Radio includes *After Independence, The Trial of Joseph Knight* and *Back Home*. May Sumbwanyambe was described by *The Scotsman* as 'one of the key creative figures in Scotland's increasingly determined effort to come to terms with its own colonial past, and particularly with Scottish involvement in slavery and the slave trade'.

Previous plays include: *Enough of Him* for National Theatre of Scotland and Pitlochry Festival; *Ghost Light* for Edinburgh International Festival and National Theatre of Scotland; *After Independence* for the Arcola and Papatango; and *After Independence, The Trial of Joseph Knight* and *Back Home* for BBC Radio 4.

Characters

Saunders – *child of the owner of the farm*
Jo – *student onion picker*
Max – *student onion picker*
Coxy – *student onion picker*
Kelly – *child of the owner of the farm, younger than all of the above*
Ali – *trafficked onion picker*
Noah – *trafficked onion picker*
Patience – *trafficked onion picker*
Asher – *trafficked onion picker, younger than the above three*
Joy – *trafficked onion picker, same age as Asher*

All characters are in their mid to late teens and can be played by any gender. Consequently, the pronouns they/them are used throughout the text, to reflect gender neutrality with a view, and on the understanding that pronouns can be assigned latterly, determined by the casting decisions made by each individual production.

Note on the text

This play is set in Lincolnshire where the playwright grew up and has been written based on the writer's own experiences of working alongside migrant workers – however, in the interests of inclusivity, and the exploration of different points of view and experiences, the intention is for any group to be able to perform this play.

For the avoidance of doubt: A lot of the reported political speech in this text is based on a speech made by Nick Griffin – leader of the British National Party – in Keighley, West Yorkshire in 2009. The speech led to him being taken to court. At the time of writing this play in 2023, ministers of the then UK government, especially in the Home Office, used identical words and ideas in relation to asylum seekers and migrants who are not white.

Note, in the interests of clarity, each scene is introduced by one of the characters speaking directly to the audience in character to establish time and place.

Note on pronunciation

Kachasu should be pronounced 'kah-chas-oh'.

1.

Asher   It's the summer of 2019. Night-time on a farm in Lincolnshire. The infinite sky is lit up by a full moon and countless stars. It looks magical.

Asher *and* **Joy** *are sat beneath the full moon and stars.*

As they talk with one another they stare upwards.

Asher   Ten times twenty is

Joy   two hundred.

Joy   Ten times thirty is

Asher   three hundred.

Asher   Ten time forty is

Joy   four hundred . . .

They trail off. They look about themselves.

No one is around.

They both look up at the night sky in silence. It is beautiful.

Enter **Patience** *dragging a heavy suitcase.*

At first **Asher** *and* **Joy** *don't hear* **Patience**, *but as they come closer* **Joy** *becomes aware and . . .*

Joy   Ten times ninety is . . .

Asher *doesn't snap out of their day dreaming.*

Joy *taps* **Asher**.

Joy   Ten times ninety is . . .

Pateince *clears their throat, announcing their presence to* **Asher**.

Asher *hesitates.*

Patience   One thousand five hundred.

Asher   One thousand five hundred . . . Right.

Joy *holds their head in their hands.*

Patience   Any danger of you two helping me. This bag is heavy.

Joy   I thought you said we had to do some maths.

Patience *carries on with the heavy bag.*

Joy *stands and goes to* **Patience**.

Asher *stays looking up at the night sky.*

Patience   Anyone would think you haven't seen a sky before, Asher.

Asher   I don't think I have. Not like this anyway.

Patience *looks about the sky also.*

Patience (*pointing out*)   Well, you see that up there.

Asher   Where?

Asher *comes closer to* **Patience** *trying to align themself in the direction of* **Patience**'*s finger.*

Patience   There. Up there.

Asher   I can't tell where you are pointing

Patience   Up there.

Asher *looks hard. Sees nothing.*

Asher   What about it?

Patience   You know what they call that don't you?

Asher *looks again closely. They squint their eyes.*

Then looks earnestly in anticipation at **Patience**.

Asher   What? What do they call it?

Patience   They call that . . . the moon.

Asher   Ha. Ha. really funny.

Patience   I thought so.

Joy *playfully slaps* **Asher** *around the head.*

Asher *tries to dodge and then tries to playfully tag* **Joy**.

Patience   Settle down.

Asher *and* **Joy** *settle.*

Patience *stands looking at the suitcase.*

They both join **Patience**.

Joy   Where did you get that?

Patience   It was left for us by the owners of the farm. They thought it would be nice for us all to have some fresh clothes.

Patience *raises their hand. They have a key in it.*

Asher *takes the key. And unlocks the case.*

Patience   Go on.

Asher *opens the case, and searches through it.*

There is nothing in it except for some clothes that are really old and far too big for them.

Asher *pulls out dresses and shirts, one after another until* they *stop and move away.*

Patience   What's wrong? Don't you want fresh clothes?

Asher   They smell like Granddad.

Joy *laughs.*

Asher   And they are all far too big.

Patience   Yes, but they will keep you warm and they're clean. Let's be grateful for these small things.

Asher   I don't want to wear someone else's clothes.

Patience   This is a lot more than we have been offered at any of the other farms.

Patience *kneels before the suitcase. They fold and pack the clothes that* **Asher** *has left on the ground. As they get to a polka dot summer dress, they stop and admire it.*

Patience   What do you think?

Joy   I like it.

Patience   You should wear it.

Joy   It suits you more. You wear it.

Joy *and* **Patience** *smile at each other.*

Joy *looks through the bag now.*

They find something – a dinner jacket.

Joy   Asher. Asher look . . .

Asher   What?

Joy   Come. I think I've found something perfect for you?

Asher *comes back to* **Patience** *and* **Joy**.

Joy *presents the jacket to them.*

Joy   See.

Asher   That is like something Grandpa would have worn.

Joy   Try it. You'll see it is nice.

Asher *tries the jacket on.*

It is several sizes too big.

Asher It makes my arms look very long.

As **Asher** *swings their arms about comically and moves about in the new jacket.* **Patience** *and* **Joy** *laugh together.*

2.

Coxy The same night at the same time – in a clearing in the woods on the outskirts of the same farm.

Four sleeping bags. **Jo** *and* **Coxy** *are sitting on the two outermost sleeping bags.*

They have been waiting for some time.

Coxy *looks across at* **Jo**, *but* **Jo** *is looking away, so they look back in front.*

After another moment, **Jo** *looks across at* **Coxy**, *but* **Coxy** *is still looking away, so* **Jo** *looks back in front*

The two really want to have a conversation about something.

Finally they finally look at one another at the same time – neither says anything, **Jo** *looks away.* **Coxy** *doesn't.*

Coxy So . . . That's where you're sleeping?

Jo Yeah, mate.

Coxy Oh.

Pause.

Jo And you're sleeping there?

Coxy Yeah. Yeah, I think so . . .

Jo *and* **Coxy** *smile to themselves.*

After a long moment.

Coxy So, where do you think Saunders is sleeping?

Jo Next to you.

Coxy No, they aren't . . .

Pause.

Jo *smiles, so does* **Coxy**. *After a moment*:

Jo I slept next to them last night. It's your turn.

Coxy Fine. Saunders can sleep next to me.

Jo *looks across at* **Coxy**.

Jo You mean it?

Coxy Yeah, I mean it.

Jo Cheers.

Pause.

Coxy Of course . . . I'm not sleeping in this bed.

Coxy *moves down one, so either side of them there is a spare bed.*

Coxy I'm sleeping in this bed.

Jo *shakes their head.* **Coxy** *feels rather triumphant for a moment.*

And then **Jo** *gets up and moves up one too.*

Now the two are next to each other and either side of them there is a spare bed.

Jo You can sleep in any bed you want, sunshine.

Jo *rolls over and lies down, before* **Coxy** *can get the chance to protest.*

Coxy *is in checkmate. A part of them admires* **Jo** *for the move, in spite of not getting what they want – to sleep further away from* **Saunders** *and their loud snoring.*

Coxy *thinks on this for a moment.*

Coxy Hey, Jo?

Jo I'm not switching with you, Coxy. I won fair and square. You're next to Saunders tonight.

Coxy It's not that.

Jo *sits up.*

Jo What is it then?

Coxy Why don't we just get rid of Saunders's bed all together? Who knows. Maybe instead of keeping us up all night with their snoring, they'll go and sleep inside their home instead.

Jo *smiles at the thought.*

Jo We can't.

Coxy C'mon. It'll be funny.

Jo *thinks on this. After a long beat.*

Jo *grabs the fourth sleeping bag and gives it to* **Coxy**.

Jo Hide it over there behind that tree.

Coxy *stands and puts the bedding out of sight.*

Jo *moves back over one and* **Coxy** *returns to the bed they were on, so there is now only one bed between them.*

The two sit in silence for a moment

Enter **Saunders**.

Saunders *sits down between the* **Two**

Jo *and* **Coxy** *share a look.*

Coxy   Stand up . . .

Saunders   I've just sat down.

Coxy *stands up.*

Coxy   That's Max's bed.

Saunders   Max's bed?

Jo   Yeah. They've already claimed it.

Saunders   You're having a laugh, right?

Saunders *turns around and looks to* **Coxy**.

Saunders   Are they having a laugh?

Coxy *shakes their head.*

Jo *grabs* **Saunders** *by the shoulders and lifts them to their feet.*

Saunders   Hey. These beds are all from the farm. They're all my bloody beds.

Coxy   Not tonight they're not.

Saunders *walks off a little. Looks around, sees no other bed.*

Saunders   Where am I supposed to sleep then? Supposed to be four bloody beds out here.

Jo *and* **Coxy** *laugh between themselves and as they are laughing* **Max** *enters.*

Max   What's so funny?

Jo *and* **Coxy** *don't stop laughing at first.*

Saunders   Oh, their majesty's here. Are they?

This sets **Jo** *and* **Coxy** *off more.*

Max *can't help but smile. They get into a bed.*

Max   This is comfy.

Saunders   This is bloody ridiculous.

Jo   What's wrong, Saunders?

Jo *giggles.*

Coxy   Yeah, Saunders, what's wrong?

Coxy *giggles too.*

Saunders *is reaching boiling point.*

Saunders   Where is the other bed? I want to know now.

Max *and* **Coxy** *can't contain it any longer; they burst out laughing again.*

Saunders   This isn't funny. I'm not sleeping on the floor. I want to know where the bloody bed is.

Everything **Saunders** *has said has made* **Jo** *and* **Coxy** *laugh that one bit more.*

Jo   There isn't one, mate.

Max   Alright. You've had your fun. Now. Tell him where the bed is.

Coxy   Honest. There isn't one, mate.

Max   I saw four beds out here earlier.

Jo *and* **Coxy** *share another glance.*

Jo   We don't know what happened to it, mate. Honest.

Saunders   You absolute liars.

Pause.

Saunders   Well, then. I'm off inside then.

Saunders *looks between* **Max**, **Jo** *and* **Coxy**.

For a long beat they give him nothing.

Saunders   Right then.

Saunders *turns to leave.*

They walk away purposefully slowly.

Coxy   Could you walk any slower? It'll be morning by the time you reach your bedroom at that rate.

Saunders *turns and glares at* **Coxy**.

After a beat **Saunders** *moves to exit again but before they can go . . .*

Jo   Saunders, wait. They put your bed through there . . .

Coxy *stares at* **Jo**.

Max   I knew it. I absolutely knew it.

Max *playfully slaps* **Coxy**.

Coxy   I didn't do it on my own. They were part of it too.

Max *turns on* **Jo** *and slaps them too.*

Jo *laughs.*

At the same time as the below dialogue. **Saunders** *goes out and comes back in with the fourth bed which they settle down next to* **Coxy**.

Max   You big fat liar.

Coxy   I'm a liar?

Max   You're both liars.

Jo   Alright, mate. I didn't even do it. It was them.

Max   Yeah, well I reckon you two are a bad influence on each other. A pair of devils both of you.

Max, **Jo** *and* **Coxy** *notice and stare at* **Saunders** *now.*

Saunders *has put their head down and is out like a light super-quickly.*

Snoring very loudly.

Coxy   How do they sleep so quickly like that? It's not normal, I tell you.

Jo   Well, goodnight then.

Max   Goodnight.

Jo *and* **Max** *lay down.*

Coxy *stays sat up and staring at* **Saunders** *snoring.*

3.

Max   The next day on the farm. The sun is shining, it's early in the morning.

We are in a large field in the countryside.

The far end of a farm. Rows and rows of spring onions as far as the eye can see.

At this side of the field teams of young people are working the land. Plucking onions from the ground, taking the root off of them, bunching them together in bundles of five and stacking them up for collection.

Amongst the people working the farm (or slightly away from the rest of the group depending on cast size) **Jo** *is crouched working hard. Plucking onions from the ground, taking the root off of them, bunching them together in bundles of five and stacking them up for collection.*

So is **Max** *at first, but as the heat begins to get to them, they stop and look across at* **Jo**.

Slightly away from the two, **Kelly** *is working too; she has her earphones in – she is listening to music.*

Max   You can't ignore me forever. You know that right?

Max *waits for a response; they get none so they get back to work*

After a beat . . .

Jo (*not looking up from their work*)   I don't know. I could try.

Max   So you can speak?

Jo   I'm trying to work. You should give it a go too.

Max *stares at* **Jo**.

Max   What's got up your nose?

After a beat, **Jo** *looks up from their work.*

They look past **Max** *and out into the field beyond, considering the people that they can see . . .*

Jo   I was listening to one of the older lot talking earlier.

Max   Were you?

Jo   The one that did the law degree, what's their name?

Max *shrugs.*

Jo   You know them, that one over there.

Jo *points.*

Max   Oh. That's Jac.

Jo   Jac. Yeah . . . they were saying their dad worked on these fields all their life . . .

Max   So?

Jo   I don't know. I just . . . Their dad worked on these fields so they didn't have to. They sent them to university and everything.

Max   Yeah?

Jo   He did everything he could so they didn't end up like himself. Look at them now, over there. Graduated from law school and stood in a never-ending field of onions.

Max   I'd rather be stood here picking onion after onion than be some scrounger on benefits or something . . .

Jo *thinks on this for a beat*

Jo   Yeah, me too.

Jo *carries on working.*

Max *watches them.*

Max   My dad reckons it's the Labour Party's fault.

Jo *grins to themself.*

Max What?

Jo What doesn't your dad think is Labour's fault?

Max Well, he's got a point, hasn't he?

Jo Labour's been out of it for ages, mate.

Max Yeah, but they should do something, shouldn't they? Stick up for the average British man and woman and that . . .

Jo Labour aren't in government

Max and **Jo** *stare at each other.*

Max My dad reckons, Boris is the only one that can sort it all out. That Theresa May, she's been just as rubbish as the rest of them.

Jo Boris? All Boris will do is talk a load of rubbish.

Max Well, the rest of them haven't done anything to help people like my dad. Have they? . . . I mean you know, with all these . . . you know . . . It's not happening by accident, they're not getting in floods of asylum seekers because they have no choice . . .

Jo Choice, Max? What choice do you think all those people picking onions on that far field have? They just want to earn an honest crust like the rest of us . . .

Max and **Jo** *stare at each other.*

Jo I'm sorry your dad can't get any work, Max. I really am.

Max I've heard them say it on the news too. The Home Secretary. What's her name. Pretty, you know . . .

Jo Patel?

Max Yea, that's right. She said it herself. We've got a duty to take every single asylum seeker whom this is the first safe country they could possible get to, so that's someone from Ireland, or someone from France, or someone from Iceland, but they've got a duty to stop in the first country they can get to, so we shouldn't take any more from Iraq, or Kurdistan, or Afghanistan, or Pakistan, or Somalia, or wherever . . . I mean they've crossed ten or fifteen countries to get here haven't they? It's not just my dad saying it.

Jo I don't think it's that simple.

Jo and **Max** *carry on working.*

Enter **Saunders**. *He stops on seeing* **Kelly** *and stares at them.*

Saunders Go inside.

Kelly No.

Saunders Go inside, now.

Kelly No.

Pause.

Saunders Dad said you're not to be out here.

Kelly So?

Saunders So you're not supposed to be out here.

Kelly What, are you my dad now?

Saunders Someone's got to be.

Kelly Don't stand so close to me, people might think I know you.

Saunders *and* **Kelly** *stare at each other.*

Kelly What are you looking at?

Saunders You're doing it wrong. You're going to have a sore hand if you carry on like that.

Kelly What do you care?

Saunders I don't.

Kelly *puts their ear plugs back in; they sing to their music out of tune.* **Jo** *and* **Max** *notice them and laugh.*

Enter **Coxy** *from up the field.*

Coxy Who's that?

Kelly *just listens to their music.* **Saunders** *stops their music.*

Saunders You better sit somewhere else.

Kelly Why?

Coxy Who's this?

Saunders Cos this isn't where the kids sit.

Kelly Free world, innit.

They stare each other out.

Coxy This your girlfriend/boyfriend?

Saunders This is my step-sibling. And they're an idiot.

Kelly Get lost. Always putting me down aren't you? Only way to make yourself feel big, is it?

Saunders Go home.

Max *and* **Jo** *have stopped working as they listen to the argument. At this point they come over.*

Max You're in my sister's class, aren't you?

Kelly Yeah.

Max Aren't you supposed to be at a school disco?

Kelly Not really my scene. I don't go round with your sister's mates anyway.

Max Why?

Kelly Got nothing in common with them.

Pause.

Coxy You want a fag?

Saunders They don't smoke.

Kelly Yes, I do.

Coxy You want a fag or not?

Kelly Go on then.

Coxy *lights a cigarette for* **Kelly**. *After one puff they have a coughing fit.*

Coxy, **Jo** *and* **Max** *hold back their laughter.*

Jo *takes the cigarette off* **Kelly**.

Jo Shouldn't smoke, you know. (*They take a puff.*) Bad for ya.

Jo *grins at* **Kelly**.

Kelly Yeah, I know.

Saunders 'Yeah, I know.' Idiot.

Kelly Shut up,

Saunders Just go home, Kelly.

Max You go home.

Saunders What?

Max You heard.

Saunders Up yours.

Max Yeah?

Saunders Yeah.

Coxy What's the matter with you? You moody prick.

Jo Want me to punch them, Max?

Coxy I feel sorry for you . . .

Kelly Kelly.

Coxy Having a sibling like them.

Kelly I know. Tell me about it.

Max What you got on your headphones, Kelly?

Kelly 'Something.'

Max Yeah? We heard you singing.

Kelly (*laughs, embarrassed*) Was you listening to me sing?

Jo Yeah, a bit. You got an all-right voice.

Kelly D'ya reckon?

Jo *and* **Max** *give each other a look.*

Jo Not bad.

Max Heard worse.

Coxy *sees the look between* **Max** *and* **Jo**

Coxy Where did you learn to sing?

Saunders I bloody hate you lot sometimes.

Kelly (*not sure if they are making fun of her*) My dad.

Saunders She's talking rubbish. You never even knew your dad.

Kelly I never said that I knew him! But my mum always said he used to sing to me, through my mum's tummy when she was carrying me.

Max Chill out, you two.

Saunders (*shouting at* **Max**) What's this got to do with you?

Max Fair enough. Jesus. Stress bag.

Coxy They're your sibling. What's the matter, Saunders? You two should try and get on. Family's important, innit?

Jo Tha's right.

Saunders They might be my family but they ain't my blood.

Kelly Slash my wrists if I was.

Saunders Let's go, shall we?

Coxy Nah, man. Ain't dark yet. We gotta wait for Robbie to get in or we won't have enough beer.

Saunders Oh yeah.

Jo I'm bored.

Max You're boring.

Coxy So where do you go out, Kelly? Ain't seen you up here before.

Kelly I ain't from round these sides.

Max Where you from?

Kelly Hull. (*Note for other productions: please change to wherever your nearest big city is.*)

Max Yeah? I don't go up north.

Kelly It's wild up there.

Saunders 'Wild.'

Jo Why?

Kelly More going on, isn't there.

Coxy You like to have a drink?

Kelly (*unsure*) Yeah.

Coxy We're all going out later. Get some beers in. Go up the park. There's a lake up there.

Kelly Yeah?

Coxy Yeah. We'll just drink. Sit about. What you reckon? You want to come?

Saunders You what? They ain't coming with us.

Coxy They can speak for herself, can't they?

Max That's right. Fancy it, Kelly?

Kelly I dunno. Yeah.

Max Sorted.

Jo Let's go now, I'm bored.

Coxy My brother won't be back yet.

Jo I'm bored!

Max Chill out, you stress head. What do you reckon your brother'll sort out, Coxy?

Coxy Dunno. Some tinnies.

Kelly Excellent.

Slight pause.

Jo Let's go.

Saunders They ain't coming.

Coxy Why not?

Saunders They don't belong up by the lake.

Max What, are you her dad or something?

Saunders No.

Kelly So shut up then.

Saunders He's gonna kill you when you get in.

Kelly I don't give a shit what he does to me.

Saunders *backs away from* **Kelly**. **Coxy** *moves closer.*

Coxy (*to* **Kelly**) You'll like it up the park. Right nice it is. You can sit out. Look at the lake. Night-time. No one knows you're there. It's alright.

Kelly Yeah?

Coxy You up for coming to the lake then?

Kelly I gotta go home first. I gotta change.

Max You got any sounds you can bring?

Kelly I got loads. Taylor Swift, Beyoncé, Nicki Minaj.

Max Nicki who?

Kelly Nicki Minaj.

Max Who's he?

Kelly You don't know who Nicki Minaj is? She's awesome she is.

Saunders 'Awesome.'

Kelly Shut up,

Saunders He knows who Nicki Minaj is.

Slight pause.

Kelly *looks at* **Max** *unsure if she's being made a fool of.*

Max We'll wait here.

Kelly I'll be right back.

Coxy Kelly.

Kelly What?

Coxy Come here.

Kelly What?

Coxy Come here.

Kelly *steps up to* **Coxy** *apprehensively.*

Coxy Make sure you do your school work before you come back out, yeah?

Kelly (*laughs*)   Get lost.

Coxy (*suddenly cold*)   Go on then. What you waiting for? Go on.

Kelly *begins to exit.*

Jo   Oy, Kelly.

Kelly *stops.*

Kelly   What?

Jo   Don't be long.

Kelly   Will you be here?

Max   Where else?

Kelly   I'll bring my phone for music.

Jo (*bored*)   Fine.

Kelly   Ain't gonna be long.

Coxy   If we're not here, the lake's just up that way.

Kelly   What over there?

Coxy   Yeah.

Kelly   Past the other . . . the other workers.

Coxy   Yeah, that's right, just past them not far, over there.

Kelly   But we're . . .

Saunders   Coxy your . . .

Coxy   What? It's past the others, I ain't saying do anything. With them. Just keep walking past them straight to the lake.

Jo   Can't miss it.

Kelly   See you then.

Kelly *exits*

Jo, **Max**, **Coxy** *and* **Saunders** *watch them leave.*

Still holding back their laughter.

Saunders   What an idiot.

4.

Coxy   Later that day. Early afternoon. The woods just beyond the limits of the farm.

There is rubbish and partying paraphernalia scattered about. Used and discarded cans of beer, sweet and crisp packets. Perhaps not broken bottles but you get the gist.

As lights up **Coxy**, **Max** *and* **Jo** *are standing by a pile of trainers and socks, their jeans rolled up by their knees. They are skimming stones into the lake.*

Behind them **Saunders** *is messing about trying to untangle a fishing rod . . . as* **Coxy** *and* **Jo** *continue skimming . . .*

Coxy   I think I just hit a duck.

Jo *smiles. Throws another stone.*

Jo   That's not a duck.

Coxy *smiles.*

Coxy   What is it then?

Coxy *throws another stone.*

Jo   I don't know. I know it's not a duck

Coxy *throws another stone.*

Coxy   Jealous

Jo *smiles again. Throws another stone.*

Coxy *throws one too.*

Jo   I've ran out of stones.

Coxy *throws a few more stones.*

Then stopping.

Coxy   That's a bloody duck. I killed a duck

Coxy *offers* **Jo** *some of their stones.*

Jo *takes them.*

Coxy *moves to throw but then . . .*

Jo   Course you did, Rambo.

Jo *and* **Coxy** *smile at each other, then continue throwing stones.*

Behind them **Saunders** *loses interest in the tangled fishing rod, stands and, coming up behind* **Jo** *and* **Coxy**, *walks to where they are standing and throws a brick into the water. We hear the sound of lots of wings flapping, a duck quaking in distress, and then silence . . .*

Jo *and* **Coxy** *stand looking shocked.*

Saunders *brushes their hands together and goes back to the tangled finishing rod.*

Coxy   Told you it was a duck.

Pause.

Jo   What you do that for, Saunders?

Saunders Do what for?

Jo You killed a duck.

Coxy Jealous.

Jo They just threw half a brick at it, what do you mean jealous? I mean there's throwing a pebble or two and there's . . . that.

Coxy *laughs.*

Jo I'm being serious, you can go to jail for that.

Saunders You can't go to jail for killing a duck.

Jo Oh yeah, who says?

Saunders I says.

Coxy *gives* **Jo** *the stones they have and sits by* **Saunders***.*

Saunders You can go to jail for killing a swan, mind.

Jo *turns around and throws a stone.*

Jo Can you?

Saunders Yeah . . . Don't know how long for like. But you ain't allowed to kill 'em . . .

Jo *throws a few more stones.*

Jo Why's that?

Saunders God knows . . . Cause they're swans and not ducks. And something to do with the Queen.

Jo *throws their last few stones into the lake.*

They wipe their hands clean on their trousers and stand looking out into the lake for a moment.

Can kill as many ducks as you like though . . .?

Saunders If it isn't on the endangered species list.

Jo *comes back to where* **Saunders** *and* **Coxy** *are sitting and also sits.*

Jo That can't be right.

Saunders I swear it. Just have to kill it humanely that's all.

Jo Like throwing a brick at its head?

Coxy *and* **Jo** *laugh.* **Saunders** *doesn't.*

Saunders It's not like I snared it or kicked it to death or something.

Jo No, mate, you just broke its neck with a brick.

Coxy *and* **Jo** *laugh again.*

Saunders Shut up.

They continue laughing.

Saunders I said shut your mouths.

They continue laughing.

Saunders It's not as if it suffered long.

Jo *and* **Coxy** *carry on laughing. After a moment so does* **Saunders**. *They all laugh together. As they slowly settle down* . . .

They sit in silence for a moment until.

Max Where do you think your sister got to?

Saunder Don't know, mate. Probably didn't come back out. Dad's not happy with her.

Max Still can you imagine if she did? Out of order Coxy telling her to go the wrong way.

They all laugh.

Coxy I can just picture her now stood there gormlessly in the middle of the field. Lost.

Saunders Serves her right. She should have listened to me and stayed at home.

Jo I mean it's not like she'd ever have the guts to go that way where all the . . . you know, where all the others are.

Coxy No chance. Everyone knows not to go over that way.

They all sit in silence for a long beat until **Saunders** *puts their shoes back on.*

They stand and stuff their socks into their pocket. And exit.

Jo *stares at* **Coxy**.

After a beat, they both put their socks and shoes on.

5.

Kelly The same day. Early afternoon. The other side of the field.

Migrant Workers *are doing the same job as the Western workers, but they seem hyper-focused. Never looking up from their task.*

Kelly *enters this part of the field, walking around looking lost. She notices the* **Migrants**.

They watch the group of **Migrants**.

After a beat **Kelly** *approaches them.*

Kelly Alright.

The whole group carry on working.

No one even looks up from their work.

Kelly *spots another group of people huddled together*

They go over to that group.

Kelly Hi, I'm Kelly . . . I'm looking for the lake . . .

Again no one from the group speaks to them.

Kelly *looks about themselves. Unsure what to do.*

Off stage we hear the sound of a whistle.

At that sound, all the **Migrant** *workers stand from their work and exit out towards the sound of the whistle.*

Kelly *watches them as they leave. They don't notice that a migrant,* **Joy***, has not left and is standing behind them.*

Joy *is carrying two beaten-up dolls that have seen some better days.*

Kelly *turns around and starts when they see them.*

Kelly Oh, you scared me.

Joy Sorry.

Pause.

Kelly *doesn't know what else to say. They stand looking about themselves.*

Joy *notices, eventually . . .*

Joy Do you want to see my ants?

Before **Kelly** *can answer.* **Joy** *turns and goes over to a small box on the floor. It is filled with 'imaginary' ants.*

Kelly *watches from where they are.*

Joy I think they might be fire ants, or something. Come see . . .

Kelly *stays where they are. Looks back over their shoulder from where they came.*

Pause.

Joy *stands, dusts themself off.*

Joy Are you gonna have a look at my ants or aren't you?

Kelly Sure.

Kelly *comes over to where* **Joy** *is standing, looks down over the box.*

After a moment.

Kelly I can't see anything.

Joy Look closer, see . . .

Joy *kneels down.*

Kelly *lowers themself but doesn't kneel.*

Joy Cool right?

Kelly *stares at* **Joy**.

Kelly There isn't anything in that box.

Joy I know. It's just a game.

Kelly Oh. Right. Well then, yes, I guess they are cool. Yes.

Joy It wasn't any trouble trapping them. I just left food out overnight and they started coming. First a just a few and then hundreds of them, you should have seen it two nights ago . . . there were thousands.

Joy *picks up some imaginary ants and offers* **Kelly** *their arm.*

Joy Do you want to hold one?

Kelly *stares at* **Joy**.

Joy Go on.

Kelly No, I don't.

Joy What don't you like ants or something?

Kelly There aren't any ants.

Joy I know there aren't. It's just a game. What, you don't play games?

Pause.

Kelly I'm just looking for a lake. Is there a lake round here?

Joy *shakes her head.*

Kelly Oh . . . of course there isn't.

Kelly *holds her head in her hands.*

Kelly I'm such an idiot.

Joy No, you're not.

Joy *puts their arm around* **Kelly** *and comforts them.*

Joy You know what always makes me feel better when I'm feeling sad.

Kelly I don't want to hold any ants right now.

Joy *smiles to themself.*

Joy Oh . . . right. You should have just said that.

Joy *goes back to their box, gently clears their arm of ants so they fall back into the box.*

Joy *goes to* **Kelly** *and sticks out their hand.*

Joy What's your name? I'm Joy.

Kelly Kelly.

Kelly *and* **Joy** *shake hands.*

Joy Nice to meet you, Kelly.

Joy *and* **Kelly** *stand and stare at each other for a beat.*

Joy I better go back or else they'll be no food for me left to eat. Do you want to play tomorrow?

Kelly Sure. If you want. Where shall we meet?

Joy (*pointing*) Up there.

Kelly By the woods?

Joy Yes.

Joy *smiles.*

So does **Kelly**.

Kelly You're definitely going to come, right?

Joy *nods.*

Kelly *turns to leave.*

Joy Kelly.

Kelly Yeah.

Joy Can you bring some food?

Kelly Sure.

6.

Asher Later that same day. Night. Somewhere in the woods beyond the farm.

Asher *stands looking out into the distance and darkness.*

Asher *is wearing clothes several sizes too big for them.*

Enter **Patience** *with firewood.*

Patience *notices* **Asher**, *holds back their laugher.*

They stand some way behind **Asher**. *Looks beyond them for a moment.*

Pause.

Asher   It's getting late.

Patience   I know.

Asher   I can barely see past those trees.

Patience   Will you stop worrying already.

Pause.

Patience   They are safe.

Asher   You don't know that.

Patience   Wherever they are. Dad's looking down on them from heaven and keeping them safe.

Asher   Like he's looking down on us?

Patience   Yes.

Asher   Well, that's done us a lot of good, hasn't it?

Patience *takes the firewood out of its basket and places it on the floor.*

Asher   Ali is back.

Patience *turns. They look out into the same darkness* **Asher** *has been staring into. After a beat they see something . . .*

Patience   Do I see someone with them?

Asher   No, they're on their own. It's just Noah.

Patience   Are you coming to greet them?

Asher *exits in the opposite direction.*

Patience *stares after them.*

Patience *collects a bottle of water from their belongings.*

Pause.

Enter **Ali** *and* **Noah**.

Patience *and* **Ali** *embrace each other. A long embrace. Eventually they step back from one another. And just look at each other. And laugh.*

Patience *looks to* **Noah** *now.*

Noah   We didn't find them.

Patience   Thank you for trying. We really appreciate your help.

Noah It is the least we can do.

Noah *nods at* **Patience**.

Noah *goes over to the fire, puts more wood on the fire.*

Patience *turns back to* **Ali**.

Patience I got you some water.

Ali *takes the water. Drinks only a little.*

Patience You should drink some more.

Ali *puts the lid back on the bottle and offers it back to* **Patience**.

Ali You finish it.

Patience You've barely drunk any.

Ali I've drunk more than enough.

Patience *and* **Ali** *stare at each other.*

Patience You're such a bad liar.

Ali *smiles.*

Ali *goes over to join* **Noah** *by the woodpile.*

Noah Is this all of the wood?

Patience Sorry?

Noah This wood. It will barely last us the night.

Patience I'm going to go and see those men. Get some more wood.

Patience *goes to where their bag is and puts away the water.*

After doing this, they find their pair of flat shoes.

Noah Is that right?

Patience How many pieces do you want?

Ali *stops organising the wood.*

Ali You want to go over there and fight with those dusty old men? For a few more pieces of wood?

Patience Sure. I don't mind.

Ali *and* **Noah** *look at each other and laugh.*

Patience I don't mind.

Noah *takes a few pieces from the woodpile. It is done.*

Ali We'll be fine. Just have to make the fire a little smaller tonight. That's all.

Ali *sits back on their haunches and starts untying the laces of their boots. Their feet are sore.*

Patience   You want some more water?

Ali *painfully pulls off a boot.*

Ali   I'm fine.

Ali *takes a breather; that one boot was hard work.* **Patience** *goes to them and starts on their other boot. Just the laces. They stop as they are untied.*

Patience   Ali, your feet.

Noah *and* **Ali** *laugh.*

Patience   They're worse than Dad's.

Ali   My feet are not worse than Dad's feet were.

Patience, **Noah** *and* **Ali** *laugh.*

Ali *and* **Patience**'s *laughter falls into melancholy as they both think about their dad.*

Noah *notices.*

Pause.

Patience *offers out their hand.* **Ali** *lifts their boot.* **Patience** *pulls it off.*

Patience *takes the boot and puts them together with their stuff. As they are doing this* **Ali** *stays looking out into the darkness of the night.*

Ali   Where's my sibling?

Patience   They're probably with the others.

Pause.

Patience   I'll go and get them if you like.

Ali   It's ok. You don't have to make excuses for them tonight. I saw them leaving as we approached.

Patience   It's not you they're angry with. Not tonight anyway.

Ali   You argued?

Patience   I told them off. All this sulking. It's driving me crazy.

Ali   The spoilt child of ours. Night after night. Thinking only about themself. They act like no one else is worried . . . I will talk to them.

Patience   That's not what I meant.

Noah *goes to* **Ali** *and puts their arms on their shoulder.*

Noah   Don't get all worked up again tonight, alright?

Ali   That is no way for someone to behave, Patience,

Noah Settle down . . . they may hear.

Ali And do not tell me they are just a child. At their age I had already . . .

Patience They are though and so are you. We all are just children.

Ali *stands and walks some paces towards the darkness of the night. They stop on the precipice of all that darkness, looking out.*

Ali We haven't been children, since the war . . .

Pause.

Patience *and* **Noah** *stare at each other.*

Noah *nods to* **Patience** *to go to* **Ali**.

Patience *goes and stands behind* **Ali**.

Patience I'm sorry, Ali, I know you're trying your best.

Ali *turns around and embraces* **Patience**.

Ali You should go back to the others. Keep warm.

Patience I'll wait with you.

Ali *releases* **Patience***; for a long moment* **Patience** *does not let go of* **Ali**.

Ali You go ahead and make sure that sibling of mine isn't getting into trouble.

Patience *finally releases their grip on* **Ali**. *They move to exit. Hesitates. Turns back.*

Ali Go on now.

Exit **Patience**

Ali *watches them leave.*

Pause.

Ali *sits by the woodpile and stares at it. Deep in thought.*

7.

Asher The same night, an open field. A large fire burns.

Lots of **Migrant Workers** *sitting around it trying to keep warm.*

In amongst them **Asher** *and* **Joy** *are playing 'tig you are it', just being children.*

Enter **Patience**. *They notice* **Asher** *and* **Joy** *playing and smile.*

Patience Oi, will you two settle down now.

Patience *lays out a rug and sits.*

Patience Come on, both of you. I want you to come and keep me warm on the rug.

Joy *and* **Asher** *do as they are told and sit.*

Patience *gives them both blankets.*

They huddle together.

Patience There that's better, isn't it?

Joy *and* **Asher** *nod.*

Patience Your sibling is back.

Joy Are they?

Patience Yes.

Joy That's good. Any news?

Patience *shakes their head.*

Joy Sorry.

Patience No news is good news, I guess.

Joy Yes.

Pause.

Joy Is Ali back too?

Patience Yes

Joy Are they coming to the fire?

Patience They are. They will be here soon.

Joy Great. I miss them.

Patience *smiles.*

Patience How was your day today?

Joy It was fine, thanks.

Patience Anything interesting happened?

Joy No.

Patience *stares at* **Joy**.

Joy *stays looking ahead.*

After a long beat of this.

Patience One of the older men mentioned that they saw you talking with one of the local workers from the other side today. At food time.

Joy *stays silent.*

Patience Is that true, Joy?

Joy   I didn't go across there, they came across here. Please don't tell Noah.

Patience   It's ok. You're not in trouble. Your sibling doesn't know. And they don't have to. But you know you can't do that right?

Joy *stays silent.*

Patience   You mustn't see or talk to that person again. Even if they come across. Do you understand?

Joy *nods.*

Patience   I'm serious, Joy. It's dangerous. Not just for you. For us all.

Joy   I understand.

8.

Enter **Joy**.

Joy   The next day. Lunchtime. The woods.

They look around, hesitantly at first, and then . . . .

Joy   Kelly . . . ?

Joy *hears no reply*

Joy   Hello . . . ? Hello, Kelly . . . ?

Joy *hears nothing again.* **Joy** *drops their head disappointed.*

After a long beat of this. **Kelly** *enters from the other side of the woods. They watch* **Joy** *for a long beat.* **Kelly** *clears their throat.*

Joy *doesn't hear, so . . .*

Kelly   Hey . . .

Joy *starts.*

Joy   Oh you scared me.

Joy *and* **Kelly** *laugh.*

Joy   I thought you were gone already.

Kelly   Not yet . . .

Kelly *and* **Joy** *smile at each other.*

Kelly   What took you so long?

Joy   There's lots more work to do today.

Kelly   Oh.

Joy   What?

Kelly   When I was just at home, I overheard my dad . . . he was saying . . . it doesn't matter.

Pause.

Joy   Did anyone see you coming?

Kelly   I don't think so . . .

Joy   I can't stay long.

Kelly   Of course you can't.

Joy   What do you mean by that?

Kelly *stares at* **Joy***.*

Kelly   I just mean don't mug me off, all right.

Joy   I don't even know what 'mug you off' means.

Kelly   It means if you can't stand to be around me then I don't need to be around you either.

Pause.

Joy   I only said I can't stay long because people will wonder where I have gone.

Kelly   Right.

The two stand looking at each other for a long moment, then . . .

Joy *looks at the bag* **Kelly** *is carrying.*

Joy   Did you bring any food?

Pause.

Kelly *searches her bag, then.*

Kelly   All I could get were these biscuits . . .

Joy *takes the biscuits. At first they eat slowly, then quicken, eating them all like some deeply savage and hungry animal. This shocks* **Kelly***. As* **Joy** *notices . . .*

Kelly   You must be really hungry.

Joy   I guess I was.

Pause.

Kelly *reaches inside her bag and pulls out two well-maintained – not new but certainly newer than what* **Joy** *had before – dolls.*

Kelly   I brought you these too . . . I haven't played with dolls for years. I thought you might . . .

Joy *reaches out to the dolls.*

Takes one of them in her hand, holds it like a cherished piece of something very valuable.

Kelly Do you like them then?

Joy *looks at* **Kelly**.

Joy They're wonderful.

Joy *grabs* **Kelly** *in a cuddle around the waist.*

Kelly (*trying to fend* **Joy** *off*) Joy, get off. Joy . . .

Joy *clings on for a long moment.* **Kelly** *gives up trying to push them off.*

Joy Hug me back.

Kelly *barely wraps one arm around* **Joy** *shoulder.*

Kelly Ok. we've hugged . . . Now, will you let me go?

Joy *eventually lets go of* **Kelly** *and steps back.*

Joy So are you going to sit down and play a game with me?

Kelly I thought you said you have to get back soon?

Joy I do. But I've got five minutes, I guess.

Kelly *nods.*

Joy We could play with my dolls, if you like?

Kelly *hesitates, then . . .*

Kelly Sure.

Joy *goes over to* **Kelly**.

Joy (*offering out a doll*) You can have this one.

Kelly *takes the doll in their hands and examines it.*

After a long moment.

Joy Her name is Josephine. She's the mummy.

Kelly *finally looks up from the doll.*

Kelly Is that right?

Joy *nods.*

Kelly Josephine . . . and does that one in your hand, does that one have a name?

Joy *puts the doll in front of her face.*

Joy My name's Rosa. I'm Josephine's daughter.

Joy *waits for* **Kelly** *to respond, they don't. After a moment,* **Joy** *comes from behind the doll and . . .*

Joy Now you . . .

Kelly *lifts the doll higher. But doesn't quite commit with the same childish abandon as* **Joy**.

Kelly Hello, Rosa . . . How are you today?

Joy I'm fine thank you . . . What do you want to do, Mummy? . . .

Kelly *hesitates, then lowers the doll.*

Joy *waits for a response but when they don't get it, they look out from behind their doll.*

Joy Don't you want to play any more, Kelly?

Pause.

Kelly I'm afraid I'm not so good at this game.

Joy You were doing just fine . . . if you don't want to play with me, you can just say you know.

Kelly *offers* **Joy** *the doll back.*

Kelly I don't know a lot about mummies . . . Mine was barely around. And when she was. She was very sad. She used to drink a lot and . . . I haven't played like that for a long time. But I really enjoyed playing dolls with you.

Joy *takes the doll back.*

Joy I'm sorry about your mum. Her being sad . . .

Kelly What's your mum like?

Joy *considers the toy in her hand . . .*

Joy My mum. She was kind. Always smiling. Even when she was tired. Even when you could tell that we were getting on her nerves. She was really patient. She would always listen. Even when we talked rubbish. Being around her, it made you feel so, so safe.

Kelly She sounds nice.

Pause.

Joy I better go.

Kelly Yeah?

Joy Yeah. Thanks again for the dolls. And the food.

Kelly That's alright.

Joy I'll see you tomorrow.

Kelly Yeah, I'd like that.

Joy Me too.

Kelly See you then

Exit **Joy**.

9.

Kelly The same woods. Around the same time of day. But several weeks later.

Off Stage we hear the sound of an adult male voice calling 'Kelly' over and over again.

Adult Male Voice Kelly! . . . Kelly come back . . . Kelly!?

Kelly *sits in the woods, crouching and trying to make themselves as small as possible.*

As they hear the voice they put their hand over their ears and close their eyes.

After a long beat of this enter **Joy**.

They see **Kelly** *and come to a stop.*

Joy What are you doing?

Kelly *opens her eyes and puts a solitary finger over her mouth.*

Off stage we hear the adult male voice. It is getting quieter and further into the distance.

Adult Male Voice Kelly! . . . . Kelly?!

Joy *comes and sits with* **Kelly**.

They both listen.

The voice is gone.

Joy Your dad doesn't sound very happy today.

Kelly He never is.

Joy Sorry about that.

Kelly It's alright.

Joy What happened?

Kelly Nothing.

Pause.

Would you come with me?

Joy What?

Kelly If I ran away . . .

Joy What happened?

Pause.

Kelly Would you come with me?

Joy Where . . . ?

Kelly I don't know . . . Away from here . . . if we had too . . .

Pause.

Kelly *and* **Joy** *stare at each other.*

Joy What is wrong?

Kelly Nothing.

Joy Then why are you crying?

Kelly I'm not.

Joy *wipes* **Kelly***'s eyes.*

Joy Funny way of not crying, all those tears coming from your eyes.

Kelly Are you teasing me?

Joy (*shrugging their shoulders*) Maybe . . . but just a little.

Kelly *smiles at this. So does* **Joy***.*

After a beat.

Joy *suddenly drops to their knees.*

Kelly Are you ok?

Joy *raises a solitary finger to their mouth.*

Kelly What is it?

Joy Shhhh . . . we're in church, silly.

Kelly *is confused for a moment, but then gets the 'game' and laughs a little.*

Joy No laughing in church.

Kelly *raises their arms in surrender then mock locks their lips and throws away the key.*

Joy *closes their eyes and holds their hands together in prayer.*

For a moment **Kelly** *stands watching them.*

Joy Come and kneel down with me.

Kelly *comes over to* **Joy***'s side and kneels.*

After a moment **Joy** *opens their eyes.*

Joy What do you think?

Kelly Of what?

Joy Of the church, silly. Isn't it magnificent?

Kelly Sure. Magnificent.

Joy I love it for its bigness, and it's old and it's got fancy windows with lots of colours and interesting pictures . . . and it's always warm, even at night. It's never cold . . . .

Kelly *looks around themself for a moment. Then . . .*

Kelly Truly magnificent.

Kelly *smiles to themself.*

Joy Do you want to pray?

Kelly Ok.

Joy *closes their eyes and puts their hands together.*

Kelly *watches them without committing to any action.*

After a moment. **Joy** *looks out the corner of their eye and . . .*

Joy You have to close your eyes.

Kelly Do you?

Joy *fully opens their eyes and throws* **Kelly** *a stern look.*

Kelly *closes their eyes finally.*

Joy And you have to put your hands together like this . . . .

Joy *demonstrates.*

Kelly *does nothing.*

Joy Hey, Kelly . . .

Kelly I can't see what you're doing, my eyes are closed.

Joy *waits impatiently. After a moment* **Kelly** *falls into a traditional shape of prayer putting their hands together.*

Joy *does the same.*

The two remain like this for a long moment until.

Joy Who is going to go first?

Kelly *(false excitement)* Oh, me, me, me, please.

Joy *silences them with a reproachful look.*

They fall back into prayer position.

After a moment.

Kelly   Well. It's been a while since I have done this . . . I erm . . .

Kelly *opens their eyes and looks across at* **Joy** *to see if they are looking.* **Joy** *has their eyes firmly closed and hands together.*

Kelly   I'd like to say thank you . . . For putting in my path. Joy . . . I'd like to say how grateful I am to meet someone kind . . . that's all. I mean. Amen.

Joy *opens their eyes and looks at* **Kelly**.

Kelly *is still looking at them. For a moment they hold each other's gaze, then . . .*

Joy   My turn.

Joy *closes their eyes again and excitedly puts their hands together.*

Joy   Dear Lord . . . I never really had a best friend. Excepting Asher of course. If you would be so kind I would like to keep this best friend of mine. They're kind, they want to play with me and aren't always thinking about what other people think or say about me. They're everything I prayed for . . . And I want to pray for my mum. I want to pray that Mum is safe and well and knows that I am thinking of her all of the time. . . . Amen . . . .

Joy *opens her eyes, happy with themselves.*

Then turns to see **Kelly**.

Joy *notices something beyond* **Kelly**.

Kelly   What is it?

Joy *points beyond* **Kelly**. **Kelly** *looks and sees . . . .*

Saunders *enters,* **Jo**, **Coxy** *and* **Max** *enter just behind them.*

Saunders   Alright?

Kelly   Yeah.

Coxy   So this is where you've been hiding after work. We've been looking for ya every day.

Kelly   Yeah?

Max   Yeah.

Pause.

Saunders   Who's your new friend?

Kelly *looks back at* **Joy**.

Kelly   I don't know. They just followed me.

Coxy *laughs.*

Coxy   They didn't.

Kelly I swear they just started coming my way. Didn't stop.

Jo, **Coxy** *and* **Max** *laugh.*

After a moment.

Coxy *walks towards* **Joy**, *has a good look at them.*

Coxy *sniffs them and turns away.*

Coxy Christ, they don't half smell do they?

Kelly No, they don't.

Jo, **Coxy** *and* **Max** *laugh.*

Jo *and* **Max** *watch on for a moment then come across too.*

Coxy I'm being serious. Don't get too close, aye.

Max *goes over to behind* **Joy**.

Smells them. Pulling a face. The smell is unbearable.

Coxy *and* **Max** *fall about into laughter again.*

Saunders *doesn't. They are the only one looking at* **Joy** *right in their face.*

Max Go on then, Jo. Have a smell. I dare you.

Jo *hesitates.*

Saunders *comes over to* **Joy**, *but then with a smile they extend their hand.*

Saunders Hello.

Joy *doesn't offer out their hand.*

The rest laugh, **Coxy** *more than* **Jo** *and* **Max**.

Max What's wrong with them?

Coxy I wouldn't get too close, Saunders. They smell like something rotten.

Coxy *laughs again. No one else does.* **Jo**, **Coxy** *and* **Max** *can clearly see* **Saunders** *doesn't find it funny.*

Kelly It's not their fault. Is it?

Max No, course not, Kells.

Coxy Blumming living in the back of that lorry. Course it isn't.

Coxy *feels the tide turn against them.*

Walks behind **Joy**.

Coxy Back of that lorry, aye? With a hundred Afghans.

Kelly They're not Afghans.

Coxy Fine, whatever they are. Back of the lorry, living like kings and queens, compared to what it's like back there in mumbo jumbo land.

Kelly Mumbo jumbo land. What century are you from then?

Coxy Give over, Kells.

Kelly No. It's so disrespectful and rude.

Coxy Look at them. They can't even understand a thing we're saying.

All look at **Joy**.

Coxy How can it be disrespectful if they don't understand?

Kelly *stares at* **Saunders**.

Pause.

Saunders What's their name?

Coxy Their name? We don't even know if they can speak bloody English. Their name they say.

Coxy *laughs to themself.*

Joy *makes no attempt to speak out.*

Saunders *goes towards them.*

Saunders What's your name? Do – you – have – a – name? Do you have a name? What's your name? Tell us your name? . . . C'mon. What's your name?

Pause.

Saunders (*pointing to themself*)   Saunders . . . Saunders . . .

Joy *looks to* **Kelly**.

Kelly *shakes her head.*

Joy *doesn't respond.*

Coxy Their name's Immy.

Jo *and* **Max** *look curiously at* **Coxy**.

Max Immy?

Coxy *smiles.*

Coxy Yeah, Immy, Immy the immigrant.

Coxy *laughs again.* **Jo** *and* **Max** *can't help but smile.* **Saunders** *doesn't.*

Coxy Tell them, Immy, better here than sleeping with tigers and stuff?

Kelly You don't even know where they're from. How do you know there's tigers there?

Coxy Oh, there's tigers. You can see it in their eyes. Big ones, aren't they? Lions and zebras and tigers, nasty ones aren't they, Immy?

Pause.

All look at **Joy**.

Joy *turns and runs away exiting the stage.*

Kelly *calls after them.*

Kelly Joy, wait. Joy, I'm sorry . . .

Max, **Coxy** *and* **Jo** *laugh to themselves.*

They all keep on laughing.

Kelly *turns on them.*

Kelly They can understand everything that you said to them. And you know what, they are a damn sight nicer than any of you idiots. The lot of you. You're just like my stepdad every one of you. Treating people like they're worthless and you are so much better than them. But you're not better than anyone.

Kelly *moves to exit.*

Saunders *shouts after them.*

Saunders Where are you going now?

Kelly To be with nicer people than you lot.

Exit **Kelly** *after* **Joy**.

Before anyone can say anything back.

Coxy *shouts after them.*

Coxy Is that where you're going is it? Well, I hope you can speak their language. Because none of them can speak yours.

Pause.

Saunders *notices the dolls on the floor.*

They pick them up. Considers them.

Jo I thought your dad said that side of the farm is out of bounds?

Saunders He did.

Jo We're all going to be in trouble if Kelly stirs them up, right.

Saunders We are.

Jo *moves to exit.*

Saunders What are you doing?

Jo I'm gonna go and get her . . .

Saunders No, you're not. We're gonna stay here. That's what we're gonna do.

Max I'm coming with you.

Coxy Me too.

Saunders *stands in their way.*

Saunders You can't.

Jo Why?

Saunders You just can't. My dad won't like it.

Pause.

Coxy Get out of the way, Saunders.

There is a stand-off between them.

Saunders *backs down.*

They all exit. Except for **Saunders**.

10.

Ali Somewhere else in the woods. Night-time.

Noah *and* **Ali** *are sitting by a small fire.*

Ali *notices something in the near distance.*

Ali There's someone just beyond the trees.

Noah Say again?

Ali We are being watched.

Noah Twelve o'clock?

Ali Go round the long way. Get a better look at them.

Noah *stands and exits.* **Ali** *goes over to the pile of belongings. Roots through them, whilst pretending to look in the wrong direction.*

After a long moment, enter **Noah** *with* **Max** *struggling to free themself.*

Noah I think I caught me a spy, Ali.

Ali *looks past* **Noah**.

Ali A quadruple of spies, my friend.

Noah *looks across as* **Kelly**, **Jo** *and* **Coxy** *enter too.*

Pause.

Ali How long have you been eavesdropping?

Kelly We haven't been. I'm just looking for . . .

Noah They're lying.

Coxy We're not. We just came to get our pal. Didn't we, Kelly? Go on tell them.

Kelly Yes, I just wanted to see Joy. Have you seen them? I need to say . . .

Noah and **Ali** *look at each other.*

Noah Definitely lying.

Ali Well, you'll just have to give them the truth serum then.

Noah *stares at* **Ali**.

Ali The Kachasu.

Noah *goes to their belongings.*

From a small bag they pull out a see-through canister that looks like it has a milk-like substance in it.

Ali *points* **Max**.

Ali You. Come here.

Max Whoa, whoa whoa . . . Just hold on . . . let me just explain . . . Because . . . I . . .

Ali I said, come here.

Max *looks at* **Coxy**, **Jo** *and* **Kelly**.

They walk over to **Ali**.

Ali *takes the canister.*

Ali If you're not lying you won't have any problem with drinking this truth serum, will you?

Max What's in it?

Ali Fermented maize, sugar. And, you know, some secret ingredients.

Coxy Max, don't do it. Saunders says they ferment anything they can get hold of.

Kelly Coxy . . .

Noah Let them speak.

Coxy They say, the really strong stuff. It turns people into zombies.

Ali *and* **Noah** *are stoney faced.*

Kelly Coxy. Do you know how ridiculous you sound right now?

Coxy I didn't say it. Saunders did.

Kelly *gives up. And throws their arms in the air with exasperation.*

Noah And they're right . . .

Ali Unless you have a pure heart.

Noah If your heart is pure, you've nothing to worry about.

Ali But if you're lying, first your tongue and then your brain will freeze. So come on, soldier, drink and let us see the colour of your heart.

Ali *holds out the canister.* **Max** *looks around themselves, as everyone watches them. They collectively hold their breath as* **Max** *clamps their nose with their fingers and drinks the Kachasu.*

A beat. **Max** *says nothing for a moment. And then a broad smile comes into bloom across their face.*

Max It's wonderful.

Noah *and* **Ali** *burst out into laughter.* **Coxy**, **Jo** *and* **Kelly** *laugh too.*

Ali *stops laughing first, then after a moment they all settle down.*

Ali Sugar and milk the most truthful drink in the world.

More laughter from the group. Which is suddenly broken by **Patience**'s *urgent entrance.*

Patience What are you doing?

Noah It's ok. We're amongst friends.

Patience Have you all lost your minds. What happens when they find out we have broken their golden rule. Huh?

Max No one is going to find out.

All look at **Max.**

Coxy That's right. We won't tell. If you won't.

Ali *and* **Noah** *look between each other.*

Ali *turns to* **Patience**.

Ali You see, little sibling. All is well.

Ali *turns back to the* **Westerners**.

Ali I need to ask you guys something . . . we're looking for a woman . . .

Patience Ali.

Ali *waves them off. Then turns back to* **Kelly**, **Jo**, **Max** *and* **Coxy**.

Ali We've been looking for our mother. In the hours when we are not working here. We believe she may have been taken to another farm.

Kelly, Jo, Max *and* **Coxy** *look between each other.*

Ali If you could help us please. Please.

Kelly Maybe we could ask my dad?

Ali *and* **Patience** *look between each other. Finally, a hint of hope.*

Kelly Do you have a picture of her?

Noah Yes we do.

Kelly Then can we . . .?

Patience It's with our belongings where we stay by the lorry. If you wait here I'll be back in a few minutes.

Kelly I can come with you and get it, save time.

Max Me too.

Jo Yeah.

Coxy And me.

Patience No. You can't come to the lorry, it's not . . .

Kelly It's not what? It's fine. We're friends. We want to help.

Ali We can trust them.

Kelly And . . . actually you can help me. I'm looking for someone too. Joy.

Patience You know Joy?

Kelly Yes. They're my friend. We play together.

Patience Joy is at the lorry. Doing what they've been told to do. For once.

Kelly Good, then let's go. I need to see them. I owe them an apology.

Patience Come this way.

They all exit.

11.

Enter **Coxy**.

Coxy The woods. Later that night. It is much darker now. The darkness of the earliest hours of a morning. Before there is any hint of sunshine. There is no moon. And barely a star can be seen. It's so dark.

Saunders *is lying down but not asleep.*

Coxy *stands over* **Saunders**, *looking down on them.*

Coxy *seems dishevelled, shocked, more subdued even – by the things that they have seen. They look around themselves. They are really troubled.*

Coxy You awake?

Pause.

Saunders Yeah.

Pause.

Saunders What time is it?

Coxy *doesn't reply.*

After a moment **Saunders** *sits up. They look at their phone, see the time.*

Pause.

Saunders What was it like?

Coxy *says nothing.*

Pause.

Saunders Where are the others?

Coxy They're coming.

Coxy *starts to cry.*

Saunders *stares at them. They don't know what to do.*

After a moment enter **Max**. *On seeing* **Coxy** *they stop.*

Max You alright?

Coxy I think so.

Max *walks over to* **Saunders**.

Max Get up.

Saunders *stands.*

Max *squares up to* **Saunder***'s face.*

Saunders *looks away as if expecting a blow to the face.*

Max Look at me. Look at me.

Saunders *looks at* **Max**. *They look at each other for a moment.*

Max Your dad. He's a . . . what's the word?

Coxy Nazi.

Saunders *looks away.*

Max Look at me.

Saunders *looks at* **Max**

Max *is crying. So is* **Saunders**.

Max He's evil, mate. Evil.

Max *walks away from* **Saunders**. *They dry their tears.*

Saunders What was it like?

Enter **Kelly** *and* **Jo**.

Pause.

Kelly They are looking for a woman. Their mother. She may be on another farm. We have this photo. I thought maybe you could speak to Dad about it?

Kelly *offers the photo to* **Saunders**.

Saunders *doesn't take it.*

Saunders *steps back. Walks off a little. Looks out into the darkness of the night.*

Saunders You guys need to think this through for a second.

Kelly We have thought this through.

Saunders Have you?

Max You weren't there, Saunders. You didn't see it. All those children. All hutched up like battery chickens. It was like something out of a horror movie.

Pause.

Saunders Best for us to just pretend none of this ever happened. Whoever they are looking for. Best for her to just disappear.

Jo Just disappear?

Max *laughs to himself.*

Jo What planet are you on? Where people just disappear.

Saunders I'm . . .

Jo She isn't some duck. That just dies.

Saunders I'm . . .

Jo And it doesn't matter. And there isn't nothing of it. She's a human being, Saunders . . .

Saunders I'm . . .

Max Your dad's lucky we don't call the police.

Saunders What! What have the police got to do with anything?

Coxy They're all just kids like us. They shouldn't be living like . . .

Saunders It can't be that bad. It isn't as bad as all that. It can't be?

Max It is! It is! It's worse than anything you can imagine. You haven't been there, you haven't seen how they're living . . . how they're dying in their own shit and misery. You haven't seen that, Saunders, because your Daddy's golden boy, always doing as he's told . . . always staying on the right side of the field. But we have seen it and so has your dad!

Saunders   Listen to me, Max. You walk around like your dad's the best person in the world. And you know what? You might even be right that my dad is the worst. But don't you act like your dad can't do anything wrong . . . what do you think happens if we call this out? How many people do you think get in trouble? How many people have worked on this farm? Seen them working on that far field. And not said two words. Two words. Except for, 'Pay me'. Your dad's worked on this farm hasn't he, mate?

Max   My dad's got nothing to do with this. What you talking about?

Saunders   Your dad worked on this farm for three years, Max. He was working here when those lorries filled with people first started turning up.

Max   He didn't know about that. He couldn't have . . .

Kelly   No one worked on this farm without knowing. Deep down inside. They all knew.

Saunders   I don't want to get in trouble. I don't want to get my dad in trouble. Or your dad . . . and I sure as he'll know none of that lot over there want any trouble. Do you understand?

Silence.

Saunders   I said, do you understand? All of you.

Jo   Yeah, we understand.

Saunders   Go to the police. Pathetic. I'm going to sleep.

A long silence.

12.

Max   The next morning. just before the sun comes up, we are all at various parts of the farm.

Jo, Coxy, Max *and* **Kelly**.

They all take their phones out.

They all ring a number. And put their mobile phones to their ears.

We hear the phone ring.

A voice at the other end of the line.

Voice   Hello. You have reached the Immigration Enforcement hotline. The Home Office takes reports of crime made by the general public very seriously. If you suspect that someone is working illegally, has no right to be in the UK or is involved in smuggling or other criminal activity, we want to hear from you. You can submit information anonymously or you can give us your name and address if you wish. We will treat any information you give us as confidential. Answer the questions as fully as you can but do not put yourself at risk by trying to find out more information.

We hear a long dial tone.

For a long beat we don't know who is calling the hotline. Then:

Max Hello . . . Mum. I need you to come and get me tomorrow.

Max *puts his phone down.*

Lights out on **Max**.

Coxy Dad. Yes could you come and get me tomorrow please?

Coxy *puts his phone down.*

Lights out on **Coxy**.

Jo *and* **Kelly** *stay in silence for a moment.*

After a long beat.

Jo *puts their phone down without saying anything.*

Kelly Yes. It's about my da . . . it's about everyone.

13.

Enter **Kelly**.

Kelly The next day. Lunchtime.

Kelly *looks around, sees the two dolls that they gave to* **Joy** *and picks them up.*

Kelly *stares at the field where the migrants normally work.*

After a long beat, enter **Saunders**. *For a long beat they watch* **Kelly**, *who continues to stare into the void left by the migrant workers.*

Kelly (*without turning round to face* Saunders, *they just know they're there*) It's so empty. So quiet.

Saunders They're gone.

Kelly *looks at* **Saunders**.

Saunders They're all gone.

Pause.

Kelly Do you know where?

Saunders *shakes their head.*

Saunders A lorry came last night. Rounded them all up.

Pause.

Saunders   You've ruined Dad by this. You do know that don't you? It's all your fault.

Kelly *begins to cry softly with muffled sobs.*

Saunders   Now you're crying.

Kelly   Can we go to the lake. I don't want to go home. I can't go home.

Saunders   Stop crying. I said shut up crying. Why wouldn't you go home when I asked you to? I'm so ashamed of you. I'm so ashamed.

Saunders *exits.*

Kelly *looks at the dolls in their hand.*

They sit and try to play with the dolls but can't quite commit to the childish abandon that **Joy** *manages.*

After a long beat **Kelly** *turns in the direction that* **Saunders** *left.*

Kelly   Joy. Their name is Joy.

End

Character Plot

	1	2	3	4	5	6	7	8	9	10	11	12	13
Saunders	☐	✓	✓	✓	☐	☐	☐	☐	✓	☐	✓	☐	✓
Jo	☐	✓	✓	✓	☐	☐	☐	☐	✓	✓	✓	✓	☐
Max	☐	✓	✓	✓	☐	☐	☐	☐	✓	✓	✓	✓	☐
Coxy	☐	✓	✓	✓	☐	☐	☐	☐	✓	✓	✓	✓	☐
Kelly	☐	☐	✓	☐	✓	☐	☐	✓	✓	✓	✓	✓	✓
Ali	☐	☐	☐	☐	☐	✓	☐	☐	☐	✓	☐	☐	☐
Noah	☐	☐	☐	☐	☐	✓	☐	☐	☐	✓	☐	☐	☐
Patience	✓	☐	☐	☐	☐	✓	✓	☐	☐	✓	☐	☐	☐
Asher	✓	☐	☐	☐	☐	✓	✓	☐	☐	☐	☐	☐	☐
Joy	✓	☐	☐	☐	✓	☐	✓	✓	✓	☐	☐	☐	☐

More information about the characters and how much they speak

Saunders – Significant dialogue and a short monologue
Jo – Significant dialogue
Max – Significant dialogue
Coxy – Significant dialogue
Kelly – Significant dialogue and duologues
Ali – Significant dialogue in two scenes
Noah – Significant dialogue in two scenes
Patience – Significant dialogue
Asher – Significant dialogue
Joy – Significant dialogue and duologues

Main Narrative Beats

1. On the farm, Asher is testing Joy on their times tables, Patience arrives with a heavy suitcase, it's clothes from the farm owners. The clothes are too big and very old, they try them on.
2. Somewhere else on the farm, Jo and Coxy and their friends are camping out. They discuss who is sleeping where, they hide Saunders's bed and tease them.
3. The next morning, Jo and Coxy and friends are picking onions. Kelly has joined them, they don't speak. Jo and Max talk about the other workers on the farm who are migrants.
4. Saunders arrives and tells Kelly to go inside, their dad said Kelly wasn't allowed to be out. Kelly is Saunders' step-sibling. Kelly is from the city, the friends invite Kelly to join them later by the lake, Coxy gives Kelly directions.
5. Later in the afternoon Saunders and friends are by the lake, they are skimming stones, Saunders throws a brick at a duck. The friends laugh about Coxy giving Kelly the wrong directions to the lake.
6. Somewhere else on the farm, Kelly is by the migrant workers. Kelly asks for directions but none of the migrant workers reply except Joy. Joy shows Kelly her imaginary ants, Kelly doesn't understand, it's a game. Joy and Kelly decide to meet up tomorrow, Joy asks Kelly to bring some food.
7. At night, migrant workers Asher and Patience are collecting firewood. Asher is worried. Some of the other migrant workers arrive, they have been looking for someone. Patience is annoyed with their sibling, they want them to grow up. All of them have grown up a lot because of the war where they came from.
8. Later, the migrant young people are sitting by the fire, Joy and Asher are playing. Patience tells Joy that the older men saw Joy talking to Kelly. Joy must never talk to Kelly again.
9. The next day, Joy and Kelly meet up, Kelly has brought food and dolls. Joy is very happy, they hug Kelly. They play a mums and daughters game, Kelly isn't used to playing. Kelly and Joy talk about their mums.
10. A few weeks later Kelly and Joy are in the woods again. Kelly's dad is shouting for her to come home. Kelly asks Joy if they will run away together. They pretend to be in a church and pray.
11. Saunders and the others arrive, they see Kelly and Joy. Coxy says that Joy smells, they bully Joy and make racist comments. Joy runs away, Kelly runs after them. Jo and Coxy decide to follow Kelly, Saunders is worried about their dad finding out.
12. In the woods, at night, Noah and Ali are sitting by the fire. They find Coxy and friends have been spying on them. Kelly just wants to see Joy. Ali gets out the 'truth serum'.

13. Coxy and friends don't know whether to believe in the truth serum or not. Ali says if they are lying their tongue and brain will freeze. Max drinks it, it's delicious. Ali reveals they are joking.
14. The two groups relax, they agree to keep this meeting a secret. Ali asks the Westerners if they have seen Ali's mum. Patience will go and get a picture of their mum from where the migrant young people are living. The western young people want to go with them, Kelly wants to apologise to Joy.
15. Late at night Coxy wakes Saunders up. The group confront Saunders about the living conditions of the migrant workers, they are horrified and upset, they blame Saunders' dad. Saunders wants them to pretend nothing ever happened.
16. The next morning, the Western young people are making phone calls, they are calling parents to pick them up from the farm. Kelly rings the Home Office, she reports what is happening on the farm.
17. The next day Kelly and Saunders are on the farm. The migrant workers have all left. Saunders blames Kelly.

Their Name Is Joy

BY MAY SUMBWANYAMBE

Notes on rehearsal and staging, drawn from a workshop with the writer led by Roy Alexander Weise held at the National Theatre, October 2024

How the writer came to write the play

Writer May Sumbwanyambe wanted to engage with an anxiety about a world that feels out of control. He was affected by his experience as a teenager working on an onion farm in Lincolnshire, and remembers it clearly. He saw other labourers, primarily people from the global majority, facing exploitative working conditions, which went unchallenged by him and others around him. Sumbwanyambe said that he regrets not speaking out against the injustices he witnessed, and the play is an attempt to challenge both his younger self and today's youth to engage with social issues and take action.

The play was also influenced by Sumbwanyambe's time as an immigration lawyer and his work with asylum seekers, migrants and marginalised people. These experiences made him think more about societal power imbalances, and the play focuses on the unspoken or ignored ethical issues in the food supply chain.

Sumbwanyambe described an essay by Arthur Miller, in which a man sees another man whipping a horse. If that man challenges the cruelty and risks a negative reaction, he has to question whether it is worth it; it is easy to walk away. But if the street is busy, there is public pressure. Sumbwanyambe reflected that this is the essence of what theatre can be; an opportunity to engage with injustice as part of a larger group.

Sumbwanyambe's writing is driven by his politics, but his aim was to embed the play's themes in the characters' experiences, encouraging the audience to see the humanity in the story.

Introductions

In pairs, find out your partner's name, pronouns and, thinking about the direct address in the play, introduce your partner as if it's a set-up for a scene that you're about to do. For example:

   Pair 1: Horror.
   Pair 2: Introduction to the last dance before being sent home on *Strictly*.
   Pair 3: Nature wildlife documentary.

One minute to prepare it in pairs and then perform to the group.

Themes

Class, race and global capitalism: The play connects global capitalism to local labour issues, reflecting how people in power exploit workers across class and racial divides.

Ethical dilemmas and complicity: How everyday choices, like what we buy or who we speak to, may contribute to oppressive systems. The play is in part about how to be a good person in society, but the characters act on complex motivations, and the play invites us to reject good vs evil narratives.

Prejudice and imagination: Imagination and empathy were central themes in the group's discussion of the play, and how a failure to empathise can lead to accepting injustices.

Youth, agency and idealism: Central to the story is the young people's desire to create a better world than the one they have inherited. They are questioning societal norms and seeking change through their own actions.

Resilience: The play also tries to find joy in the midst of sorrow, and is ultimately a story of young people finding value and connection.

Home: The characters in the play are navigating trauma, dislocation and an attempt to find stability.

Approaching the play

Politics are built into the dramaturgy of the play, and the focus of the productions should be on the personal and relational dynamics between the characters. The characters' ethical dilemmas are meant to open the audience up to empathy and self-reflection, in the hope of prompting the audience to consider their own societal responsibilities. The question for the groups is: how do we introduce the audience to the humanity in the story and allow them to make up their own political mind?

Before rehearsal: Lead director Roy Alexander Weise suggested that the directors write a list of all the challenges that the play might bring up, including creative and pragmatic challenges.

Research: Sumbwanyambe suggested that there is a degree of education that should be done with every group around the historical, social and political context of the play, but not to bog them down in the research. Instead try to find entry points of context that will work for those young people. There may be useful videos made by young farm workers on YouTube and TikTok.

Mood boards: Invite the young people to print out their research and stick it up.

Conversation: Weise said that directors will have to hold court with their young people. Directors don't have to have all of the answers, but they do have to be able to signpost them in the right directions. Unpack the central idea of how capitalism is working using stories that we all connect to, for example fast fashion.

Farming

Sumbwanyambe spoke in detail about his experiences farming, which provided useful context for the play and could feed into research.

In the late 1990s/early 2000s, from the age of 16 until he was at university, Sumbwanyambe would go home to Lincolnshire in the summer and work on farms and down at the docks. During spring onion season the farms would recruit heavily. Minibuses would be sent round the villages to collect the young farm workers. Once you're used to the system you jump in, they drive you, you get out and get started straight away on the farm. The work is manual: you collect ten onions, bunch them together, cut off the roots and repeat until you have 50 bunches to fill a box. You got ten pounds for every box, which was good money for a teenager. The farm is split up into big fields, so there were other fields nearby.

Sumbwanyambe observed a difference in atmosphere between the fields. On the side of the farm where he worked, you would arrive, have a chat and there was a slowness and calm to the day. There were old hands who worked every season, who give the young people stick; it's a friendly atmosphere. You never meet the owners of the farm, and you stay one step removed from the people that own it.

On the other side of the farm, a lorry would turn up delivering lots of adults, mainly people from the global majority, to work. Periodically, a forklift truck would arrive on this side of the farm with empty crates on. There followed a mad rush to try and get hold of as many crates as possible. Sumbwanyambe saw people trying to grab boxes before the truck had stopped moving. He remembers the spectacle, and wondering what was going on.

Sumbwanyambe realised as an adult that the workers in the other field were trafficked, and were deliberately given too few crates to make them work faster because they had targets to meet. It was a deliberate and calculated way to coerce these people into working harder. People on the farm were aware of what was going on, but nobody said anything. Sumbwanyambe recalls a kind of gallows humour amongst the Western labourers. Nobody did what the young people in the play do; nobody went across the field.

Sumbwanyambe reflected that being a playwright opens up space to ask questions that you might not have asked at the time. He thought about how these exploitative practices operate within a wider system. Supermarkets put so much downward pressure on farmers that they are forced to make tough decisions, and the average person doesn't think about the consequences of these consumer choices; they are motivated by giving their child a diverse, but affordable, diet, for example. The corrupting power of the supermarkets, the manic logic of globalisation and the practicalities of capitalist food chains make it complicated, and the pressures on the different sectors of farming are growing, combined with the reluctance of British people to do this kind of work.

There is a lack of agency when it comes to our participation in these structures of oppression, and the play explores how to be a good person in a broken system.

Structure, style and transitions

Direct address

The direct address is intended to empower the performers to claim the setting of the play, create a direct relationship with the audience and communicate that they are in charge. It also invites a stripped-back production style, which asks the audience to actively participate in the creation of the story from their seats, using their imagination to set the scene. This production style can also help to deliver a truthful exploration of themes of exploitation through character agency rather than physical resources. It is also intended to be practical for companies with different resource levels.

Transitions

Weise emphasised the importance of transitions, and reminded participants that from the moment the audience arrives to the moment they leave, everything that happens on stage is the director's responsibility. He advised not to treat the transitions like commercial breaks where they wait for the play to start again.

Some things to consider when creating transitions:

- A stripped-back production allows for transitions that rely on text and imagination
- Directors should take nuggets of the story and eke them out in the transitions
- Tone in transitions is critical; whether scenes are cut sharply or left to linger affects storytelling, and can be used to allow something from a previous scene to hang in the air, or for the production to leap to the next moment of action
- Changes in environment need to be clear, and these transitions can layer storytelling elements such as movement and direct address
- Find the moment where the language of an environment switches really clearly
- If your physical transition happens on stage it needs to be part of the storytelling
- The movement of objects can be used as part of storytelling. Consider the quality of this movement; are objects being discarded or carefully collected?
- The only way that you can work transitions is to practically do it
- When working on transitions, create what you think the final image of the previous scene is and what you think it looks like at the start of the next scene
- Ultimately, don't drown the story of the play. The transitions should not be the most exciting element of a play, and sometimes brilliant work is invisible

Physicality

Weise led the group through some physical tasks to start to explore ways to stage the play.

He reflected that rhythm and physicality are important in establishing setting. Work on building an ensemble can really support with this. It can also support the group to work together to find out what you're trying to portray in each scene. This can stop the actors jumping to conclusions and coming to fixed decisions.

Exercise: Flocking

The group stands close together in a group. One person becomes the leader, and the rest of the ensemble must copy their movements.

Exercise: Jumping in time

The company stands in lines of three. The first line jumps while counting one to eight. On eight they spin to face the next row, who immediately start jumping and counting. When the final line has finished their sequence, they start again with (e.g.) six and the sequence goes back down the rows. This can be adapted to use any length of sequence and any tempo.

Counting exercises and rhythm-focused games reflect the physical and repetitive nature of labour. Ensemble games are also helpful for getting proximity and encouraging young people to get closer to each other. It also supports the young people to trust each other; working towards a goal as a group.

Physical actions that might be found in the play

- Bend to pick something up with your right hand, turn and put it behind you.
- Forklift trucks arriving, and pallets are being repeatedly unloaded.

Ideas for how this movement language could tell the story

Using different tempos and rhythms for the two groups could be an effective way to create a strong distinction between the two; one is relaxed and the other is frantically trying to unload boxes.

This could be used to stage a scene where the entire ensemble is picking onions, for example simultaneously in two lines. With a cue like a clap, everyone but the characters in the next scene carry on with the movement, and the scene happens over the top.

Or, the ensemble continues the gesture while moving upstage, and the two people in the scene stay still and speak the dialogue. Alternatively, the scene could take place downstage, and the people pulling onions slowly stop and watch them when something shifts in the scene.

Using movement to shift audience focus and alter tone uses the actors' physical presence to support storytelling without the use of technical elements.

The group also explored changing the environment through physicality by being given ten seconds to walk into the centre of the room and take on the physicality of a hot day.

The action of picking onions

Sumbwanyambe explained to the group that you are either sat on your bottom or kneeling. You cut the ten spring onions against your thumb. After two or three days you develop a callous and get better at cutting quickly. Sumbwanyambe said he is sick of onions!

It's worth considering the mess of it. Do they do their work in a delicate way? Or maybe they can't touch their faces because their hands are dirty. How do they say hello to each other? How do they touch each other when they are working?

If this is your life, you do the work with a different energy than the person for whom it's a temporary vocation or seasonal one-off.

Some people just turn up because they want money to buy weed. As soon as they've made their money they sit back and chill. What is each character's relationship to the work? How did they get there? Each character has a different journey to get to that place.

There are lots of opportunities to deliver story through how the characters do the work, and details are something you can get your young actors excited about.

Language

The language in the play is naturalistic, but introduces themes that are there to be invested in; for example, the first line of direct address where Asher describes the sky – the small, the tiny and the ordinary could become massive, big and majestic. There is also symbolism in the name Joy, which invites us to think about the poetic space of the play; how does joy exist and survive within that space?

There is no swearing in the play; instead tension should bubble within the subtext. For example, a character's bravado might be an attempt to deflect uncomfortable truths. The migrant characters all speak in clear English, which challenges assumptions about the language abilities of migrants, and is true to the multilingual experience of many people. Weise observed that some people in previously colonised countries have a wider vocabulary than native speakers.

When the migrants speak to each other, perhaps in their own language, the way they speak is less formal, and becomes more formal when they're talking to the Westerners. The Westerners' language involves more colloquialism and contraction. Perhaps there are subtle ways that the language of the two groups can get closer together over the course of the play?

Accents

The group experimented with ways to differentiate between the trafficked workers and the westerners. A scene was read in a range of configurations; using RP, Northern accents, non-British accents to distinguish between the groups. The impact of these choices was discussed:

If the characters all have the same accent, then the story becomes about the similarities between the characters and their humanity. It invites everyone to be seen through the same lens. If you hear different accents, more emphasis is placed on what divides the characters. It was also noted that accents denote place, but also class.

Some of the choices felt unsettling, like hearing the migrants with received pronunciation, which might challenge the audience's notion of stereotypes. What impact would this have? Weise spoke about Brecht and the use of *Verfremdungseffekt*, a deliberate theatrical choice to make the familiar feel strange. These choices could invite the audience to be part of the action because the artifice is broken.

If you're making an impactful choice then you have to back it and be consistent.

Representing the migrant experience

You might feel a huge responsibility that you have to hold up this under-privileged experience, but that this story is asking us to look at all the experiences. Those students whose parents might represent the migrant experience should be able to sit in the room proudly and feel that they've been represented in a fair way.

Companies must make thoughtful choices about what voices represent which experiences. Consider who you invite the audience to see as a victim, and which character's suffering you invite the audience to see. It is important to remember that all of the characters are trapped in this system. There is just as much weighting to Kelly's pain, as there is for Joy looking for their mum.

It is important not to lose sight of the joy in the play. Find humour and celebrate the resilience of the characters.

It is left deliberately ambiguous where the migrants are from. Words like *kachasu* suggest East Africa, but Sumbwanyambe believes it is not helpful to be too specific. Any group should be able to meet the play and feel empowered to shape the narrative.

Somewhere there has been a disruption which means people can no longer live there.

Characters and characterisation

The challenges of the play include: how do I make it so that my audience feels a connection, whether we believe it's right or wrong, to every character in the story? How do I fall in love with the dynamic of these young people? How do we make it impossible to write anyone off, so that we're always changing our minds about these characters?

The characters have lived experiences that the young people will not have had, but it is still possible and important for the performers to empathise; it is not necessarily the events of that experience that are important, but the emotional journey and the emotional truth. The performers will identify with things like loss and grief, and will be able to find those parallels.

Playwrights are trying to convey change – to show a journey of change in each individual character and story. A challenge for the actors is making the leap that they have seen the lorry first-hand, that they are transformed and that everyone can see that transformation.

The friendship between Joy and Kelly is the core relationship of the story. To all intents and purposes, they should not be able to connect, but they are able to find a way around it, to find a sense of play and compassion.

In the play, it is the Western teenagers that seem to be carrying more baggage, despite the adversity the migrant kids have faced. Is the baggage because of the perspective that these young people have?

Everybody sees themselves as the hero of their own story. If you're too honest with yourself, if you don't build resistance and be kind to yourself, you will crumble. It's not that people who do morally reprehensible things are trying to deceive you, it is that they are lying to themselves. There is a sense that there are no good guys and bad guys – this is a very complicated situation and most people are trying to make the best choices that they can.

Notes from a discussion about the central characters led by Sumbwanyambe:

Joy

Joy really misses their mum. Joy's instinct when it comes to playing is to play mums and children. At first Kelly doesn't understand this, but eventually they do. Could Joy's mask be their happiness?

Kelly

Kelly is really affected by the trauma of their experience. Their father's not around, and there is a relationship between their mum and Saunders' dad. Their father hasn't treated his child or mother well. Kelly's been dislocated, and this isn't really their home. They have an ability to play and access a childlike abandon. Some of Kelly's actions are driven by their loneliness and a desire for connection; they find Joy because they get lost looking for a lake. They are aware that they are an outsider trying to find their place. The biggest obstacle that Kelly has is that they're self-conscious. They start off with a mask, but they learn that they don't need to do this, they can be a functional person in the world without changing themself in some way.

Saunders

Saunders comes from a broken family. Their mother is no longer around, but they've formed a very close attachment to their father who they have modelled a lot of their behaviour on. To prevent them seeing their dad as a villain, they must lie to themself and believe their dad is a good person. They want to be respected, they want to be loved by their peers, they want to be listened to, but they don't necessarily have the empathy or the natural charisma to inspire that confidence. They are never more on the defensive or as repulsive than when their step-sibling is prodding them, because on some level their step-sibling knows the truth of how messed up their life actually is. Saunders knows that their step-sibling could ruin them and the public image that they're trying to present in an instant.

Jo

The one person in the play who thinks 'what's going on here is more complicated than what you think it is'. Jo is level-headed and morally grounded, aware of their limitations and perceptive of others' bravado. They are much more informed and not on either side of the extremes. They have a slightly better sense of the world and how little they know. Maybe they're going home and having good conversations. This gives them the moral conviction to challenge Saunders. But they still hang around with Saunders, Coxy and Max.

Coxy

Coxy is confident in their simplicity. They are like their dad: good-looking and seem charming. They are not weighed down by complexity; what you see is what you get. They are not an onion, there are no layers to them – it's all there on the surface. They're a good soldier, but not a general. They're not someone who's going to think about strategy.

Max

Max is visibly more antagonistic. They are angry and blame the whole world but themself.

Patience

Patience has been forced to become an adult even though they are still a child. Patience is Ali's sibling, but they're performing certain roles that the absent mother would have been.

Ali

Ali has also had to become an adult too quickly, and has had to take the lead in terms of disciplining their sibling. Children who take on responsibility have to code switch between playful childishness and responsibility.

Asher

Asher has been spoiled because their siblings have taken on so much for them. They have maintained a sense of childish wonder and energy.

Staging the characters

Character statues

In the workshop, as the group talked through the characters, one person was a statue and another was a sculptor, moving them into a statue of the character in 90 seconds.

Choices around how much space the characters took up, the placement of their arms and hands, their eyeline and so on revealed information about who these characters are, and how they might present themselves.

When the statues are in place, invite the performer to imagine what their character might be saying at that moment.

The way that you combine the characters in a picture has a big impact on how we read those characters, and a lot of storytelling is done through proximity. Someone entering into a scene more antagonistically combined with someone standing confidently or calmly can change a dynamic really significantly.

After the first stage of this exercise, layer the pictures with additional characters and invite the cast to make observations about the frozen stage pictures.

Character story sentences

Choose one character from the story and imagine that the whole play is called that character's name, e.g. 'KELLY'. Finish the sentence 'KELLY, the story of the person who . . .', and come up with a sentence about something that they do, and the choices they make. This will allow you to boil down what you understand their journey is from the beginning to the end.

Sometimes young people can do a lot of really detailed character work, but it ends up being quite internal. Finding ways for them to translate their thinking to the stage so that they can physically embody their character and the changes they go through is important.

Casting

The play is written to encourage flexibility in terms of casting, but casting decisions which will impact on the dynamics of the play should be made consistently. For example, the direct address could be given to another group of actors, who could function as witnesses, like a Greek chorus. Choices like this will impact on which characters have the 'perspective' on the action of the play. Any big choice just has to be made with commitment. Gender will also alter the dynamics, and age will have status implications.

Production, staging and design

The staging is intended to be minimalistic, and Weise advised participants to make the productions as analogue and self-contained as possible. Understated design will also allow for focus on character relationships. This challenge will stretch the company to think about the task of communicating the story as actors.

Creating the world of the play

How can you pull imagery from the story to establish the overarching themes? What are the visual motifs and the physical setting?

Start by doing scene breakdowns: list all the locations and the characters that are onstage in each scene. Find images of what each of those settings looks like.

How can you communicate the farm?

- Could the characters move through the audience to evoke a wide expanse of field? There could be a sense that there is a likeness between the audience and the characters.
- A childlike design, like a toy farm speaks to the 'play' of the characters; their imagination and the game of it.
- There is a lot of greenery – the design could just be 30 green chairs, and all the action they have takes place over the chairs.

You don't need complex sets to invite the audience to look for symbolism; 30 green chairs could be chairs in a classroom, a toy-like design could be a potent statement that the world they create is imagined by children. A box of clothes could be the one design element, and the symbol that you weave through the piece. Everything we do in theatre is poetic; the audience is not supposed to see exactly the location of the scene, as in film.

Exercises for use in rehearsals

To get the group's attention:
Clap once if you can hear me ****clap****
Clap twice if you can hear me ****clap/clap****
Clap three times if you can hear me ****clap/clap/clap****

Status exercise: Actors play scenarios – e.g. A wants B's shoes, B doesn't want to give them – using playing cards to represent status. A new card is taken for each line, and you have to adapt your delivery to meet the status as denoted by the card.

Status as a journey: Map a character's status journey across the story. Ask your actors to rate their character's status at the beginning, middle and end of the play. You'll start to see a really interesting shape.

Status and inequality are themes that run through the play. Status should be seen as a dynamic, evolving trait shaped by experiences. Directors can experiment with physical proximity and interactions to communicate status among characters.

Understanding status is really going to help to show those distinctions in character. Their stories will start to play out.

Sharing work with the audience

Scene at a distance: Play an intimate scene far away to explore voice and physicality in a large space. Teach the company to want to share their work.

They must imagine and share their work with the room. Teach them the value of making sure that they're trying to touch as many people in the room as they can. That is about desire. Give your actors the desire to want to do everything in their power to ensure that their work is being communicated to the audience.

Question and answer with May Sumbwanyambe

Q: What is the significance of the religious moment in the play?
A: The religious moment is open to interpretation. The key thing about that scene is that it says something cultural – there is still that propensity to go to church, or to the mosque. It makes a clear cultural distinction between the Western characters and the trafficked characters, and there is something really beautiful about the connections between characters. It is an invitation between someone who does believe something and someone who does not.

Morality and philosophy are more guiding notions in the play than religion.

Q: What do you want audiences to leave with?
A: To reflect on the humanity, that's the key. By not going across the field and not speaking out, I denied the humanity of the people across the field. This is an attempt to challenge the young person I was and say, 'That's not good enough, you should have gone across the field. You should have valued your own interest.' But the play should not be accusatory. We're all partners in whatever this is. We're all part of this system.

From a workshop led by Roy Alexander Weise
With notes by Lucy Allan

Ravers
by Rikki Beadle-Blair

Rikki Beadle-Blair MBE is a writer, director, composer, choreographer, designer, producer and performer working in film, theatre, television and radio. He has written and directed more than forty plays over the last 20 years along with several feature films, shorts and TV episodes and series. He is the recipient of several awards including the Sony Award, the Los Angeles Outfest Screenwriting and Outstanding Achievement Awards, an MBE for contributions to drama and an honorary doctor of letters from the University of Warwick. Rikki Beadle-Blair is a committed mentor to many actors, composers and directors around the world. From 2010, he has been hosting the annual UK Black Pride event as well as voguing balls around the country.

Characters

Ali
Robin
Quinn
Shiloh
Jamie
Jackie
Avery
Joey
Asa
Taylor
Sam
Drew
Lennox
Kerry
Blake
Pat
Dylan
Jude
Jordan
Parker
DJ/MC
Police

Ravers is about a group of teenagers who identify as 'neeks' (nerds and geeks) who gather together with the intention of holding a 'sober rave' in a park overlooking their neighbourhood(s).

There are 21 characters which can be played by – or as – any gender.

Characters can be combined for smaller casts or divided for larger casts.

It can be set anywhere – a city, a town, a village or suburb. Directorial/collective choices can be used to mould the play to fit any creative vision, observation or exploration of class, race, sexuality or youth culture tribe(s). Language can be adapted – 'aren't' can be become 'ain't' or 'int' 'ent' or whatever accent or register. 'Innits' can be attached, slang can be adapted, swearing can be added, music can be chosen to fit. This is your play now. Be as personal, creative, interpretative or literal as you want to be. As long as you don't trash any other group of young people, it's great. Be free.

All assemble as **Ali** *sets up the phone for a timed selfie. It's awkward. These people are mostly not friends. And the ones who are friends struggle to appear at ease with each other. Or themselves.*

Ali Ready?

Grudging grunts and half-committed murmurs.

Ali Counting down . . . Four, three . . . two . . . . say Rave!

Few – if any – convincing smiles.

All Raaave.

Flash.

Start music.

Relieved, the group disperses. Some nodding. The odd foot-tapper. Only one or two are inclined to be ravers at this stage.

Stop music.

Clearview Park, daytime

Ali *holds a phone.* **Robin** *watches supportively.*

Ali I can do this.

Robin You can do this.

Ali Definitely. I can do this, right?

Robin Right. Definitely. Do it.

Ali I'm doing it.

Ali *presses record.*

Ali Yo.
(*Snaps off recording.*) No!
(*Cringing hard.*) No no no no no! Okay!
(*Presses record.*) Hi! Er, hey! Er. Urrr!
(*Presses record.*) What is *wrong* with me?

Robin You're just being you.

Ali Thanks.

Robin I'm not saying that's a bad thing. Though you are.

Ali Am I? Oh, God, I am saying that aren't I?

Robin Yep. And what's the point in saying that?

Ali Um ... there's no point in saying that ...?

Robin After all, who are you doing all this for?

Ali Not me.

Robin Not you?

Ali Course not!

Robin Why not?

Ali Well, maybe I'm doing this for ...

Robin ... Someone like you?

Ali ... Like us. I'm doing this for people who are like us.

Robin Which includes you.

Ali Okay, fine. What's your point?

Robin That you just be you. And you'll be relatable. Or at least be comfortable.

Ali Be comfortable

Robin Or at least get comfortable.

Ali Being me?

Robin Well, you want people like you to be comfortable with themselves, right?

Ali Riiiight ...

Robin That's the mission, right?

Ali Right.

Robin And if you can't do it for yourself, how you gonna do it for them?

Ali Okay, inspirational grandma.

Robin Just say what you would want to hear the way you'd wanna hear it.

Ali Hmm. Do I love or hate the fact that when you talk rubbish it somehow randomly ends up making sense?

Robin Years of counselling. It's a blessing and a curse.

Ali Whatever. Just remember – if anyone asks, I'm the smart one.
(*Recording on.*) Hello. Are you always the designated driver? The only one who can remember what happened last night; what got broken or stolen? Are you the only one who doesn't get the joke when everyone around you is laughing? Who has to pick everyone up and is always the last one home? Who's only been invited because you're the one who'll remember how you got there and how to get home? Because you're the one with parents that can trust you not to crash their car? Well, this is your night. A night without any intoxication or inebriation, just big bass vibrations offering you a natural high. Wear your glasses proudly on your blissful face and your bumbag

unashamedly around your waist. Hold your soft drink up to the UV light and robot-dance until your two left feet are bleeding through your scuffed and battered un-branded trainers. This is a nerd alert for all the nice well-behaved 'kids' who are too often in bed by midnight on a Friday. No more wasting time wondering what it's like to be physically co-ordinated, supremely uninhibited, blissfully narcissistic, confident and popular.

Tonight is the night when self-consciousness is sexy, social awkwardness is swag, and painful shyness disguised as a time-consuming dedication to quantum physics, classical music and calculus is the real cool. That's right! If you've been recommended to be on this secret message board, it's because, you, my geeky friend, are cool. Here's the address and the coordinates. Come as you are, comfort is style, bring your sustainably sourced low-carbon refreshments in a reuseable bottle and let the wreck-heads find their own way home tonight. You are busy. You are unofficially invited here to Clearview Park and you are officially invited to Clarity.

Ali *stops recording and looks at* **Robin**.

Robin   Wow. You did it.

Ali   I did it. Send?

Robin   Send.

Ali *presses send. Everyone's phones light up.*

Ali   We're doing it.

Music.

More dancing than before.

Stop music.

Shiloh's Room

Shiloh *pulling out a buzzing phone.*

Quinn   So?

Jamie   Well?

Shiloh   Soooo . . . Well, this is it!

Jamie   What? For real?

Quinn *holds out phone,* **Jamie** *snatches it and reads:*

Jamie   'You are officially invited to Clarity'?!

Quinn (*looking over* **Jamie**'s *shoulder*)   'The night of our lives'?

Jamie   Could it finally be . . .? A miracle?

Quinn Yeah, for Shiloh.

Jamie Oh. Yeah.

Shiloh Read the bottom bit.

Jamie 'Admit three.'
(*Looks up*.) Enough, no more! I believe!

Quinn And you're sure this means us?

Jamie There are three of us.

Quinn It was sent to Shiloh.

Shiloh That's us. Who else would they think I'd go with? My mum and dad?

Jamie/Quinn Weeelllllll . . .

Jamie Let's face it, you might.

Shiloh Well, I'm not going with Mum and Dad, I'm going with you.

Quinn Which is basically the same thing.
Oh, snap! What will we wear?

Shiloh 'Dress Code: Come as You Are.'

Quinn We can't come as we are. We'll get bottled.

Shiloh We'll just put our hoods up and wear shades.

Quinn At night?

Jamie Ravers wear shades in a coal-mine.

Quinn At least try to make sense. What ravers have you seen in a coal-mine?

Shiloh Jamie's just saying they wear them everywhere. Do you have to be so literal?

Quinn Well, excuse me for bothering with boring old reality.

Shiloh Do you want to be a virgin forever?

Quinn What's wrong with virgins?

Shiloh Do you want to be a virgin forever?

Quinn Why are we chastity shaming?

Shiloh Do you want to be a virgin forever?

Quinn No.

Shiloh Then stop being such an uptight anal retentive and get with the program! We have an official invite that says come as you are and we are going as we are and when we get there we are gonna have a good time. Is that understood?

Jamie Ay ay, cap'n! I for one am officially down for a good time.

Shiloh How?

Quinn What do you mean, how?

Shiloh It's a dry rave.

Jamie Sober rave. Crucial distinction. And we don't drink.

Shiloh Yeah, but everyone else does. Usually. And they won't be.

Quinn So?

Shiloh So everyone's going to be as socially awkward as we are.

Jamie Okay, that is potentially grim.

Shiloh Don't you start! Do you really have to poison the only oasis in the desert, Quinn?

Jamie You can't poison a mirage.

Shiloh We have a actual real-life invitation!

Quinn To a rave.

Shiloh Yes, a rave!

Jamie A rave, yay!

Quinn Which is what?

Shiloh A dance.

Jamie A dance, yay!

Quinn And we don't dance.

Silence.

Shiloh We dance.

Jamie In front of people?

Silence.

Shiloh My mother has a hip-flask.

Quinn It's a dry rave.

Jamie Sober rave.

Shiloh Whatever.

Quinn We can't bring booze to a booze-free rave!

Jamie Actually, to be fair, we're probably the only ones who can.

Shiloh Exactly! Who's going to suspect three legendary virgins?

Jamie Our tipsy is basically everyone else's sober. We'll be even.

Shiloh We might even be the wildest ones there. How's that for a rebrand?

Quinn So, we're drunk-dancing?

Shiloh Well, maybe tipsy dancing.

Quinn No hip-flasks.

Jamie All in favour?

Shiloh and **Jamie** *raise their hands.*

Jamie Outvoted! Plus, my parents have a drinks cabinet –

Shiloh Ok-AY!

Quinn – A drinks cabinet? –

Jamie Please don't start, Quinn, you're too pretty to hate. We are going to be the life and soul of Clarity.

Quinn What could possibly go wrong?

Shiloh If we're lucky. Everything.

Music.

People are getting into it gradually.

Almost all are moving now. Some more confidently than others . . .

Stop music.

Graveyard

All HURRRGHHHHH!

Jackie, Avery, Joey, Asa and **Taylor** *all vomiting loudly and violently. They come up for air . . .*

Jackie Oh my God!

Avery I'm sweating!

Joey My throat hurts!

Asa It's all down my front!

Taylor Well, I feel sooo much better.

All HURRRGHHHHH!

They all vomit again. Come up again.

Avery This is getting a bit boring now.

Jackie How is there anything left?

Asa It's up my nose!

Joey I want my mummy!

Taylor I am definitely fine now.

All HURGGGGGGGHHHHH!

Jackie Surely that has to be all of it . . .

Asa Are we done?
(*Looking round.*) We done?

Joey I am so done.

They get to their feet to try their wobbly legs out.

Avery Uhh! I can smell my own breath!

Asa We reek!

Taylor *produces more alcohol.*

Taylor Here you go!

The others cringe and recoil. Urghh!

Avery Is that alcohol?

Joey Away, Satan!

Taylor *commences gargling with the alcohol.*

Jackie Oh my days, what is wrong with you besides everything?

Taylor I'm giving myself a desperately needed mouthwash!

Asa You swallowed!

Taylor Ooops! Oh well.

Taylor *offers it out. Another group cringe.*

Avery After your vommie lips have been on there? Yum yum, yes please.

Joey Can we go home now?

Taylor It's only seven o'clock, y'lightweights!

Jackie Am or pm? It's feels like we've been out forever.

Asa No one's gonna let us in anywhere in this state are they? IDs or no IDs.

Joey Home time!

Avery Whose genius idea was it to sit around drinking in a graveyard anyway?

Taylor This is pre's! You have to have pre's. Club and pub drink are unshushtainably un-unacheptable.

Asa Like your pronunshishachion.

Avery They'll never let us in anywhere in this state anyway.

Taylor We've blatantly chucked the bulk of it up, we'll be sober in a minute.

Joey I'm texting my mum to pick us up.

Jackie Oh, thank God for your mum!

Joey She's probably driving round and around in the people carrier waiting to hear from us.

Asa As usual.

Taylor We can't go home now! Not this time. It's Jackie's birthday!

Jackie Well, let's not make it my funeral, yeah? Text your lovely non-judgemental mummy, Joey.

Avery Why do we always let Taylor get us into this mess?

Taylor 'Cause you love it.

Avery I'd love it considerably more if I could actually be allowed entry to somewhere and actually socialise.

Taylor Oh, we soshcialize! I pershonally am sochializality itself!

Asa See? We should have gone to Clarity.

Taylor Don't talk wet. They're a bunch of melts.

Jackie (*indicating all of them*) Um . . .?

Avery Actually, melts are hot. That's why we're melting.

Asa They're literally organising secret nerd raves.

Taylor They're not allowing drink!

Asa Like I said, we should have gone to . . .

Joey Mum's not answering! How dare she have a life?!

Avery Walking home, then?

Jackie Happy birthday to me.

Taylor FINE!

All eyes on **Taylor**.

Taylor You've talked me into it.

Asa Into . . .

Taylor Clarity. You've talked me into clarity.

Avery Is that even possible . . .?

Taylor I am prepared to hide my alcohol and tone down my tipsiness and dig deep down into my inner nerd so that young Jackie here can celebrate this milestone in style. That's friendship. Happy birthday, Jackie, mate.

Jackie Er, thank you . . .

Taylor (*raising a toast*) To Jackie!

Others . . . to Jackie . . .

Taylor *necks the drink.*

Music.

Everyone is moving now.

Stop music.

Sam's Family Home

Sam (*exiting*) Dad, I'm going! What?
(*Returning*) Dad, what? I was halfway out the door, what? I did say. I said I'll be back at one o'clock. Dad! You know nothing gets started till midnight! I promise I'll text you on the hour every hour. Seriously? Okay – firstly – does anyone actually say wasted any more? Secondly, I won't get wasted. Because I won't. Because (a) I don't drink and (b) I don't take drugs and (c) this is a no drinks no drugs party and (d) because I'm not you. I'm not saying there's anything wrong with you, you're the one saying you couldn't be trusted. Drew doesn't drink or take drugs either. How do I know? We don't sit around asking each other why we don't take drugs, we just don't. And you know Drew's obsessed with not polluting that precious amazing brain. No, I wouldn't take 'em no matter who I was with – look, I'm confused – are you saying you *want* me to get drunk and stoned tonight? What? When? No, what I actually said was, 'No matter who I was out with'. Dad, I know what I said, and anyway, whatever, 'cause even if I was going out with someone or anyone, it wouldn't be a big deal. 'Cause I'm not you, Dad, and I'm not Mum and if I ever go out with anyone, I'll make sure we actually genuinely like each other. Oh, so you can talk to me however you like but I can't be honest with you? Daaad! Where you going? Fine go to your room, you spoiled brat, I'm off out.

(*Silence*) Dad, I'm sorry. That was out of order. No, it was, 'cause it hurt you and I don't want to hurt you. Yeah, I know you don't want to hurt me either. Neither does Mum. We're all just working it out as we go along, right? Look, I have to go. And you have to let me go, okay? It's just a dance. I promise I'll call you.

If I'm not too off my face. Joke! Sorry, I'm a teenager. It's my duty to wind you up. See you later. I love you. Sorry. I'm a teenager. It's my job to emotionally manipulate you. Plus I actually sort of mean it. Okay. I'm going before the cringe kills me. Yes! I-will-call-you! Just please please please whatever you do, do not call me.

Start music.

Some people are dancing with each other now.

Stop music.

Drew's Family Home

Drew It fits fine, Mum. It does. Well, I don't know do I?? I don't wear stuff like that. Stuff is not an insult, Mum. It's not a judgement. Everything is stuff. What do you really want me to say, you look pullable? "He's gonna love it, Mum, he's gonna salivate like a pitbull seeing a steak or a brand new bell toy. He's gonna think all his Christmases have come at once and he's pulling a cracker. He's gonna love you, Mum and you'll get back together." Nah. When I get back from this jog, I'm probably gonna go for an early night. I am! I'm not! Why would I lie to you? Okay, to be fair, I am lying to you 'cause I don't want you to go all weird and start prying for further details. Because it's none of your business. And 'cause I just wanted something for myself. If something happens tonight, I don't want advice or an interrogation or cheer-leading or anything. I just want this to be mine and Sam's. I mean, obviously I'll tell you everything in a week's time, when Sam drops me for liking a Taylor Swift track or whatever, just like I tell you everything else.

But just for tonight, I don't want to be the Mind Sports Brain Olympics kid, I don't want to be your pride and joy or your best friend, I want to be a teenager and sneak out and have secrets and look innocent at breakfast, while a ton of fresh memories, physical sensations and contradictory emotions churn around inside me. Is that weird? I hope so. I want to be weird and feel normal. Have a good night, Mum. Can't wait to hear about it. And if Dad disappoints you for the thousandth time, text me, yeah? I'll be right here.

Music.

The vibe is lifting. People are dancing together – some even with people they don't know.

Music stops.

Library

Lennox *checking watch.*

Lennox   Right! 7.30!

Kerry   7.28.

Lennox   Whatever, no one's coming now, are they?

Kerry   We close at 8.

Lennox And no one's been in since 6.
I'll do the shutters
You fetch your keys.

Kerry Just go ahead without me.

Lennox And leave you here in this prison? What kind of monster do you think I am?

Kerry Libraries are the opposite of prisons.

Lennox Then why do they have bars on the windows?

Kerry Books are the spaces between bars.

Lennox Oh, mate! Serious cringe!

Kerry Pretending you don't like books won't you make you cool, you know.

Lennox And what does pretending you like books get you . . .?

Kerry We're not pretending, Lennox.

Lennox . . . overlooked, ostracised, uninvited. Respected by professors for being as reliable as prefects, and reviled by peers for being neeks. And now by some bizarre miraculous typo of fate we've finally been invited, we're still stuck here in the empty library categorising and alphabetising other people's life stories. There's some things no book can teach. How to dance. How to kiss. How to be in a sea of sweaty bodies and just be young. All the years we've spent reading about youth, we've just been getting old. It's got to stop, Kerry. And it's got to stop now.

Kerry Can it stop at 8 o'clock? I like this job.

Lennox They don't even really pay you!

Kerry They do though.

Lennox Not really though.

Kerry They pay *us*. 'Cause you work here too, Kerry.

Lennox To hang out with you. But you actually mean it. You're the deputy duty manager, for crying out loud.

Kerry So are you.

Lennox Yeah, but I don't wear the name badge. When they promoted me I blocked out the trauma.

Kerry You love books, Lennox.

Lennox Slander!

Kerry You love books!

Lennox Comic books!

Kerry You're here on your days off.

Lennox Trying to get my best friend to take the opportunity to hang out with me in the real world. That's what this invitation is to, Kerry – the real world. How often does something cool come up for the geeks and the neeks? Well, this is it. We won't be the only bookworms, we won't be the only ones sober, we won't be the only weird ones.

Kerry I hadn't thought about it like that.

Lennox And now?

Kerry (*weighing it*)   ... We won't be the weirdest ones in the room ...

Lennox Well, I didn't actually say that ...

Kerry What if someone comes in?

Lennox No one's coming in.

Kerry A student on a deadline.

Lennox They can google.

Kerry Someone lonely who needs company.

Lennox It's a library, not the Samaritans!

Kerry You know that's not true. You know that a library is more than a library and that librarians are more than librarians.

Lennox I wish! God, how deeply I passionately wish. Everyone I've ever met over forty says that life goes by in a blink of an eye, that youth is wasted on the young and in this case they are right, we are wasting it, you and me with our retro clothes and our mental health priorities, our constant anxiety about the environment and our hypocritical romanticised obsession with printed paper books. And while our parents and grandparents and great-grandparents overflow with their countless glorious, decadent, shamelessly shameful memories we are dying here, Kerry. Rotting in a library on a Friday night. And no one's coming in!

Enter **Blake**.

Blake Hi.

Lennox You are kidding me.

Blake Oh, sorry ...

Kerry No! Hi!

Blake	**Kerry**
... are you ...	It's okay!

Blake ... not open?

Kerry No. We are not not open we are definitely open, can we help you?

Blake   Well, I was actually just looking for somewhere to charge my phone.

Lennox   Seriously, you have to be kidding me . . .

Kerry	**Blake**
Sure! We can help you with that. Do you have a charger lead? We have some in lost property if you . . .	I don't want to be any trouble, it's just that I'm on a low battery and the Maps app uses up a ton of juice.

Lennox *holds out a charger unit and lead.*

Lennox   Here. It's yours, take it.

Blake   I can't take your charger lead.

Lennox   It's not a problem. Take it and go where you're going. Please take it.

Blake   Thanks.
(*Plugging it in*) But I really only need it for a few minutes so I can check the directions on Maps. This place is a bit of a mare to pinpoint. But if the destination is clear view – then how hard can it be to find?

Lennox   Clear view?

Blake   Yeah, have you heard of it? I'm going to this, um, thing – this rave – called Clarity – and my friends have all dropped out – so I'm going solo and freaking out – but I'm going – Like I am so going – 'cause, you know, there's more to life than studying, right? And where else am I gonna meet weird teetotal neeks like me? . . . Right?

Blake *takes in* **Lennox** *and* **Kerry***'s staring faces.*

Blake   . . . What?

Music.

Dancing.

Music stops.

Just Outside Clearview Park

Parker *and* **Jordan** *both looking around, then looking down at their phones, adjusting to face fresh directions. Then looking up and seeing each other. Shy awkward smiles. Then looking down. Then* **Parker** *looks up.*

Parker   Um . . .

Jordan   Mmm?

Awkward.

Jordan   You're wondering if we're –

Parker (*overlapping*)   – if we're looking for the same thing – same er –

Parker/Jordan   – Place –

Jordan   Yeah. Clarity.

Parker   Which is meant to be at –

Jordan   – Clearview.

Parker   Which is somewhere here.

They look around perplexed.

Parker   Behind the locked gates?

Jordan   It's a park – I think.

Parker   Who locks a park?

Jordan   People round here? I dunno.

Parker   Guess illegal raves aren't popular with the authorities.

Jordan   Is it actually illegal? I mean, there's theoretically no drinking, so . . .

Parker   Is it even really about the drinking? I dunno. Maybe it's the music.

Jordan   Maybe it's young people having a good time. That's always been an issue. Punks. Mods and rockers, hippies, nineties ravers, hip-hop, garage-heads, grime spitters, they kept shutting all that down.

Parker   'Cept the people who lock up parks today used to be mods and ravers.

Jordan   Why do people forget what it was like to be young?

Parker   Maybe some people never felt young. They were outside of all of that and felt shut out.

Jordan   Or maybe they looked young and went through the motions, but never really fit in.

Parker   I'd feel better if one other person was heading the same way. Do you know anyone else who's going to this?

Jordan   Only you.

Parker   Well, that's someone, yeah? We should climb the fence.

Jordan   We should, shouldn't we?

Parker   Over the locked gate and into the possible park.

Jordan   I'm pretty sure it is a park.

Parker   There's a grassy hill on the other side.

Jordan   A hill makes sense. Clearview Hill.

Parker   And climbing locked gates and fences . . .

Jordan   . . . also makes sense.

Parker Okay. Okay. Okay?

Jordan I'm okay. Are you okay?

Parker Yes, Yes, I'm super okay, I'm just having – (*Gasping for air.*) A moment.

Jordan Oh! Oh oh oh! Are you having a panic attack?

Parker Just a . . . It's no big . . .

Jordan Oh, we need a bag!

Parker *produces a paper bag.*

Jordan Oh, okay! Um, do you need me to . . .

Parker*'s head shakes no, breathing into the inflating, deflating bag.*

Jordan Is it working?

Parker It'll take a minute. Please. Go ahead, without me.

Jordan I don't mind waiting.

Parker But if we arrive together, people will think we're . . . together and you don't want that.

Jordan I don't mind that.

Parker Trust me. You don't want that.

Jordan Well, let's walk up together when you're ready and just arrive separately like we don't know each other.

Parker We don't know each other.

Jordan See? Perfect plan.

Music.

The dancing has real joy now.

Music stops.

Clearview Park

Pat *waiting. Checks watch. Sighs. Pulls out phone as* **Dylan** *and* **Jude** *arrive.*

Dylan No phones!

Pat (*putting phone away*) I was checking the time.

Dylan You're wearing a watch.

Jude You've really got to lie harder if you want to get anywhere in life.

Dylan You were about to call us, weren't you?

Pat You're half an hour late!

Dylan And of course you were half an hour early. Phone off!

Pat It's off!
(*Shows phone*) See?

Phone rings.

Jude Ooopsy.

Dylan *snatches the phone. Looks at it. It's not ringing.* **Jude** *reaches into* **Dylan***'s pocket, pulls out a ringing phone.*

Jude Ooops.

Dylan *gives* **Pat***'s phone back and answers the culprit phone.*

Dylan I said don't call me, Mum!

Everywhere phones are ringing, people find their phones and start switching them off.

Pat She's just worried.

Jude Just doing her duty.

Dylan Shame she didn't worry about doing her duty when she was our age.

Pat They protested in their day! Well, my mum did. That's why she's so worried.

Dylan And what did she achieve? The mess the world's in now that we've been stuck with. Actually, now you mention it, didn't your mum and dad actually meet at a protest?

Jude Oh, they certainly did that.

Pat Jude . . .

Jude You're not ashamed, are you? They're not.

Dylan Do I smell a juicy narrative?

Jude They told me they met when she was a protester and he was in the military.

Dylan You mean like at a protest?

Jude Affirmative.

Dylan You mean he arrested her?

Jude And they fell in luuurve.

Pat Jude!   **Dylan** Noooo!

Jude And he basically became a double agent.

Dylan Shut UP! You're kidding me?

Jude Nearly went to prison for it. Powers that be hushed it up and he was encouraged to 'retire'.

Dylan Okay, that's kind of cool, can't lie. You come from good stock, little Paddy.

Pat Don't call me Paddy. My name's Pat.

Dylan Sorry, Patty!

Pat Pat.

Dylan Fine, Patsy. Protest, just don't arrest me, soldier. And definitely don't fall in love with me.

Pat Trust me, you're safe there.

Dylan (*miming arrow to the heart*) Ouch. The neek has a knife!

Pat Stop it. Is your phone off?

Dylan (*switching it off*) Yes, boss!

Pat So, are we doing this or what?

Jude Easy, tiger . . . we wait for the sign.

Pat Oh yeah! Duh! The sign!

Jude Meet at the monument, wear a key ring on your backpack, switch off your phone and any traceable device and wait for the sign.

Dylan And what's the sign again?

Loud scratching – everyone jumps.

DJ/MC (*testing mic*) Check-check-check. One-two, one-two testing never resting perpetually investing!

Welcome! To Clarity!

Kick drum pulses and echoes . . .

DJ/MC An organically spaced out safe space you don't need to get wrecked in to connect. So, this is your moment to find your partner or partners or your own solo space and get ready to make this patch of the universe your stamping ground and get ready to celebrate!

DJ/MC *drops the beat. It's basic but insistent.*

People start to move with the various levels of commitment/certainty we witnessed earlier

Shiloh/Jamie/Quinn

Jamie Oh boy, here we go . . .

Shiloh This is it.

Quinn Shiloh, where's that hip-flask?

Shiloh I thought you said you weren't into –

Quinn Never mind what you thought I said! You said you were bringing your mum's hip-flask!

Jamie Quinn, calm down.

Quinn You calm down. This is an emergency! What about your tragic family drinks cabinet?

Shiloh You know what I think?

Quinn Since when did you decide to think?

Shiloh I think you were right. We don't need it.

Quinn Since when do you listen to me, you treacherous snake!

Shiloh I mean, look around you, what do you see? It's just people moving about.

Jamie The thing is, though, they're moving to a beat.

Quinn Okay, let's go.

Shiloh And what's a beat?

Quinn What the hell are you on about? Why are we even still here?

Jamie A beat is a rhythmic division in music or poetry.

Quinn Oh my God!

Shiloh And if memory serves me, most standard dance tracks are 120 beats per minute which breaks down into –

Jamie – Units of four – or twos,

Shiloh (*trying while speaking*) – so if we just move our feet to the even numbers regularly –

Jamie – Most people are emphasising beat two and four –

Shiloh We may not be dancing,

Jamie/Shiloh But we will be moving!

Quinn Traitors! Don't leave me behind!

Jamie I think you can do this!

Quinn Oh God! Hip-flask! Hip-flask! Hip-flask! (*Increasingly to the beat.*) Hip-flask! Hip-flask-hip-flask-hip-flask!

Shiloh You're moving!

Quinn Shut up, I hate you! Hip-flask-hip-flask-hip-flask!

Jackie/Avery/Joey/Asa/Taylor

Taylor   Okayyy, so this was unexpected.

Joey   I know right?

Avery   No cider, no alcopops.

Asa   Just us.

Jackie   Dancing.

Asa   You're actually quite good, Tay!

Taylor   So are you, Asa!

Jackie   We all are! This might be alright!

Avery   Who knows! We might make new friends!

Joey   Do I still smell of sick?

Jackie   If we dance enough, we might sweat it off!

Jordan/Parker

Jordan   Hi. Again.

Parker   Hi.

Jordan   I was . . . thinking . . . wondering . . .
If it would be okay . . .

Parker   Okay!

Jordan   . . . I mean probably perfectly comfortable here, dancing on your own, which is fine, cool, you don't look awkward at all – which is amazing – but you see, I . . .

Parker   I know! There's always that weird moment where you step onto a dance floor or into an area that's been designated – for – dancing and it's like you step out of one reality –

Jordan   – daily reality –

Parker   and into dancey reality –

Jordan   and usually you're with a few companions – and so your initial awkward twitches blend in –

Parker   – and no one notices you struggling to find your feet like a new-born baby cow –

Jordan   – and even after that, dancing on your own can be great – if you're on your own –

Parker   – but it's so much better if you fall into rhythm with someone else – trading moves, mirroring shapes and

Jordan – losing self-consciousness – so it's cool? If I dance near you?

Parker I thought you'd never ask.

DJ/MC Yes, yes, yes, best believe, whatever your label or lack of it, you do not need it here and now, where every one of us has assembled with one universal ulterior interior motive: To dance!

DJ drops the bass . . .

Music: Building, escalating.

DJ/MC To move! To get lost in the beats. High on this hill, deep in this long grass amongst these tall trees, under this canopy of stars all glowing and scintillating and objectively beautiful. Tangled up in the rhythm like lazy loafers in Sunday sheets. Exploring all the ways we can move our bodies. Lifting our hands and faces up to the follow-spot ring-light full-moon, like shameless pagans and righteous believers have done since that prehistorical time we first fell in awestruck love with the night sky.

Falling into trances, quieting our screaming shouting minds as our primordial instincts reawaken like dinosaurs in thawing ice, lighter on our feet that any mere human has ever imagined we could be. . . . We move!

Through a night without labels categories or competition or insecurity or negotiations or divisions or inhibitions. One night without worrying about the plight of the planet or politics or economics or career prospects or the need to be cool – or sexy – or reckless – or responsible or acceptably beautiful, or intimidatingly intellectual, or inspiringly rebellious or self-consciously different or desperately anonymously reassuringly normal – one night when there is no weird. No wondering what we look like in the mirror or what we sound like when we speak or whether we can sing on the note or if anyone anywhere is impressed by us or laughing at us or judging us or even noticing us. Just one unique night in which we're utterly unafraid to be our barefoot selves, dancing however we want to dance! Moving however we feel like moving! Knowing what it feels like to just be alive!

Almost everyone dances now – getting into it.

Flashing police light . . .

Music stops.

Police (*off stage*) This is an illegal gathering. You must disperse immediately. Repeat: This is an illegal gathering. Disperse immediately.

Pat/Dylan/Jude

Dylan Oh! Migod!

Jude Whose idea was this?

Dylan I'm calling my mum.

Pat Okay. Everyone chill.

Jude Um, since when do you say 'chill'?

Pat It's not like they've stormed in and kettled us.

Dylan What's kettling?
(*To phone.*) Switch on, you lazy piece of crap!

Jude It's when they surround you and you can't get away.

Dylan Oh my God!

Pat It's not violent, it's just frustrating.

Dylan Nah, matey, I get claustrophobic at open-air festivals. We're going.

Jude It does seem sensible.

Pat They're just trying to scare us.

It's not like we're storming parliament.

Dylan Exactly. We're here to have a laugh, not start a revolution.

Jude Is a dance worth getting in trouble for?

Pat Good question!

Dylan (*to phone*) Come on!

Pat If it's not important, then why are they here?

Dylan Don't know. Don't care.
(*Into phone.*) Mum?

Pat *takes the phone.*

Dylan Excuse me?

Pat Why are we here?
(*Into phone.*) Excuse me, Miss Farmer, Dylan'll be with you in just a moment.
(*To* **Dylan/Jude**.) Why are we here?

Dylan Not to pay tribute to your militant parents. I told you – to have a laugh.

Jude To have fun.

Dylan Don't you start! And don't look at me like that, this is not fun!

Jude Thing is, how will we know what this is we don't stay? Maybe having fun is our revolution.

Pat Right. My parents weren't actually freedom fighters in like South Africa, or anything.

They used to go on marches and chant and do sit-ins and kiss-ins for a whole bunch of causes because they believed in stuff and because they wanted to be with friends that believed in stuff too. I mean they got arrested but they had a good time. Now they're kind of boring but at least they've got some cool posters and t-shirts and some great stories. What have we got?

Jude This. We've got this.

Pat And this might be our great story.
Are we gonna run away from it?

Dylan *snatches the phone back.*

Dylan Sorry to bother you, Mum. I'll call you back.

Some others are starting to disperse, some staying put.

Dylan Oy! Where're you lot going?

Asa Somewhere else.

Jude What's wrong with here?

Kerry It's illegal and surrounded by feds.

Pat How is this illegal?

Robin Exactly, It's a park!

Ali It's a public space. That's why we chose it.

Quinn That's true. This land is publicly owned.

Lennox I think you'll find that's 'state-owned'?

Joey Well, that's us, yeah? We are the state.

Avery Are we though?

Jackie When have any of us paid taxes?

Joey Well, we're going to, aren't we?

Avery Are we really, though?

Shiloh Not if we can help it, I suspect.

Avery My dad hasn't paid taxes in years.

Quinn Well, my mum has. Both of my parents have.

Asa Actually, we all have. As in the public have. I mean, VAT's a thing, right?

Robin Right! We own this space. There's no gate, no locks.

Jude They're not going to let us stay here.

Joey Why not? We're not creating a disturbance just by being here.

Taylor Not right now we're not.

Jordan So we wait until they're gone, fire the music back up and cane it until they come back?

Jamie And what do we do in between?

Drew Hang out?

Sam Hang out?

Parker Get to know each other.

Dylan Mate! This is supposed to be a rave!

Jude And what's a rave without music?

Pat Like, what's the number one element?

Jordan/Parker People.

Surprised, they glance at each other.

Jordan Basically, it's about homo sapiens getting together and getting in sync.

Parker We're the special ingredient. The number one element.

Joey So – 'homo sapiens', basically 'vibeing'?

Parker Yeah – I mean I guess – vibeing, yeah.

Ali Well, that was actually the point to be fair. To bring people together. And for them to experience each other sober, which I know is cheesy . . . but actually you know what? I don't care. I love a bit of cheese, vegan cheese – but yeah. Basically, I'm cheesy. I believe in human unity and if that's corny or cheesy I do not give a monkeys.

Robin I love the way you think you're swearing when you're not.

Avery You're the organiser?

Taylor The ringleader?

Robin Yes.
(*Nudges* **Ali**.) Yes.

Ali Yes! I mean, yep, er, yeah. . . . I'm the perp. The perpetrator.

Pat Cool.

Ali Yeah, I am cool. I'm my own cool.

Robin Which is the coolest of the cool.

Ali Yeah, I'm a nerd and a geek – a neek, if you will – but who isn't? We're all in our heads these days, aren't we? Glued to computers and excruciatingly socially awkward when encountering the slightest threat of actual eye contact with another actual human, even the ones who can fake enough swag to mask it. We're all of us OCD and obsessive about something. Trainspotting, dungeons and dragons, sci-fi, pop culture, trivia, fashion, cars, books, astrology, astronomy, skateboarding, some inexplicably popular sport . . . it's a world full of dweebs and all the really cool people own their dweebiness and can see it in others. So I activated my dweeb-dar and sent out this invitation to all of you because I think you're as big of an anorak as I am and I wanted us to have our Dork Pride. So, I say bun the police – in a nice way – and we stay and we reclaim this space – just a bunch of specky young 'uns hanging out and stuff and getting to know each other. 'Cause neeking out together with or without music . . . is lit.

Robin *sits down decisively. Gratefully* **Ali** *sits too.*

Asa   So what, this is a sit-in? Like in the sixties?

Pat   I dunno, this isn't exactly Greta Thunberg, is it?

Jordan   We could glue ourselves to the grass.

Jordan   Sounds effective.

Parker   Or we can just hang out.

Avery   In the park.

Joey   At night.

Sam   Like young people are doing all over the world.

Blake   But aren't they usually drinking cider or smoking zoots?

Shiloh   Weellll . . .

Quinn (*glaring at* **Shiloh**)   No!
(*Realising everyone is looking*) Nope! Not in like, super-religious parts of the world.

Blake   Well, but most people in most places . . .

Quinn   Drinking is illegal in like fourteen countries – like most of India – and there's a billion and a half people in India alone. And in some other places where it's not illegal, like Norway and Sweden and Turkey, it's so mad expensive it might as well be.

Asa   Since when did something being illegal stop people going for it?

Dylan   That's what makes it fun though, right?

Jude   Exactly! Which is why all over the world at this very moment, kids are going through their parents' drinks stash and pouring 'em into . . . what are they called, again . . . those little skinny tins you hide in your sock. . .?

Shiloh   A . . .

Shiloh *holds out a hip-flask.*

Shiloh   . . . hip-flask?

Everyone looks at **Ali** *who does not move.*

Pat   Well, there's probably enough in there for one decent sip each.

Dylan Paddy . . .

Pat It's Pat. And it is getting a bit chilly. . . . What?

Jude Like it ever stops at a sip.

Pat Well, it'll have to this time, won't it?

Ali (*wearily*) Will it? Anyone else brought a bottle?

Five more bottles are revealed.

Jude We are teenagers, remember! We sneak bottles into places – school, church, bedrooms, sports events, you name it, it's what we do – find new places to get pissed and throw up.

Lennox And what's wrong with that? This is a rave not a book club. Teenagers get tipsy. Teenagers get cheeky and extra and out of order. Teenagers get grimy.

Kerry Not just teenagers – all-agers. For every place where it's illegal, how many places are people drinking or smoking or eating mushrooms? In Catholic church everyone has a sip of wine at morning mass. Getting wavy is as human as it gets.

Taylor That's true. What's wrong with wanting to escape for a bit? What's wrong with fun?

Dylan Oh my God, remember fun?

Taylor That thing people used to have before everyone made careers out of having opinions and brutal judgements of everyone else? That's why we're here, right? To take a mini-vacation from our brains and just let go for a bit.

Blake Yeahhhh . . . but is getting hammered, succumbing to acute alcohol poisoning and waking up in the back of an ambulance with vomit in your hair while realising you've swallowed your tongue actually fun though?

Shiloh It doesn't sound boring.

Taylor You do realise it is possible to have a bevy without passing out, needing emergency services?

Jude Though that does legit sound like a good night out.

Taylor That people have been known to actually go out and have one drink or three, and even a pill or two and stay conscious and hang out and have a laugh like a normal person?

Asa Or! That is it possible to just be your un-self-medicated self and still have a laugh? Seriously when was the last time you went out and had 'fun' that didn't require getting bladdered?

Kerry 'Bladdered?'

Blake Okay, boomer. How old are you, again?

Asa Blasted, bombed, hammered, mashed, mortalled, mullered, slaughtered, sloshed, smashed, soused, trashed, wrecked, mega-wavy ... wasted.

Blake Drama queens. Blimey.

Asa When was the last time you kissed anyone for the first time and you were actually sober?

Dylan What?

Asa Have you ever had the courage to go for that first kiss with no drink or pills involved?

Jude When I was twelve. It didn't go well.

Pat That's the problem with real life. It doesn't go well without a bit of assistance.

Jamie Are you trying to say it goes better when you're wavy?

Pat Are you saying I'm the only one who thinks that?

Jamie I mean, maybe it feels better for a minute or an hour or, if you're lucky, an evening –

Asa – and then comes the morning –

Joey – Uhhh, the morning! –

Asa – And you're back where you started –

Avery – With a hangover.

Blake At least you had the evening though, right? Some of us have never even had that. Some of us just have a 'real life' that's crap 24/7. The hangover without the high.

Quinn And the opportunity to actually do something about real life to be fair.

Blake Like what for instance?

Lennox Isn't getting wavy doing something about it?

Avery Feeling like you're dealing with something isn't the same as actually doing something about it, though, is it? Like if someone's bullying you or getting in your face, what does getting off your face do?

Drew Well, at least you're doing something to make yourself better.

Sam Thank you! What's wrong with feeling better for a change?

Lennox That's not confronting anything or reporting anything or actually getting away from the situation for real. Real life requires real action. Real action creates real change.

Blake You make that sound nice and easy.

Ali Maybe real life doesn't have to be easy, maybe it just has to be real.

Quinn That's the problem with our generation though, and I don't mean people our age, I mean, more or less everyone who's alive right now. We want everything easy and we want it now.

Sam What's wrong with that though?

Drew Life is now, isn't it?

Asa Why should it have to be hard?

Jude It's not for long, let's face it. That's what all the older people I know say.

Taylor That's nice and cheerful.

Pat Maybe it's all over anyway. For all of us. Maybe this mess we're living in is the end of the real life – as everybody disappears into carefully filtered social media avatars that are prettier than them, better made up than them, fitter and thinner with a smaller waist and bigger bum or boobs or pecs or hair, smile or lips and that have more friends than they'll ever need or actually talk to or even meet.

And in just few more years none of us will know what anyone outside of our close family actually looks like, and even then, we'll all have undergone so much surgery that we'll have forgotten our own faces and even our best friends won't be able to remember or recognise us. Not that any of that matters because we'll never be in the same place as anyone at the same time. Not at school, not at work, not in bed, nowhere, but anyway we'll never look in an actual mirror, just our photoshopped digital reflections in our phones and screens and dysphoric perceptions and projections.

Dylan Yikes.

Robin Maybe indeed. And maybe this silly little suggestion-slash-dream of a drink-free, drug-free rave is our invitation to do something radical. To actually be together and talk and flirt and dance without distortions or filters. And that's why just for one night under the stars and trees on real live grass, we agreed to do without so much high tech crap and just be actually totally 100 per cent present in actual three-dimensional real life.

Silence.

Jamie I've got Haribo.

Jordan *sits.*

Jordan I've got Percy Pigs.

Parker (*sits*) I've got Fruitella.

Lennox (*sits*) I've got Squashies!

Everyone sits.

Pat/Dylan/Jude Sugar high picniiiiiiiiic!

Sweets are shared. The almost silence filled with the sound of sweet eating.

Ali Thank you.

Pat So . . . we talk? Communicate?

Connect? *All look at* **Ali**. **Ali** *shrugs a semi-yes.*

Asa Sounds good to me.

Taylor What do we talk about?

Ali We can talk about whatever we like talking about.

Shiloh (*getting up*) Okay, you know what, I'm going home before my folks realise I'm AWOL.

Robin Or whatever we don't like talking about.

Shiloh *stops. Ears prick up all round.*

Robin What are the things we never talk about? To anyone. What does nobody – even our best friends – know about us?

Blake I don't have any friends. I don't know why. I want to. I think people have tried. I've tried. But nothing sticks. It's not like I'm always picked last for teams or games or anything. I'm good at stuff. People like me. I get invited to stuff. Like tonight. We'll hang out.
  (*To* **Lennox** *and* **Kerry**.) We'll smile next time I see you at the library. There'll be small talk. But that'll be it. We just won't gel. I'm like that shadow in *Peter Pan* that cannot stick to Peter's feet.

There's pics of me all over social media but almost every one is with someone different. Everybody's buddy, nobody's bezzie. Popular pariah. And that's okay. At least I'm never actually alone. I suppose.

Quinn And you're a okay dancer.

Blake Oh! Thanks. So are you.

Quinn I am aren't I?! Talk about something I never ever thought I'd say. I just looked around and watched and copied and I really got into it!

Jamie We all did!

Shiloh I did say we could dance.

Quinn Yeah, but you were lying then, and now it's . . .

Quinn/Shiloh . . . Truuuuue!

Quinn I know, right? I mean who woulda thunk that we were funky?

Jamie Why does no one tell you that music is basically maths?

Quinn It's like, oh my days, we're made for this!

Shiloh   We're a crew! Alright, cringe alert, we're overdoing it now . . .

Jamie   No! We are owning the cringe without fear or shame.

Quinn   Let the whole world cringe at our dancing feet. We are a crew!

Shiloh   The cerebral crew!

Jamie *takes a group selfie of the trio throwing up gang signs.*

Quinn/Jamie/Shiloh   Bow down, bitches!

Sam   I'm not a nerd.

All eyes on **Sam**.

I'm a fraud. I don't find math sexy. I don't make hilarious lame jokes about chemistry, I can't code to save my life and I don't love the smell of a brand new book. I've never played chess, *World of Warcraft* or *Dungeons and Dragons*. Rubik's Cubes scare me, quantum physics confuses me – or is that the other way round? – and it's not my ambition to be on University Challenge. I hate *Doctor Who*.

Gasps.

And *Star Trek* and *Lord of the Rings* and *Star Wars*. I don't speak Klingon or Elvish or Dadsat. I don't love cosplay or making stuff out of Lego or wearing bow ties. I don't need contact lenses, cause my glasses are fake. I'm a fake. I'm so uncool. I'm not even genuinely uncool. I'm fake uncool.

Asa   You wear fake glasses?

Sam   Yep. I mean I know not all neeks wear glasses and that's reductive stereotyping and all that, but . . . yeah. Clear lenses.

Asa   Why?

Drew   To make me feel better?

Sam   Actually – to make me feel better.

When we got talking on the coach to the Science Museum and I realised you were actually looking forward to it and that somehow you'd assumed that I was as into it as every other misfit who'd signed up,

I was gobsmacked. No clue what to say to you, and so I made the worst joke ever . . .

Drew   'I was reading a book on helium – I couldn't put it down.'

Sam   . . . and you laughed.

Drew   It was funny.

Sam   And then you said,

Drew   'What did the tectonic plate say when it bumped into the other tectonic plate? "Sorry – My fault!"' And you said . . .

Sam   'What's the quickest way to determine the sex of a chromosome? Pull down its genes!'

And your expression went totally blank and I had to scramble to explain that obviously I knew that sex and gender are two different things and you were still like stoney-faced and I'm thinking, 'Oh my God, Comrade Wokedy Woke-Woke, lighten up! . . . please . . . lighten up, . . . and just then you looked me in the eye and said . . .

Drew   'You're funny.'

Sam   And it suddenly hit me that I might just about get away with fooling you into thinking I was your intellectual equal and you might actually tolerate my company on a longer-term basis.

And so I went online and bought a light sabre, a Rubik's Cube and a pair of specs – and here we are.

Drew   Wait, are you seriously claiming you're not a neek when you're legitimately brilliant at Rubik's Cube?

Sam   Honestly? Conquering that nearly killed me.

No one is impressed.

Seriously! Took me hours!

Ali   Try weeks.

Sam   Really?

Avery   All those YouTube tutorials!

Drew   Wait, you're not saying you learned to draw for me?

Sam   Well. No. I've always drawn.

Drew   And you're an amazing artist.

Sam (*to everyone*)   Is art nerdy?

Drew (*to everyone*)   Comic books.

Taylor   Like, graphic novels?

Sam   Er, yeah.

Jordan   Well, what's more neeky than that?

Sam   Fair point. But . . .

Robin   You realise that it's not being crazy good at something or knowing stuff that make you a neek, right? It's wanting to know stuff so badly that you can't stop yourself finding out everything you can about it.

Sam   So jocks are neeks?

Parker   Jocks are MAJOR neeks.

Jordan You have to be.

Drew But you do know that if you weren't a neek I'd like you anyway, right?

Sam Really?

Drew Not that we'll ever know. 'Cause you are a neek!

Sam So basically you're saying we were made for each other?

Drew I know. We're a bit ridiculously young.

Sam But you're saying . . .

Drew We were made for each other. Yeah. For now.

Sam Now is fine by me.

Taylor Ugh! Spare my poor stomach, please and change the subject!

Police (*off stage*) This is an illegal gathering!

Groans and some muted defiant reactions. Some nervous faces.

Lennox (*mutters*) Oh, for crying out . . . .

Police Disperse immediately!

Lennox Shut up!

Lennox *leaps up.*

Police	**Lennox**
If you do not disperse immediately, you will all be subject to arrest.	SHUT UP!

Lennox FOR WHAT?

Lennox *grabs the DJ's mic (if there is one).*

Lennox For what? For dancing? For having friends and making new ones?

The others encourage, some timidly, some a bit more loudly. 'Thank you! You tell 'em! Preach! Yes!' etc.

Lennox For taking a few minutes off from the mind-numbing tedium of living up to your vision of the perfect offspring? You disperse! You go home and for once in our lives, stop embarrassing me!

Silence.

Dylan Wait. You're serious?

Pat That's actually your . . .?

Lennox Yep. Breaking news. My parents are police officers. Both of them. You want secrets. Beat that.

Silence.

Asa My mum's a prison officer.

Pat Mine's a school principal. At my own school.

Dylan Shall we go now?

Jackie Well, these are all important jobs. Good intentions. Keeping society going. I mean, seriously, what would we do without them?

Lennox I know. I know it's all good intentions. And I'm still feeling a way about it. Pathetic. Messed up. Embarrassed for being embarrassed. Ashamed of being proud. Ashamed of knowing that one day I'll probably do the same. I'm always saying I won't. Especially when we're arguing and I'm being a brat who needs to score my points. I tell my folks and myself every day I'd rather die than end up as a uniformed enforcer, 'just following orders'. But, let's face it – I will be. Because I know my parents didn't become coppers because they were dickheads who were bullied in school and crave power over other people, but because even though they're a pair of dinosaurs who vote for all the wrong people for all the wrong reasons they basically want to do the right thing. And because, even though I'm too chicken to tell even my best friends what they do for a living, I basically think they're – in a weird way – sort of cool. And if I follow in their footsteps, I might be even cooler. Which is our job as offspring, right? To try to be even cooler than our parents and succeed or fail with the best intentions. Oh my God, what am I even saying?

Kerry Basically, you're saying you are on the side of the so-called law.

Lennox What, wait, No! Well . . . Not this law. I mean we need laws, obviously – I suppose – but definitely not this law, fundamentally.

Kerry Well, you're saying that even though not 'fundamentally' you ultimately believe that us not being allowed to get together and dance is basically the police trying to do the right thing.

Parker Police don't make laws.

Kerry The government then.

Jordan That pesky state again . . .

Kerry You trust that 'every law is always made for the common good with the best of intentions', like fascists, oppressors, manipulators and hypocrites simply don't exist. As if old people don't seem to totally forget what it's like to be young, or don't get bitter because they were neeks when they were young and missed out on all the fun and can't stand to see their kids seizing the freedom they were scared of. So you're gonna give up and shrivel and slink back home to an early middle-age and a spiritual grave. Is that it? Is that what we're meant to do with our tiny window of youth? Protest on Saturday but basically refuse to rebel?

Lennox I'm sorry, I never told you, Kerry.

Kerry Oh, I knew what your parents are, Lenny. I'm not actually stupid. I just didn't know you were one of 'em.

Lennox And you're not one of yours? The librarian who grew up in a house of books and bookworms? And least I'm trying to break us both out of the cocoon.

Kerry Yeah, but deep down do you believe there should be laws against dancing?

Lennox Well, you know, people do live round here.

Kerry Oh, right.

Sam And people do need their sleep –

Pat – specially old people.

Kerry Why? Because they're knackered from having had their fun when they were young?

Blake But you were just saying yourself that they missed their chance to have fun.

Kerry I know what I said! I don't have to be consistent! 'Cause I am young!

Lennox Exactly! We're supposed to be loud and obnoxious and shockingly selfish.

Kerry We're supposed to say, think and do appalling things that'll make us cringe in twenty years' time.

Lennox We're supposed to stay up too late and drink too much –

Kerry – and make terrible mistakes and get arrested for doing stupid stuff and learn the hard way –

Lennox – or be obsessively teetotal and totally judgemental and a little bit jealous.

Kerry It's our duty to sneak out to the park with our mates and dance all night and wake up feeling like rubbish and walk home 'cause we've lost our phone and can't pay for the night bus.

Lennox We're meant to scoff at wisdom and guidance, embarrass them publicly so we can get grounded and slam doors in a series of teenage tantrums before we inevitably give in and grow up to become them.

Kerry We were born to drive our parents to their wits' end because we're as stupid and reckless and beautiful and feckless as they used to be.

Jude Wow.

Shiloh Okay.

Lennox I never said I wasn't stupid and reckless too. And I never said I was giving up and going home. Just 'cause I'm embarrassed about being embarrassed doesn't mean I'm not glad to be here with you. Are you embarrassed to be here with me?

Kerry Yes and no and maybe. Like I said, I'm inconsistent.

Lennox Me too. Consistently.

Dylan Okay. I'm confused. You're staying? (*Looking around.*) We're staying? We stay?

Asa We stay. And we rave.

Jude Um, call me old fashioned and repetitive, but I still reckon that a rave requires music.

DJ/MC Music? Not a problem. Never was. I think it might be time for a little bit of 'high-tech crap'. Everyone got headphones?

People nod, shrug, hold up their headphones.

Lennox I lost mine.

Jude I've got a spare.

DJ/MC Everyone got their Bluetooth working?

General assent. Smiles breaking out as people realise what's happening . . .

DJ/MC Search for DJ/MC Squared . . . And connect . . . Cool?

Thumbs go up, people put their headphones on and earbuds in . . .

DJ/MC . . . Sweet.

DJ/MC *spins the track we can hear it playing tinny through all the headphones as everyone starts to move in their own way.*

Sam Hi, Dad!

Drew Hi, Mum!

Quinn Sorry I'm late.

Jackie Well, actually, I'm not sorry I'm late . . .

Blake . . . just sorry I'm later than I promised.

Joey And I'm not gonna lie . . .

Dylan . . . Like I usually do . . .

Lennox . . . 'cause I have had THE most INCREDIBLE time.

Ali I sort of kind of . . . actually arranged a rave in the park!

Robin And people actually came!

Avery And you know what?

Parker I think I maybe might have met someone.

Jordan And I think they might have actually met me!

Kerry And we actually talked about stuff.

Asa Agreed about stuff.

Kerry Disagreed about stuff!

Jude And laughed about stuff.

Pat And Mum! Dad!

Shiloh We actually danced!

Jamie In front of people!

Taylor And it was amaaaaaazing!

DJ/MC Check-check-check. One-two, one-two! This tune goes out live.

Ravers Live!

DJ/MC Live and acoustic.

Ravers Live and acoustic!

DJ/MC Live and acoustic and amplified.

Ravers Live and acoustic and amplified!

DJ/MC This tune goes out loud and acoustic and spiritually amplified to the young and the young at heart. This is an open invitation to move your body any way you want to, with anyone who wants to move with you to any rhythm you choose. This tune is spinning to welcome you to yourself and your freedom.

Ravers Freedom!

DJ/MC Welcome to freedom!

Ravers Welcome to freedom!

DJ/MC Welcome!

Ravers Welcome!

DJ/MC and Ravers To clarity!

Music exolodes into full volume. Everyone is dancing.

Together.

End.

Character Plot

	Opening	Clearview Park, Daytime	Shiloh's Room	Graveyard	Sam's Family Home	Drew's Family Home	Library	Just outside Clearview Park	Clearview Park	Shiloh/Jamie/Quinn	Jackie/Avery/Joey/Asa/Taylor	Jordan/Parker	Pat/Dylan/Jude
Ali	✓	✓											✓
Robin	✓	✓											✓
Quinn	✓		✓							✓			✓
Shiloh	✓		✓							✓			✓
Jamie	✓		✓							✓			✓
Jackie	✓			✓							✓		✓
Avery	✓			✓							✓		✓
Joey	✓			✓							✓		✓
Asa	✓			✓							✓		✓
Taylor	✓			✓							✓		✓
Sam	✓				✓								✓
Drew	✓					✓							✓
Lennox	✓						✓						✓
Kerry	✓						✓						✓
Blake	✓						✓						✓
Parker	✓							✓				✓	✓
Jordan	✓							✓				✓	✓
Pat	✓								✓				✓
Jude	✓								✓				✓
Dylan	✓								✓				✓
DJ/MC											✓	✓	✓
Police											✓	✓	✓

More information about the characters and how much they speak

The characters are grouped with the other characters they generally appear with. In the opening and final scene, all characters (probably with the exception of the police) are onstage.

Ali – Significant dialogue and two long monologues
Robin – Significant dialogue and a short monologue

Quinn – Significant dialogue
Shiloh – Significant dialogue
Jamie – Significant dialogue

Jackie – Significant dialogue
Avery – Significant dialogue
Joey – Significant dialogue
Asa – Significant dialogue
Taylor – Significant dialogue

Sam – Two long monologues, several short monologues and significant dialogue
Drew – Long monologue

Lennox – Significant dialogue and medium-length monologue
Kerry – Significant dialogue and medium-length monologue
Blake – Some dialogue and short monologue

Pat – Significant dialogue and long monologue
Dylan – Significant dialogue
Jude – Significant dialogue

Jordan – Significant dialogue
Parker – Significant dialogue

DJ/MC – Various DJ-style monologues

Police – Short lines, could be created via sound or voice over

Main Narrative Beats

1. Everyone takes a selfie, they are at a rave. Ali and Robin make a video to advertise that the rave is alcohol free. At Shiloh's house, some friends watch the video, they decide to go.
2. In a graveyard some friends are vomiting, they have been drinking alcohol. They decide to hide their alcohol and go to the rave. Sam is at home, they reassure their dad about the rave.
3. Drew is at home, they talk to their mum about the rave, they are going to meet Sam.
4. Some other friends are working at the library, they say they might close early and go to the party, someone comes in to the library to charge their phone, they're also going to the rave.
5. Outside the park Jordan and Parker bump into each other, they're both going to the same rave, the park is locked.
6. In the park Pat is waiting for their friends, Dylan's mum is ringing, Jude explains their parents met at a protest. Pat tells them to put away their phones.
7. The DJ announces the beginning of the rave, Shiloh, Jamie and Quinn are looking for a hip-flask, they try to dance
8. The friends who were vomiting are at the rave, they're dancing. Jordan and Parker bump into each other again, they talk about dancing. The DJ talks about being free to be yourself at the rave.
9. The police arrive, they try to stop the rave. Pat, Dylan and Jude panic, Dylan tries to call his mum. Pat says their parents used to protest and sometimes got arrested.
10. Most people stay at the rave, the police won't scare them off. They are going to stay in the park, play the music and enjoy themselves as soon as the police have left.
11. Ali reveals that they are the organiser of the rave. They are a nerd, they wanted to bring people together, to chat and hang out without alcohol.
12. Several people reveal that they have brought alcohol, some of them find it hard to socialise without alcohol. Pat thinks it's better to hang out together rather than be on phones and screens.
13. They are offered sweets by other people and decide to talk to them. Blake struggles to make friends, Sam has been pretending to be a nerd.
14. The police try and disperse the group. Lennox stands up to them, their parents are police officers. Kerry and Lennox discuss whether they are like their parents or rebelling against them.
15. They restart the music, on headphones this time.
16. Each character talks about the rave to their parents, they had the most amazing time.

Ravers

BY RIKKI BEADLE-BLAIR

Notes on rehearsal and staging, drawn from a workshop with the writer led by Phyllida Lloyd held at the National Theatre, October 2024

How the writer came to write the play

During lockdown during the Covid-19 pandemic, Primrose Hill Park – usually open 24/7 – was closed at night. Young people, who would normally gather there to play music, dance and socialise, found an essential part of their lives restricted. Despite these closures, they would still climb over gates to be together, seeking a place where they could fully express themselves.

The park attracts teenagers from all backgrounds, nationalities and ethnicities; it reflects the diversity of London. This setting felt ideal for a play that could resonate universally and be adaptable for youth companies across the country.

Today's young people have fewer public spaces to gather freely, making it harder for them to assert themselves in the world. This play aims to explore that struggle.

The play combines a courtroom drama backdrop with a trial, where each character grapples with asserting themselves while navigating complex personal relationships.

It highlights the essence of a rave: strangers coming together, sharing stories, laughter and movement. In club culture, dancing is about feeling the music – you belong simply by being into it.

The play is about giving yourself permission to be authentic and allowing others the space to do the same. Art embodies the freedom to be oneself, while also inspiring others to embrace their own identities.

'Maybe we should just make our own cool. Which is my recommendation to the whole world: make your own party.'

(Rikki Beadle-Blair, 2024)

Exercises for use in rehearsals

Writer Rikki Beadle-Blair led a couple of warm-up games that he frequently uses when working with young people:

Exercise: Owning the space

- Move through the space as if on a runway. Encourage the group to be as big and bold with this as possible.

Beadle-Blair spoke about how this is the first thing he'll do when performing in a new space. He'll walk the entire stage space as if it's a runway so he can own the space. This way, it becomes an extension of him and helps with confidence.

Exercise: Stop/Go/Jump/Clap

- Move around the room in any direction. Make sure to not just walk in circles, keep your journey interesting. Notice where no one else in the group is going, find new uncovered ground to move in
- 'Stop' is a command to freeze in the space. 'Go' means continue moving
- 'Clap' means clap three times as a group. 'Jump' means jump on the spot three times as a group
- Once the group were comfortable with these commands, Beadle-Blair reversed the meaning of the commands. So 'Stop' means 'Go' and vice versa. 'Jump' means 'Clap' and vice versa.

Exercise: One, two, three

- In pairs, stand facing each other. The aim is to say 'One, two, three' on repeat with each person taking one number at a time
- See how fast you can go without making a mistake
- Beadle-Blair stopped the group and asked a pair to demonstrate. He commented on the level of teamwork and connection that's required to keep the game going
- Replace saying 'One' with a clap. So it goes: '[clap], two, three'
- Beadle-Blair asked the group to consider if it was 'Easier or harder? Is it because it's two languages? Your job is to keep the script going and not let the audience know that you sometimes don't know what you're doing.'
- Replace saying 'two' with a stamp. So it goes '[clap], [stamp], three'
- Replace saying 'three' with a body wiggle (e.g. a shimmy)
- Once the pairs had a few minutes to try out this non-verbal version, Beadle-Blair asked a pair to step into the middle and demonstrate. He pointed out the pressure that's immediately put on with an audience present and so when the pair messes up, they're to turn and bow to the audience who will cheer enthusiastically. The pair then go again, aiming for a stronger and better version
- By bowing to the audience and continuing the game, it invites the actors to embrace failure and encourages resilience.

For Beadle-Blair, a rehearsal room that feels free is a loud, chatty one where everyone feels like themselves. These games are intended to be silly so as to help less confident/more shy participants come out of their shell.

Exercise: Building character

Seven levels of tension

Lead director Phyllida Lloyd stressed the usefulness of building a vocabulary with the ensemble. Exploring tension levels allows the actors to find the characters' varying energies and how they develop over the play.

Each level has a physical definition and a sound. There's a tendency to just commit to the physical and forget about the sound, but it's important to start vocalising the soundscape around and in your body from the beginning.

After spending a couple of minutes on each level, come to your feet and have a brief reflection on how that felt in your body and voice.

Level one – *Pond life*
Lie on the floor. You're an amoeba. A big amorphous jelly. Use breath as you imagine your limbs moving in the jelly. Spend some time experiencing what pond life is for you.

Level two – *Stoned dude*
You're walking through a frat house the morning after a big party. Your head is aching, all noises are too loud. As you move through the house, you pass other 'stoned dudes'. How do you greet each other? What's the sound? There might be some grunting and heavy breath.

Level three – *Stage management (can adapt to a more familiar context)*
This is the most neutral state of tension. Move through space efficiently, setting up the room for the day. Waste no energy and be strategic as you move through the space. Ensure to make eye contact. Use the phrase 'Good morning. Thank you.' as a starting point for efficiency in use of voice.

Level four – *Toddler*
Move around as if you're on your way to do something, but get distracted easily. Can't focus on anything for more than a second or two at a time. All light and airy. Make use of levels. There's no threat of violence in this tension state.

Level five – *Disturbance*
In this state, a threat is imminent and there's a build of panic. Play with the sense of warning and alarm in the voice and body. Explore a jagged change of dynamic in the space – a sudden interruption to moving around the space.

Level six – *Pandemonium*
The panic increases significantly. This state should be orally earsplitting. The action is to terrify each other in whatever scenario is most appropriate (e.g. there's a bomb on the bus, the police are about to arrest the group).

Level seven – *Kabuki (in theatrical terms)*
It's very hard to just jump into this tension state. It helps to start in level three in which you are going about your business efficiently, then suddenly notice the incredible threat near you. Practise reacting with a loud intake of breath followed by a paralysing stillness and tension of the body. This happens when the facilitator claps their hands.

Once the group has tried this a few times, add in the exploration of the 'release' right after, as if the threat has completely dissipated. Focus on the loud exhale and take in the people in the room around you to share the experience.

Once each tension state has been explored in turn, start in level two – don't forget the sounds! – and work through them with the whole group, jumping up and down between the tension states.

These can be completely customised to your group. What Lloyd finds helpful is once the vocabulary is set up, you can then use it as a shorthand in your direction of the group without much discussion. It's all about altering and playing with energy and levels of tension in the space.

Exercise: Improvising levels of tension

To put these into action, Lloyd played an improv game. With a chair in the space, three volunteers entered and were assigned a character: a teacher and two students. The scenario was to discuss what had just happened in the playground. The teacher was assigned a tension level three, first child a tension level two and the second child a tension level four. The scene played out and a couple of minutes in Lloyd asked volunteers to assign new tension levels to see how it would impact the direction of the scene.

Exercise: Listening and response

This exercise highlights the importance of listening, not just speaking, within a monologue. It also helps in developing the backstory and character relationships.

- In pairs, choose a monologue to a parent: Sam (page 415) or Drew (page 416). Person A reads the monologue as the character, and Person B plays the role of the character's parent.
- Improvised parent dialogue: Identify and insert conversational 'beats' where the parent might naturally respond. Improvise these responses, or write them alongside the text for structure.
- Watching some examples back, the exercise demonstrates the interplay between spoken monologue and implied response, adding depth to character motivations and parent-child dynamics.
- This exercise is especially valuable with a longer rehearsal period, allowing actors to craft nuanced portrayals through in-depth exploration of the monologue's underlying backstory.

Staging options and spatial dynamics

- **Proscenium arch (end-on stage):**

    Option one: Characters interact as if they're in the same room, with a fourth wall maintained. This set-up focuses on authentic, private exchanges.

Option two: Characters face out towards the audience, each in their own spotlight, simulating separation while allowing audience engagement with each character individually.

- **Theatre in the round:**

    Playing across the space: In this configuration, characters maintain eye contact across the stage, which enhances the intimacy of the exchange for an audience encircling them.

Each spatial set-up brings out instinctive responses from actors, prompting varied pacing, blocking choices and tension-building based on distance.

Lloyd also prompted the actors with a **character focus** for the scene, e.g. the teenager's focus is on leaving (heading to a gig), while the parent's goal is to hold their attention. Experiment with distance and 'point of concentration' by positioning the characters across the space, amplifying the emotional stakes.

Once the actors have built an understanding of the parent's response, move the parent actor into the audience:

- **Step one:** Actor playing the parent sits in the audience, speaking lines out while the actor on stage directs their monologue towards them. This set-up gives the actor on stage a point of focus.

- **Step two:** Parent remains silent, letting the monologue carry with implied responses. The actor keeps the rhythm, listening and 'waiting' for responses to maintain the conversational feel without the parent's actual voice.

Comments and further thoughts from Phyllida Lloyd

Actors facing the audience, especially in the parent-directed monologues, helps connect with parents in the audience and creates a meta-narrative about generational dynamics.

Listening should be visibly active; when playing to the parent, actors must maintain a sense of urgency in their actions, making pauses powerful. Avoid drifting or 'meandering'.

Assigning specific **actions and objectives** keeps the actor's intentions directed and intentional.

Ball-passing exercise: For shorter rehearsals, use a ball game where actors pass a ball, committing to a purposeful action when throwing, e.g. I warn you. This keeps physical engagement high and prevents the scene from feeling like casual conversation.

Additional exercises for rehearsals

Exercise: Hotseating

- Place a character in the 'hot seat' and have the rest of the cast ask them a rapid series of questions about their background – aim for about 100 questions. This

method helps to quickly build a backstory and encourages instinctive choices without overthinking
- As other characters learn about a character's background, it naturally enriches their relationships with that character.

Exercise: Text detective

- Take on the role of a 'text detective'. Create lists and write down everything a character says about themselves and others
- Use this approach to add depth and flesh out each character.

Exercise: Status

- Status is an essential concept in this play. Consider: What status am I giving to others in each scene?
- For example, in a scene with four characters, assign each a status level (one to four). Each character should know whose status they are trying to elevate
- This technique adds rich layers to the scene and helps the audience engage more deeply with the story and characters.

Staging the ensemble

Library scene staging (p. 417)

Lloyd's set-up of the exercise:

- Divide cast into four groups; each group stages the scene differently with ensemble members supporting the central characters (Avery and Lennox)
- Key questions:
  - What is the ensemble's spatial configuration?
  - How does the ensemble interact with the scene – are they acknowledged by characters or remain background?
  - What transitions help the ensemble support the scene's emotional and visual flow?

Group feedback and observations:

- **Ensemble as landscape:** Keeping the ensemble onstage as 'human landscape' provides energy and visual depth, making set pieces less necessary
- **In-the-round benefits:** Enhances character connections and natural movements; ensemble energy is more dynamically distributed and responsive
- **Directional note:** Ensemble physicality should support but not overshadow the main action, avoiding over-emphasis.

Monument scene staging (p. 428)

Lloyd led this as a group exercise:

The scene reveals a meeting point at the monument; six volunteers positioned themselves in the centre of the room and formed a monument structure.

Playing with configurations:

In the round: Ensemble gathers in the centre with chairs, creating a monument that Pat, Dylan and Jude approach. One ensemble member from the monument acts as a DJ when prompted.

Proscenium arch: Ensemble positioned behind the main action; one participant cues the ensemble on key visual moments inspired by the scene's text.

Group feedback and observations:

- **Need for visual interest:** The scene requires an engaging focal point to sustain interest and tension
- **Dynamic ensemble movements:** In the round, the ensemble's formation is more visually and emotionally compelling, enhancing audience engagement with the main characters
- **Using student input when creating the scene:** Allows exploration of important visual beats and brings fresh interpretations, especially in ensemble-heavy scenes.

Key staging takeaways from the ensemble exercises

- **Spatial configuration**
- **Proscenium arch vs in the round:** In-the-round staging promotes natural character movements and keeps audience engagement high, whereas proscenium setups can create more formal, static dynamics
- **Ensemble:**
  - Use the ensemble as 'human scenery' to create an active, flexible set that's both visually compelling and cost-effective
  - Ensemble members' movements and positioning should reflect characters' internal states, enhancing the emotional undercurrent of scenes
  - The ensemble should embody the mood without overpowering; balance is crucial to avoid 'over-egging' the scene.
- **Audience relationship:** Decide if ensemble members will interact with the audience or remain in the background, especially when depicting large-scale scenes like libraries or monuments
- **Transitions:** Smooth transitions between ensemble states (e.g. dance to stillness) are critical to maintaining the scene's rhythm and preventing distractions.

Scene-specific enhancements:

- **Library scene:** Experiment with configurations that allow fluid transitions into and out of the library set-up, letting the ensemble amplify the mood without detracting from Avery and Lennox's status dynamics
- **Monument scene:** Ensure visual interest through intentional ensemble formations and a focal point (e.g. the DJ) to anchor the scene's energy.

Focus: Tackling the second half of *Ravers* (from p. 425)

The group explored how to address the main challenges in the final section by clarifying story beats, character dynamics, and pacing to ensure stakes and engagement.

Working as a whole group, the session's aim was to solidify story architecture and critical scene transitions. Throughout the afternoon, Lloyd fostered an open, collaborative environment with emphasis on shared ownership of all characters.

Proscenium setting: Experimenting with character arrangement and beats in a proscenium arch layout.

Groups and pairings:

- Ali and Robin
- Blake, Kerry and Lennox
- Asa, Avery, Joey and Taylor
- Jamie, Quinn and Shiloh
- Jordan and Parker
- Dylan, Jude and Pat

Given circumstances: Scene involves high-stakes 'siege' moment with police presence, requiring heightened tension and maintained sense of emergency.

Key directions:

- Police proximity and presence remain constant
- Amplify stakes and urgency through lighting, sound and character tension
- Consider adding lines to clarify the police as a stand-off threat.

Character intentions and reactions:

- **Dylan:** In extreme distress, tension level six
- **Pat:** Attempts to calm Dylan, exerts pressure
- **Jude:** Wavers between stances.

Scene markers and key beats:

- **'Who owns the place?':** Identified as the first major beat by Lloyd
- **Snapshot moments:** Encourage characters to find moments that feel natural and cohesive within the scene
- **Driving force:** Assign actors responsibility for propelling specific sections, cue 'baton handover' moments for seamless transitions

- **Police cues:** Directors add sound cues to simulate police presence, forcing group reaction and maintaining stakes
- **Space command:** Actors use lines to establish physical dominance or vulnerability
- **Movement with purpose:** Enter with purpose, reinforce who is attacking/ wanting attention from whom.

Exploring the alcohol bottle in the scene as a focal point:

Exploring rules and hierarchies: Define group norms (e.g. rave rules, alcohol stance) for deeper character-driven interactions.

- Explore how the drinkers and non-drinkers interact differently – start with heightened body language showing their individual attraction/repulsion to the object. Allows exploration of internal character conflicts
- Each actor explores an individual relationship with the bottle, adding complexity and variation to each character's journey
- Consider whether characters actually drink or simply use bottles as symbolic props.

Experimenting with transitions between groups and moments within the scene: Private vs public moments:

- 'I'm not a nerd' speech (p. 435): Initially performed as a private confession, transitioning to a more public, press-conference style
- Lloyd reflected on how the scene works best with a single transition from private to public; avoid frequent shifts to maintain emotional impact
- Confession moments as public revelations to maintain stakes within the group's shared trust
- Always interesting to note who stays silent in a scene and why – encouraging actors to make active choices
- **Shift focus with lighting:** Use lighting to separate smaller groups, focusing the audience on key characters during breakaway moments.
- **Proxemics:** Vary physical distance to manage tension, avoid close positioning to preserve language impact.

The final part of the play can be guided by focusing on **clear story beats** that the cast can anchor to, in order to help convey the narrative arc cohesively.

Costume

How can costume be used to guide the audience through the characters' transitions over the evening?

Consider the phases:

- **Private moments:** Characters as we meet them individually.
- **Ritual preparation:** Characters dressing for the event.

- **Revealing their true selves:** Characters in costumes that reflect who they are.

How can costumes support this structure?

What will help keep the ensemble anonymous when needed, while allowing them to stand out as individuals at other times?

Group suggestions:

- *Ensemble*
    - Characters could dress with the mindset 'This is what a raver looks like' and interpret it as they understand the term
    - Utilise hoodies to provide uniformity in ensemble scenes; actors can pull up hoods to create an anonymous, cohesive look
    - Colourful sunglasses could add to the uniformed anonymity in ensemble moments, adding a pop of colour and energy.
- *Individual and group styling:*
    - Consider having the set and costumes evoke the rave atmosphere right from the beginning, leaning into an abstract and vibrant aesthetic
    - Allow young people in the cast to design their own costumes to reflect personal style or fandom, making each character distinct
    - Each 'geeky' group might wear a uniform or themed attire based on what they 'nerd out on', bringing out individuality within the collective.
- *Environmental considerations:*
    - Decide whether the setting is indoors or outdoors, as this could influence costume choices
    - Consider the seasonal context – is it summer, autumn, etc.?
    - Could the location be specific to your area, grounding the play in a familiar or recognisable setting for the audience?
- Are you working with characters that feel distant from the performers' actual identities, or are you encouraging the actors to explore a version of themselves? Are they leaning into a parody, or playing it closer to reality?

Question and answer with Rikki Beadle-Blair

Directors discussed in small groups what they *NOTICED, LIKED* and *WONDERED* about the play as a way of framing the Q&A:

- *NOTICE*: A couple of questions about specific aspects of the play
- *LIKE*: what you celebrate about the play and what you're excited about
- *WONDER*: interpretations of the play that you would like more information on or are curious about

Q: Why the choice to not hear the parents' response in the monologues?
A: The play is their world without their parents' voices. The actor can decide what tone the parent in the scene is using with them, a great opportunity for them to do it collectively or individually.

Q: How do you feel about adapting the colloquial language to suit the group?
A: I'm willing for you to bend and slash the play. I'm very clear about the language I'm using, but my ultimate aim as an artist is to set people free. There's a whole range of abilities and confidence that young actors have and so adapt it to your group's needs, as long as you're not slandering a specific group of people.

- If you want to add swearing in, do
- Put your own slang in
- Change accents to whatever suits the group best
- Names are gender neutral so you can choose the right person for the part
- You can make it a much smaller cast by combining characters, or split characters for a larger cast
- There's also space for non-speaking characters.

I want them to feel challenged but comfortable with the piece. Investigate, explore and find pleasure for the team making the production.

Q: Do you envision the scenes at the start as flashbacks?
A: Yes, that is the structure. But you could also change it to being chronological. You decide.

Q: Characterisation: did you envision it as entirely naturalistic, or is there space for heightened characters?
A: It has to be fun and true to the actors. I recommend letting your cast inspire you and ask them what they're interested in, most people respond to having a voice and being asked. Different scenes could have different styles because they're individual lives and experiences. Ask 'How does each character feel about going to the rave?' and see where that takes you.

Q: When working with the idea of nerds and geeks, how much do we lean into the full blown stereotype?
A: There are 21 characters and so they can be 21 different versions of geeks/nerds. Most people think of themselves on some level as a geek/nerd – car geeks, video-game geeks, fitness geeks, etc. – let the group decide what kind they each are. And then add on the complex layer that within each group, you can still feel like an outcast. A lot of these characters are going through this identity crisis.

Q: Is the DJ character a 'neek'?
A: I think being a DJ is very neek-y. There are different types of DJs – what type does the actor want to be? Also it's worth mentioning all the characters can embody the DJ by splitting the lines, or shared between a few people. The DJ is the spirit of possibility.

Q: We're working with a smaller cast. Do you have any leanings for which characters could be amalgamated?
A: Any of them. Create a timeline for the new character so the through-line is clear. People can multi-role as well. If you need to amend some lines to make that amalgamation clear, feel free to do that.

Characters such as the DJ, or Robin and Ali who have a significant amount of lines, can be split. In terms of combining characters, consider also that an actor could take on two characters and talk to themselves in the scene, reflecting on how much we talk to ourselves.

Q: Any tips on how to make the large debate monologues in the second half of the play less intimidating?
A: Workshop specific reactions to the debate from individual characters (e.g. some are bored, sleeping, raging). Try it like a courtroom drama. It's a good challenge for them. An exercise on how to loosen up an actor with a big speech, get them to teach the speech to the rest of the group. Line by line, word by word, sound by sound. It's about de-centring their fear and/or overwhelm and making it about teamwork. You could also break it down into story beats and find the team captains for each section.

Q: And how do you deal with the more intricate moments of the last 15 pages?
A: I recommend the clapping exercise in which the actor has to clap on each syllable they speak. It allows them to feel and see each syllable. It's a way to engage with the text and take it away from any shyness or inhibition, and helpful for big chunks of text. A key thing to remember is that they won't learn it until they understand it.

Q: The character whose parents are police officers – what were the choices of that backstory?
A: I'm interested in stories that haven't been told before and characters dealing with experiences that are huge to deal with (e.g. gay parents, immigrant parents). And there's a shame around having police officer parents that's not discussed much. I wanted to challenge that prejudice and defend that position. It's worth asking, 'Do we believe in representation? Is it for only a particular group of people?'

Q: Does it have to be in a park?
A: Not at all. It could be a car park, shopping centre, an empty building – wherever the police would shut down if young people were trying to have a rave.

Q: Does the soundscape of the play have to be specifically rave music?
A: Not at all. Whatever works for the group. You could set up a shared playlist that the cast can contribute to.

Q: What's the catalyst for Ali and Robin to create the rave? Is it an open invite to the rave?
A: Every human can identify with the struggle of self-acceptance. I wanted to put the characters in a situation where they were trying to give themselves permission to do something that isn't about what's expected of them. They don't want to be their parents' version of 'good', they want to assert themselves without permission from others, or alcohol. They've chosen creativity as a door into the world and themselves.

Q: Does the Jordan and Parker meeting at the rave have a romantic vibe?
A: There's definitely something there, but it could be romantic or platonic. Let the actors find the reasons and backstory on why those characters don't want to be seen together – what's the fear? Do tone down the relationships if the actors aren't comfortable. Let them guide you.

Q: I'm struggling with the idea that the characters say they can't dance but the play invites lots of physical movement?
A: Explore with the cast what awkward dance moves could look like. It doesn't have to all be big movements, some people are just 'nodders' on the dance floor. Ask your company and they'll tell you how to get there.

Q: You mention phones at the start of the play – what are the tech possibilities?
A: Be as creative as you want. Use what you have. There are lots of avenues to explore how you stylise a phone – miming, lighting, sound, using the torches, etc. You could also go big on the tech and use projections (pre-recorded live streaming or actually live) – a perfect opportunity for the tech kids in your group to geek out. Strip the tech down or build it up as much as you want.

A closing comment from Phyllida Lloyd:
It is an incredible gift to have genuine permission to explore and play. Notwithstanding the permission you're given, discipline will set you free. Cut, paste, amalgamate – get all that stuff organised, and then commit. To maximise rehearsal time, prep beforehand so you can get the cast to play and make offers in your sessions.

From a workshop led by Phyllida Lloyd
With notes by Roberta Zuric

Mia and the Fish

by Satinder Chohan

Satinder Kaur Chohan is a writer from Southall, West London, whose stories largely focus on hidden global majority worlds and characters. A former recipient of the Adopt a Playwright Award, her plays include *Zameen*, *Made in India* and *Lotus Beauty*. Audio dramas include an adaptation of Pam Gems' *Camille* and *Southall Uprising*. She has also worked with and written extensively for young people. Plays for young people include an adaptation of *Gulliver's Travels* with co-writer Mike Kenny, at Bolton Octagon; *Crossing the Line* for Hampstead Theatre's Heat & Light company; *Half of Me* for Lyric Hammersmith and at various 'Made in India' venues; *Potato Moon* for Tamasha and Migration Museum; and an audio adaptation of *The Girl of Ink and Stars* for Sparks Arts for Children. She is currently developing various theatre, film and fiction projects.

Characters

Mia, *14, refugee*
Samaki the Fish/Narwhal
Halima, *15, Mia's sister, refugee*
Paz, *15, all-round Mr Popular*
Anika, *15, Halima's best friend*
Eleni, *15, teen eco-warrior*
Talia, *15, surfer girl*
Faiz, *15, asylum seeker, student/part-time café worker*
Nova, *15, serial dater*
Zuri, *15, social media addict*
Crony One/Two/Three/Four/Five

Beach-goers, *various ages*
Protestors, *various ages*
River-goers, *various ages*
Students/Cronies, *14–15-year-olds*
Nova's Girlfriend/Boyfriend *(non-speaking)*

This is a play inspired by the Indian myth 'Manu and the Fish'.

In the world of the play, **Mia** *and* **Halima** *are (war/climate change) refugees from an unspecified country. Research can be undertaken to settle on a country of origin.*

Samaki the Fish *can be made of recycled materials or a movement ensemble, growing bigger and smaller, size-shifting and shape-shifting like a Chinese dragon. Samaki can be voiced by a single or several voices. In realising this concept, be as experimental and creative as possible. The name Samaki is pronounced 'Sama-kee'.*

All parts can be played by anyone, unless specifically stated for reasons of gender or heritage.

With reference to playing K-pop in the production, groups will be responsible for acquiring the rights and permissions for any music played. It is also possible to access music that is 'free to use' and this might be preferable.

Regarding the use of words recognised as slang, groups are free to change the words to something more appropriate to them and their community.

In the script, end of line dashes can variously denote continuing a previously interrupted line, an interruption, interjection or dramatic pause.

Forward slashes between two or more characters on a line denote them speaking at the same time.

Prologue

Darkness. Waves crash against the shore. The wind swirls. Seagulls squawk. Lights up to reveal **Mia** *and* **Halima**, *dishevelled, shivering and huddled together on a beach.*

Halima   Mia, it's ok. These are pebbles. We're on dry land. We're safe. Come . . .

Halima *gets up and walks ahead.* **Mia** *follows.* **Halima** *raises her hands in the air.*

Halima   'Refugee, refugee, refugee . . .!'

Torch lights appear out of the darkness. **Mia** *hangs back slightly and pulls out a multi-coloured tusk-like object from her pocket. She holds it and kisses it.*

Mia   Thank you, Dad.

She puts the object back in her pocket and follows **Halima**, *raising her hands in the air.*

Mia   Refugee, refugee, refugee . . .

Scene One

The beach, afternoon.

A few months later. A scorching winter heatwave. Waves crash against the shore. Under an apocalyptic sun, fiery smoke clouds drift by. On one side, **Halima** *waits to join the group, as* **Mia** *trails behind, beachcombing. On the other side,* **Paz, Zuri** *and* **Anika** *sunbathe and phone scroll,* **Faiz** *studies, as* **Talia** *towels down. Other young* **Beach-goers** *play, sunbathe, chat, scroll on phones, take selfies, listen to music, dance, eat ice-cream, hang out.*

Halima   Mia, please! Hurry up!

Mia   After the bombings, the sun and skies would smoke up just like this – remember?

Halima   We're missing all the food and fun!

Mia (*resumes walking*)   Fun? Really?

Halima   They're our friends.

Mia   *Your* friends.

Halima   Could be yours too . . .

Mia   I'll never be friends with Paz, or any loudmouth like him.

Halima   You promised.

Mia   I've tried.

Halima Try harder. Try to fit in more. You two just got off to a bad start.

Mia There won't be a restart.

Halima Mia, it's been a few months. This is our new home now. We have to make it work.

She approaches the group, as **Mia** *lags behind.*

Halima Hey, everyone!

The group distractedly wave.

Anika Halima, you're late!

Halima Sorry. Mia was locked in the bathroom.

Paz I thought your sister was an expert at escaping.

Faiz I thought you were an expert host, making everyone welcome.

Paz This isn't my lame beach party – I'm just bankrolling it and providing the resources, as usual.

Zuri And we're so glad you did!

Halima Mia's glad she's here now, aren't you?

Mia Mm . . . hmm.

Anika (*to* **Halima**) Saved you a spot . . .

Halima *sits next to* **Anika**.

Faiz (*gesturing to* **Mia**) Want to sit?

Mia (*standing awkwardly apart*) I'm good here, thanks, Faiz.

Halima So where's this barbecue I've heard so much about?

Talia (*looking around*) Oh, um . . . /

Halima I'm starving!

Faiz Sorry . . . /

Zuri (*holding out empty hands*) Just crumbs and embers left.

Paz – cos we gorged all the food!

Mia (*to* **Halima**) Can we head back home then?

Halima (*sotto voce*) No! . . . Remember what we talked about?

Anika (*offering* **Halima** *a wrapped napkin*) I saved you something . . .

Halima (*unwrapping cake*) Anika, you star!

Paz Baked by the master chef himself.

Mia Oh yeah – who's that then?

Paz Doh, the supremely talented Paz of all trades – and top grades.

Mia *scoffs.* **Halima** *offers cake to* **Mia**, *who declines.*

Halima (*eating*)   Master chef, this cake is bussin'!

Talia (*laughing*)   'Bussin'?

Zuri (*laughing*)   Is it?

Anika *hugs an embarrassed* **Halima**.

Mia   You're not meant to have beach barbecues – they're banned.

Paz   So are small boats crossing the English Channel.

Faiz   That's out of line, Paz.

Mia   Small boats are way less dangerous than small minds.

Paz   Is it?

Halima (*defusing the situation*)   Weather's cray!

Anika   Yeah, steamy, sultry wintry sea, soaring waves –

Talia (*readying her surfboard*)   – perfect for surfing!

Zuri (*to* **Talia**)   Going in again, so soon?

Talia (*to* **Zuri**)   Wanna take another dip with me?

Zuri   I should cos this wildfire smoke's really messing up my skin . . .

Talia   It'll be winter again before we know it . . .

Zuri   – but I've got to tan tan. So in a bit. (*Snapping a group selfie.*) 'Hola Heatwave' everyone!

All (*except* **Mia**)   'Hola Heatwave!'

Halima (*to* **Zuri** *and* **Paz**)   Glowing tans.

Zuri   Bronzing till the sun goes down.

Mia   Winter sun drops faster than a summer one.

Paz   Ok, Doomsville, we're only on day one of a ten-day winter heatwave.

Shaking her head, **Mia** *wanders off to beachcomb, leaving the others to chat.*

Zuri   Soon, my glowing tan will dazzle even more followers than Paz –

Paz   When I'm shades ahead?

Zuri   We'll see hot stuff.

Halima   Talking of hot stuff, where's Nova?

Anika (*pointing*)   Over there, chatting up another double squeeze.

Nova *chatting with a girl and boy nearby.*

Zuri They literally just app'd and met them.

Halima Thought they were with Ivo and Latika yesterday.

Talia Keep up, that was yesterday . . .

Paz (*distracted by his phone, excited*) Oh yeah! Just as I predicted . . .

Zuri What now?

Paz My crypto stock's skyrocketing – and I've nearly perfected 'Shadowtime'.

Faiz 'Crypto shadow' what?

Talia Your rank new aftershave?

Paz For the gazillionth time, 'Shadowtime' is my Gen Z snowflake survival app.

Anika What you on about now, Paz?

Faiz Something to do with AI?

Paz Luddites. Worse than my parents. It's my new ground-breaking app. You describe your dark mood and my app offers instant solutions for all your moody generational woes –

Talia Aww, you care?

Paz As if. It's a money spinner.

Mia *rushes back, excitedly, as the others exchange glances.*

Mia Halima! I just saw the exact same fish that was circling the dinghy –

Halima What?

Mia That multicoloured fish – that was – circling –

Halima Sure, Mia – the exact same fish . . .

Mia Come and see!

Halima (*to* **Mia**) Thought we were all going for a swim?

Faiz (*closing his books*) Mia, I'll take a look with you.

Mia (*deflated*) It's fine, Faiz.

Faiz Got to head off anyway . . .

Mia It's probably swum away by now . . . Where you off to?

Faiz Got to pick up Mum's prescription before my café shift . . .

Mia How do you juggle all that? Study, work, care for your mum . . .?

Faiz Only me to do it.

Eleni *rushes on.*

Eleni Oh right – so we're all busy burning up the beach are we?

Zuri Lighten up, Eleni –

Eleni We'll all light up once the planet's fully dry roasted –

Paz Go guilt trip somewhere else.

Eleni A peak heatwave in December?

Zuri A cool light 'n' smoke happening, bronzing my skin, burning up my socials –

Eleni An alarming abnormal new normal.

Paz Cool! Another mood for my app! 'Today, I feel a bit abnormal new normal . . .'

Eleni It's not the only abnormal stuff happening.

Anika What now?

Eleni A big company is deep-sea mining out there.

Faiz What's 'deep-sea mining'?

Eleni Drilling the seabed for natural resources.

Mia They're drilling holes into the seabed?

Eleni Word is they've been secretly blasting holes for months. Wiping out marine life, releasing toxic stuff into the water, wrecking ecosystems we don't even know exist yet –

Talia Not on my surf turf!

Eleni Yeah, we need to protest!

Zuri After the heatwave.

Eleni 'After'? This is why there's a heatwave! Look, the sea is like a giant carbon sink, soaking up our excess heat and carbon emissions –

Paz No, that's farty Mia's fault –

Faiz Shut up, Paz.

Eleni The carbon sea-sink slows down climate change. If we disrupt that process, climate change gets way worse.

Nova (*joining, to* **Eleni**) You're squawking louder than the seagulls.

Eleni Cos no one's listening, Nova. We have to stop deep-sea mining now!

Talia I'm tired of putting out fires lit by 'grown-ups' –

Halima Grown-ups will always drill profits from wherever –

Anika – whatever they can –

Mia – till they've blasted the life out of everything.

Eleni   Not if we *all* protest.

Talia (*to* **Eleni**)   Come on, surf some winter waves with me –

Eleni   Soon, there won't be any waves left –

Talia (*running to the sea*)   Then I best get my fill!

Anika   Just have to wait for the greedy grown-ups to die before we take over.

Eleni   We won't have a planet left by then.

Paz   It's way more resilient than you all think.

Mia   Eleni, I want to help.

Halima   You do?

Eleni (*to* **Mia**)   I'm planning a beach protest for tomorrow. (**Eleni** *holds out her phone.*) Give me your number, message you later?

Halima   Yes, please!

Mia *taps in her number and passes back* **Eleni**'s *phone.*

Eleni   Thanks, Mia, I'll message soon. (*Leaving.*) And you beach bums – you're not off the hook!

Paz (*to* **Mia**)   Suck up.

Mia   You wouldn't understand altruism even if I tried to explain it.

Halima   Mia!

Mia (*to* **Halima**)   I'm going beachcombing.

Nova   That's a thing?

Mia   Yeah, where we used to live.

Zuri   Instagrammable?

Halima (*to* **Mia**)   Just . . . hang here with us.

Mia   Our dad, our sisters, brothers and us used to comb the beach for objects – Halima, remember the whale poo?

Halima (*sharply*)   No.

All (*except* **Halima**, *laughing*)   Huh? / What?

Mia   We'd go beachcombing for 'ambergris' – basically, sperm whale poo.

The group laugh and make 'ugh/ew' sounds.

Mia   It's used for pricey perfumes, more precious than gold.

Paz   Whatever rocks your crappy boat . . .

Faiz (*to* **Mia**)   I'll search for whale poo with you.

Paz   Stealing Nova's chat-up lines again?

Nova *mock wrestles a laughing* **Paz**.

Mia   Thanks, Faiz, but I need to find materials for my art project too. Might be a while.

Faiz   No worries. Happy beachcombing . . . and I'll see you lot tomorrow.

Mia   Don't forget your mum's prescription.

Faiz   Heading there right now.

Mia *and* **Faiz** *walk off in opposite directions.*

Paz   Aww, I smell a whiff of whale poo romance. Weirdo . . .

As **Mia** *walks off, the group laughs loudly behind her.*

Scene Two

The beach, same afternoon.

In a secluded spot by a rockpool, **Mia** *beachcombs, picking up shells. A voice.*

Samaki (*off stage*)   As-salamu alaykum.

Mia (*looking around*)   Faiz? . . .

She continues beachcombing.

Samaki (*off stage*)   Mia!

Mia (*bemused*)   Faiz, is that you?

Mia *takes out and checks her phone, before putting it away.*

Samaki   Down here.

Mia   Down . . . where? . . .

Samaki   Here, in the sea –

Mia   But there's no one . . . (*Spotting a multicoloured fish.*) You – ? You're – talking . . . to . . . me?

Samaki   Yes!

Mia   No . . . oh no . . .

Samaki   Please, don't be scared!

Mia   No – no – fish don't talk.

Samaki   I had to get your attention somehow, cos swimming in circles isn't cutting it –

Mia   It was you? Circling the dinghy?

Samaki Course it was me!

Mia This is not normal. This is not –

Samaki Mia, please –

Mia What? How do you know my name?

Samaki Doh, from the dinghy.

Mia Nope, still not normal.

Samaki Mia, you have to save me –

Mia 'Save' you? Me?

Samaki See anyone else chatting with sea life round here?

Mia This isn't real . . . this isn't . . .

Samaki Please, take me from the sea, to somewhere safe.

Mia But the sea is your home.

Samaki Before the drilling, toxic plumes or big fish kill me.

Mia Wait – the deep-sea mining?

Samaki There's no more silence down here. No more darkness. Just constant banging and clanking. Ringing in our ears. We can't hear each other talk. Heavy drilling is throwing up all sorts, clouding the water, choking and smothering us. And the big fish are taking it out on the small fish. Sleep-deprived, angry, they're more savage than ever. Mia, if I go back in there, I'm finished.

Pause. **Mia** *pulls out a water bottle from her bag.*

Mia I can't believe I'm – (*Holding the bottle.*) Will this work?

Samaki Scoop me up!

Mia (*scooping* **Samaki**) In . . . you . . . go . . . You ok in there?

Samaki Safer than I was.

Mia So what's your name, talking fish?

Samaki Do I need one?

Mia If we keep talking, I'd like to be on first-name terms.

Samaki Ok . . . Call me – 'Fish'.

Mia Catchy – but how about (*thinking*) . . . 'Samaki'? From the Arabic word for 'fish'.

Samaki Ohhh . . . I like it.

Mia Ok, Samaki, I'm carrying you home.

Samaki Thank you, Mia. One day, I'll repay your kindness.

Mia No need, Samaki. No need.

She carries the bottle carefully across the beach, homewards.

Scene Three

The beach, next afternoon.

The winter heatwave continues. Drifting wildfire smoke veils the sun and beach in a sepia glow. Led by **Eleni**, *the group join other* **Protestors**, *waving placards including 'Stop Mining the Seafloor! Stop Wanting More More More!', 'Planet and People Before Profit!', 'No Deep Sea Mining! No Drilling! No Overfishing!'. They chant slogans including 'Stop the Drilling! Stop the Sea Life Killing!' and 'Protect Marine Life! Stop Ocean Crime!'.* **Beach-goers** *variously chat to, applaud and ridicule* **Protestors**. **Zuri** *takes a group selfie, as* **Paz** *ducks.*

Zuri Shout 'Stop the Drilling' everyone!

All (*waving placards*) 'Stop the Drilling!'

Halima Send me for my socials?

Eleni/Anika/Faiz/Nova/Talia For mine! / Mine too!

Zuri Your likes and followers are gonna soar!

As the protest continues, the group except **Eleni**, **Faiz** *and* **Mia** *down placards.* **Halima** *plays K-pop on her phone, heading off with* **Anika**. **Talia**, **Zuri**, **Nova** *and* **Paz** *tag along behind them, chatting and checking their phones.*

Anika (*to* **Halima**) K-pop dance practice?

Halima I've got some slick new moves!

Mia Hey, come back everyone!

Eleni Can we keep this protest going please? It's only the first one –

Paz – and probably the last.

Mia We've got to strike while the planet's hot!

Paz (*to* **Mia**) Bad luck, 'Suck Up'. I'd explain the laws of motivation and rewards . . . but you wouldn't understand. (*To* **Eleni**.) You can count on us, when you make it worth our while again.

Eleni I bought you all ice-creams . . .

Talia Should have bought them *after* the protest.

Eleni You're not all doing this for me or for the short-term rewards.

Zuri Kind of were . . .

Nova (*laying down his placard*) We'll plant these placards right here, so people can pick them up if they want.

As they leave, everyone except **Eleni** *and* **Mia** *lay down their placards in a pile.*

Eleni Great, now just litter the beach.

Zuri We're so caring, we're sharing.

Faiz Eleni, sorry, I've got to get to work.

Eleni Protest tomorrow?

Faiz (*leaving, taking his placard*) Mos def! See you, Mia.

Mia (*waving to* **Faiz**) Try and rest up later!

Everyone leaves. **Mia** *protests alone with* **Eleni**.

Eleni Tough to save the planet when no one really believes it's in danger.

Mia Sun's even hotter and fierier today.

Eleni A 'climate con', 'nothing to do with me' they say.

Mia Till their house burns down, gets blown away or swept away by floods –

Eleni Listen, ignore Paz.

Mia That's as easy as ignoring a climate disaster.

Eleni (*giggling*) He's definitely easier to deal with.

Mia (*giggling*) You think?

Eleni Hey, how's your new home?

Mia Mrs Carter's all right. Supportive. (*Laughs.*) But an awful cook.

Eleni Not what you're used to?

Mia Dad caught fresh fish every morning. Then Mum spiced it up –

Eleni Your dad was a fisherman?

Mia Yeah. Sometimes, Halima, our brothers, sisters and me would go out on the boat with him.

Eleni Must have been fun.

Mia We loved it. He loved it. We all thought we'd never stop loving it.

Eleni Sorry, I didn't mean to . . .

Mia It's fine. I think about them all . . . all the time. Halima doesn't like to remember . . . but I can't ever forget all those happy times before . . . (*Pauses.*)

Eleni It's ok. You don't have to –

Mia The drought came first . . . Not enough water or food . . . Then floods hit, swept away everything – our home, most of the town . . .

Eleni I'm so sorry . . .

Mia Violent civil war broke out, the government lost control, fought back, dropped bombs, fired bullets . . . My Dad and the other fishermen waved white flags but it didn't matter – (*Tearful.*) . . . We lost everything – everyone . . .

Eleni *holds* **Mia**.

Mia We have to succeed.

Eleni We will.

Mia We've a saying back home – 'Listen to the Earth and you'll hear the voices of all living things bound together. Those voices will show us the way.'

Eleni Then let's crank up the volume!

Mia How?

Eleni For starters, I've got a local newspaper contact. (*Rushing off.*) I'll chase them right now, make them listen!

Mia Amplify the climate emergency!

Eleni It can't wait!

Scene Four

Mia's *bedroom, late afternoon. A week later.*

In school uniform, **Mia** *rushes in with an armful of beachcombing objects which she spills on the floor. She slides out a fish bowl from under her bed.* **Samaki** *has grown.*

Samaki (*bashes its head*) Ow!

Mia Careful!

Samaki I can't stop the ringing in my ears, I keep bashing my head –

Mia Sorry I'm late.

Samaki – and I'm starving.

Mia We had another deep-sea mining protest today –

Samaki A week of protests? Excused!

Mia Then I had to beachcomb, plus find you fresh plants –

Samaki What's on the menu today?

Mia (*dropping plants in the bowl*) Plastic free, toxic free . . .

Samaki (*gobbling*)   Yum!

Mia   Slow down, Samaki!

Samaki   How was school?

Mia   Kids losing their cool in the heat. Big fish circling. Paz targeting me for cheap laughs –

Samaki   Just swim away from him.

Mia   I've swum right to the edge.

Samaki   Swim over, like I did.

Mia   Sounds dangerous.

Samaki   Not if there's a safe place to swim.

Mia   There isn't.

Samaki   What about your beach friends?

Mia   Halima's friends.

Samaki   Yours too if you try.

Mia   I'll always be a fish out of water.

Samaki   Not if you do what I did. Find a friend.

Mia   I did. You.

Samaki   Aww . . . (*Bashes its head.*) Ow, this bowl!

Mia   Samaki? Are you – bigger?

Samaki   This bowl definitely feels like it's shrinking, fast . . .

Halima *rushes in, spotting the beachcombing heap.* **Mia** *quickly hides the bowl under the bed.*

Halima   Mia, what's all this rubbish?

Mia   It's not rubbish. I'm taking it to school tomorrow for my art project.

Halima   You better – or Mrs Carter will have a meltdown.

Mia (*showing her designs*)   Here, just rough sketches –

Halima (*softening*)   Rough . . .?

Mia   – and ta-da! (*Revealing the tusk-like object.*) The centrepiece!

Halima   That weird pointy thing?

Mia   The one Dad found and gifted us.

Halima (*admiring the sketches*)   Not gonna lie – this is actually really good . . .

Mia   Thanks, sis.

Halima So, can you help Mrs Carter with dinner? Anika's coming over.

Mia I need to get on with my artwork.

Halima You're the master chef in this house.

Mia The only master chef in this house. What's she trying to mess up now?

Halima Fish pie.

Mia No way.

Halima Why not?

Mia I've given up eating fish.

Halima But you love fish!

Mia That's why I'm not eating them any more.

Halima Why you acting strangely?

Mia I'm acting responsibly.

Halima Suspiciously.

Mia Ethically.

Halima What are you hiding?

Mia Nothing.

Halima *snoops behind* **Mia** *and slides out the bowl.*

Halima A fish?

Mia The exact same one that circled our dinghy when we arrived!

Halima What? Don't be ridiculous.

Mia It's the same one!

Halima How can you tell?

Mia The colours – and – it told me.

Halima Excuse me?

Mia (*holding up the bowl*) Samaki, this is my sister Halima. Say 'Hi'.

Halima 'Say hi?'

Swimming around, bashing the sides of the bowl, **Samaki** *is silent.*

Mia Samaki's a talking fish.

Halima Uh, fish don't talk.

Mia That's what I thought.

Halima Nor does this one.

Mia Samaki called out to me, even knew my name. We've been talking since I saved it.

Halima 'Saved it'?

Mia From the deep-sea mining.

Halima You for real?

Mia Samaki, say something. Halima won't tell anyone.

Halima You're freaking me out.

Mia I swear Samaki was talking before.

Halima First thing tomorrow, drop that fish back in the sea.

Samaki Don't listen to her, Mia!

Mia There! Did you just hear Samaki speak?

Halima No, I didn't . . .

Mia Samaki just said –

Halima Mia, I know it's been a tricky few months settling in. But please, stop hiding, try harder, make friends – real human friends. Everyone's been so welcoming. Act weird and distant, people will act the same way back.

Mia Please don't tell anyone about Samaki.

Halima Why would I tell anyone my sister's new best friend is a talking fish?

Mia Cos you blab to your friends about everything.

Halima Trust me, I won't breathe a word. So let the past go, give thanks for being safe here – and go help Mrs Carter. Anika will be here soon.

Halima *exits.*

Mia Samaki, why didn't you talk to Halima?

Samaki Even if I did, she wouldn't hear me.

Mia Now she thinks I'm even crazier than before.

Samaki I'm even bigger than before, so before I crack through this bowl, take me somewhere bigger?

Mia Samaki, eat less! . . . (*Pause.*) Ok . . . after dinner, I'll move you in the dark (*thinking*), to the river.

Samaki And make sure Mrs Carter drops fish from the menu, once and for all.

Mia Anything else your Royal Samakiness?

Samaki More plastic-free plants?

Scene Five

The river, next afternoon.

The smoky winter heatwave continues. **River-goers** *relax by the river, hang out, tap and scroll on phones. The group are part of a bigger protest at the river's edge, distractedly waving placards, texting and scrolling on their phones.* **Mia** *approaches.*

Eleni (*leading*)/**All** (*chanting*)   'Stop the Drilling! Stop the Sea Life Killing!' 'Stop Mining the Seafloor! Stop Wanting More More More!'

Paz (*spotting* **Mia**)   So, fair-weather weirdo decided to turn up?

Halima (*waving*)   Mia, over here!

Mia *joins, as everyone, except* **Paz** *greets her.*

Paz   Bored of changing the world already?

Mia (*ignoring* **Paz**)   Sorry I'm late everyone. School biz.

Paz   Quit trying while you're behind.

Faiz (*offering* **Mia** *a placard*)   For you.

Mia (*taking the placard*)   Thanks, Faiz!

Eleni (*to* **Mia**)   We're working the riverfront today, to keep the protests moving.

Mia   Great idea! . . . Oh Eleni, you nailed it with your interview quotes!

Eleni   You read the article?

Mia   Downloaded it first thing.

Eleni   Thanks! (*To* **All**.) Cos no one else did . . .

Faiz   Swear I bookmarked it for later.

Mia   We've got to keep the pressure on – can't stop protesting till they stop drilling.

Paz   Says the part-time protestor. We're all stopping soon. My crypto stock's still soaring and I've got more pitch meetings for my app –

Faiz   I've actually got to get home to cook for Mum –

Nova   And I've got another date with my hotties!

Anika (*to* **Nova**)   Another? When's the wedding?

Talia   And I need to buy that budget surfer gear the oldies refuse to pay for.

Paz (*to* **Talia**)   Crypto King will lend you cash.

Talia   Really, Paz? Promise I'll pay you back soon as I can.

Zuri   Eleni, after these amateurs have left, let's glue you to a rock in protest. I'll take pics, stick them on my soaring socials –

Eleni – and I can send them to the newspaper!

Zuri I've even got glue!

Eleni Let's find a rock for later!

Eleni *and* **Zuri** *exit, as the others start scrolling on their phones, chatting between themselves.*

Faiz (*to* **Mia**) You weren't in art class today. I saved you a seat.

Mia Sorry, should have told you. I got moved up.

Faiz Wow! You're in the A stream now!

Anika That's you top in Art, English, Maths, Science –

Talia Sweeping the board!

Paz Grade inflation to make Weirdo Misfit feel like she belongs.

Faiz (*to* **Paz**) Feeling the heat, cos you're no longer top of the tables?

Paz Get a grip. No one gets higher grades than me at year's end – when it counts.

Anika We'll see then, won't we?

Paz Yeah, she'll be sobbing, while I'm basking in top grade glory!

Faiz Maybe not this year . . .

Paz (*to* **Faiz**) You're always playing catch-up – what do you know?

Faiz I know the teachers have started judging works for the art prize. Mia, they were raving about your piece. I thought it was beautiful too.

Mia You saw it?

Faiz What was that twirly, rainbow-coloured centrepiece?

Mia Something my dad found, beachcombing with us.

Faiz What is it?

Mia No idea. When Dad gave it to me, he wouldn't tell me what it was. He said it was for me to discover, as I discover the world.

Faiz You carried it all the way here?

Mia The only thing I carried from home.

Paz Bet it's trash, like your artwork.

Faiz Paz, mate, I hope you never experience losing everything, like some of us.

Paz When the first of many apps is gonna make me more rich and successful than I already am?

Faiz Shame it won't change how ignorant and xenophobic you are –

Paz Me? With the friends I have?

Faiz Threatened by a smart, unique girl who washed up here with nothing but is trying to make something of herself? Threatened just cos she doesn't live or play by your rules?

Paz She's doing more than all right, stepping on other people's toes.

Faiz Your insecure toes.

Mia Faiz, please leave it.

Faiz (*to* **Paz**) You've got all you need, yet you want more. There's enough to go round.

Paz Deep-sea mining's happening because there isn't enough.

Faiz Cos people like you plunder for more, hoarding, never sharing.

Paz This is a small island.

Faiz Filled with too many small-minded people like you.

Paz Simmer down, Faiz – that's why I'm selling an app and you're working several jobs to make ends meet.

Eleni *and* **Zuri** *return.*

Eleni Er, the protest, people? Or no iced lattes.

Paz Actually, the more I learn about deep-sea mining, the more I like the idea.

Mia Troll.

Paz (*ignoring* **Mia**) If we want things like eco smartphones or electric cars, we'll need to find natural resources to meet demand – the seabed's rich, untapped . . .

Mia The seabed is for sea life, not us. Their home, not ours.

Paz It's our planet – we're the big fish making the big decisions.

Mia Humans need to stop wanting so much.

Faiz Yeah, we've uprooted enough people for greed, power, profit. So now we start on sea life?

Paz Deep-sea mining's actually more sustainable than land mining –

Eleni Don't greenwash, pretend it's a green alternative when it isn't! We need real green solutions like recycling, urban mining –

Paz And it's got a smaller carbon footprint than other mining, so time to tap tap tap away!

Talia Then why you protesting against it?

Paz Doh, Eleni's free iced lattes. If the mining companies paid me, I'd support them too.

Mia And I'm fair-weather?

Paz (*squaring up to* **Mia**) Don't tell me what I am or I'm not.

Talia Touché, Harris.

Mia 'Harris'?

Paz Yeah, my name. Your problem?

Mia In the article, the mining company CEO's surname is also 'Harris' –

Paz Common surname in our country.

Mia No – you're definitely related.

Eleni *immediately scrolls her phone. The group crowds round and peers over.*

Zuri Paz . . . isn't that your dad?

Paz No.

Nova Really looks like him . . . .

Paz Well, it ain't.

Anika Don't even try –

Talia Seriously, Paz?

Paz O . . . k . . . minor detail.

Faiz Pretty frigging huge.

Paz Just keep it on the down low, alright?

Eleni Then tell him to stop.

Paz I'm a happening man of vast influence but even that –

Talia You've got a direct line.

Paz Surfer girl, you're always arguing with your parents. Listen do they?

Anika At least talk to him.

Paz It's a multi-billion-pound operation – he's not the only one in charge.

Mia 'CEO'? Bet 'Crypto King' holds some sway.

Paz (*squares up to* **Mia**) You don't get to say what happens here!

Mia Cos the likes of you do? Wrecking the sea? Our planet?

Halima (*to* **Mia**) Behave.

Paz Listen to your smarter sister, who knows how to fit in.

Mia Fit in with you? You could make a real difference. But people like you profit from destroying eco-systems to prop up your own ego-system. Your dad must be very proud.

Talia/Zuri/Nova   Ohhh . . . /

Eleni   Yeah! /

Faiz   Right! /

Anika   Uh-huh. /

Halima (*angrily to* **Mia**)   That's enough!

Paz   At least I have a dad.

The group, except a shocked **Halima** *and* **Mia**, *collectively gasp.*

Faiz (*tries to intervene*)   That's bang out of –

Paz (*in* **Mia**'*s face*)   Little girl, learn your place in the pecking order.

Mia (*teary-eyed, in* **Paz**'*s face*)   What if I don't?

Halima   Mia, home! Now!

As the group look on in silence, **Mia** *shakes her head at* **Halima** *in disbelief and rushes off.*

Scene Six

The river, same afternoon.

Mia *walks along the river's edge, looking for* **Samaki**.

Mia   Samaki? Samaki?

Samaki *peers out of the river.*

Mia   Samaki, you won't believe what Paz just – (*Gasps.*) Woah – you're even bigger!

Samaki   Something unnatural in the river water . . .?

Mia   Stop eating so much!

Samaki   Mia, you have to move me again.

Mia   To where? How?

Samaki   Wheelbarrow again? . . .

Mia   Right – it's time to go back.

Samaki   Oh no, please, not the sea . . .

Mia   What else can hold you?

Samaki   But the drilling, big angry fish –

Mia   Samaki, I'll do all I can to stop the drilling. But look – you're the big fish now.

Pause.

Samaki Yeah . . . yeah . . . I am, aren't I?

Mia Big enough to make waves if you want.

Scene Seven

School art studio, next day lunchtime.

Paz *and a few* **Cronies** *circle* **Mia***'s artwork, laughing, messing around, taking silly selfies with it.* **Paz** *picks up the artwork, deliberately drops it, breaking it, to more laughter. He snaps off the tusk centrepiece.*

Paz Let's see that upstart refugee shine without her precious piece.

The **Cronies** *laugh and take photos of* **Paz** *doing silly poses with the centrepiece.*

Crony One Looks good on you!

Paz Better on me than her stinky canvas.

Crony Two You're a walking work of art, Paz!

Paz Think she can just sail in here and rule our joint?

All Cronies Upstart! Upstart!

Paz Behave how she wants? Speak to me how she wants, like yesterday?

Crony Three Teach her a lesson!

Paz (*pocketing the centrepiece*) Mine now!

Crony Four Yeah, she should know who's boss!

Paz Let's see her get top prize now.

Crony Five Paz, mate, maybe leave that here?

Paz I'm not stealing, just borrowing, till the judging is over. Right, let's get fish and chips!

All Cronies (*chanting*) Fish and chips! Fish and chips!

As **Paz** *and his* **Cronies** *are about to leave,* **Mia** *enters.*

Mia What are you doing in here?

Paz (*pushing past*) Out my way.

Mia (*blocking him*) You don't even do art.

Paz Our country is a free country – people can come and go where they like.

All Cronies Yeah!

Mia *gasps as she spots her damaged artwork on the ground. She picks up the pieces.*

Mia (*shaken*)   You did this?

Paz (*brushing her off*)   That's your kiddie doodle trash?

Mia   How could you do this?

Paz   I didn't do anything, did I gang?

All Cronies   No!/Nah!

Paz   Your installation 'art' was already playing doormat on the floor.

Mia   Where's my centrepiece?

Paz   Deep in whale poo?

The **Cronies** *laugh.*

Mia   Wrecking things – runs in the family, does it?

All Cronies   Ooooh!

Paz *squares up to* **Mia**. *Pause.*

Mia   Your grubby fingerprints are all over this.

Paz   My dad knows people in high places – and this isn't your home. Mess with me, you'll be on the first boat back out of here. (*To the* **Cronies**.) Gang, let's get lunch.

Paz/Cronies (*exiting chanting*)   Fish and chips! Fish and chips!

Paz *and his* **Cronies** *leave.* **Mia** *holds her broken artwork and sobs.*

Scene Eight

The beach, afternoon, a few days later.

Mia *walks along the coast, looking for* **Samaki**.

Mia   Samaki? Samaki?

Samaki (*peering out*)   Mia, where have you been? It's been days.

Mia   Staying well away from the world.

Samaki (*rising out of the sea*)   Now really isn't the time.

Mia (*seeing* **Samaki**)   What the –? You're bigger than a great whale!

Samaki   So big, I'm ready to knock those mining ships right out of the water.

Mia   After that, please knock Paz right out, too.

Samaki   I didn't think you'd get here in time.

Mia   You need to eat less.

Samaki You need to be ready.

Mia Why? What will Paz do next?

Samaki Mia, listen carefully. Get ready to say goodbye to the world as you know it.

Mia Goodbye to this cruel world? Gladly.

Samaki Word in the sea is that a huge violent storm is brewing – and very soon, it's hitting the whole planet.

Mia Good. People deserve what's coming to them.

Samaki A storm so big, it will cause a great flood that will submerge even the highest mountains, every inch of land and desert, sweeping away life everywhere.

Mia Yeah – I'm deffo down for a people 'n' planet refresh.

Samaki You can't give up now.

Mia Tired of keeping my head above water.

Samaki Not the time to indulge dark moods.

Mia This isn't a passing mood Paz's lame app will solve –

Samaki You're happy to lose Halima too, for ever?

Pause.

Mia Obviously not, even if she doesn't always stand up for me.

Samaki Then you have to survive.

Mia How?

Samaki Find a big boat –

Mia (*laughing*) I can't just magic a boat –

Samaki I'll find you a boat.

Mia Really? Dad always promised me a boat . . .

Samaki – then fill it with your nearest and dearest –

Mia Ok, Halima, you and er –

Samaki You need water, food, plants, seeds, supplies –

Mia (*sarcastically*) No problem, I'll just rustle all that up.

Samaki Then when the storm hits, I'll reappear to you as a narwhal with a tusk.

Mia Wow, end-of-worldie floods, body makeover and a fish facelift, too?

Samaki Once you're secure on the boat, look for me. When I signal, get out on deck, throw the ropes, loop them over my tusk and I'll steer your boat through the storm.

Mia Samaki, has all that drilling gone to your head?

Samaki When the storm finally stops and the flood recedes, I'll lower the boat to safety.

Mia Or is it the toxic plumes?

Samaki Mia, this is End Times.

Mia Food coma?

Samaki End Times.

Mia You're serious?

Samaki Take heed, Mia – or ignore at your peril.

Pause.

Mia Fine! I'll come back soon. Armed with Mrs Carter's humungous patio umbrella.

Samaki With loved ones and supplies.

Mia How do I convince Halima to help me stock a random boat?

Samaki You'll find a way, use your smart brain. But time is short – so hurry!

Mia (*running off*) Oh, Samaki, the things you make me do . . .

Samaki End Times, Mia! End Times! Our whole world is about to be washed away . . .

Scene Nine

The beach, late afternoon, a few days later.

A movement sequence as the ensemble create the boat on stage, using recycled props and materials needed to survive a flood. In the ongoing heatwave, the group (except **Paz**) *fix up the boat.*

Mia I really need to find that lost centrepiece.

Halima I said I'd help.

Mia It's been days already.

Halima Your art teacher said she'd help too.

Mia I bet Paz took it.

Halima He said he didn't.

Mia Please, just stop sticking up for him.

Halima I've put a message on my socials as well. Now come on, let's finish fixing your latest crazy beachcombing find.

Mia (*lowering her voice*) How did you persuade everyone to help?

Halima Same way Eleni and Paz get them on side.

Mia Pizza?

Halima You're paying for it.

Mia Fair enough. (*Pause.*) You didn't tell Paz about today, did you?

Halima You asked me not to.

Mia Thanks, sis.

Halima Just keep smiling. But please, don't mention talking fish or apocalyptic floods. Be cool.

Mia As if I could ever be you.

Halima Sooner this day's over, the better. Then maybe you'll calm down about End Times and come back to your senses. No sign of storm clouds – if anything, it's getting hotter out there.

Mia Sorry. I've just been under the weather lately –

Halima No pun intended?

Mia Missing home . . .

Halima I get it. I feel it sometimes too.

Mia You do?

Halima Let's finish up before it gets too late.

Eleni (*approaching*) Mia, where did you *really* find this awesome boat?

Mia Told you – beachcombing. We learnt from the best – our dad, (*to* **Halima**) didn't we?

Halima (*looking around*) Right, I think we're nearly done.

Zuri (*taking a photo*) Selfie ahoy, Boat People!

All (*tools in hand, posing*) Selfie ahoy!

The group apply finishing touches to the boat.

Zuri This boat pic best rack up more views than Eleni's rock pic.

Eleni Glad that being stuck to a rock, cautioned by police, then grounded for a month, works for you.

Zuri I'm so gonna catch Paz up.

Halima (*to* **Eleni**) So your parents don't know you're here?

Eleni I snuck out, Talia snuck out –

Talia Stormed out. They blew up at me again about being a surfer girl –

Mia But it's so kick-ass.

Talia But not a respectable career.

Faiz (*checking his phone*) Hey, Mia, Mum messaged – needs me home. How shall I finish painting this bit?

Mia If you've time, another quick DIY vid?

They watch his phone together, soon distracted by **Anika** *and* **Nova** *carrying boxes.*

Mia Wow!

Anika More blankets, sleeping bags, warm clothes, canned food, utensils, candles –

Mia You're all incredible!

Nova No, not us.

Anika These are the last of Paz's contributions –

Mia What? (*Looking at* **Halima**.) I thought he didn't know about today.

Zuri Oops sorry, didn't realise today was a secret –

Mia I don't want his stuff here.

Halima Sure about that?

Mia The hand that bites me feeds us?

Eleni Yes – we're gonna keep milking his guilty handouts.

Faiz Guilt? He'll just lord it over the rest of us.

Talia Doesn't he anyway?

Anika Might as well profit like he does.

Halima (*taking* **Mia** *aside*) Mia, let's just gracefully accept this –

Mia 'Gracefully' – after what he said and did?

Halima The rest of us could never pull all this together.

Pause.

Mia Fine – as long as he doesn't show up . . .

Anika (*lowering a box*) Last box – books and board games donated by all –

Zuri Er not me – cos this ain't the twentieth century . . .

Eleni (*admiring the boat*) No . . . this is just a great hideout –

The group stand back to admire the boat.

Talia A cocoon from parents who think we're Gen Z snowballs that need firming up –

Mia An escape when we're feeling low.

Faiz A quiet study space.

Anika A date night boat –

Zuri – a banging party boat!

Nova I'll invite all my paramours!

Talia All of them? And sink the boat?

Eleni Yes! A *Rainbow Warrior* protest boat!

Zuri Nabbing that hashtag name!

Eleni Too late. *Rainbow Warrior* was a famous Greenpeace boat, protesting against nuclear testing in the Pacific, blown up and sunk by the French government.

Zuri On second thoughts . . .

Paz (*clambering on, staring at* **Mia**) Who's blowing up boats then?

Mia *glares at* **Halima**.

Paz Only dropping in – on my way to an all-expenses-paid dinner, to sell my app.

Halima Paz, thanks for the supplies.

Paz Just house clutter. But when you're all done fixing this boat, let's sell this piece of junk, share the profits.

Faiz Nah, your dad's raking in enough profits.

Paz Hard to believe this was a random find . . .

Zuri It was begging Mia for some TL 'Sea'. TL S.E.A., geddit?

The group fake laughs.

Nova (*styling his hair*) Right, best get ready for my big date night . . .

Talia Ugh, spare us any details. /

Anika Halima, still coming over to meet the fam?

Halima Just try and stop me! /

Zuri (*waving his phone*) Paz, watch out, I'm chasing you down on followers.

Paz In your Insta dreams.

Mia (*agitated, to everyone*) Please, can we just finish the boat?

Nova Aye-aye, Captain Antsy.

Mia (*suddenly stopping*) Oh no . . .

Halima What?

Mia The temperature's dropping.

Paz No – cos my app says still hot.

Halima/Zuri/Nova/Talia/Anika/Faiz And mine/Mine too.

Eleni No – it's definitely dropping . . .

Zuri Heatwave's over?

Talia Nooo, winter surfing's over . . .

Faiz (*arms aloft*) Laterz to sweaty patches!

Eleni Seasons are back in sync!

Anika (*nudging* **Halima**) And cosy winter nights are in –

Nova (*nodding*) Oh yeah . . .

Zuri (*comparing with* **Paz**) My tan wins –

Paz Says someone in permanent filter mode?

Eleni Damn, it's freezing.

All Yeah/It's cold . . .

The group grab jumpers from a box.

Paz (*looking through a porthole*) Check out the massive storm clouds!

The group rush to the portholes.

Mia (*looks at* **Halima**, *concerned*) It's about to pour.

Crashing thunder and lightning.

All Woah!

Torrential rain falls. A violent storm swirls outside.

Nova Monster storm!

Halima Just a little rain.

Zuri It's torrential.

Paz I'm off, before it gets worse.

Faiz Me too – Mum's alone, not well –

Nova I've got to get to my double date too –

Talia   Guys, you can't go out in this.

Faiz   It looks really bad out there . . .

Nova   I don't wanna mess up my hair . . .

Paz   – or turn up drenched.

Halima   Just wait it out –

Anika   – it'll pass soon.

Paz, Nova and Faiz wait to leave. The group glance between their phones and the portholes. Pause. Phones beep.

Talia   Parents ordering me to get home asap.

Eleni/Zuri/Anika/Nova   Mine too.

Faiz (*on his phone*)   Mum's not answering.

Halima (*to* **Mia**)   Mrs Carter messaged us to get an Uber home.

Mia   We can't move in this.

Anika   Not when it's hammering down.

Phones continue beeping.

Zuri   Oh, severe weather warnings now.

Faiz   Flood ones too.

Halima   It'll be over soon.

Paz   Sure will with 'danger to life' storm warnings.

Anika   Weather forecasters are always wrong.

Eleni   Warned you all about the heatwave – now a storm, floods . . .?

Paz   Oh drop it –

Talia   Everyone, calm down, we'll leave when it passes.

Booming thunder and blinding lightning alarm the group, glued to beeping phones.

Faiz   It's getting worse.

Mia   Sounds like Earth's cracking open.

Zuri   Or this boat's cracking open.

Paz   This piece of junk better hold out.

Nova   We'll soon find out . . .

Halima   We did all the repairs –

Anika   – only small jobs left.

Mia (*moving*) I'll check for leaks.

Halima (*moving*) I'll help.

Halima and **Mia** *check the edges of the boat.*

Faiz Mum's still not answering . . .

Paz (*holding up his phone*) Shit! Roofs blown clean off, power cables snapping –

Nova (*holding up his phone*) – cars, buses, trains – washed away . . .!

Zuri (*holding up his phone*) Er, houses and people too . . .

The group collectively gasps. Pause.

Eleni Government's just declared a State of Emergency.

Mia 'Emergency'?

Anika Always overreacting.

Zuri People being warned to stay indoors.

Eleni (*holding up her phone*) Oh God, it's not just here – it's a global storm!

Talia Sahara's being deluged.

Halima Himalayas too –

Nova Aussie Outback –

Zuri Death Valley . . .

Eleni Earth was going to hit back at some point.

Paz Had to be while I was stuck on this damn boat.

Eleni End Times.

Paz Oh, shut up, Doomsday.

Zuri Nooo! I've lost reception!

All Oh no – me too!/Me as well!/Mine's out!/Mine too!

Talia What do we do now?

Nova I'm an atheist but – start praying?

Anika Look, we've sent enough messages –

Talia – everyone knows we're here.

Halima Once the rain calms, we'll all just get Ubers –

Mia (*concerned*) Then we'll all be back home in no time, won't we, Halima . . .?

With louder thunder and brighter lightning, the boat begins to rock precariously. The group freeze, exchanging terrified glances.

Scene Ten

The boat, same evening.

Torrential rain. Crashing thunder and lightning.

A movement sequence involving the group trying to withstand the turbulent rocking and shaking of the boat in the raging storm and great flood. **Mia** *scrambles to a porthole.*

Scene Eleven

The boat, outer deck, the same night.

In the violent storm, **Mia** *is on the outer deck, struggling to loosen the ropes.*

Mia (*shouting*)　Almost done, Samaki! Almost . . .!

Faiz *runs out after* **Mia**.

Faiz　Mia! Get back inside!

Mia (*struggling to untie the ropes*)　I have to free the boat!

Faiz (*trying to stop* **Mia**)　What? No!

Mia　We need to move –

Faiz　No, we don't!

Mia　– or we'll drown in this flood!

Faiz *and* **Mia** *struggle, pushing and pulling at the ropes.*

Mia　We need to move with the waves!

Faiz　We need to stay right here till morning! Till somebody comes! They'll know we're missing, send help!

Mia　No, Faiz, it's too late!

She pushes **Faiz** *aside, throwing the loosened ropes into the sea.*

Mia　This is our only chance!

Faiz　No, Mia! What have you done?

Scene Twelve

The boat, same night.

The storm continues raging. The group surround **Mia**, *who sits in the centre, her head buried in her knees.*

Zuri You psycho!

Nova What's wrong with you?

Anika What were you thinking?

Paz She wasn't.

Talia I can't believe –

Faiz You've just set us adrift in a giant flood.

Zuri With no signal.

Nova No power.

Faiz No way back.

Eleni (*to* **Mia**) You're not alone here – you should have asked us all first.

Faiz Mia, my mum, she's sick, helpless, alone . . .

Talia All our families.

Paz Is it cos you don't have a family?

Pause.

Zuri Might as well have just thrown us all overboard.

Nova We should throw her overboard!

Paz Cos she's one messed up little . . .

Halima Stop! Listen to the storm. Look at the flood outside. It's only getting worse. I think my sister was right.

Anika Seriously, Halima?

Halima If we'd stayed there, this flood would have swept us away –

Talia Like now?

Halima We would have drowned there.

Paz Bullshit!

Nova You don't know that!

Anika How can you say that?

Halima Ever seen a raging storm or flood like this? Before everything cut out, you all saw this storm and flood slam the whole world from the Himalayas to the Aussie Outback. Sometimes, water is safer than land. Mia might just have saved all our lives.

All Oh come on!/What?/Please . . .

Paz On what planet?

Halima Like Eleni said, this could be End Times.

The group reel in disbelief.

Eleni Really not the time to quote me . . . /

Nova What? /

Talia Oh my days! /

Anika You for real?

Zuri You're as batshit crazy as she is.

Paz (*to* **Halima**) When I said you're the smart one – I take it all back.

Faiz Mia, I thought I knew you – but how can I ever forgive you?

Paz (*to* **Halima** *and* **Mia**) You two, get a grip. It's just a giant storm. When it's over and we're back in the world of the sane, I'll sue you both for false imprisonment. Then send you both straight back to where you came from.

Suddenly, the boat lurches and the group falls in all directions. **Mia** *scrambles to look through the porthole. Quietly, she begins to mutter something over and over, gradually getting louder.*

Mia Swim, Samaki, swim. Swim, Samaki, swim. Swim, Samaki, swim . . .

Scene Thirteen

The boat, day.

The storm continues raging. The boat rocks in the great flood. Some of the group still look shocked, bereft and sit under blankets, trying to console each other as their new reality sinks in. Others try to busy themselves reading and doing chores.

Faiz So far from people, lives we love –

Talia – from all we've known . . .

Eleni – all we might have become . . .

Pause. **Paz** *runs on, chased by* **Zuri**.

Zuri He's stealing food – again!

Paz I'm not!

Anika You two, stop!

Zuri *wrestles a snack from* **Paz**'*s jumper.*

Zuri (*holding the snack aloft*) Bingo!

Nova Nope, not playing bingo again, however much you beg and plead.

Eleni Paz, we're rationing!

Paz I'm starving!

Talia We all are.

Paz I paid for most of this and I've been most generous sharing . . .

Anika Here we go . . .

Paz I catered, I cook –

Talia We all take turns –

Faiz Hold us all together, don't you?

Paz Protest back there, happy to devour my mining money here.

Eleni No ethics in survival.

Mia (*joining, to* **Halima**) I've cleaned the toilet, shower – anything else?

Halima Thanks, Mia – you've done more than enough again today.

Paz It will never be enough.

Mia *sits by the porthole, watching* **Samaki** *steer the boat through the flood outside.*

Eleni Zuri, stop wasting the generator to charge your phone.

Zuri That phone was like fam to me.

Talia No matter how many times you try, it's never coming back.

Zuri TikTok . . . Insta . . . Snapchat . . . X . . . damn, even Facebook . . .

Nova Netflix –

Paz KFC –

Zuri Nando's –

Nova Maccy D's –

Paz – even Chicken Cottage –

Talia We had it all . . .

Pause.

Zuri Btw, Faiz has been recharging his phone too.

Eleni What? /

Anika Faiz!

Paz Then I'm gonna use it for my Shadowtime app too – and charge you all food rations to use my app.

Talia Cos we'll be queuing up.

Faiz I only did it to see Mum, before I lose sight of her, for ever.

Anika Faiz, we know – but we're dangerously low on everything.

Eleni Right, blanket generator ban. Everyone goes through me.

Faiz And I was tallying how long we've been here, on my phone –

Eleni Pen and paper perhaps?

Talia How long's it been?

Faiz It's been raining fifty days, fifty nights –

Nova Not God's biggest fan but – isn't this all meant to be over by now?

Paz Not till we're forced to eat each other –

Eleni Nope – vegan for life.

Paz Mia's dead meat first.

Faiz God! When is this going to end? . . .

Talia We stink –

Nova – we're starving –

Anika – sleep deprived –

Zuri – screen deprived –

Eleni – suffocating in here –

Paz (*staring at* **Mia**) And every friggin' day, she just sits there, muttering to herself, waving out the porthole, oblivious to what she's done.

Zuri Why do crazy kamikaze people always take others down with them?

Nova Luring us onto a crashing sea to nowhere –

Paz (*confronting* **Mia**) Why didn't you get the help you clearly needed?

Mia *moves away from* **Paz**.

Paz All this just to get us to feel your pain? Your loss? Your sadness?

Paz *pulls her back, before* **Mia** *struggles free.*

Paz Cos if it is, I'll charge up my Shadowtime app for your rations, get you better.

Mia *scoffs.*

Halima (*intervenes*) She's kept well out of your way.

Paz Well out of my way only if we throw her overboard. Can we?

Halima (*moving* **Mia** *aside*) Help me prepare dinner.

Mia (*sotto voce to* **Halima**) Every day, I sit by the porthole, urge Samaki to keep swimming, to keep us safe. What's the point? Keep us safe for what? Is this how it will be? For the rest of our lives?

Paz (*shouting at* **Halima** *and* **Mia**) Don't you two dare sneak any food –

Halima Paz, just stop!

Paz Monitor them!

Paz, **Zuri** *and* **Nova** *circle* **Halima** *and* **Mia**.

Halima Everyone, please! We need to figure out a better way to be on the boat together. Who knows how long we'll be here?

Paz We wouldn't be here if it wasn't for you two.

Zuri (*to* **Halima**) Who put you in charge anyway?

Nova (*to* **Halima**) Yeah, you'd do well to stop right there.

Paz Lured us on the boat, threw the ropes –

Eleni Paz, you're on loop again –

Paz – the way that waste refugee girl looped our lives into an unending loop of doom?

Zuri Drowning us in her lies –

Nova – her delusions –

Paz – her madness!

The boat rocks violently and hits something. A huge crunching sound.

Eleni Shit!

Halima What's happening?

Faiz (*spotting water*) Boat's sprung a leak!

Eleni (*looking around*) Water's coming in!

Halima Quick! Grab buckets, pots, pans, anything!

The group scream and panic, slipping and sliding, trying to block the leak.

Anika It's no good!

Paz The boat's sinking!

Zuri We're sinking!

Halima Keep trying!

Nova No, we all need to get off the boat!

Zuri Or we're gonna drown here!

Talia This isn't working!

Halima Just try!

Anika Block it!

Nova Oh God –

Paz – this is it!

Zuri Jump!

Zuri *and* **Nova** *try to run off, as* **Eleni** *and* **Talia** *restrain them.*

Eleni Nova, no! /

Talia Zuri, get back!

Mia *rushes out onto deck.*

Mia Samaki! (*Off stage.*) Samaki!

Paz What's she doing?

Eleni Stop her!

Halima No, let her go!

Faiz Halima!

Mia (*off stage*) Samaki, help!

Suddenly, **Samaki** *appears above the sea, over the boat, stunning the group.*

Paz What the hell is that?

Eleni A giant fish?

Talia A whale?

Nova It's massive!

Anika With an epic tusk!

Halima A narwhal . . .

Zuri A what?

Halima A narwhal –

Faiz – a unicorn of the sea . . .

Nova That's what hit us?

Paz Or attacked us?

Halima No, it didn't hit or attack us – but it might just save us!

Mia *rushes back.*

Mia Chuck everything non-essential overboard and keep bailing out the water!

Everyone except **Paz** *begin throwing objects overboard.*

Paz (*to* **Mia**) Listen to you?

Halima Paz, please, we need your help!

Mia We've got to lighten the boat! We're too heavy. Samaki says they can't do it alone, we have to help –

Anika Samaki?

Faiz Who the hell's Samaki?

Mia The talking fish out there.

Pause. The group stops in disbelief. **Halima** *nods.*

Paz What the –?

Zuri You're frigging crazy!

Eleni Mia –

Mia Samaki's seen a mountain peak, they'll tow the boat up to it but we have to help.

Zuri Nah –

Talia – this is mad.

Mia So, after everything, we're all just ready to sink and drown?

Pause. The group freeze for a moment.

Paz Let's listen to the talking fish!

The group throw more objects overboard.

Mia Swim, Samaki, swim! Swim, Samaki, swim! . . .

Led by **Mia**, *the group start chanting 'Swim, Samaki, swim' together, whilst continuing to bail out water and discarding their belongings. Then – an even louder big bang. All is still for a few moments.*

Faiz Is that it?

Zuri Is it over?

Talia Are we safe?

Nova Did the talking fish save us?

Anika We should head out and check.

Halima Yeah, let's go and find out . . .

Pause. Everyone hangs back.

Paz Let's just turn back –

Anika Now?

Paz And go home.

Halima How exactly?

Paz Mia's talking fish can take us back, like it got us here.

Eleni (*ignoring* **Paz**) Right, who steps out first?

Zuri Go first, get eaten . . .?

Nova Yeah, best watch out for wild animals –

Paz – and wild people, like Mia? . . .

Talia Don't drown, get burnt or iced to a crisp.

Paz (*pointing at* **Mia**) She got us here. Shouldn't she go first? Then we blindly follow? Oh wait – we did that once and look where we ended up.

Nova Paz, if we're gonna survive this, let's drop the Mia-baiting, mate.

Zuri Yeah, let's focus energies on getting through this.

Paz *is taken aback.*

Mia I'll go.

Halima Sure?

Mia *nods. The group parts to let her through. Taking a deep breath, she opens the door and steps out into bright sunshine. Pause. Everyone waits.* **Mia** *rushes back in.*

Mia We're on dry land! Come on, it's so beautiful out there!

Suddenly, **Paz** *roughly pushes everyone aside and dashes off the boat without looking back.*

Talia Paz! /

Eleni Where you – ? /

Faiz Wait! /

Anika Not alone! /

Halima Paz!

Epilogue

The new world, two weeks later.

*Clear sunny blue skies. Calm waves caress the shore. Birdsong. In various groupings (***Mia** *and* **Faiz**, **Halima** *and* **Anika**, **Eleni** *and* **Talia**, **Nova** *and* **Zuri***), everyone converges together from different points (perhaps laying down and sorting through some materials).*

Mia We found more driftwood towards the east.

Halima Us too, towards the west.

Eleni   We found odd bits all around we could use.

Faiz   Find enough, we can start building here.

Nova   Finally move off that stinky boat.

Talia   Hey, it's been good to us.

Zuri   We've found more materials, but anyone found Paz yet?

Eleni   After his epic runner from the boat?

Anika   Just hope he's safe.

Nova   He's a survivor . . .

Pause.

Talia   Two weeks on – no sign of Paz, still no sign of other people.

Halima   At least the sea's been calm.

Anika   No storms at all.

Nova   Retweet to that.

Zuri   X . . . oh I miss X . . .

Eleni   Let's not –

Mia   Skies are still so sunny and clear, we could see for miles where we were –

Anika   Yeah, same on the west side too.

Talia   Sea's so clear too – so when can I surf these aqua turquoise waters?

Faiz   Once we make you a driftwood surfboard strong enough.

Eleni   Sea's so clear you can see rainbow-coloured fish from here.

Mia (*to* **Faiz**)   What about the rainbow-coloured birds we saw?

Faiz   Loudly singing, then gently (*teasing* **Zuri**) 'tweeting' –

Zuri   Oh, come on, Faiz!

Eleni   The animals, insects – it's just buzzing with new life round here.

Halima   We even saw electric-coloured plants –

Anika   That actually reach out and buzz you!

Zuri   We found some new fruit trees –

Nova   Tasted delicious!

Talia   So where's our fruit?

Zuri   We had to taste test first –

Nova   – if we're still ok later, we'll do a group walk and fruit feast before sundown.

Eleni Great idea!

Halima Shouldn't everything have been washed away?

Mia Instead, it's thriving.

Pause.

Faiz How will we keep living in this new world?

Anika Figure it all out as we go?

Zuri We might kill each other long before that.

Halima Law numero uno – let's try not to do that.

Mia Trust we'll find our way –

Faiz – and trust we'll find everything we need.

Eleni Only if we work together, take only what we need from around us, putting back as much as we take.

Pause.

Zuri I just wish we knew where we were –

Talia – where home is –

Faiz – even if there's a home to go back to . . .

Eleni If there's still a world back there – family, friends, technology – they'll find us.

Halima If they never come, we'll know.

Nova Till we know, we don't know?

Mia Even if we made it back, the Old World's gone. We have to build a New World. Not only what we think it should be for us – but what it needs to be for all that lives and breathes in it. How we all live here – our planet, our future, our humanity, depends on us. This isn't a survival of the fittest anymore. This is a survival of the nurturers.

Faiz *hugs* **Mia**. *A group hug circles them, before gently coming apart.*

Eleni Carry on beachcombing for materials closer to the boat?

Halima Meet back here with smaller bits, collect the big stuff later?

The group nod in agreement, separating to beachcomb in different directions. **Mia** *walks off and spots* **Samaki**.

Mia Samaki, you're back!

Samaki We're all rising back up now . . .

Mia (*looking out*) Wow, look at all you fish.

Samaki   Don't even let the others think about eating us all!

Mia   Hey, I got fish dropped from Mrs Carter's menu, didn't I?

Samaki   You did. So keep reminding them it's our world as much as yours.

Mia   All of ours.

Samaki   This time, we'll all be speaking up.

Mia   We'll be listening . . . You look smaller . . .

Samaki   I'm on the New World diet.

Mia   Snap!

Samaki   No more growing too big for the pot that holds any of us.

Mia   Knowing when to stop?

Samaki   Because greed and selfishness destroy worlds –

Mia   – and compassion and connections create them.

Samaki   We're all bound together.

Mia   This time, we won't forget.

Samaki   It's time for the big fish to protect the small fish.

Mia   Just the way you did.

Samaki   Only after you did it first, Mia.

Mia   Samaki? (*Pause.*) Is it really only us now?

Samaki   You're the only human survivors. The last of the Old World. The first of the New World.

Mia   How will I tell them?

Samaki   Carefully – and in time.

Mia   Don't abandon us too.

Samaki   As if I ever would! I'll come up again soon.

Mia *waves off* **Samaki** *and continues beachcombing. Pause.* **Paz** *approaches.*

Mia   Wow, you're back?

Paz   Think I'd have survived alone?

Mia   We thought we might never see you again.

Paz   Just needed some time out – to think.

Mia   You? Think? About? . . .

Paz   I'm sorry, Mia.

Mia *stops* and *stares at* **Paz**.

Mia   For what?

Paz   How I treated you.

Mia   How's that, Paz?

Paz (*shuffling around*)   Badly.

Mia   I was struggling so much – and you – you made everything way harder than it ever needed to be, pushed me right to the edge.

Paz   I know.

Mia   You made me feel painfully alone, singled out, picked on, ridiculed, pushed around, my efforts to fit in, offer something, be something, just be safe, literally smeared and stamped on.

Paz *looks sheepish.*

Mia   Are you fully feeling yet how painful it is to be taken from your home, thrown into a strange, unstable world, while you desperately try to find your footing?

Paz *nods.*

Mia   Sucks, doesn't it?

Paz *nods. Pause.*

Mia   Paz, we're all refugees now. Nowhere else to go, except towards each other.

Paz   I'll try to do better.

Mia   'Try'? No. Do better. Or there's no hope for all of us – and it's all any of us really have right now.

Paz   I promise.

Pause.

Paz (*holding out the tusk object*)   I think this belongs to you . . .

Mia *gasps as she takes the tusk, holds it and, eyes closed, kisses it. Pause.*

Mia (*opening her eyes*)   Why did you take it?

Paz   I'm sorry.

Mia   But why?

Paz   I don't know . . .

Mia   My father gave it to me. It's all I had of him, of our life before.

Paz   I should never have taken it. Something so precious.

Mia (*looking at the object*)   Ah – the tip of a narwhal tusk.

Paz (*looking at the object*)   Yeah . . . just like the giant talking fish.

Mia   Dad's tusk or Samaki's tusk – to live in a new world, we can't step on others to survive and thrive. Take care of others, they will take care of us back.

Paz   Keep leading the way, Mia.

Mia   No. No one leads here – we're all in this, together. Us, the planet, every living thing in it.

Paz   Together.

Mia   Come on, let's beachcomb our new world – together.

As **Mia** *and* **Paz** *rejoin the others, the group beachcomb for a new world.*

End.

Character Plot

	Prologue	1	2	3	4	5	6	7	8	9	10	11	12	13	Epilogue
Mia	✓	✓	✓	✓	✓	✓	✓	✓	✓	✓	✓	✓	✓	✓	✓
Samaki	☐	☐	✓	☐	✓	☐	✓	☐	✓	☐	☐	☐	☐	✓	✓
Halima	✓	✓	☐	✓	✓	✓	☐	☐	☐	✓	✓	☐	✓	✓	✓
Paz	☐	✓	☐	✓	☐	✓	☐	✓	☐	✓	✓	☐	✓	✓	✓
Anika	☐	✓	☐	✓	☐	✓	☐	☐	☐	✓	✓	☐	✓	✓	✓
Eleni	☐	✓	☐	✓	☐	✓	☐	☐	☐	✓	✓	☐	✓	✓	✓
Talia	☐	✓	☐	✓	☐	✓	☐	☐	☐	✓	✓	☐	✓	✓	✓
Faiz	☐	✓	☐	✓	☐	✓	☐	☐	☐	✓	✓	✓	✓	✓	✓
Nova	☐	✓	☐	✓	☐	✓	☐	☐	☐	✓	✓	☐	✓	✓	✓
Zuri	☐	✓	☐	✓	☐	✓	☐	☐	☐	✓	✓	☐	✓	✓	✓
Cronies	☐	☐	☐	☐	☐	☐	☐	✓	☐	☐	☐	☐	☐	☐	☐
Beach-goers	☐	✓	☐	☐	☐	☐	☐	☐	☐	☐	☐	☐	☐	☐	☐
Protestors	☐	☐	☐	✓	☐	☐	☐	☐	☐	☐	☐	☐	☐	☐	☐
River-goers	☐	☐	☐	☐	☐	✓	☐	☐	☐	☐	☐	☐	☐	☐	☐
Students	☐	☐	☐	☐	☐	☐	☐	☐	☐	☐	☐	☐	☐	☐	☐
Nova's Partners	☐	✓	☐	☐	☐	☐	☐	☐	☐	☐	☐	☐	☐	☐	☐

More information about the characters and how much they speak

Mia – Significant dialogue
Samaki – Significant dialogue – could be shared between multiple people
Halima – Significant dialogue
Paz – Significant dialogue
Anika – Significant dialogue
Eleni – Significant dialogue
Talia – Less dialogue but in multiple scenes
Faiz – Significant dialogue
Nova – Less dialogue but in multiple scenes
Zuri – Less dialogue but in multiple scenes
Cronies – Couple of lines
Beach-goers/Protestors/River-goers/Students/Nova's Partners – non-speaking roles, could be created by a small group or large chorus

Main Narrative Beats

1. Mia and Halima have arrived on dry land. They are refugees. Mia finds the tusk her dad gave her and kisses it.

2. A few months later, Halima is meeting her friends on the beach. Mia is beachcombing. There is a heatwave. Mia sees the fish that she saw in the dinghy. Eleni tells the group about the deep-sea mining. She's planning a beach protest for tomorrow.

3. Mia goes beachcombing. She shares that she and Halima used to look for whale poo with their dad. There is a precious substance in it. The group think it's gross.

4. Later on at the beach, Samaki the fish starts talking to Mia. Samaki needs help. The sea is full of toxic waste and bigger fish. Mia puts Samaki in a bottle and takes him home.

5. The next day at the beach, the group are protesting the deep-sea mining. They give up quickly. Eleni is frustrated. Mia stays to protest. She tells Eleni about life back home and fishing with her dad. When the drought and floods hit, Mia and Halima became refugees.

6. In Mia's bedroom, Samaki has grown bigger and he is hungry. Halima comes in. She sees Samaki. Mia tries to get Samaki to speak to Halima but Halima can't hear.

7. The next day at the river, there is more protesting. Mia arrives. She wasn't in art class. Faiz asks about her art project. The tusk is in it. Paz makes ignorant comments. Faiz defends Mia.

8. Paz says he supports the deep-sea mining. The others realise that Paz's dad is in the newspaper. He is the CEO of the mining company. Paz is rude to Mia and Halima about them not having a dad.

9. Later at the river, Mia goes to speak to Samaki. He has grown again. He needs to go back to the sea.

10. At school, Paz and his cronies are in the art classroom. They laugh at Mia's art and break off the tusk. Mia comes in and realises what they've done.

11. At the beach, Mia is looking for Samaki. He's bigger than a whale. Samaki tells Mia a great storm is coming. Mia needs to find a big boat and fill it with her friends, food, water and seeds. When the storm comes, Samaki will return as a narwhal with a tusk.

12. A few days later, the group are preparing the boat. Mia needs to find her missing tusk. Paz feels guilty and so has paid for supplies. Torrential rain starts falling.

13. The storm gets worse. The group are on the boat. Mia unties the ropes and frees the boat. They are floating on the sea. The others are furious. They need to get home.

14. Fifty days later, still on the boat, the group are arguing about food and charging phones. The boat hits something and starts to leak. Samaki, now a giant narwhal, appears. He will tow the boat to a mountain. There is a crunch. They are on dry land. Paz pushes past everyone and runs off.
15. Two weeks later, the group are looking for driftwood and fruit trees. It is beautiful. They are working together. Samaki appears. He is smaller. He tells Mia they are the only survivors. She will tell the others soon.
16. Paz returns. He needed time to think. He apologises to Mia. She explains how small he made her feel. Paz gives back the tusk. They will beachcomb together.

Mia and the Fish

BY SATINDER CHOHAN

Notes on rehearsal and staging drawn from a workshop with the writer led by Tinuke Craig held at the National Theatre, October 2024

How the writer came to write the play

I was inspired by an ancient Indian flood myth, and wanted to think about non-Western modes of dramatic storytelling. Taking elements of the myth and adapting them for a contemporary story about our precarious world and a more compassionate new one. Myths have a timeless message. 'Manu and the Fish' is about the law of the fishes, where big fish eat the small fish, similar to the law of the jungle; a dog-eat-dog world, in which the strong dominate those (seen as) weaker. We use animalistic phrases like these to describe ruthless human survival instincts, alongside the idea we are more civilised than the animal world. But we actually need to work with nature and the animals, protect and respect them, instead of arrogantly separating ourselves from them or placing ourselves above them.

Another core element is the idea of refugees – the message of the play is also that we should look after those more fragile and vulnerable than us (like refugees), and make a conscious choice to do so. But it's not just about Mia and war refugees. Sadly, successive waves of global conflict refugees are now being overlapped by waves of climate refugees. I wanted to make that connection between refugees, war, the environment and climate change.

The idea of refugees also relates to teenagers. In a way, we are all refugees from our childhood, having to move into adulthood, sometimes painfully. We have to shed our younger selves and experiences, accepting and relinquishing the past, to grow into a new, older skin.

Samaki the fish is a refugee too. I introduced deep-sea mining into the play because this rapacious attack on the ocean will likely happen at some point. How long is our voraciously profit-hungry society going to hold off drilling into the ocean to plunder its untapped precious seabed resources, displacing and destroying the deep-sea life that lives there? So it's also about animals as refugees, nature as a refugee, fish as refugees. It's important that a production explores these ideas around being a refugee in an uncertain, unstable world and finding one's place within it.

The play is also about community and the difference between eco-systems – where nature works in harmony – and ego-systems – where individuals are driven to exploit and destroy. Eco-systems vs ego-systems is a lynchpin of the play. It's about the importance of community working together and forging connections. Hopefully that will be reflected in the ensemble work in the production and the teenagers learning to work together as part of the story.

(Satinder Chohan, 2024)

What would make a successful production for Chohan?

A successful production creates a dramatic eco-system of sorts, connecting the ancient myth to our contemporary world, connecting the overarching themes to conflicting feelings and emotional states in the play, connecting different beings and different refugees – before dramatically manifesting these in a holistic, universal whole.

Sound might also play a part in the story. The deep-sea mining and its sounds interferes with the communications and frequencies between sea animals. Their homes become a 24/7 construction site or even like a war zone, as the constant drilling blows up the seabed, fatally disrupting sea life.

A production might also think about how it can use recycled materials, and keep to the themes of the play by thinking about how to avoid consumerism (or over-consumption). For example, is the fish made of recycled materials? How can the ensemble reflect the ideas about the importance of community? How can you manifest a community in this play and present it for an audience?

Approaching the play

Lead director Tinuke Craig talked about how useful a director's manifesto is when approaching a play. This means asking yourself the question: what do you want the show to do? This is the start of creating a directorial magnetic north for yourself, somewhere to come back to when it's tough, or you get lost.

Craig shared three questions with the group that can help in creating your director's manifesto:

Why this play?

Why now?

Why you? (Why your young people and you as a director?)

Craig then shared a new set of questions to consider as a director approaching the play.

Which are the three moments this play lives and dies by?

What is the 'five-star' moment?

What is your company's superpower?

What is your company's kryptonite?

Here are some of the group's answers:

What are the live or die moments:

- Samaki the fish (especially when it grows and changes)
- Prologue
- The storm
- Paz's apology
- The destruction of Mia's artwork
- The moment where everyone turns on Mia

Five-star moments:

- The storm
- Samaki the fish

It is also worth asking the question: What can you deploy to make sure your five-star moments land?

Superpowers and kryptonite (relating to your cast and how you might solve them):

- Learning lines – how can you make this part of rehearsals?
- Short lunchtime rehearsals – how can you break the play up into chunks and let the cast come prepared to do that scene week by week?
- No puppetry/movement experience – can you start exploring these elements first?

Concepts and style

Craig talked about how helpful it can be to have a clear concept when directing a show. She talked about how a good production becomes great when we have rules so that the whole production feels cohesive. And, if you have clear rules, you can break them. Director Thomas Ostermeier said: The audience don't need to understand the rules, as long as they understand the game.

Exercise: The execution gap

Craig shared an exercise by director Sasha Wares called 'The Execution Gap' which can help you define your concept by running the play through the following binaries or scales. With all of these, you will probably be somewhere on a scale between the two extremes, but you might decide to place your production at one extreme or the other.

You ← → The Text
Literal ← → Abstract
Then ← → Now
Digital ← → Analogue
This Room ← → That Room

You ←→ The Text

Who's in charge? You or the text? If it was a Shakespeare play; is the show reverent to the text or is Shakespeare dead in your production? Most of you will exist somewhere on the continuum. The group talked about the difference between dialogue and stage directions; some say the dialogue is something to honour completely and stage directions are a playful invitation. Whereas others see playing with the text as helping their young people to access it, particularly when language barriers might be at play. If you are working with a living playwright then text is extremely important.

Literal ←→ Abstract

To continue with the Shakespeare example, a literal version would be creating Elsinore photo-realistically, as much like watching it in the 1600s as possible. Abstract could be the version where the set is a white box covered in blood, maybe it's set in Hamlet's head. For *Mia and the Fish*, literal would be creating a super-realistic set for each scene with a bed for Mia's bedroom or an actual fish in a fish tank which is moved round the stage. Whereas abstract might be the actors creating the fish using phone lights or a person just wearing a sign round their neck saying fish. Where do you want to be? Again, you will probably be somewhere on the scale and not at an extreme. Some of the group talked about using the abstract for the magical/epic elements like the fish and sea, while the young people are more naturalistic.

Then ←→ Now

Do you want it to be set when it was written/intended or now? Craig thought it's most likely to be set now, but the question is: *how* now?! With *Mia and the Fish* it's slightly dictated to be now or a little in the future, but how much does it need to feel that way? You could definitely play with having anachronistic elements to bring out the ancient myth. One participant suggested music might help to bring out the ancient myth.

Digital ←→ Analogue

How do you want to use technology in the show? Will it be fully digital, hyper-analogue, absent of any technical elements, or somewhere in between? For *Mia and the Fish* it was suggested a version where there is a filmed CGI fish scene projected on a big curtain, or an analogue version with a tiny puppet fish in a cup of water, or a whole ensemble playing the sea. Analogue is useful if you don't have that much access to technology. You can play with sticking clearly in one camp except for one section or scene. One participant talked about how using analogue or digital to create a sensory experience for your actors can help them immerse themselves.

This Room ←→ That Room

Are the audience and cast in the same room, or are the stage and the auditorium two separate rooms? This is somewhat dictated by your venue, but you could challenge it with design elements or lighting. It's worth thinking about your duty of care to both the cast and the audience – this might inform your 'this room/that room' choice – for example if this is a really important moment for your young people to share how they feel with their parents and carers, you might want your show to be more 'this room'. Do you want your audience to feel refugee-like?

Participants shared some ideas for *Mia and the Fish*'s storm scenes (scenes ten to 12).

- One group used props to create the sound world, building the noise through umbrellas, then flapping cloth, banging sticks and banging of ear defenders. These created the rattling of the boat, the rain falling, the waves hitting and the wind. It built up slowly.
- Another group used ropes tied around themselves to create a boat and a state of tension. They then dropped to the floor as the scene changed, and began tapping the floor in a building energy. They wanted to create the erratic nature of a storm.
- Another group used the ropes to create the shape of the boat with oars at the side and the umbrella.
- Another group talked about how you could create the smell of an ocean.

Getting people on board

Craig asked the group to think about:

- Reluctant casts (or young people you want to potentially cast)
- Reluctant parents/guardians/carers
- Reluctant school or theatre management
- Reluctant community

How do I convince senior management teams in schools and youth theatres?

Some of the group came up with this:

This cross-curricular project will champion and develop the Voice 21 Oracy initiative and highlight the cultural capital of the school as demanded by OFSTED. We'll ensure accessibility to the project for pupil premiums students to release budgets. It will cover key areas of the PSHE and Humanities curriculums in an innovative and efficient way.

Below shows the intersection between story and the curriculum:

- The story begins with two young children arriving in a new country, having been forced out of their home by conflict and climate crisis.
- Following this, a group of young people establish a peer group with a hierarchy, based on prejudices, privileges or lack of, and existing relationships. This links very closely to the social skills and anti bullying areas in our PSHE curriculum.
- One of the children, Mia, meets Samaki, and her eyes are opened to the prospective changes with regards to climate change and energy consumption, and this ties in with the geography curriculum and all the initiatives undertaken by the school with regards to environmental impact and the work of our sustainability ambassadors.
- There is then an extreme weather event, which forces a diverse group into

working together as a community which leads to a greater understanding of each other's cultural experience. Vital for us in this area, due to our refugee population.
- They arrive at a new land with lessons learned, a clear demonstration of the importance of education to our students.

How do I convince the local community to engage?

- Tell them the story quickly and include the most dramatic moments, especially ones which they would be intrigued to see on the stage: 'This is the story of two refugee sisters who arrive in a new place. One settles in easily, but the other doesn't. The lonely one meets a fish who tells her about a threat to the seas. The fish warns her of a flood, and she begins preparing and gets her friends on board a boat in time to escape a storm. The fish helps them survive and start a new world'
- Free drinks if you have the budget for it
- Big posters for the event and placards from the play
- A promise of glitz and a good night out.

How do you persuade reluctant young people to join or engage with the project?

- The promise of a performance
- Explain the story in relatable terms and start with a cliffhanger from the end:

  A group of young people, all on this boat in the middle of the ocean, there's a big storm. All the adults are gone and they have to survive. But let's start at the beginning: two refugee sisters are stranded on a beach without anything, but the scary thing is that there is another storm coming. The older sister is making friends, but Mia is isolated and alone, and during a lonely walk along the beach she meets a sea creature who is facing the threat of extinction and losing its home, because of human behaviour. The sea creature can shape-shift. It can only talk to Mia, and no one else believes her when she tells them about it. The creature warns her of the coming storm, and with its help she is able to get her sister and friends on to the boat. No one else in the world is ready, so these young people have to survive together

- Contextualise it 'The play is inspired by an Indian myth'
- Then ask for their help: 'How do we put this on the stage? This is going to be so challenging! Shape-shifting creatures, boats, storms. I need your help. We need to work together to tell this story'
- If you think they might need a little extra persuasion, then offer them exciting tools to play with, like puppetry or movement.

How do you persuade reluctant parents of your cast?

- Connect it to the curriculum: 'This play thinks about global citizenship, mental health, privilege, prejudice, geography, and more, so relates to many elements of the curriculum'
- Talk about how a project like this can build key life skills: 'However, working on this play is something which stretches beyond the curriculum, and will give them something which they might not get from their grades. The person with the best story is the most powerful communicator. It also promotes collaboration and working together as a team'
- Give them a brief summary of the story: 'This play begins with two sisters who are refugees washed up on the shoreline, and put into foster care. One sister settles in, but the younger one, Mia, struggles to make friends. She misses her old home and father very much.'

Structuring the rehearsal process

Scheduling and managing time is a big part of the director's role. Craig talked about how she splits up rehearsals into four quarters. Here are the main things that the group thought would go in each section.

Stage one

- Learning music
- Establishing roles/expectations
- Blocking
- Character
- World building – exploring character, voice, space, working as an ensemble
- Read through
- Establishing theatrical language
- Trying scenes
- Movement

Stage two

- Blocking
- Stumble through
- Staging
- Trial and error (all the way through but especially in this stage)
- Movement

Stage three

- Putting it all together
- Working on choreography
- Stumble through

Stage four

- A run-through where the directors have to keep their mouths shut and the young people have to problem solve if it goes wrong
- Problem solving
- Practise using microphones
- Run-throughs
- Tech rehearsals
- Dress rehearsal

Rehearsal processes can be complicated and participants shared some worries they had about their groups for some team troubleshooting.

When people don't turn up for rehearsal
Use character plots to help you make contingency plans for what you can do with all the different eventualities. Other cast members may be able to jump in and understudy.

You're not getting through all the material fast enough
Work out what you need to compromise on, so if there was going to be a dance number at the end, maybe that has to be cut because people are absent, and the focus is more on the core elements of the text.

Casting

Some participants were worried about white washing and tokenism in their casting. Chohan noted that: 'Mia and Halima were originally written to be from Syria or Lebanon, and driven from there by bombs and war, but this isn't vital in the casting or the way your production presents them.'

Characters

Mia

Mia is brave, bold and has a strong moral compass, but she's also in a new place where she doesn't understand the rules or connect with people. Mia is vulnerable. She is still grieving her old life and her lost family members, in particular her dad. This is why she carries around the memory of him in the tusk he gave her. Even her artwork is a shrine to this memory.

Halima
Halima is eager to please and fit in. She is the one more welcome in a xenophobic society. She wants to make a new life.

Samaki
Samaki and Mia are parallel characters – both are displaced from their homes by explosions and destruction of the environment. Is Samaki a figment of Mia's imagination? Mia definitely sees a fish from the boat, but is Samaki simply born of trauma experience and created from the narwhal tusk she has from her father? Samaki grows from a smaller fish to a large narwhal throughout the play, and is magical so it's up to you how you present Samaki. It is likely Samaki will need more than one person involved.

Paz
Paz is Mia's opposite: he's popular, smart, egotistic, entrepreneurial, a go-getter. Set up to work in this egotistical, individualistic society. He has to be charismatic to get away with his horrible vibes. It is unclear at the end how genuine he is, but the stark reality is that he has no choice but to return to the group and work with them in the new world. You can explore how genuine you want him to be, and how much he really has changed at this point in the production.

Anika
Anika is attracted and drawn to Halima, there is definitely a potential blossoming romance here.

Eleni
Eleni embodies the teen eco-warrior model. She cares about the planet, and is tarred with the same brush that many eco-warriors are. She is determined and passionate.

Talia
Talia is a surfer girl. She's from a religious conservative background and is rebelling against her family with her surfing.

Faiz
Faiz has a job alongside school and is a carer for his mother. He cares for Mia and connects to her, potentially he's sweet on her. He faces the clearest loss when the rest of the human race is destroyed, and is the most betrayed by Mia. He was from an asylum-seeker background in an early version of the play, but this is not vital, though it could be an explanation for why he understands Mia.

Nova
Nova is a serial dater and atheist, who (perhaps) wants to be in a (loving?) relationship. He also props up Paz with Zuri, till a new undeniable reality sinks in.

Zuri

Zuri is an image-obsessed social media addict, who wants to be more popular than Paz, always looking for validation outside himself.

Ensemble

Beach-goers, protestors, cronies are just some of the roles your ensemble might play. They might also play nature at other moments, or the elements of the storm.

Exercises for use in rehearsals

Warm-up games

Favourite thing in the space

Get your cast to walk the space; as they do they should look around the room and notice the space, focusing away from the other people and at the room itself. Get them to find their favourite thing in the room, but keep walking. Stop them. Ask them to take a step towards their favourite thing. Then another. Has anyone else picked the same thing?

Pass the clap/click

While walking the space get your cast to pass a clap. You have to clap to send it and clap to receive. Ask them to think of this clap as heavy and pretend it takes effort to toss it to the other person. Then once they are comfortable, introduce a second move. Pass the click. Again you click to send and click to receive, but this time they are light and they float so they take longer to reach the other person. How many claps and clicks can your group comfortably sustain?

Traditional Indian storytelling

Workshop notetaker Stephanie Kempson spoke about an Indian traditional art concept called *Rasas*, which influences Indian storytelling, music, theatre, painting, sculpture and literature. The word literally translates as 'juice, essence or taste' but it is essentially an aesthetic which creates a specific feeling in a spectator. There are nine *rasas* and, though they vary throughout schools of thought in India, they generally are:

The Loving (Romance, love, new life, new beginnings)

The Comic (Laughter, amusement)

The Furious (Anger)

The Piteous (Compassion, mercy)

The Disgusting (Disgust, aversion)

The Horrifying (Horror, terror, fear)

The Heroic

The Wonderful (Amazement, magical, sublime)

The Peaceful (Peace, contentment)

Understanding these *rasas* can be a useful way of getting your company to think about how they want the audience to feel at each moment of the play. In groups, introduce the *rasas*. Assign each group a *rasa*, then get them to make a still image which will evoke that feeling in their audience. Then share them and get people to guess which mood each picture creates in them. If they are really good at this, then you can also get them to think about what they might change in a picture to switch it to a completely different *rasa*. Or give them two moods and ask them to make a wordless scene which starts as one mood and then switches to another, and get your audience to guess which ones they are.

You can then apply these *rasas* to the play. Which feelings do you want where? Where do you want them to feel one *rasa*, and where do you want a mix? For example, how do you want an audience to feel at the beginning in the prologue? Do you want to evoke The Piteous in that first scene? Or would you like the audience to feel The Furious and The Heroic for these girls too? You don't need to be limited to one at a time, as we rarely feel emotions one at a time, but having a clear aim will help your company build the mood of each moment.

Playing with props

Craig introduced some props into the room, which included umbrellas, ropes, flowers, wooden sticks, ear protectors and eye protectors. Groups were formed and then each group gathered some props to explore how they could use them for the storm. It's useful to think how props can be used differently throughout the play. Maybe you could ask your company to think of where else they might be useful?

To make sure each group got a fair mix of props, Craig suggested letting one person from each group go up at a time. With each visit they could only get two props for their group. You can repeat the visits until the props are gone or everyone has what they want.

Question and answer with Satinder Chohan

Q: Why do the group hang with Paz?
A: Various reasons: he's inexplicably popular, smart, savvy, he pays for stuff, he's an old friend, he keeps things interesting, they don't mind him and have fun with him despite his unlikable characteristics.

Q: Should we see grief from the survivors? Is everyone else gone?
A: Definitely. Everyone dies apart from this group of lone survivors. It's up to you how much the characters (apart from Mia who knows the truth) understand this.

Q: What is the flood myth's purpose as a story?
A: Flood myths are a cleansing, and in this story, we are plundering the oceans and that's the beginning of a very slippery slope that ends in a huge global storm and flood. In this particular version of the flood myth, Manu saves the (small) fish, and the

(fortified, bigger) fish returns to save Manu. Humanity is saved because of this kindness, creating a new hopeful society. Take care of nature and nature will take care of us back.

Q: How do I find hope at the end of this story?
A: Hope can be found in community and everyone working together, especially when we move from the survival of the fittest to survival of the nurturers in the new world. For me there is a moment where Nova and Zuri say 'enough' to Paz, and without support Paz loses his power. Then he runs away (into the wilderness?) and realises he can't go it alone, coming back to the group, changed. While Mia doesn't totally forgive him just yet, there is a glimmer of hopeful connection between Mia and Paz at the end.

Q: Why does the storm happen?
A: The deep-sea mining destabilised everything, and greedy humans in this profit-seeking world have disrupted and disrespected nature, triggering the unsettled seabed to cause a devastating global storm and flood. We mess with nature at our own peril.

Suggested references

The podcast *This American Life* has a very interesting episode (841: My Senior Year) on the experience of Gazan young people who were on exchange in the US from just before the war breaking out in 2023. It talks a lot about the dissociation of being in a new country, while losing your home.

From a workshop led by Tinuke Craig
With notes by Stephanie Kempson and Freyja Winterson

Fresh Air

by Vickie Donoghue

Vickie Donoghue is a writer from Essex working across stage, screen and radio. Her plays include *Mudlarks* at the Bush Theatre; *Tender Loving Care* at the New Theatre Royal, Portsmouth; *Aperture* at the Royal Court Theatre London; *The Path* at HighTide Festival; *The Electric* for Paines Plough and the Royal Welsh College of Music and Drama; and *The Witch Finder's Sister* and *The Flood* at the Queen's Theatre, Hornchurch. Radio includes *The Gift* and *The Piper*, a ten-part podcast drama co-written with Natalie Mitchell. Vickie Donoghue was an Associate Artist at the Mercury Theatre and a Paines Plough Playwright Fellow. She was longlisted for the Evening Standard Theatre Awards as Most Promising New Playwright and was shortlisted for the Royal National Theatre Foundation Playwright Award.

Characters

1927

Doris
Joan
Jack
Albert
Billy

2024

Alisha
Millie
Lee
Holly
Erin
Charlie
Brian

Notes

- The play is set in One Tree Hill, Langdon Hills, Essex. It's well known for being one of the most haunted woods in England. There have been stories of people bursting into tears, shocking screams from within the woods and chilling stories from those who have visited. Children from an old tuberculosis sanatorium are supposed to haunt it.
- There is no set age for the contemporary children or the ghost children – they can be played by any age between 13 and 18. The contemporary children all attend a local Pupil Referral Unit but have come from separate schools.
- Have fun with the ghost children. They are playful, immature and naïve.
- How you achieve the ghostly effects is open to artistic interpretation. However, it is important that at no point are hands put on any part of another performer, and certainly not around someone's neck to enact the supernatural phenomenon of choking and suffocation.
- Charlie and Lee support West Ham but please feel free to change this to an appropriate team for your area. This can also include changing the A13 and the references to Plaistow to somewhere more local that will resonate with your community.

Scene One

One Tree Hill, Langdon Hills, Essex.

A clearing in a wood.

Four children (one girl, three boys) sit on chairs set out away from each other. There is one empty chair.

The girl, **Joan**, *has severe bobbed hair with a blunt fringe. She is wearing a pinafore dress and tights. The boys (***Albert**, **Jack** *and* **Billy***) are wearing jumpers, shorts and long socks. They have a short back and sides hairstyle with a side parting.*

We can't see their faces as they read large books.

The sound of breathing. Big deep lungs full of breath. The song 'Oranges and Lemons', sung slowly and distorted by children can be heard amongst the trees, mixed with giggling and whispering.

When the children speak, it is whispery and quickly as though they might get caught. When they speak, we get a small glimpse of their pale faces.

Joan   Lungs full of glass.

Jack   Skin and bone.

Albert   Shrinking so they can't see us no more.

Billy   Mouth full of blisters.

Albert   Mouth full of blood.

Joan   Coughing until it hurts.

Jack   Coughing until your insides come out.

Albert   Hidden. So we can be forgotten.

Joan   Hidden. So they can't catch it.

Jack   Hidden. So that we don't exist.

Billy   Day after day. The same.

Joan   Sit still.

Albert   Don't move.

Joan (*whispers*)   Don't speak.

There is a noise, people coming. Still from behind their books, they all hold their breath and listen.

Billy (*whispering*)   Too long, we have played in these woods.

Albert (*whispering*)   Too long, we have called this home.

Jack (*whispering*)   Too long, we have played alone.

A girl, **Doris**, *who has a severe bobbed hair and a blunt fringe, runs on, then stands listening. She is wearing a pinafore dress and tights. There is something odd and otherworldly about her. Her lips are dried shut with blood.*

Doris *wipes the blood from her mouth.*

Doris Come. We will breathe again.

Joan Today? We do it today?

Doris One by one we will take them.
We don't have long.

Billy Who?

Doris Doesn't matter. They don't need it.
They don't want it. Ungrateful and clueless.
This is our chance.
Their air will be our air.

They all stand up, put their books on their chairs and face **Doris**. *Blood pours from their mouths as they all smile at her . . . and disappear.*

Only **Doris** *remains.*

Alisha *runs on but does not see* **Doris**. *She has been running for a while and stops to catch her breath.* **Alisha** *hurriedly looks for something.*

Doris *watches her and smiles as she reveals she is holding a flag . . . and then . . . just like that . . . she disappears.*

Millie *enters, immaculately clean.*

Millie What you doing? Alisha?
We're not running.
We're not doing this whole thing running. That is not happening.

Alisha Er, it's a race.

Millie We're *not* running it.

Alisha Fastest wins.

Millie But you're the only one that can do 'fastest'.

Alisha You did cross-country for your school.

Millie Yes, and I would vape halfway round the course.
We are not running.

Alisha Oh, for God's sake.

Millie Come on, Alisha. No one can go at this pace.
And anyway, the other pupil referral teams haven't even set off yet.

Alisha It's a staggered start, yes, but we still need to go for it. We can do this. I know we can.

Believe and achieve.

Millie   What?

Alisha   Believe and achieve.

It hangs in the air.

Millie   Seriously?
We're not running. We can't. What about the others?
Brian's lost his shoe.

Alisha   Oh my God. We're a joke.

Millie   The minute he started it just shot off.

Alisha   We haven't even found the first checkpoint and we're a joke.

Millie   Scrabbling round in the brambles he is.
He's never going to find it.

Alisha *runs on the spot.*

Alisha   Run on the spot, Mills, or you'll get cold.

Millie   No. No, thank you.

Lee *enters. He's been running and is very out of breath. He holds an orienteering map.*

Lee   Smells . . . smells like shit.

Alisha   What does?

Lee   The . . . the air.

Millie   Only since you arrived.

He flips her the finger.

Lee   Do you know what, since I've not been doing PE, I cannot run for shit.
I'd still beat you all in a race, obviously.
Although, the team from Tilbury look a bit sporty.

He does a hacking noise as he's about to spit.

Millie   If you spit one more time, I'm going to throw up.

Lee   Phlegmy.

Millie   You're disgusting.

Lee   You're welcome.
Why we stopped?
Come on!

He goes to run off.

Alisha   Think this is it.

Millie   What is?

Alisha   This. The first checkpoint.

Millie   Well, where is it?

Lee *stops and inspects the map he has been holding.*

Lee   Don't think so, mate.

Alisha   It was by the start of the dense forest bit, that's in dark green and it's just before you turned right for the lake. That is the light blue bit.

Lee *is looking all over the map. It's clear he can't see what she's talking about.*

Alisha   Let me actually show you.

She grabs the map off **Lee**.

Lee   Er, I'm in charge of the map.

He grabs the map back off **Alisha**.

Alisha   Er, since when!

Millie   In charge of the map? Can you hear yourself?

Holly *enters. They don't even notice her.*

Millie   Is it a massive problem if I said that I need a wee.

Alisha   Gonna have to hold it in.

Millie   Are you joking?

Lee   Do it behind a tree.

Millie   Absolutely not.

Alisha   Get a bladder infection then.

Lee   Why didn't you do one before we set off?

Millie   Didn't like the look of 'em.

Lee (*struggling with the map*)   This map is a joke.

Millie   Oh my God! Have I got mud on my trousers?
Alisha, can you check, babe?
Is there mud there?

Alisha *begrudgingly looks. She can't see any mud on* **Millie**'s *trousers.*

Millie   I don't know if I can do this. Is there definitely no mud, babe?

Alisha   You know when you get a new pair of trainers, and no one has trodden on them yet? That is the feeling I get when I'm near you, Millie.

Lee   Someone really needs to push you over.

Millie Yeah, and someone really needs to kick you in the bollocks.

Erin *enters holding a bug and looking well pleased with herself.*

Erin Most haunted woods in England.

Lee No it ain't.

Millie They are. Man at the start said. Gave us the map and the compass.

Alisha No he didn't.

Millie (*to* **Alisha**) You didn't hear cos you were competitively stretching with Lee.

Alisha You're making it spooky by saying stuff like that.
It's just trees. And . . . and . . . green stuff.

Millie And a sanatorium.

Lee A what?

Alisha What's that?

Millie Dunno.
Sounds clean though.

Erin In 1927 a sanatorium, a hospital, was built for kids from West Ham who had contracted TB. Tuberculosis.
Twenty children are said to haunt these woods.
People are said to have felt cold. Burst into tears.
Been possessed and started talking funny.

Lee I often feel like that stood next to you, Millie.

She gives him the middle finger.

Erin Some people have felt like someone is stood next to them.

Alisha (*shudders*) Stop it.

Erin Apparently, if you stand still for long enough one of them is meant to come and hold your hand.

Alisha I said stop it!

Millie Erin?

Erin Yeah.

Millie What the bloody hell are you holding.

Erin Stag beetle. I'm well pleased. Look at it!

Millie Don't come near me, babe. That's disgusting.

Erin Got a hurt leg. Look.

Alisha You know this is a race, Erin. Put it down.

Millie Urgh, keep it away from me, babe.

Erin The trees must be oak.

Lee I'm sorry but who gives an actual shit?

Erin That's . . . that's where stag beetles live.
Oak trees.
Cool, isn't it? Being out here. With them.

Alisha Look, can we stop all this chit chat and hurry up. The team who come after us will be here soon.

Millie God. Embarrassing.

Lee No, they won't.

Alisha Sorry?

Lee The other team. Won't come this way.

Alisha Why?

Lee Told 'em, I knew where they lived and if they went the same way as us I'd mess them right up.

Alisha Ahh, that's sporting of you.

Lee Want to win this or not?

Millie Not as much you, clearly.

Alisha That's how they all think we'll win it, Lee. Cheating. Lying. Mucking about. How about we try and do it . . . you know . . . like we're meant to.

Lee And how's that going so far?

Erin Did you know they spend most of their lives underground. As larvae.

Lee Look. They wouldn't be coming this way anyway as it's the wrong way. They will have made the first checkpoint and already be heading to the next. I guarantee.

Millie So what is the actual point then?

Alisha I'm telling you, this is the first checkpoint.

Lee Well, where is it then, Alisha? Where?

Alisha It's clearly been knocked over or something, dickhead.

Lee It's not here.

Charlie *and* **Brian** *enter; they are covered in mud.* **Brian** *is hobbling as he is wearing one trainer and a lady's flip-flop.*

Charlie *is wearing a West Ham shirt and a huge West Ham rucksack.*

Brian Yeah, thanks for waiting everyone.
Appreciate that. Yeah, cheers.

Alisha   It's a race, Brian.

Charlie   I think I knelt in fox poo and we couldn't actually retrieve the trainer. Massive fail.

Millie   You stink.

Brian   Look, I know this don't look great, but at least we can continue. We're here. In it to win it. Let's do this. Yeah!

Silence.

Alisha   In a woman's flip-flop?

Brian   Found it in the bushes.

Alisha   We need to find the flag.

They all start looking for the flag. **Holly** *has found a weird doll thing made of sticks and leaves and pops it in her bag.*

Millie (*jiggling*)   Did I say I need a wee?

Lee (*to* **Charlie**)   Nice shirt by the way. What about the West Ham game on Saturday. See the West Ham game on Saturday? Charlie?

Pause.

Charlie   Sure.

Lee   Should have buried them.

Charlie   Definitely.

Alisha   It should be here.

Millie   What should be?

Alisha   God's sake . . . the flag.

Lee   You need to stop thrashing about in the bushes and find a route. Use the map. It's about logic. Thinking. I am the only one here who has grasped that bit of this . . . this . . . what the hell is it called . . . the . . . that we're meant to be doing?

Silence. They look at each other and shrug.

Lee   The name of it, people!

Holly   Orienteering.

Silence as they all look at **Holly**. *Surprised to see her there.*

Lee   Yeah. That.
We've come here to win.
To outwit the other PRU groups.
To prove ourselves.
Right?
Right?

Oh my God . . .

All Right.

Lee Come on. We're bloody doing this.
(*He looks at the map.*)
Fucking bunch of bellends. The lot of you.

Silence.

Alisha Lee. You do know the map's upside down, right.

Lee Fuuuuuck!

He throws the map on the floor. **Alisha** *retrieves it and looks at it.*

Erin I'm sorry, if this isn't the spot, and if the flag's not here, then we're lost.

Millie Lost!

Erin Lost.

Alisha We are not lost.

Brian (*panicking*) Oh my God.

Lee Well, we still might come second. Even third maybe. But let's not think about that. Lost is a bit strong.

Erin No, lost. Lost. We don't know where we are.

Lee Shit.

Brian Shit.

Lee Shit. Shit. Shit.

Brian (*panicking*) We don't know where we are.

Alisha I don't believe this. I'm not having it.

Lee Could murder a Maccy D's.

Millie Wish we had our bloody phones – this is so messed up.

Alisha It would be cheating, Millie.

Lee Did you see the bloke's face when we handed them in. Smug prick.

Holly, *who has been looking at her phone, quickly smuggles it into her pocket.*

Brian Don't . . . don't really like not knowing where I am.

Erin We could just find the next checkpoint.

Charlie I knew I should have signed up for the go-karting.
Didn't even know what this was.

Lee You would have been shit at that and all.

Erin   I said, we could just carry on. To the next checkpoint.

Alisha   What?

Erin   We could –

Alisha   I heard what you said – it's the worst idea, ever.

Millie   I need a wee.

Charlie   Could just head back the way we came.

Lee   What? To the start? Are you for real? To the start! We're not total bloody losers, Charlie.

They all look at each other.

Lee   He is. I ain't.

Charlie   Going home and going back the way we came is the only sensible thing anybody has said all day.

Lee   That rucksack is the most sensible thing I've seen all day.

Millie   Oh my God!

Brian (*panicking*)   What??

Millie   I have got mud on my coat.

Alisha   I say we move on. Keep moving. The flag's not here so . . .

Erin   That's what I –

Lee   Without knowing where we're heading to?

Alisha   Moving forwards is better than going backwards.

Charlie   Going forwards: imminent death. Backwards: car park, home, bed.

Millie   Will it wash out?

Holly *has found a stick that looks like a sword.*

Alisha   We have to keep moving.
I'm getting cold. Our muscles are going to be getting tight. Could go into spasm.

Brian (*panicking*)   Into what?! What's a spasm?

Lee   Charlie will be all right, he ain't got any muscles.

Charlie   I hate you. I actually hate you.

Alisha   Well, I'm going to find the checkpoint. I'm not giving up.

Lee   Why would we follow you? You led us to the wrong bit, make out you're some kind of map genius and then worry about us getting cramp?!

Alisha   Severe cramp can lead to tears in the muscle fibres, causing bruising, swelling, loss of strength and then scar tissue forms and then the muscle never fully

regenerates leading that muscle to being prone to future injury.
Do you want that?
It can take weeks, even months to recover, maybe even leading to surgery.
That is no laughing matter, Lee.

Lee   Right.

Erin   Erm . . . well . . . I've got the compass so we can easily figure this out.

Lee   This is winding me up.
Come on, then, Alisha.
Which way, map nerd? Come on. Which way?

Alisha   Erm, this way. Let's just go this way.

She has marched off.

Erin   But I've got the compass. We should check which way is north before we –

Alisha (*shouting*)   Come on.

They all look at her as if they are going to murder her, especially **Erin**, *but they quickly follow behind.* **Holly** *finds something else unusual in the leaves and quickly squirrels it into her bag before leaving.*

Lee *pushes* **Charlie** *over.*

Charlie   What you do that for?

Lee   Just wanted to know what you got in that sensible rucksack.

He checks the others have gone then pulls the rucksack off **Charlie** *and tips the whole thing onto the floor.*

Charlie   Stop it! Don't! Why would you do that!

He starts hurriedly trying to get it all back in the bag.

Lee *spots something and picks it up.*

Lee   What the hell is this?
(*He reads the packet.*)
Kendal Mint Cake.

Charlie   My mum packed it. They . . . eat it when they . . . climb Everest.

Lee   Everest!
Your mum got a nosebleed at the top of the Eastgate car park! We're in some mouldy woods not –

Charlie   Give it back.

Lee *spots something exciting and picks it up.*

Lee   He's got a whistle! He's got a bloody whistle!
(*He blows it hard a few times.*)
Is anyone coming?

(*He listens.*) Oh dear.
Oh, hang on, (*shouts.*) everyone stop panicking, Charlie's got a plaster. He's got a plaster, we're going to be all right.

Charlie *starts putting everything back into his rucksack but can't find something.* **Lee** *just watches him.*

Lee   Come on, mate. Hurry up.
Pick it all up. That's a good boy.
Never good for the ones at the back.
Bad things happen to the ones at the back.
You've watched *Scooby Doo*, right?

Charlie *is now frantically searching for something.*

Charlie   What have you done?
What have you done?

Lee   What?

Charlie   Where is it?

Lee   Where is what?

Charlie   My pen.

Lee   A pen.
What, you going to do a bit of writing while you're down there.

Charlie   My dad gave it me.
I can't find it, Lee. You don't understand.

Lee   Does your pen have West Ham on it too?
(*Silence.*)
Who do you think they'll put up front on Saturday then?
(*Silence.*)
Come on, Charlie boy. Perfectly legit question.
Who's going to score a goal for us?
Huh?
Do you need to ask your dad?
Probably need to give his shirt back and all.

Charlie   At least I have a dad.

A long silence then **Lee** *runs off.*

Charlie   Shit.
(*Shouts.*) Shit!

Standing in the shadows, just visible, are two girls, **Doris** *and* **Joan**. *They watch him.*

Joan *is holding* **Charlie**'s *pen.*

They slowly approach him until they are standing next to him. He can't see them.

Doris *holds his hand.*

Blackout.

Scene Two

Alisha *runs into another clearing. She hurriedly looks for a checkpoint. Nothing. She picks up a stick and starts angrily whacking it at the ground.*

Watching her curiously from the shadows is **Doris**.

Erin *enters waving the compass around and still holding the stag beetle.*

Alisha *stops whacking when she spots* **Erin**. **Alisha** *catches her breath and her composure.*

Awkward silence.

Doris *disappears.*

Erin   Meant to be doing us good all this.
You know. Out and about.
All Bear Grylls.

Alisha   No good if we don't win.

Erin   Really?

Alisha   Unthinkable if we don't even finish.
How would you tell your mum and dad about today?
How would you describe it?

Erin   I won't . . . I don't think I'll even . . .
I mean, I'm not even sure if they know I'm doing this.

Alisha   Oh, my dad does.
My dad will be waiting in the car park.
First words that will come out of his mouth.
Where'd you come?
Where'd you place?

Erin   Surely that all stopped when you got selected.

Alisha   Got worse.
The academy this. The academy that.
Just wanted to play football.
Not lose friends.
Not . . . talk about it 24/7.
Not . . . be all I am.

Erin   I've always wondered how someone like you ended up with us.

Alisha   . . .

Brian *enters limping and rubbing his foot followed by* **Millie**, **Lee** *and* **Holly**.

Brian Can we just stop. I need to stop, this flip-flop is really rubbing.

Alisha Play hard, win easy, Brian.

Brian How do people actually wear these things. It just keeps shooting off.

Millie Urgh, Erin. Still holding that creature.

Erin Did you know the big antler horns at the front are there just to scare you off. They would never hurt you. Never bite.

Brian Where's Charlie?

Millie What do you mean, where's Charlie?

They all suddenly notice he's gone.

Brian I mean, where's Charlie! Lee? Where's Charlie? He was with you.

Lee No he weren't. I don't know where he is.

Erin Is it me or is it getting dark?

Millie I don't like this.

Alisha Where is he?

Brian Why does no one know where he is?

Lee Who cares?

Alisha How long has he not been with us?

Millie He was right behind us.

Erin They say people have gone missing in these woods.

Brian (*panicking*) Oh my God.

They all shout 'Charlie', except **Lee**. *Nothing.*

Lee Perhaps he's gone for a wazz.

Erin Or headed back to the start.
He said about doing that, didn't he?

Millie How does he even know where the start is, it all looks the bloody same.

Brian (*shouts*) Charlie!

Alisha I'm sure he's fine.

Brian (*shouts*) Charlie!

There is a noise in the bushes.

Millie What was that?

Brian Oh God, what?

Millie Feel like we're being watched.

Lee Bet it's the other team. Probably watching us and pissing their pants.

Millie They're going to watch me piss mine in a minute if we don't hurry up and get this over with.

Brian Can't breathe.

Alisha Come on. We need to keep moving.

Alisha *starts to leave.* **Brian** *is struggling to breathe, and it gets progressively worse as the scene goes on.*

Erin Erm, that's north . . . Alisha, the next checkpoint is –

Brian (*panting*) What about Charlie?

Erin We need to be heading east. Alisha?

Alisha Fine. East. North. Whatever. Can we just go please.

Erin But you are literally just guessing where you are going?

Alisha I'm using the map.

Erin Which you use in conjunction with the compass.

Alisha Whatever, Erin. Can we just go!

Brian Did I say that I'm struggling to . . . to get air in.

Erin But we need to . . . if we head east, we should come across at least one checkpoint, possibly two.

Lee What would be the bloody point of that? We have to do them in order.

Erin To get help. We need help, Lee.

Lee Help?

Alisha Why do we need help?

Millie Brian's having a moment in case anyone's noticed.

Brian (*gasping*) I'm all right . . . Just –

Alisha We need to win, Erin.

Lee We need to win.

Erin Do we though?

Lee/Alisha Yes!

Millie I thought we'd already lost?

Erin We have the dibber, we check in at a checkpoint, any checkpoint, they know where we are then, they'll come and find us, find Charlie and then we can go home.

Millie A clean toilet.

Lee Big Mac.

Erin And we never have to speak of this again.

Alisha We still have a chance. I'm not giving up.

Millie Even if it makes everyone miserable.

Lee (*to* **Erin**) Why have you got the dibber?

Erin The man . . . the man give it me.

Millie I want to go home. The mud is freaking me out. I keep looking at it.

Brian Really, really can't breathe.

Erin All the time we have the dibber, we're all right.

Lee Give me the dibber.

Erin Why would I give you the dibber?

Lee Because I should have the dibber.
Give me the dibber.
(**Erin** *doesn't move.* **Lee** *moves towards her.*)
Give me the dibber.

Erin *doesn't move.*

Erin I ain't scared of you.
I'm not here because I drew dicks on tables and threw wet tissue on the ceiling of the toilets.
I did something. Actually did something.
So, no. You do not get the dibber.

Lee Why are you here?

Erin *won't answer.*

Lee *moves towards her and swipes the beetle out of her hands.*

Erin Hey! Why'd you do that?
It's injured.

Lee *stamps on it. There is a silence.*

Then **Erin** *screams. Then* **Millie** *screams.*

Brian It's on your shoe. It's still on your shoe.
It's still alive! Oh God, I'm going to pass out.

They all scream. Except **Holly***, who just stands there.*

Alisha Everybody stop. Just stop. Stop!
They stop screaming. **Brian** *can hardly breathe.*
Brian, breathe.

Millie, hot wash and some Daz, your coat will be fine.
We came to win this together. Right?
They made us do this, because, I don't know, they think it will be good for us, or something.
So, we should at least try to accomplish this.
Finish it.
Brian. Breathe.
Together.
Even you . . . (*points to* **Holly**.) What's your name again?

Holly *stares at them.*

Alisha   Fine. Whatever.
We've missed one checkpoint. Doesn't matter.
We don't give up. They are expecting us to give up.
We carry on.
We have to carry on.
We have to do this.
Even if it's horrible.
Even if the mud's looking at us funny.
Even if we can't breathe.

The sound of breathing through the wood.

Millie   What. The hell. Is that? I don't like it.

Alisha   Let's go. Come on.

Brian *is really struggling to breathe.*

Erin   We need to give him a minute. Alisha.

Millie   Alisha.

Alisha   For God's sake . . . Fine.
One minute then everyone. Take some water. Take a moment. Maybe have a stretch.
We've still got this.
We can do it.

Lee   Anyone got anything to eat?

Holly *stuffs a custard cream biscuit she's been casually eating into her mouth and turns her back to swallow it quickly.*

Erin   You all right, Brian? Easing?

Brian *nods.*

Holly *finds an old skipping rope in the mud.*

Lee   Brian.

Brian   Yeah.

Lee   Talk to me about your trousers.

Brian What?

Lee Talk to me, tell me . . . you know . . . what they are?

Brian Corduroy.

Lee Wow.

Brian Incredibly hard wearing and I think it makes me look like –

Lee A dick?

Brian Lee! I was going to say Jarvis Cocker.

Lee Who?

Brian Oh don't, Lee.

Erin I don't know who that is either.

Millie Me neither.

Brian Oh don't. I can't bear that you don't know who he is. He's . . . he's just the best.
I listen to him as I go to sleep. He has a podcast.
His voice . . . it's magical.
In fact, I listen to him if I know I'm going to get a bit, you know, stressed. Pop me headphones on and there he is.
His old man voice . . . it's soothing.

Lee You make me feel weird, Brian.

Millie You feeling better now, babe?

Brian *nods.*

Millie Thought you were going to pass out back there.

Brian I . . . wanted to say something, actually. To you all.

Alisha Please, we really need to get going.

Lee Oh God, here he goes, he's making a bloody speech.

Brian I'm worrying . . . because . . .
Well . . . they've said I can return to school.
That I'm on the mend and –

Millie No way!

Erin That's brilliant.

Brian Thank you.
The episodes . . . the anxiety . . . they're getting less.
Less and less. I've got things in place . . . strategies . . . and they seem to be working. Most of the time.
I've had to sort of prove I'm all right. You know. These past months.

And . . . I am. I've been fine. I've been good.

Erin You tried going back, though?

Millie I couldn't do it.

Brian One day a week.

Alisha That's brilliant, Brian.

Brian It's been great.

Lee Wouldn't go back if you paid me.

Brian But I need to have my attacks under control.
You know.
So . . .

Erin So . . .?

Brian Well. I need you to say I didn't have one today.
Or . . . I suppose . . . don't mention it. When we get back.

Lee *If* we get back.

Brian Is that ok?

Alisha Course.

Lee Don't know about that, Brian.
That's called lying.

Brian I need to get back, Lee.
I need at least two As and a B. To do what I want to do.

Erin Of course, Brian.

Alisha Why wouldn't you go back, Lee? Too scared?

Millie Won't have him.

Lee .

Millie Wish I could go back.

Erin You might one day, Mills.

Lee I ain't lying, Brian.

Brian You lie.

Lee No, I don't.

Alisha You ate Millie's sandwiches on the way here and denied it even though you had egg mayo all round your chops!

Millie Knew it.

Lee No, I never.

Brian You lie because it's easy.

Lee I was top set for everything. Top set.

Brian Another lie.

Lee You don't know nothing.

Alisha Why you here then?

Lee I don't need to tell you.
Don't need to tell you nothing.
Can we just go, please?

Alisha Why you here?

Lee You don't know me.
You don't know me.

He gets up and starts to go but doesn't have a clue which way to go.

Erin We know why he's here.
He's the student you dread sitting next to.
The student who always kicks off.
Distracting. Destructive.
They get into trouble and drag you down with them.
The idea of rules riles them.
We all know why he's here.

Lee Rules.
Rules. Rules. Rules.
'Refused a reasonable request'.
Not handing my phone in. My *own* property.
Someone, not me, threw a chip, so we all get blamed. Whole table in solitary.
Excluded for reasons that never, never reflect what actually happened.
Feel like I'm smashing me head on a wall over and over and over.
Couple of us are mucking about, someone gets hurt, pushes me, and I flip. Assault.
Assault?!
On me own again.
And isolation means I've missed loads. Loads.

Millie We all have.

Lee I don't know what the teachers are banging on about.
I'm not used to it being hard.
And it's really hard.
Struggling to understand. And I don't like it.
So . . . you know . . .
Don't bother.
Teachers all acting like they were expecting this.

Millie Hate that.

Lee Then . . . me mum gets in from night shift. twelve hours.
Looks after babies in ICU.
I feel bad. Well bad.
Can't look at her over breakfast.
I'm straight back to school in the morning.
All the promises. Knuckle down.
Keep your mouth shut. I will. I try.
I promise.
Her face. All I can see.
I love my mum.
(*Pause.*)
But . . . just can't stay on the right side.
Rules. Rules. Rules.
I just can't . . .
And . . . just like that I'm out on my ear.
And I'm trudging through a wood with a dodgy looking map and a boy in corduroy and I don't want to be here but . . . I . . .
I can't be doing it no more.
Exclusions and isolation. Isolation.
I can't . . .
I'm done sitting on my own.
I'm done being on my own.
I'm done.

He runs off into the woods. They are all stood there stunned.

Millie Do you think we should . . .

Alisha I found a flag! I've found a flag!
This is a checkpoint!
(*She waves a checkpoint flag around.*)
Oh my God! Yes!
We're on the right track.
I knew we were.
Yes!

Millie What about Lee?

Alisha Who's got the dibber then?
Let's get the map out, let's look. If we can work out the next checkpoint, we might have a chance.

Millie I think we should go after Lee.
Alisha? I think we should go after Lee.

Silence.

Alisha No.

Millie Alisha, this ain't about orienteering, or whatever it's called, no more.

Erin Did anyone else feel cold then?

Millie This is about getting found.
We just want to get found now, Alisha.

Alisha No. No, no, no. We keep moving, we'll find the end.
And they'll be waiting for us.
Medals. And claps on back. And cheers.
And and shock. Shock that we actually did this.
Who's got the dibber?
Give me the bloody dibber.
(*Silence.*)
(*Shouts.*) Who's got the dibber?

Erin It . . . it was in me pocket.

Alisha Was?

Erin Must have . . . must have fallen out.

Alisha I don't believe this.

Erin I'm sorry.

Brian *is struggling to breathe again.*

Brian My chest hurts again.

Alisha I can't believe this.
How hard is it to hold a bloody dibber?

Erin I'm sorry. I'm sorry, Alisha.

Pause.

Alisha What are we going to do now?

Brian Can't breathe.

Millie We go after Lee.

Alisha No.

Millie We go after Lee, Alisha.

Erin We go after Lee.

They all head off in the direction of **Lee**, *except* **Brian**.

Brian *doesn't move as he's struggling to breathe.*
*Doris appears from the shadows. She has the dibber in her hand. She smirks. She beckons the others (***Jack**, **Billy**, **Albert** *and* **Joan***) from the shadows. They are all wearing their nightwear now and are freezing.*

Doris *then slowly approaches* **Brian** *and sucks all the air from him.*

Scene Three

Alisha, **Millie**, **Erin** and **Holly** *enter to the sound of breathing.* **Holly** *is holding a weird ball thing she's found.*

Millie (*shouts*)   Lee!

Erin   Does the air . . . sort of feel cold?

Alisha   No.

Millie   Where's Brian? Wasn't he with us?

They pause. Wait. Where's Brian? The sound of someone blowing a whistle.

Millie   Oh my God, what is going on?

Alisha (*shouts*)   Brian!

Silence. Then a noise from the bushes.

Millie   What the hell . . .

They are scared and huddle closer together.

Millie   Feels . . . so weird out here.
The trees are . . . weird. Everything is just . . . weird.

Alisha (*whispers*)   There is someone there.

Erin   They were strapped to their beds, day after day.

Millie   Who?

Erin   The children.

Alisha   Shhhh.

Erin   Left to . . .

Millie   Left to what?

Alisha (*jumps*)   Ow! Who did that?
Ow!
Someone's pinching me. Stop it! Who did that?

There is another strange noise from the bushes.

Alisha (*whispers*)   Shitting hell.

Erin (*whispers*)   These are their woods.
Possessed by their spirits.

Alisha (*whispers*)   Ow! Stop it! Who's doing that?

Millie (*whispers*)   We need to leave.

Erin   We need to leave before . . . before they . . .

Millie Before they what?

Alisha I'm sorry, but what the hell is in that bush.

Lee *jumps out of the bushes making them all scream.*

Millie Oh my God, you absolute idiot.

Alisha What are you doing?

Lee *holds up* **Charlie**'s *bag.*

Lee Found it on the ground back there.
He would never . . . Charlie wouldn't just leave his bag.
His dad . . .
He'd never leave it.

Alisha We need to get out of here. Now. Something's not right.

They begin to all head in the direction they were heading before.

Erin We're going the wrong way.

Alisha No, we're not.

Erin I did say. A while back.

Lee You may have, but no one listens to anything you say as it is incredibly boring.

Millie I really, really need a wee. It's actually hurting.

Alisha What way do you suggest then?

Lee I tried every way, but it all ends up back here.

Alisha For God's sake.

Millie I can't go on. I need a wee so badly it hurts.

Lee Go then!

Millie I just need someone to come with me.

Erin Just make sure you don't hold hands with anyone.

Millie Please.

Alisha No.

Millie Please. Someone.

Alisha You've got thirty seconds.

Millie Just stand near me.

Alish No.

Millie I'm scared.

Erin It's too weird, Millie.

Millie It's nearly coming out.
(*No one moves.*)
I hate you. I hate you all.
(*Still no one moves.*)
I don't do anything on my own.
I don't even go upstairs.
I can't go to sleep without the landing light on.
Please.
I make my mum stand outside the toilet while I go.

Lee What?

Millie I sort of, need to know where she is. All the time.
All the time.
For a long time, I didn't even like her going out.
I would cry when she left the house. Cry.

I would wake up, in the middle of the night and panic about where she was. I don't do that any more. Obviously. Well, I do, sometimes, but I never tell her. Because I'm meant to be getting better.
I am better.
I am better.
(*Pause.*)
I still go up and down the stairs five times before I go out the front door.
And I'd still rather breathe in second-hand air and curtain twitch then . . . than do this.
But I came.
I came. And I'm here.
But, I just can't, can't do a wee in the woods.
Please.
(*Silence.*)
Oh my God it's coming out!
It's coming out!

She runs into the woods.

Silence.

Lee Think she'll be all right?

Silence.

Alisha What do you think's happened to Brian?

Lee How long's he not been with you?

Alisha How am I meant to know? He's your friend.

Lee Let me just tell you that he is not my friend.
None of you are.

Erin So busy worrying about winning, we've left people behind.

Alisha It's all we've got.

Erin   It's all *you've* got.

Alisha   I got asked to leave. OK?

Apparently stamping on someone's ankle after you've fouled them and they've thrown themselves on the floor is not appropriate. So. Here I am. Running around a wood with a load of people I don't know.

Pause.

Erin   You have to wait for people, Alisha.

Alisha   No, no you don't, Erin. You don't *have* to. Push on. Push forward. Sit back and wait, let life happen around you, you end up setting fire to things.

Erin   That has nothing to do with this.

Lee   Was that you? Was that you! I read about that!

Erin   Leave me alone.

Alisha   We should just go. Before . . .

Lee   Before what?

Alisha   I don't know. Something's not right.

Erin   What about Brian? Charlie?

Alisha   We were never going to make it with Brian.

Lee   He had a bloody flip-flop on, Erin.

Erin   And he was still trying.

Lee   Let's just go, Alisha.

Erin   What about Millie?

Lee   Oh shit, yeah, what about Millie?
(*Shouts.*) Millie! You alright?

Alisha   They are all just holding us up.

There is a girl's scream from the woods.

Erin   What was that?

Lee   Millie!
(*Shouts.*) Millie!

He runs into the woods after **Millie**.

Alisha, **Erin** *and* **Holly** *are left stood there.*

Erin   Did not see that happening!

Alisha   Just us then.

Pause.

They look at **Holly**.

Erin *is shaking the compass. The sound of breathing again.*

Erin   This is weird. This is really weird.

Alisha   What?

Erin   The compass isn't working.

Alisha   What do you mean the compass isn't working?

Erin   It's . . . it's not . . . it's just spinning round. Round and round.

The sounds of 'Oranges and Lemons . . .' sung slowly and distorted by children can be heard amongst the trees, mixed with giggling and whispering. They are coming.

Erin   What's that?
What's going on?
(*Shouts.*) Who's there?
Who's there!

Alisha   Run! Just run!

Erin *and* **Alisha** *run but something inhabits them.*

They turn and look at **Holly**.

They approach her singing – but it's not their voices.

Erin/Alisha
Here comes a candle
To light you to bed
And here comes a chopper
To chop off your head.

Holly *spots* **Doris**, *the girl with her mouth dried shut with blood. She has been watching them and giggling. She holds their map up and rips it to pieces.*

Then darkness. Screams echo and spin around the wood.

Scene Four

Holly *stands alone. Scared.*

From the darkness **Doris**, **Joan**, **Albert**, **Jack** *and* **Billy** *appear and slowly surround* **Holly**. *All of them are wearing nightwear. They are freezing and look very unwell.*

All
Oranges and lemons
Say the bells of St Clement's.

You owe me five farthings
Say the bells of St Martin's.
When will you pay me?
Say the bells at Old Bailey.
When I grow rich,
Say the bells at Shoreditch.

Holly *suddenly looks directly at* **Doris**. *They all stop.*

Doris *is taken back. Shocked.* **Joan** *whispers something in her ear.*

Doris   Can . . . she see us? Can you see us?

Holly *nods.*

Billy   No, she can't.

Holly *swings her head to look directly at him. He jumps back in surprise.*

Doris   Doesn't change anything.

Joan   We must do it.
We must still do it.

They move towards her but stop when she speaks.

Holly   Who . . . who are you?

A beat. They all look at **Doris**, *to check they're allowed to speak. But* **Billy** *ignores this.*

Billy   Billy. Billy Corrigan.

32 Anne Street. I've got enough brothers to form a football team and we'd beat anyone who dared to challenge us.

Jack   I live with me old man in The Black Lion.
It's on the High Street.
You'll know it. Hear it before you see it.

Albert   Me and Mum doss down with me Auntie Peg on Pelly Road. Do you know her?
She don't like me much.

Doris   Doris Callow.
Upstairs flat. Seaton Street. Plaistow.
I can still remember what it looks like you know.

Joan   Don't talk to her. Just do it.

Albert *has pulled a packet of custard creams out of* **Holly**'s *pocket.*

Albert   What are these?

Holly *snatches them back.*

Holly What's... what's wrong with you?
What you doing here?

Billy We've been done in from the darkness we inhaled.

Joan The smog.

Doris The foul air we once breathed back home.
The coal fires we huddled around.
The dirt kicked about on our streets.

Jack But I've still got it. It's still here.
In me lungs. In me bones. In every breath.

Doris They call me a vampire.
With every cough more splutters out of me.
Tastes disgusting an' all.
Like metal.

Billy (*to* **Holly**) You've got legs like a left back – She's strong, Doris. She's strong.
Bet you couldn't beat me in an arm wrestle though.

Holly I... well... my mum falls on the floor a lot. So I have to... you know... makes me quite strong I suppose.

Billy I'd still beat ya.

Jack I could arm wrestle me dad and win every time.
I'd drag the beer barrels down to the cellar on me own if he was still sleeping off the night before's shenanigans.
Stand on a stool and unlock the top bolt so punters could get their hands on the first pint of the day.
Man the bar if he never appeared.
I'd pull him to bed, stair by stair if he'd collapsed on the parlour floor taking off his boots.
Give me a pipe and they'd have called me Popeye.
But then...

Joan Doris...

The sounds of air being sucked inwards fills the air, swirling around the trees.

Holly What was that?
I need to get out of here.
I need to go home.

Joan You don't get to go... not any more.
No one will miss you.
That's what you said, Doris.

Doris No one will miss her.

Holly My mum would miss me. She needs me.

Doris But we need you.

They all move a step towards her.

Holly Need me for what?
Please. She's really ill.
What if she falls. What if she can't get up.
I'm all she's got.

Albert What's she like?

Joan Albert! Don't.

Albert I want to know.

He moves towards her.

Holly She . . . erm . . . she drinks . . . and then . . .
She's got brown 'air. With bleached ends.
She doesn't wear make-up. She doesn't like it.
Erm. She . . . I don't know.
Please. I'm all my mum's got.
Don't hurt me.

Joan Albert misses his mummy.

Albert No, I don't.

Doris He does.

Albert I don't.

Doris You do!

Albert I used to hear her voice in me sleep.
But now . . . it gets weaker and weaker.
I'm worried . . .
What if I . . .?

Doris Albert.

Albert How can I forget that voice?
That voice would shout down the street, 'Get in for tea now, Albert Crosby'.

Jack Everyone could hear your mum's lungs bellowing.

Billy Louder than the ship horns down the docks.

Albert But I can't hear it. Can't hear it no more.
That voice, that voice would whisper good night in my ear as I pretended to be asleep.
That voice, that voice would tell naughty jokes round the kitchen table.
A laugh like a dirty old docker.
That voice. She could sing like a bird.
I can't hear it no more.

Joan My parents would come once a month.
We all knew what that meant.

Doris Stop it, Joan. I don't like it.

Albert We all knew what it meant.

Doris We all knew what it meant, Joaney, but . . .

Joan If the air has done its magic job, you never see them.

Billy *is looking around, as if someone is coming.*

Billy (*whispers*) Stop it, Joan.
They'll tie ya to the bed again.

Albert Shhhhhhhh.

Doris You're the only one that gets restrained, Billy.
Arms and legs, kicking the nurses.

Billy Dreaming I'm Syd King, mate.
Running towards goal and walloping it into the right top corner.
Syd King was West Ham, West Ham was Syd King.
Cut me open I bleed claret and blue.

Joan You weren't asleep. Your peepers were wide open.
I saw 'em.
(*Coughing.*)
You knew what you were doing, Billy Corrigan.

Billy It was that spiteful matron. Pinches when no one's looking.

Doris I hate her.

Joan Pinches little naughty children that no one will miss. That disappear and nobody bats an eyelid.

Doris My mother and father never visited me.

Albert Probably enjoying the peace and quiet.

Doris Close me eyes I can't see 'em no more.
I don't think I'd recognise them if they bothered to come.

Joan My parents would drag themselves up here.
A day's wages.
To be by my side.
(*Coughing.*)
Dad not really knowing what to say.
Mum stroking the top of my hand. I did like that.
But no words. What is there to say?
(*Coughing violently – then blood comes out her mouth.*)

Doris Joan!

Billy   Do it, Doris. You got to do it.

They all breathe in and step closer to **Holly**. **Joan** *is struggling.*

Holly   What . . . what do you want?

Doris   We want what you have so freely.

Albert   What you waste.

Jack   What you take for granted.

Doris   Wheeled us outside first thing. Crack of dawn.
To breathe it in.
Breathe it in.
Breathe it in.

They all stop and breathe. Through the trees we hear the distorted sound of breathing.

Holly   Breathe what in? I don't . . .

Albert   Shhhhhhhh!

Doris   Breathe it in.

Joan (*whispers to* **Holly**)   Breathe it in or they'll tell you off.

Holly   Breathe what in?

Joan   It is good for you.

Billy   It is good for us.

Joan   It will cure us.

Jack   It is our only hope.

Doris   And the sunshine. The sunshine will kill the stuff . . . the . . . the grot that's got inside us.
The bugs.

Joan   The germs.

Doris   That's what they say.

Joan   Weak.

Billy   Strapped to our beds.

Albert   Strapped to our chairs.

Jack   My bones ache so much at night I don't get a wink.

Doris   They give us a tablet that gives us blisters in our throats.

Billy   And they burst. And they taste disgusting.

Doris   And when you wake up in the morning . . . all the blood has got stuck round your mouth. Dried it shut.

Jack Which can be a good thing if you sleep in the bed next to Doris.

Joan The open air, it's meant to increase our appetite.

Doris Our spirits.

Albert Our strength.

Billy So we can play.

Jack We just want to play.

Doris But we can't.

Joan We're trapped in these woods.

Albert Only ever allowed to look at it.

Doris We want to be free.
You can set us free.

Holly Set you free? To what? Play?
I'll play with you. Look.

She tips out of her bag their homemade toys she found in the woods. **Holly** *holds up a football made from a pig's bladder.*

Billy My ball!

Doris Who cares? You know why we're here. Billy?

Holly It stinks.

Billy Pig's bladder.

Doris Billy.

Billy The only thing I brought with me. It was a prize for winning the 1927 Boleyn championship.

Holly A pig's bladder?

Billy I scored a goal with that against –

Doris It doesn't matter. We don't need these things where we're going. We will have the real things not pretend made from muck.

Holly *holds up a crown made from twigs and leaves.*

Joan Doris, look! Queen of the fairies you were! That took you so long to make. She would hide it under her pillow so matron couldn't find it.

Doris It's just twigs.

Holly *holds up the rudimentary wooden sword and* **Albert** *grabs it off her.*

Albert King Arthur's sword that I was going to use against the Vikings that sailed up the Thames to attack us.

She holds up **Jack**'s *skipping rope.* **Jack** *snatches it out of her hand. He is overjoyed to be reunited with it.*

Jack Yes! Where'd do you get that? It was me sisters'. Want to play?

Excitedly, **Jack** *and* **Joan** *start turning the rope.*

Holly I mean . . . it's been a long time and skipping wasn't something I did much as a kid.
Slides. The swings. The roundabout.
Bulldog. I did all that. But then . . . Mum . . . it all kinda stopped. Got complicated. Shopping. Cleaning. Errands. That's me now.

Albert You said you'd play with us.

Doris This is a waste of time.

The skipping rope turning is the only sound.

Holly *thinks about what to do; she is terrified.*

Billy Go on, girl!

She takes a deep breath and runs into the ropes and starts jumping.

All
    Teddy bear, teddy bear, turn around.
(**Holly** *turns around successfully.*)
    Teddy bear, teddy bear, touch the ground.
(**Holly** *touches the ground.*)
    Teddy bear, teddy bear, show your shoe.
(**Holly** *shows her shoe.*)
    Teddy bear, teddy bear, that will do!
(**Billy** *runs into the rope and joins* **Holly** *in the skipping.*)
    Teddy bear, teddy bear, go upstairs.
    Teddy bear, teddy bear, say your prayers.
(**Joan** *runs into the rope and joins* **Holly** *in the skipping.*)
    Teddy bear, teddy bear, turn out the lights.
    Teddy bear, teddy bear, say good night.

The skipping is exhilarating and joyful, and they laugh and have fun.

All
    Teddy bear, teddy bear, say good night.

Joan *collapses.*

Holly Oh my God.

She rushes to **Joan** *and confidently puts her in the recovery position.*

Billy Just do it, Doris!

Albert Do it now, Doris.

Jack You have to do it, Doris.

Holly Do what?

Jack One more and we are done.

Holly She's choking on the blood.

Albert One more and we can all go home.

Holly We need to keep her airways clear.

Billy Just one more.

Suddenly, in the darkness we see **Erin**, **Millie**, **Lee**, **Brian** *and* **Alisha**. *Frozen. Gasping for breath. Unable to take in air into their lungs.*

Holly Oh my God. What have you done?
Let them go! Let them go!
What are you doing to them?

Doris You don't understand.
They're not your friends.
They trudge. Moan. Never looking up.
Never breathing it in.
You and your friends don't need it.
We need it.
We need it. We need to go home.
But we can't . . .
Not without . . .

Without moving any closer to **Holly**, **Doris** *slowly raises her arm and outstretches her hand out towards* **Holly**.

Billy Do it, Doris.

All Do it!

Holly *begins to choke and suffocate.*

Doris Your air . . . will be our air.
Your air . . . will mean we can live again.

Holly (*gasping, she grips her neck*) No. Stop! I can't . . .

Millie, **Lee**, **Brian** *and* **Alisha** *writhe with pain.*

Joan *begins to stand up.*

Billy Yes, Doris! It's working.

Holly *desperately trying to breathe.*

Holly Wait, you haven't played *my* game.
Stop. Please. Let me show you my toy.

She scrambles in her pocket and retrieves her phone. Gasping for breath, she types something into it and the screen lights up. The ghost children step back. Aghast.

Jack What's that?

Billy It's a trick.

Holly It's not. It's a toy. My toy. Please. One more game.

Joan Don't trust her. Don't stop, Doris.

Holly Let me show you. Look.

Jack What does it do?

Holly It can take you anywhere. Show you the future. Your future.

Jack *and* **Albert** *tentatively move over to* **Holly** *and peer at her phone. They are a combination of intrigued, frightened and in awe.*

Jack Pictures. Moving pictures.

Albert Maybe we could play one more game and then go? Doris?

Doris *suddenly stops choking* **Holly** *and releases her.* **Holly** *quickly types into the phone.*

Holly Home . . . your home isn't home any more.
It's doesn't . . . exist.
It not there.

Jack What? What's she going on about?

Holly The Black Lion.

She shows him the screen.

Jack That ain't my pub. Where's the horse and carts?
Where's the people?
Where's me old man?

Holly Quiet round there now. Only suits from the city.
Football on a screen.

Billy Football on a what?

He goes to look at the phone screen, but **Holly** *quickly changes it and shows it to* **Billy**.

Holly Anne Street.

Billy That ain't Anne Street.

Holly Your house is now . . . a coffee shop.
The streets paved. Rushes of people walk past. No room for football. No room to play.

Billy You're lying.

Holly *types something else and holds it up for* **Albert** *to see.*

Holly Pelly Road. One-bedroom apartments.

Albert *looks in horror at the phone screen.*

Albert No. Where's me mum? Aunt Peg?

Joan Don't listen to her.

Holly This is what it is now. It's changed.
The home you so long for is just a building.
A shell filled with other people's belongings.
(*She shows them the phone screen again.*)
This is now. My present.
Look at how everyone is dressed.
Please. Please believe me.

Doris And Seaton Street? What's happened to Seaton Street?

Holly *types 'Seaton Street' in and looks. She pauses.*

Holly Its . . . it's a car park.

Doris No.

Holly Home . . . it's gone . . . not there any more but it's . . . it's not *where* you want to be it's *who* you want to be with.

Joan We are forgotten.

Holly The people you need are waiting.

Albert Where?

Holly Just need to breathe. Really breathe.
The air you need is right here.
It's time for these woods to belong to someone else.
It's time for the air to fill other lungs.
It's time to rest in peace. For all of you.
For everyone.

Joan I wanna go home.

Holly Close your eyes. Do it. All of you.
(*They all close their eyes.*)
Breathe in.
(*They all breathe in. Pause.*)
Who do you see?

Albert Mum. She's singing. It's beautiful.
'Hush. little baby . . .'

We hear 'Hush. Little Baby' whisper through the trees. **Albert** *takes a big breath and disappears.*

Billy I see . . . I see all my brothers and sisters. The whole team. Waiting. No one in goal. I'm not going in goal.

He takes a big breath and disappears.

Jack Me old man. Beer in his hand.
Keeps looking at his watch.
Waiting. He's waiting for me.

He takes a big breath and disappears.

Joan My mother and father. They are crying.
They have their arms wide open. Reaching|. . .

She takes a big breath and disappears.

Only **Doris** *is left.*

Doris I'm scared.
No one . . . no one will be . . . I wasn't missed.
I know that.
No one missed me. But . . . I bloody miss them.
Eight brothers and three sisters.
I miss them more than mother and father.
I would put the little ones to bed every night.
On me own.
I cry every night when I think about their faces.
'Teddy bear, teddy bear . . .'
Kiss them goodnight.
One by one. On every cheek.

Holly You can do it, Doris.
Time to say goodnight.
Breathe in.

Doris *closes her eyes.*

Holly They're waiting. Can you see?
They're all waiting for you.
Breathe in.

Doris *breathes in and disappears.*

As she does **Erin**, **Millie**, **Lee**, **Brian** *and* **Alisha** *collapse to the floor.*

Scene Five

A clearing in the forest.

In the middle stands **Holly**. *She is out of breath. Around her, on the floor, are five piles of nightwear that the ghosts were wearing.*

Lying on the forest floor are the bodies of **Brian**, **Millie**, **Lee**, **Erin** *and* **Alisha**.

Brian *stirs and sits up.* **Holly** *and* **Brian** *look at each other.*

Holly All right?

Brian Yeah. Think so. You?

Holly *nods.*

Brian Never thought I'd sleep outside. In a wood.
Weren't too bad.

Millie *stirs. She is covered in mud and has got sticks and leaves in her hair.*

Millie All right?

Holly Yeah. You?

Millie Yeah.
Dunno . . . I feel like I've really connected with nature.

Brian You look like you've connected with nature.

Millie I'm zoning that out, Brian. I'm zoning it all out.
Is it really bad? Don't answer that.
No, actually, has anyone got a mirror?

Holly Really best you don't look.

Millie I don't even know who I am any more.
But . . . I dunno . . . I think I like it.
I've got dirt under my actual nails! Look!
Lying here. Looking up at the trees.
It's . . . sort of beautiful.
I reckon . . . No . . .

Brian Go on.

Millie I think I could go camping.

Brian Behave.

Millie I do.

Holly I'd come with you.

Pause.

Millie Would you?

Holly Yeah.

Lee *stirs but doesn't move.*

Lee I'm so hungry.

Alisha *stirs.*

Alisha Feels like something has died in my mouth.
(*She sits bolt upright.*)
Has something died in my mouth?

Millie Oh my God, has something died in your mouth?

Brian We haven't had anything to drink in a long time.

Lee *still doesn't move.*

Lee I've ripped me Adidas. Big hole in me knee.
Any holes in the old corduroy, Brian?

Brian No. Very much still intact, Lee.

Lee Literally never felt this badly hungry in all my life.

Erin *stirs. As she slowly stands up, we see she has fashioned stag beetle antlers on her head from twigs.*

Brian Erin?

Holly You ok, Erin?

Erin Six years.
Six years the little stag beetle grub hides in the rotting wood. Waiting.
Not bothering anyone.
Just going about their business.

Holly You ok?

Erin Hidden underground. Growing bigger and stronger.
But when they are ready . . . when she was ready to leave, it was too hard.
(*Pause.*)
I . . . I didn't want to go.
Didn't know anyone.
Didn't like the uniform.
Didn't like the teachers.
(*In her hand is a lighter, which she flicks on and off.*)
So, the little Billywitcher builds a cocoon around herself. A grub. Reading books.
Staring at screens.
Buried in the mud, it is peaceful there.
(*She flicks the lighter on and off.*)
But the grub is forced to go. To emerge.
To transform.
When she is not ready.
I wasn't ready.

Brian What senior school did you have to go to?

Erin Woodlands.

Alisha Oh God.

Erin The noise was unbearable.
The little grub had to fight, every day, but she didn't know how to. So . . . I . . .
She flicks the lighter on and holds it.

Lee You burnt the sports hall down.

Erin Yeah.

Lee Shit.

Erin It felt so good.
The flames, big fat flames washed away the . . . the tension. The anger . . . it all just disappeared.
But . . . left with nothing.
Asked to leave.

Lee What about your parents. Did they . . .?

Erin Work in London. Get home late. Never see them.
Just me.
Got a Ring doorbell so they know I'm home.
So, this thunder beetle went in search of mates.
It's little wings barely holding the weight of its tired body.
It flung itself through the air . . .
And hoped . . . and hoped . . .
(*She looks at them all.*)
And found them.

She throws the lighter away. **Alisha** *comes over to her and gives her a huge cuddle.*

Lee Sorry. Sorry for treading on the bug thing.
I don't know why I . . .

Erin It's ok.

Brian Are you sorry for the comments you made about my corduroy?

Lee No.

Brian Will you lie about me having a panic attack?

Long pause.

Lee You ain't ready, mate.
Sorry.

Millie You will be, Brian. You'll get there.

Lee I want to know why she's here.
(*He points to* **Holly**.)
What did you do? It's only fair.

Holly I'm a ghost.
(*Pause.*)
Constantly off. Continually not there.

I struggled in every day but then the virus hit.
It was a relief. I like staying in.
I'm the best at staying in.

Millie Me too.

Holly Continued absence and then . . .
We moved house. So.
Mum never enrolled me in a new school.
And I never went back.
I don't stop. Things to do. Places to be.
Collect medication. Clean. Make dinner.
I'm a whizz at a shepherd's pie.
I'm terrible at changing the beds.
(*Pause.*)
I'm an empty seat in a class that goes unnoticed.
I'm a name on a register that no one can remember.
Apparently, I have 'fallen through the system into a black hole'.

I'm a ghost.
Fading. Fading away.
Until . . . Until this . . . Until now.
Pick me up on a Wednesday. In a van.
Forced to hang out with people who don't even look at me.

Brian Sorry.
I . . . I don't even know your name.

Holly You do. They say it every time we have to attend these things but none of you . . . *none* of you . . .

Millie It's Holly.
I listen.

They smile at each other. There is a noise that spooks them all and then suddenly **Charlie** *appears. A long silence.*

Charlie I ran.

Brian We thought you were dead.

Lee No we didn't.
You ran off. Didn't join in. Didn't turn up.
Like you always do.

Charlie I could hear the A13. Rumbling.
Thought. I'll just bloody walk home.
I gave up. On this. On you lot. 'Like I always do.'

Lee Told you.

Charlie Two hours later. I'd only just made it to the services.

Lee Idiot.

Charlie Nearly been run down by three lorries and a tanker.
But there it was.
The sign.

Brian What, from God?

Charlie No. The big yellow M sign, you dickhead.
Lighting up the sky and making me . . . making me think of you pricks titting about in the woods.

He holds up a bag of McDonald's.

Lee Oh my God. Oh my God. I can't believe it.
I can't believe it.

Charlie (*to* **Lee**) Sorry . . . you know . . . for saying about your dad . . .

Lee *bear hugs* **Charlie** *for a long time.*

Lee Did you get a Big Mac?

Charlie *nods.* **Lee** *hugs him again.*

Brian Is he crying?

Lee I'm not crying.

Alisha He's crying.

Lee Yeah, all right, I'm crying.

He rips into the bag and bites down on a burger.

Charlie Two-hour walk back here, probably stone cold.

Lee Don't care.
(*He suddenly remembers he's wearing* **Charlie**'s *West Ham bag.*)
Got your bag.

Charlie Keep it.

Lee What? But your dad.

Charlie Can't keep pretending.

Lee What that you're secretly a dirty Tottenham fan?

Charlie Can't keep trying to ram goal-scoring facts and figures into a brain that is just not into it.
Can't keep trying to please him, by being him.
Time to get me head down. Make him proud by . . . doing this. Properly. Completing something. Turning up.

Lee To be fair, it's boring when you're not there.

They hug again.

Charlie Oh, you know the car park is literally just there.

Lee What!

Alisha Really?

Charlie Yeah.
Our parents are all sat in their cars.
Bit worried. We've been ages.
Well, not Erin's. They did phone my dad to see if we could give you a lift home though.

Erin *rolls her eyes.*

Charlie Come on. Let's go.

Alisha Charlie. Was my dad there?

Charlie Yeah. Well worried, mate.

Alisah Really?

Charlie Really.

He nods and **Alisha** *smiles.*

Car horns honk.

Brian Last ones standing.

Charlie The man who runs it said he's never had a team not complete the easy course in all the years he's been running it.

They hug one another and start to leave but stop when **Holly** *speaks.*

Holly Stop.
(*Pause.*)
Just wanna . . . sort of say . . .
Does, anyone, sort of, wanna come back?
Like tomorrow.
Come back here tomorrow.

Silence.

Brian Here?

Holly Yeah.

Lee And do what?

Holly Dunno. Go for a walk.
Muck about.
Build a den.

Silence.

Alisha Sure.

Holly No running. No . . . competing just . . . you know.

Alisha Sure.

Brian I will.

Lee I will. This is the longest I've gone without getting in trouble.

Millie I will, I'll come, Holly.

Lee You're coming because I'll be there.

Millie I am really not.

They slowly leave until just **Holly** *remains. She gathers the ghost-children's nightwear and her custard creams out of her pocket and buries them.*

Holly Teddy bear, Teddy bear . . . say . . . good night.

End.

Character Plot

	1	2	3	4	5
Millie	✓	✓	✓	✓	✓
Alisha	✓	✓	✓	✓	✓
Lee	✓	✓	✓	✓	✓
Holly	✓	✓	✓	✓	✓
Erin	✓	✓	✓	✓	✓
Charlie	✓	☐	☐	☐	✓
Brian	✓	✓	☐	✓	✓
Doris	✓	✓	✓	✓	☐
Albert	✓	☐	☐	✓	☐
Joan	✓	☐	☐	✓	☐
Billy	✓	☐	☐	✓	☐
Jack	✓	☐	☐	✓	☐

More information about the characters and how much they speak

Millie – Significant dialogue and medium-length monologue
Alisha – Significant dialogue and multiple short monologues
Lee – Significant dialogue and very long monologue
Holly – Minimal lines until the end, long monologue
Erin – Significant dialogue, long monologue
Charlie – Significant dialogue in two scenes, short multiple monologues
Brian – Significant dialogue, long monologue
Doris – Significant dialogue, short monologue
Albert – Significant dialogue in one scene, short monologue
Joan – Significant dialogue in one scene, short monologue
Billy – Significant dialogue in one scene, short monologue
Jack – Significant dialogue in one scene, short monologue

Main Narrative Beats

1. In the woods, the ghost children are waiting, they want fresh air. The modern-day young people are in the woods, they are orienteering. Erin tells them it's the most haunted woods in England, in 1927 there was a kids' hospital for tuberculoisis, now 20 children haunt the woods
2. The group are lost, Charlie thinks they should go back to the start, Alisha marches off, the others follow, Lee pushes Charlie over, Charlie has a backpack with sweets, and a whistle.
3. Charlie can't find his pen, he's stressed out, the others have left. Two ghost children arrive, they have the pen, they hold Charlie's hand.
4. The group are looking for the checkpoint, they notice Charlie has gone. It's getting dark, they panic. Brian is struggling to breathe, the group argue about what to do next, Alisha tries to calm everyone down. They hear breathing sounds.
5. Brian wants to return to school, his anxiety is getting better. He asks the others to keep this panic attack secret.
6. They talk about going back to school. Millie wishes she could go back, Lee struggled with the rules, he kept getting in trouble. Lee runs off.
7. Alisha finds a checkpoint flag, the group can't find the dibber so the adults won't be able to find them. Brian can't breathe, the group follow Lee, Brian is left. Doris appears with the dibber, the other ghosts are there too. Doris sucks all the air from Brian.
8. The orienteering group are in a new part of the woods, they are looking for Brian. Erin starts talking about the children in the tuberculoisis hospital, they had horrible experiences. Lee jumps out, he has Charlie's bag.
9. Millie needs a wee, she can't go unless someone comes with her, she can't be on her own. Millie runs off. The group hear a scream in the woods. The compass has stopped working, they hear children's song and giggling in the woods.
10. Erin and Alisha try to run but they have ghost voices, they sing to the others. Holly sees Doris the ghost, Doris rips up the map. Darkness, there are screams.
11. The ghosts are surrounding Holly, they are haunting her. Holly can see the ghosts, they are surprised. Holly asks the ghosts who they are, they tell their stories, they breathed bad air, they were ill. Holly just wants to go home to her mum, the ghosts want Holly's air.
12. The ghosts remember their parents, and being in the hospital, it was horrible, they were taken outside to breathe the fresh air, they just wanted to be free.
13. Holly says she will play with them, she has been collecting their toys in the woods. She has found their skipping rope, Holly skips with them. Joan collapses, the ghosts need to take Holly's air to save Joan.
14. Holly sees her orienteering friends, they are frozen, gasping for breath. Doris starts to take Holly's air. Holly takes out her phone, she tries to distract the

ghosts with pictures of their home town, she shows them everything has changed. Holly tells the ghosts to take a big breath, they disappear.

15. Holly and the orienteering group are in the woods. They are waking up, they are all ok. Erin explains she found school hard, she burned down the sports hall. Holly says she cares for her mum, she stopped going to school.

16. Charlie appears, he walked to a service station and got McDonald's. The car park is just through the trees, their parents are waiting. They make plans to meet again tomorrow. Holly says goodbye to the ghosts and buries their belongings.

Fresh Air

BY VICKIE DONOGHUE

Notes on rehearsal and staging, drawn from a workshop with the writer led by Stef O'Driscoll held at the National Theatre, October 2024

How the writer came to write the play

The play came out of Vickie Donoghue's desire to write a tightly plotted play for a compact-sized cast, allowing the young actors to engage with fully rounded characters.

'One of my favourite films is *The Breakfast Club*, and my favourite theatre is when you take a group of people, put them in a space they can't get out of, lock the door and throw a bomb in – that essentially is *Fresh Air* if you strip it right back. That's the theatre I really love. You have time to really get to know the characters and go on a huge journey with them.'

The ghost story elements came out of her curiosity about a real place, One Tree Hill, where East London children were sent to treat their tuberculosis in the 1920s, and which now has the reputation as one of the most haunted woods in Britain. As she researched accounts of children sent to the sanatorium there, she saw so many parallels with the challenges facing contemporary children, particularly those who have been removed from mainstream education.

'It is a play about playing and playfulness – and how playing is disappearing from children's childhoods. Children are not encouraged to play, they're forgetting how to play. The children don't quite know what to do when they're out there in nature with no phone and no adults, so we go on this journey to see what happens.'

Donoghue summarised the play with a single sentence: 'By getting lost they find themselves.'

Approaching the play

Exercise: Welcome Icebreaker

- In a circle, everyone takes turns to say their name, their pronouns, and their favourite horror movie.

In addition to introducing the participants to each other, this exercise generated a list of potential horror references to research. There were also many moments of connection and recognition between individuals with shared memories of different horror movies.

Exercise: Unlock the play

This activity 'crowdsources' ideas from the cast to build their understanding of the play's themes and context.

- Opposite ends of the room represent 'Agree' and 'Disagree'
- In response to a statement, participants move to positions at or between the Agree and Disagree spaces that best capture their opinions
- Select participants to explain their choices
- Participants can move position if they change their mind after hearing different opinions
- Ask follow-up questions based on their responses.

Responding to the statement, 'Kids do not play as much as they used to', most of the participants placed themselves in the middle of the room between the two poles of Agree and Disagree. Many felt that young people still play but very differently to children of the past, and that much of this play is mediated through (and restricted by) screen-based technology. Covid, parental safety concerns, adult disapproval, limited outdoor space and the disappearance of boredom were also cited as factors that have changed how today's young people play.

Research

O'Driscoll briefly described the earliest steps of her directing process. Following her initial conversations with the writer, she enters 'Research Mode' to help her consider how she might approach staging the script. In the case of *Fresh Air*, she would research the specific real locations and lives that Donoghue took as inspiration for the play. All of this would enrich her understanding of the possible world she can create on stage with a young cast.

Exercise: Research mode

- In groups of five, share something you have researched or something you would like to learn about the world of this play.

Exercise: Video night

- Share a scene or episode from a programme or movie that connects to the themes or world of the play. Alternatively, direct the cast towards where they can find and watch it in their own time.

In this workshop, O'Driscoll shared an excerpt from the BBC comedy *PRU* in which, like the protagonists of *Fresh Air*, the young characters go orienteering in the woods. She highlighted potential discoveries from the video: the contrast between Donoghue's delicately observed characters and the more heightened comic figures in *PRU*; also, the use of specific language and slang as an expression of their backgrounds and context of the story.

'The detective work'

This is O'Driscoll's personal framing for script analysis or table work, as, in her words, 'all the clues are in the script.' Sharing her process, she described starting off with uniting the script, breaking down the scenes into shorter moments – units – in which the mood, focus or dynamic of the scene has changed. These more manageable chunks help actors track shifts in their character's motivations or objective and their overall journey through a scene.

Certain beats signal a change within a unit:

- Character entrance or exit – changing who is interacting in the scene.
- Changes in topic – characters steering the interaction in a new direction.
- New discovery – as this shifts the characters' understanding and emotions.
- Outside intrusion – such as a gunshot, weather event, voice afar, etc., changing the focus and priorities of the characters in the scene.

Some moments can be ambiguous (for instance, when information is new for some characters but not others) and O'Driscoll advised discussion with the actors and potential differentiation between the performers, i.e. a moment might be a unit change for one character but not another. She was also mindful that not all young people may find this analytical process helpful and would prefer something more physically active and practical.

Actioning

Actioning is a technique that offers the actor tools to play each line of a text with specificity. It encourages accurate and dramatic communication between characters by articulating in plain, immediate language what one person is trying to do to another person. You could introduce it to a young cast in the form of a fun and active game.

Exercise: Click game action style

- Half the group observe while the other half play the game
- Players stand on their own throughout the space
- The first player passes the focus by making eye contact with another player and clicking (or clapping if they cannot click) in their direction
- The second player clicks to receive the focus, makes eye contact with another player, clicks at them, and so on
- Once confident with this, the group can pass the focus/clicks while circulating around the space

- Ask players to send the click with a specific action (e.g. Push, Comfort, Confront) and for receiving players to respond to these actioned clicks truthfully
- Practise with similar but separate actions (e.g. Comfort and Soothe) to discover the nuance and subtle differences between them.

O'Driscoll described how she uses actions to note all the actors she works with – young, experienced, professional and non-professional alike – as it allows her to be specific and avoid giving restrictive line readings. She recommended *Actions: The Actor's Thesaurus* by Marina Caldarone and Maggie Lloyd-Williams (available as paperback and app) as a timesaving resource for both actors and directors. It gives performers options that are accessible and meaningful to them – for instance, 'enchant' might not resonate for a young person but 'attract' or 'amuse' or 'hypnotise' might.

Exercise: Would you like a coffee?

- Participants work in pairs: A and B
- A asks B, 'Would you like a coffee?'
- Ask actor A to pick an objective for the line – for instance, 'I want you to be relaxed', 'I want to show you I am a caring person', etc.
- They then pick an action word that helps them achieve their objective. It must be a transitive or active verb ('a doing word') and is always in the present tense (e.g. for the objective 'I want you to be relaxed', they might choose the action 'befriend')
- Actor A tests their objective and action on the line by saying it to actor B
- Now ask actor B to pick an action for their response to the line.

Observations: the line provoked completely different facial expressions from B depending on action; the meaning of the words can be flipped by the action; different actions can introduce pauses or intonations that carry subtext; unhelpful actions can highlight something unexpected and interesting about a moment.

Encourage young people to be playful with actioning rather than look for the 'correct answer'. Keep the exercise practical, experiment with different actions and discuss them with the actors afterwards. While some directors action every line, this might be counterproductive for young performers; instead, you could apply it purposefully on lines where the actors might be stuck, using it as a tool to better understand the line and find alternative ways of playing it.

The actioning mantra

One thought. One sentence. One breath. One action.
We choose an action for each whole thought.
A whole thought is comprised within a whole sentence.
This sentence should be spoken with one breath.
And each breath should contain one action.

Character

Returning to the idea of 'The Detective Work', O'Driscoll described hunting for clues about each character in the text.

Exercise: Character lists

- Each actor goes through the script making a list of facts about their character
- They then make a list of things other people say about their character
- Finally they list any remaining questions they have about their character.

Sometimes there are key pieces of backstory that are left ambiguous by a text (usually indicated by an unanswered question). Consequently the director and actors may have to make choices about what they think has happened to the character before the play or off stage. To help actors make these choices, 'fill in the gaps' to make fully rounded human characters, O'Driscoll suggested giving them some structured provocations (in this case, formatted as a questionnaire) to help collect and shape their thoughts.

Exercise: Character development questionnaire

Each actor can complete this form for their character. Questions and provocations might include:

- What is your name? Nickname? How did you get this nickname?
- What is your age? Birthday? How do you feel about your age?
- Height? Hair colour? Presentation? Weight/body shape? Complexion? Vocal quality? Posture? Health?
- Draw your character detailing specific features
- Draw your character's family tree/network
- How do you feel about your individual family members? What are your relationships like?
- Draw or list some of your character's favourite memories
- Do/did you have any dreams? When do/did you feel most happy?
- Where and who do you live with? How do you feel about it?
- Who do you most admire?
- What is your favourite possession?
- What is your greatest responsibility?
- What is your biggest fear?
- What makes you dream?

These choices can be further embedded in the actor's performance using the interview or interrogation exercise 'Hot Seating'.

Exercise: Hot seating

- An actor embodies their character and responds in role to questions posed to them by the director or other cast members.

Take time to debrief after the exercise; as the actor's responses were improvised, some may be worth remembering, others may no longer be helpful. It is fine to change opinions on further reflection. 'Hot seating' may be used to complement the character questionnaire or as a more practical way of finding responses to the same questions.

Exercise: Improvisations

- Pick a specific character relationship or element of backstory that you would like to know more about (e.g. Erin's relationship with her absentee parents)
- Set up a charged situation in which both characters want different things (e.g. Erin's mum is in a hurry to get to work. Erin has not seen her for days. They meet outside the bathroom door)
- Cast the improvisation (e.g. the actor playing Erin plus a volunteer to play her mum)
- Equip the actors with all the facts they need to play the characters accurately
- Give the actors an objective for the scene (e.g. Erin's mum: 'I need to get to work')
- The actors play the scene
- Debrief afterwards about any discoveries made during the improvisation.

In our session, the participants discussed potential improvisations that they could offer to their young people, including:

- A day in the life at the sanatorium, in which the children discuss what they have left
- What was the morning routine of the 2024 children before they arrived at the woods?
- What was the conversation with Alisha's dad afterwards?
- A conversation between Charlie and his dad on match day
- The journey of the 2024 young people to the woods
- The parents of the 1927 children explaining why they need to go to the sanatorium
- A headteacher explaining to one of the 2024 children why they have been excluded
- A day during lockdown in which Millie is dealing with her OCD
- Charlie's journey between appearances in the play.

Exercise: Character playlist

- Each actor decides their character's favourite songs, their song for heartbreak, their song for anger, etc.

Movement

Exercise: Leading strings

In contrast with the earlier psychological entry points to character, O'Driscoll introduced this as a practical, physical way of discovering how a character might move and interact with the world.

- Actors walk around the space. As they move, ask them to check in with how they are walking: Are you heavy or light on your feet? Where do you lead from? Is your head held quite high?
- Ask the actors to imagine that they have a piece of string attached to their chest. When it is pulled, what does this do to your body?
- Ask the actors to intensify the effect using a sliding scale: If this is a level five, what happens if it increases to level seven?
- Further provocations: How does that make you feel? Who walks like this? What happens if the level increases to ten? Decreases to three?
- Ask actors and observers to note what they see and experience during this variation
- Then ask the actors to imagine being led by their nose, their hips, their eyebrow, their own choice of body part. Again play with the level of intensity and take note of observations between variations.

Observations: a plethora of characters was created very quickly; lots of humour and playfulness; potential ambiguity – leading from the chest might suggest confidence, entitlement, or a front, a mask; slow pace suggested presence and grace, fast pace suggested anxiety; brought to mind toddlers discovering their bodies for the first time – children take up more space, as we get older we make everything smaller.

Exercise: Laban Efforts

This draws on terminology and principles established by the movement practitioner Rudolf von Laban to analyse how we move in our bodies:

The Eight Efforts: Punch, Slash, Dab, Flick, Press, Wring, Glide, Float

The Four Components:

- Direction: Direct or Indirect
- Speed: Quick or Sustained
- Weight: Heavy or Light
- Flow: Free or Bound

O'Driscoll shared her use of these tools to help actors discover how they might move as a character.

- Actors walk around the space

- Tell the actors to physicalise one of the Efforts through their movement – for instance, Punch
- Support the actors with details of each Effort's components (e.g. Punch: Direct, Quick, Heavy, Bound)
- Adjust the level of intensity with the earlier one to ten scale
- Further provocations: How do you walk as a Punch? Can you say the line 'Would you like a coffee?' as a Punch?
- Ask actors and observers to note what they see and experience during this variation
- Repeat for different Efforts at different levels, noting differences between the movements and other effects generated.

Observations: physicality forms the voice; again, the variety of characters produced; haunting yet youthful movements; felt supernatural and real at the same time; allowed us to play with scale and intensity; put in mind wearing the wrong clothes in the woods (e.g. Brian's flip-flop, Millie protecting her trousers); the subtlety of certain movements.

O'Driscoll offered this exercise as a potential means of discovering the ghost children's physicality and movement style. After investigating what Effort (or combination of Efforts) best suits the ghosts, directors could potentially add in the 'Leading Strings' exercise: Where do you lead from when you have a pain in your chest?

Exercise: Non-contact fight choreography

Noting that the ghosts do not touch their suffocation victims, O'Driscoll used the following activity to investigate how you might find creative solutions to this challenging staging provocation.

- Participants work in pairs: A and B.
- They mirror each other, with A as leader, B as mirror.
- Then A asks B for consent to touch them. They send an impulse to B with a light touch of the hand on an appropriate part of the body. B responds in kind to the intensity of the impulse.
- A and B step away from each other. A now sends non-contact impulses across the space towards B's body.
- Encourage participants to experiment with the different strengths of impulse directed at different parts of the body – a slap across the face, an upper cut, a kick to the knee, a grab of the neck.

Observations: removing the naturalistic element made it far more interesting to watch.

Transitions

When thinking about transitions, identify the 'thread of the show', its heart, and focus on how transitions can support and emphasise that. So in the case of *Fresh Air*, if you agree that it is a play about playing, the job of transitions is to help tell that story, as well as the practical business of moving props, set and people. How much story is at the director's discretion; it might be that the play is best served by a clear change in energy or atmosphere.

Exercise: Flocking

This is an ensemble-building exercise that can be applied to transitions.

- A group of participants stand facing the same direction, with the leader at the front
- As the leader moves, the others move also, as if they were one
- When the group faces another direction, a new leader emerges at the front. The group now follows their lead
- Add atmospheric music to bring a horror movie atmosphere and tension for the participants to respond to
- Offer the group horror references (*The Ring*, zombies) to interpret and generate potential images and movements for transitions.

One participant asked how to make the flocking shapes tighter and more cohesive. O'Driscoll acknowledged that teenagers do not always feel comfortable being close to others. Her solution is to devise games, such as Human Tangle, where the group stands shoulder to shoulder in a circle and must hold hands with others in the circle (not the people standing next to them), choosing a different person for each hand and untangle themselves without breaking the chain of hands. The actors have no choice but to be tight beside their peers and, in so doing, become less conscious of the close contact. Images of small spaces can be useful motivators: 'You are all in a lift.' Another participant suggested the game Islands, in which the whole company has to fit on four (later, far fewer) sheets of newspaper whenever the trigger word 'Shark' is called. Everyone has to survive in order to win the game, encouraging the group to squeeze together, lift and carry peers to ensure that no one is touching the floor. A sense of competition can also be helpful: for the sake of winning a team challenge to make, for instance, an Eiffel Tower with their bodies, young people will push through their self-consciousness.

One participant expressed some anxiety about making characters disappear on stage. O'Driscoll wondered whether darkness could be useful here, depending on your resources and ability to achieve a proper blackout in your venue. Flocking could act as this 'darkness', covering and consuming individuals within the mass of bodies. When the flock dissolves, the stage is left changed. Another theatrical idea is for a character's key costume items to be removed before the actor has walked off stage – the performer is still visible but the character has disappeared. Above all, O'Driscoll encouraged playful experimentation with different stagings in the rehearsal room; to not be scared by the creative challenges of Donoghue's script but rather embrace them.

Sound

O'Driscoll shared three online videos that demonstrated the expressive potential of sound. The first showed the same scene from the horror movie *Creak* with and without music.

This simple side-by-side comparison emphasised the difference designed sound and musical composition can make to building atmosphere and tension.

The second video demonstrated the work of a Foley artist with a specialism in horror movies. The short film highlighted how subjective sound (placing us in the character's point of view) and sounds coming from objects or beings out of view can intensify the audience's feelings of dread. Clear contrasts – for instance, between a pronounced accent sound followed by silence – also heightens our sense of suspense.

The final video focused on successful (and less successful) jump scares in horror movies to examine how tension rises and is released within such storytelling. It argued that fear is generated in the build up towards a bad event, identifying approaches such as: using 'breadcrumbs' or sound motifs to signal the presence of an unseen threat; employing misdirects to prevent audiences anticipating jump scares and reveals; limiting what the audience can see (often with darkness) to increase their sense of vulnerability; and deploying a 'sting' or sudden shocking sound effect to elevate their anxiety. Being economical with jump scares and other horror effects will also make them more effective.

Sustainability

When spending limited resources on set, props, costume and transport, O'Driscoll asked 'What is essential to your piece?' In the case of *Fresh Air*, it might be ensuring that the two time periods are distinct; alternatively, it might be creating the atmosphere of being lost within the woods. She reflected on whether it was possible to imply and evoke things like the forest through the actors' performances, their movement and behaviour, rather than literally represent the trees with expensive physical set.

Exercise: What is it?

- Everyone stands in a circle, with a bottle (or another commonplace object) at the centre
- Participants take turns to step into the centre of the circle and use the object in ways that imply it is something other than a water bottle
- The other participants name what they think the transformed object has become
- Bottle transformations included: a toothbrush; the torch from the Statue of Liberty; a hairbrush; a telescope; a golf club; a microphone; corn on the cob; a rugby ball; a harmonica; the monolith from *2001: A Space Odyssey*; a campfire; an Oscar.

Through the resourcefulness and creativity of the group, the bottle was transformed into 30 completely different props by the power of their imaginations and commitment of their improvisations.

O'Driscoll alerted the group to Pigfoot Theatre Company, which is committed to making theatre with the least carbon impact possible. Their online resources share their methodology for sustainable theatre-making, with approaches such as: reducing electricity consumed; using public transport whenever possible; and hiring, borrowing and buying second-hand design materials.

Question and answer with Vickie Donoghue

Q: Why are the children reading books at the start of the play?
A: So this came from a photo of the sanatorium that I found, of a girl sat outside peeking over the top of her book. The children were strapped to their beds and chairs and had to do everything from those positions. But the books are also a little bit of a device because, as this is horror, I didn't want to see the ghosts at the beginning. So the books are to hide them.

Q: Would it be okay to use puppets as the ghosts?
A: I think so. As long as you don't show everything straight off. Let's not throw all of our goodies into the start of the play!

Q: What was your intention in writing characters from a PRU (Pupil Referral Unit)?
A: It's kids who are isolated from society, which was what the tuberculosis children were. I read a lot of interviews with kids from PRUs and that isolation came through so much, even before they are put into PRUs – it spirals so quickly until they are completely removed from society. It's also the idea of 'fixing' children – 'fresh air, come on, outside, isn't nature wonderful!'

Q: How would you like the audience to feel about the contemporary kids?
A: I would like the audience to be surprised by them. PRU kids get quite a bad rep, stereotype-wise. We're all human. These kids are just human beings who are struggling.

Q: How long have the PRU kids known each other?
A: Not very long. They're awkward and a bit clumsy with each other because they don't know each other very well.

Q: Can we make our own decisions about the characters' backstories, such as Lee's relationship with his dad?
A: I know their relationships with their parents but it's not in the text so it's up to you to decide what these relationships are.

Q: Is there a reason why Erin has swapped schools?
A: I think she can't deal with the transition from primary to secondary school.

Q: Are the contemporary children from the same area in Essex?
A: Yeah, pretty much. They've come from different schools, possibly different areas.

Q: Can we adapt the play's setting or would you prefer it to remain in Essex?
A: No, I'm totally up for that. Change the motorway, the football shirt, those kinds of local details. You want to spend time with the kids getting to grips with the story and characters, not trying to do Essex accents. Go for it.

Q: How Essex do you want the contemporary kids to be?
A: Do what you feel is right. I always worry when people say 'Can I do proper Essex?', it's going to go all 'Cor blimey, guv', so as long as it's not that. I would think about

what you need to do to make that distinction between the two different groups of kids, the differences in how they speak. Leaning into one or both of the accents might help you find that distinction.

Q: How do you feel about the dialogue being adapted to the cast's local dialect or slang?
A: I think you can change the odd word as long as the rhythm of the line or the meaning of the sentence isn't changed.

Q: Are you happy for us to swap in alternatives to swear words or using the Lord's name in vain?
A: Of course, absolutely. Take the words out and ask the actors to put in insults they are more comfortable with.

Q: What was the intention behind the stag beetle metaphor for Erin?
A: Stag beetles are fierce but won't actually hurt you, just as Erin is perceived as fierce but wouldn't harm anyone. Also, stag beetles are really crap at flying, so they sort of hurl themselves through the air, and I feel that's a little bit what Erin's doing.

Q: Is Holly a bridge between the ghost and contemporary worlds?
A: In our contemporary world, we call kids like Holly 'ghost children' – they've slipped through the administration of school and authorities. She is the only one who can see the ghosts because she is the modern-day equivalent. No one remembers her name, no one sees her until the end of the play. She's my main character in a way but doesn't say anything for so long. So it's a challenge to make sure she's seen and has a presence on stage before she speaks. We've got to feel her frustrations. She does not want to be there at the start, she does not want to be with these people. I think she's quite a solitary person, probably fairly comfortable in her own skin and own company – although I think spending time with these people has given her a breath of fresh air, a new lease of life and energy. That's the journey for her.

Q: Of the ghost children, Doris seems the closest to the contemporary children. Do you see her as being older than the others or different in some way?
A: I am not so worried about her age, so much as her maturity. She's been brought up mothering younger children, so she has a maternal quality and maturity that others haven't got. There is a connection between her and Holly – Holly is looking after her mother, Doris her siblings.

Q: Do you imagine the ghosts as abstract or as real children?
A: A bit of both, really. The main difference is they are very naive and clearly from a different era. I imagine them moving differently, even if they weren't ghosts, because of the time period, the different mannerisms of 1927. Another layer is tuberculosis – it's a pretty awful thing to have and there's lots of physical stuff that comes with having it. They're really poorly, especially Joan.

Q: Do you envision the ghosts as eternal spirits but living with pain?
A: I think so. It's so part of them. They cough up blood regularly, it's not a big deal to them. I think for horror, it's good to make the rules of your world. One of the rules could be that they feel the pain of their illness.

Q: Are the ghosts trapped in a loop or a moment?
A: The supernatural allows you to do whatever you want. I imagine them playing in the woods and unable to leave. They're trapped in that bit that the contemporary kids find them in and unaware of the passage of time. But they don't want to be there – they want to go home.

Q: Do you see the ghost children doing this over and over again to young people who visit the woods?
A: Yes, they're playing with who they find – whoever is brave enough to visit. They're quite mischievous.

Q: Do you envisage the ghosts playing with the 2024 children all the time?
A: There is a moment with Brian, when they stand next to him and attempt to hold his hand. But I think that is just that standalone moment. When the ghosts are there, the energy changes in the world – I really like the difference between this and when the ghosts are gone and we are left with the contemporary children.

Q: While the ghosts hold hands and share objects with the living, during the attempted suffocation, they do not touch the contemporary children. What are your thoughts on what is shared between the worlds?
A: I thought it was an interesting challenge for the ghost children to suck the air out of their victims' lungs without touching. Touch is limited in the play between the living and dead but when they do, it's electric.

Q: What is the significance of 'Oranges and Lemons' to the ghost children?
A: To me, it's a little link to home, to East London.

Q: Do you think this nursery rhyme would still work in other areas of the country?
A: I found it really hard to find a song that sat with their world and their location and that time period but was also spooky and childish.

Q: With 'Oranges and Lemons', we have ideas about using harmonies, clashing harmonies, singing it live in different areas of the auditorium. Can we be creative with the music?
A: Yes, go for it!

Q: Do you want us to sing 'Oranges and Lemons' only or can we bring in other nursery rhymes?
A: I was trying to avoid 'stereotype' nursery rhymes that are often used in horror. I landed on 'Oranges and Lemons' as it isn't used as often and has that link to where the kids are from. My gut is saying just stick to that one.

Q: Could we use a different nursery rhyme?
A: I think that is a non-negotiable for me.

Q: Would it be okay if half the cast played the forest as a kind of sentient being, underlining the words of the ghosts?
A: I think so, as long as the story doesn't change. It sounds amazing.

Q: How do you feel about two actors speaking the ghost children's lines simultaneously or as a slight echo?
A: As long the narrative is intact and the characters are not diffused – as an effect only.

Q: Where does the animosity of the ghost children towards the modern children come from?
A: Doris has been watching them on the first bit of their orienteering and to her they're these energy-less, lifeless forms.

Q: Do the female ghosts have to have blunt fringes or is this a style or energy that you are looking for?
A: More of an energy to show the time period. No bad wigs!

Q: As clothes may get stained when characters are coughing blood, could I make blood stains part of the costume design from the beginning of the show?
A: Yes, I think they would probably look like that actually.

Q: Would you be happy for us to make the ghost children look less naturalistic with grey make-up?
A: Yes, as long as it is not over the top.

Q: Is it important that the ghost characters have different costumes at the beginning and end of the play?
A: The sanatorium kids were often just left outside in nightdresses in winter. Breathing fresh air and feeling the cold – the elements – was the cure. It breaks my heart! The idea of nightwear is about vulnerability and suits where the characters are at the end.

Q: If resources are tight, would it be okay if the 1927 characters are always in nightwear?
A: I would prefer it if you found a way to make the costume change work, as the difference and contrast takes us to two separate places emotionally.

Q: Can we use video, projection or pre-recorded elements in our productions?
A: I think so as long as it's not changing the narrative or the characters' journeys. It could be a really exciting way to think about set and the environment.

Q: I'm working with a dance teacher to bring as many young people into the show as possible. How would you envisage adding movement to your storytelling?
A: I think it goes back to what we started the day with, which is play. There is an opportunity for ensemble work with the ghosts, stuck in a loop of playing in these woods. There are choral elements, like singing 'Oranges and Lemons'. Thinking about transitions, ask yourself what is at the heart of the piece and what is the movement language that can physicalise that. Always tell the story through transitions, whether that's moments of play or an epic ghost ensemble.

Q: Are you happy for the ghosts to be played gender-blind?
A: Yes.

Q: What are the most essential things to cover in a short rehearsal period?
A: I think it is about how you structure rehearsals. What tasks can be done in between sessions? So, instead of doing the character development document in the room, can they do it as homework? If you are working with only two actors in a scene, can you give creative tasks to the other young people? Can they devise an offer for a different scene that you can tweak later? Block the show as quickly as possible. I would focus most on character and lines – once they understand their characters, everything else will fall into place.

Q: What does the theme of class mean to you within the world of this play?
A: For the contemporary kids, it's about them coming from an urban environment and going to this wooded space, it's about how it affects them. But as for the characters', particularly class, backgrounds, it's open – although I think for the ghost children it's pretty clear. It's important to me that the PRU kids all come from different places – they're a bit of a mix.

Q: What are your thoughts on the theme of gentrification in the play?
A: It was exciting to imagine being brought up around Shoreditch in 1920 then going back and looking at it now. And likewise One Tree Hill and all of that area is so different to how it was back then. This idea that Essex is this magical place that can heal you – I love it! It is interesting how London was so congested and people moved out to Essex and actually a lot of Essex is now very much like London. So it is a bit of a nod to that.

From a workshop led by Stef O'Driscoll, assisted by Janisè Sadik
With notes by Stewart Melton

Participating Companies

#TeamDrama, Roding Valley High School
20Twenty Connections
1812 Youth Theatre
Abbey Grange Academy
Aberystwyth Arts Centre Youth Theatre
Acorn Young People's Theatre
ACS Cobham HS Theatre Company
ACT Youth Theatre
Actors Workshop
Alderbrook School
Altrincham College
Amersham School
Angmering Connections, The Angmering School
Apollo Theatre Arts
Arts Outburst
Arts1
artsdepot Young Company
Artz Centre
Ashford Youth Theatre Company
Atlantic Coast Theatre Co.
Attleborough Youth Theatre
AYT, Ardclough Dramatic Society
BCA Perform, Beamont Collegiate Academy
Berkshire College of Agriculture
Berzerk Productions
Bideford Youth Theatre Company
Bishop Luffa 6th Form
Bishops High School
Black Box Theatre Company, Coulsdon Sixth Form College
Bloxham School
Bodmin College
Boteler StageCraft
Bournside Ensemble
Brassneck Youth
Bright Minds Youth Theatre
The BRIT School
Bristol Free School
Bristol Institute of Performing Arts
Bristol Old Vic Young Company
Brockhill Park Performing Arts College
Burton College
Callywith college
CAPA College
Cardinal Wiseman Catholic School
Carmel Performing Arts
Cast Youth Theatre
Cavendish School
Central Foundation Boys' School
Central Youth Theatre
Chatham and Clarendon Grammar School
Chelsea Academy
Chichester Festival Youth Theatre
Chickenshed Young Company
Churchill Theatre Young Conmpany
City of Norwich School
Cockburn John Charles Academy
The Sir John Colfox Academy
Colmers School and Sixth Form
Coombe Dean School
Corn Exchange Newbury Youth Theatre
The Courtyard Youth Theatre
Crescent Arts Youth Theatre
Crewe Lyceum Theatre Senior Company
Crieff High School
Crooked House Theatre Company
Croydon Youth Theatre Organisation
CWC Company, City of Westminster College
Darrick Wood Secondary School
Delanté Détras, Hall Cross Academy
Dembe Academy
Denbigh School
Deptford Green School
Derby Youth Theatre
Dorchester Youth Theatre
Dorset Drama Academy
The Dorset School of Acting
The Drama Studio
Duckegg Theatre Acting School Limited
The Earls Courtiers
Eastbury Drama Group, Eastbury Community School
Eastern Angles
The East Sussex Young People's Theatre
Ebbsfleet Academy
Egerton Rothesay School
Elthorne Park Youth Theatre
Ever Unique Productions
Everyman Youth Theatre
Evolve Performance Hub
Exeter Northcott Young Creatives
Felpham Community College
Flourish Youth Theatre

Flying High Young Company
Fowey River Academy
Fred Longworth High School
FSG Players, Folkestone School for Girls
The Garage
Gateshead College
Gladesmore Community School
Glasgow Acting Academy SCIO
Glenthorne High School
Gordano School
Grand Young Company
Greenford High School
Guild of Players Youth Theatre
Gulbenkian Young Company
Habs Hatcham Company, Haberdashers' Hatcham College
Hackney Shed Collective
Haggerston School
Halesowen College
Hamilton District Youth Theatre
Harris Lowe Performance Company
Hastings Theatre Company, East Sussex College
Havant & South Downs College
Haywards Heath College
Hayworth Players
Helsby High School
Holcombe Grammar School
HOME Young Company
ICA Riot Grrls Drama Crew, Irlam and Cadishead Academy
Ignite Youth Theatre
Imaginarium Young Actors
Inspire Performing Arts, Coventry College
InterACT Youth Theatre
Inverclyde Youth Theatre (Kayos)
The Island Free School
Jarrow School
JCoSS, Jewish Community Secondary School
JK Theatre Arts
John Smeaton Academy
The Joseph Rowntree School
Kensington Arts
Kettering Science Academy
KEVICC, King Edward VI Community College
Kindred Youth Theatre
Kinetic School of Performing Arts
Kingsthorpe College
Knightswood Secondary School
Kola Nuts
Largs Academy Theatre Company
Lewisham College
Lipson Cooperative Academy
The Loft Arts
Longfield Youth Company
LORIC Players, South Wirral High School
Love Theatre Jersey
The Lowry Onstage Company
Lowther Youth Theatre
LSC Expressive Arts
M6 Theatre Company
Make Your Mark Theatre Company
The Marlborough School
Mayflower Youth Theatre
Middleton Technology School
The Mill Youth Theatre
Mulberry UTC
The Mullion Collective
Mull Youth Theatre
Multiplicity Theatre Company
New College Leicester
New Vision Theatre Company
Newcastle Performance Academy Acting Company
NGA Theatre Company
Norlington School
North Lindsey College
The Norwood School
Nottingham College Actors
Nottingham Playhouse Connections Company
NPA Theatreworks, Noodle Performance Arts
Oasis Youth Theatre
Octagon Theatre Bolton
Oldham College
Oldmachar Academy
Open Door Drama Youth
Orange Tree Young Company
Ormiston Rivers Academy
Ousedale School
OX2 Collective
PACT Theatre Company, Soham Village College
Page2stage Performing Arts
Pegasus Performing Arts
Perfect Circle Youth Theatre
Pike and Musket
Pitlochry Festival Theatre
Plashet School

Platform Theatre Arts
PlayActing Youth Theatre
Plympton Academy Company
Poole High School
Queen Elizabeth's Girls' School
Rainham Mark Grammar School
Ricards Lodge High School
Riverside Youth Theatre
River Tees Multi Academy Trust
The Robinson Drama Academy
Roundwood park school
Royal & Derngate Young Company
Rugby Connected Youth Theatre
Saracens High School
Sharples School
Shenfield Sixth Form Theatre Academy
SHS Acting Company, The Stourport High School and Sixth Form College
Sidney Stringer Actors, Sidney Stringer Academy
Silhouette Youth
Sir William Ramsay School
Skegness Academy
SLBS Youth Theatre, Simon Langton Grammar School for Boys
Sleaford Little Theatre Academy
South Hunsley School
Southfields Academy
Spotlights Community Youth Theatre
SRWA Theatre Company
St Catherine's College
St John Plessington Players
St Joseph's Boys' School
St Laurence School
St Mary's Youth Theatre
St Paul's Way Trust School
St Peter's Pathway
St Thomas the Apostle College
stage@leeds Young Company
Stagedoor Learning
Steel Valley Beacon Arts
Stockport Academy
Stockport Garrick Youth Theatre
Stockton Riverside College
Straffan Drama Club
Strive Drama
Suffolk New College Performing Arts
The Swanage School
Swanshurst School
Taunton Brewhouse Youth Theatre
TDMS Collective, The De Montfort School
Telford Priory School
Theatre Glo
Theatre Peckham's Young Actors Company
Theatre Royal Youth Company
Theatre School of Scotland Ltd
TheatreWorks Deal
Threefold Theatre CIC
Torch Youth Theatre
The Totteridge Academy
Towers School and Sixth Form
Tramshed
Trinity Youth Theatre
Trowbridge PPA 2025
Uckfield College
Upton Court Grammar School
Urswick Youth Theatre
Uxbridge High Theatre Company
Waterford Youth Arts
Watford Grammar School for Girls
West Yorkshire Drama Academy
Westacre Theatre
Westborough High School
White City Youth Theatre
Winstanley College
Winton Community Academy
The Witham Youth Theatre
Wollaston School Theatre Company
Woodmansterne School
Worcester Theatres Young Rep Company
The Workshop
Wyke Sixth Form College
Wykham Park and Futures
Yew Tree Youth Theatre
York Theatre Royal Youth Theatre groups 1 and 2
Young Actors Theatre Islington
The Young Creatives Portsmouth
Young Dramatic Arts
Ysgol Aberconwy

Partner Theatres

Aberystwyth Arts Centre
artsdepot
Beacon Arts Centre
Blackpool Grand Theatre
Bristol Old Vic
Cast Doncaster
Chichester Festival Theatre
Crewe Lyceum
Derby Theatre
Exeter Northcott Theatre
The Garage, Norwich
Gulbenkian Theatre
HOME Manchester
Kiln Theatre
Lighthouse Poole
Lowry, Salford
Lyric Theatre, Belfast
Lyric Hammersmith
Newcastle Theatre Royal
North Wall Oxford
Nottingham Playhouse
Pitlochry Festival Theatre
Queen's Theatre Hornchurch
Royal & Derngate
Sherman Theatre
Soho Theatre
Southwark Playhouse
Theatre Peckham
Theatre Royal Plymouth
Tramshed, Woolwich
Trinity Theatre, Tunbridge Wells
Worcester Theatres
York Theatre Royal

National Theatre Connections Team 2025

Kirsten Adam — *Head of Young People's Programmes*
Ola Animashawun — *Connections Dramaturg*
Finley Neilens — *Connections Coordinator*
Praise Okeowo — *Young People's Programme Assistant*
Jenny Wilkinson — *Project Producer, Connections*

Alice King-Farlow — *Director of Learning and National Partnerships*
Virginia Leaver — *Deputy Director, Operations*
Liza Vallance — *Deputy Director, Programmes*

Workshop notes edited by Kate Budgen
Character plots and narrative beats created by Freyja Winterson
Special thanks to all the young companies who took part in development workshops on these plays

The National Theatre

National Theatre
Upper Ground
London SE1 9PX
Registered charity no: 224223

Director of the National Theatre and Joint Chief Executive
Indhu Rubasingham
Executive Director and Joint Chief Executive
Kate Varah

Performing Rights

Application for permission to perform, etc. should be made before rehearsals begin to the following representatives:

For *YOU 2.0*:
Haworth Agency
158b Kentish Town Rd
London
NW5 2AG

For *Normalised*, *The Company of Trees* and *Ravers*:
Bloomsbury Publishing
50 Bedford Square
London
WC1B 3DP

For *Brain Play*:
Casarotto Ramsay & Associates Limited
3rd Floor, 7 Savoy Court
Strand
London WC2R 0EX

For *Saba's Swim*:
Independent Talent Group Ltd
40 Whitfield Street
London
W1T 2RH

For *No Regrets*:
The Agency (London) Limited
24 Pottery Lane
Holland Park
W11 4LZ

For *Their Name Is Joy* and *Mia and the Fish*:
Berlin Associates:
7 Tyers Gate
London
SE1 3HX

For *Fresh Air*:
Curtis Brown
Cunard House
15 Regent Street
London
SW1Y 4LR